KB091636

문제풀이책
2

내신공략 중학영문법의 구성 및 특징

시리즈 구성

내신공략 중학영문법 시리즈는 중학교 영어 교과과정의 문법 사항을 3레벨로 나누어 수록하고 있으며, 각각의 레벨은 **개념이해책**과 **문제풀이책**으로 구성됩니다. 두 책을 병행하여 학습하는 것이 가장 이상적인 학습법이지만, 교사와 학생의 필요에 따라 둘 중 하나만을 독립적으로도 사용할 수 있도록 구성했습니다.

개념이해책은 문법 개념에 대한 핵심적인 설명과 필수 연습문제로 이루어져 있습니다.

문제풀이책은 각 문법 개념에 대해 총 3단계의 테스트를 통해 체계적으로 문제를 풀어볼 수 있도록 구성되어 있습니다.

특징

❶ 최신 내신 출제 경향 100% 반영

– 신유형과 고난도 서술형 문제 비중 강화

점점 어려워지는 내신 문제의 최신 경향을 철저히 분석·반영하여 고난도 서술형과 신유형 문제의 비중을 더욱 높였습니다. 이 책으로 학습한 학생들은 어떤 유형의 문제에도 대처할 수 있습니다.

– 영어 지시문 문제 제시

영어로 문제가 출제되는 최신 경향을 반영하여, 일부 문제를 엉어 시시문으로 제시했습니다. 문제풀이책의 Level 3 Test는 모두 영어 지시문으로만 제시됩니다.

– 독해 지문 어법 문제 수록(문제풀이책)

독해 지문에서 어법 문제가 출제되는 내신 문제 스타일에 익숙해지도록, 독해 지문과 함께 다양한 어법 문제를 풀어볼 수 있습니다.

❷ 개념이해책과 문제풀이책의 연계 학습

문법 개념 설명과 필수 문제로 구성된 개념이해책으로 문법 개념을 학습한 후, 다양한 문제를 3단계로 풀어보는 문제풀이책으로 복습하며 확실한 학습 효과를 거둘 수 있습니다.

❸ 성취도 평가와 수준별 맞춤형 학습 제안

문제를 풀어보고 나서 점수 기준에 따라 학생의 성취도를 평가할 수 있습니다. 개념이해책에서 Let's Check It Out과 Ready for Exams 점수를 합산한 결과에 따라 문제풀이책의 어느 레벨부터 학습하면 되는지 가이드가 제시됩니다. Review Test에서는 일정 점수 이상을 받아야 다음 챕터로 넘어갈 수 있습니다.

❹ 추가 학습을 위한 다양한 학습자료 제공

다양하게 수업에 활용할 수 있는 교사용 자료가 제공됩니다. 다락원 홈페이지(www.darakwon.co.kr)에서 무료로 다운받으실 수 있습니다.

STUDY PLANNER

CHAPTER 01 **문장의 형식**	학습일	
UNIT 01	월	일
UNIT 02	월	일
UNIT 03	월	일
Review Test	월	일

CHAPTER 02 **to부정사**	학습일	
UNIT 04	월	일
UNIT 05	월	일
Review Test	월	일

CHAPTER 03 **동명사**	학습일	
UNIT 06	월	일
UNIT 07	월	일
Review Test	월	일

CHAPTER 04 **현재완료**	학습일	
UNIT 08	월	일
UNIT 09	월	일
Review Test	월	일

CHAPTER 05 **조동사**	학습일	
UNIT 10	월	일
UNIT 11	월	일
UNIT 12	월	일
Review Test	월	일

CHAPTER 06 **명사, 부정대명사**	학습일	
UNIT 13	월	일
UNIT 14	월	일
Review Test	월	일

CHAPTER 07 **수동태**	학습일	
UNIT 15	월	일
UNIT 16	월	일
UNIT 17	월	일
Review Test	월	일

CHAPTER 08 **관계사**	학습일	
UNIT 18	월	일
UNIT 19	월	일
UNIT 20	월	일
Review Test	월	일

CHAPTER 09 **비교 구문**	학습일	
UNIT 21	월	일
UNIT 22	월	일
Review Test	월	일

CHAPTER 10 **형용사, 부사, 분사**	학습일	
UNIT 23	월	일
UNIT 24	월	일
Review Test	월	일

CHAPTER 11 **접속사**	학습일	
UNIT 25	월	일
UNIT 26	월	일
Review Test	월	일

CHAPTER 12 **의문문**	학습일	
UNIT 27	월	일
UNIT 28	월	일
Review Test	월	일

CHAPTER 13 **가정법**	학습일	
UNIT 29	월	일
UNIT 30	월	일
Review Test	월	일

SCORECARD

PASS 기준: Level 2 → 25점 이상, Level 3 → 41점 이상, Review Test → 60점 이상

CHAPTER 01 **문장의 형식**	Level 2	Level 3
UNIT 01	/ 30점	/ 50점
UNIT 02	/ 30점	/ 50점
UNIT 03	/ 30점	/ 50점
Review Test		/ 70점

CHAPTER 02 **to부정사**	Level 2	Level 3
UNIT 04	/ 30점	/ 50점
UNIT 05	/ 30점	/ 50점
Review Test		/ 70점

CHAPTER 03 **동명사**	Level 2	Level 3
UNIT 06	/ 30점	/ 50점
UNIT 07	/ 30점	/ 50점
Review Test		/ 70점

CHAPTER 04 **현재완료**	Level 2	Level 3
UNIT 08	/ 30점	/ 50점
UNIT 09	/ 30점	/ 50점
Review Test		/ 70점

CHAPTER 05 **조동사**	Level 2	Level 3
UNIT 10	/ 30점	/ 50점
UNIT 11	/ 30점	/ 50점
UNIT 12	/ 30점	/ 50점
Review Test		/ 70점

CHAPTER 06 **명사, 부정대명사**	Level 2	Level 3
UNIT 13	/ 30점	/ 50점
UNIT 14	/ 30점	/ 50점
Review Test		/ 70점

CHAPTER 07 **수동태**	Level 2	Level 3
UNIT 15	/ 30점	/ 50점
UNIT 16	/ 30점	/ 50점
UNIT 17	/ 30점	/ 50점
Review Test		/ 70점

CHAPTER 08 **관계사**	Level 2	Level 3
UNIT 18	/ 30점	/ 50점
UNIT 19	/ 30점	/ 50점
UNIT 20	/ 30점	/ 50점
Review Test		/ 70점

CHAPTER 09 **비교 구문**	Level 2	Level 3
UNIT 21	/ 30점	/ 50점
UNIT 22	/ 30점	/ 50점
Review Test		/ 70점

CHAPTER 10 **형용사, 부사, 분사**	Level 2	Level 3
UNIT 23	/ 30점	/ 50점
UNIT 24	/ 30점	/ 50점
Review Test		/ 70점

CHAPTER 11 **접속사**	Level 2	Level 3
UNIT 25	/ 30점	/ 50점
UNIT 26	/ 30점	/ 50점
Review Test		/ 70점

CHAPTER 12 **의문문**	Level 2	Level 3
UNIT 27	/ 30점	/ 50점
UNIT 28	/ 30점	/ 50점
Review Test		/ 70점

CHAPTER 13 **가정법**	Level 2	Level 3
UNIT 29	/ 30점	/ 50점
UNIT 30	/ 30점	/ 50점
Review Test		/ 70점

개념이해책과 문제풀이책 연계 학습법

개념이해책으로 문법 개념 학습

문제풀이책으로 문법 개념을 복습

QR코드를 찍으면 개념이해책 문법 설명이 보여요!

개념이해책 Let's Check It Out과 Ready for Exams 풀고 점수 합산

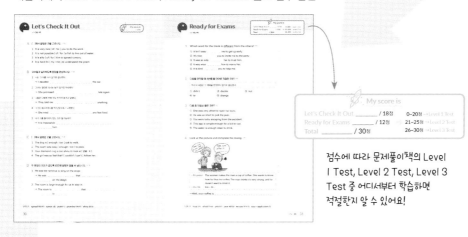

점수에 따라 문제풀이책의 Level 1 Test, Level 2 Test, Level 3 Test 중 어디서부터 학습하면 적절한지 알 수 있어요!

챕터 내용을 모두 학습한 후 Review Test 풀기

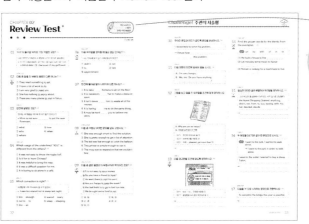

패스하면 문제풀이책의 Review Test도 풀어보고, 그것도 패스하면 다음 챕터로 넘어가요!

문제풀이책의 구성

문법 개념 요약

개념이해책에서 학습한 문법 개념이 표로 더욱 간결하게 요약 제시됩니다. 핵심 용어가 빈칸으로 처리되어 있어서 학생들이 직접 내용을 채워 넣으며 개념을 복습할 수 있습니다.

개념이해책 연계 학습용 QR코드

QR코드를 찍으면 개념이해책 문법 개념 설명 페이지로 연결되어 내용을 즉시 확인할 수 있습니다.

Level 1 Test

학습한 문법 사항을 간단히 확인할 수 있는 드릴형 연습 문제입니다.

VOCA

문제에 쓰인 주요 단어가 정리되어 편리하며, 문법과 단어 공부를 같이 할 수 있습니다.

Level 2 Test

중간 난이도의 문제를 풀면서 앞에서 배운 문법 사항을 실제 문제 풀이에 적용하는 연습을 합니다. 객관식과 주관식 서술형이 50% 정도로 섞인 내신 유형 문제로 구성되어 있습니다. 지시문은 한글로 제시됩니다.

My score is

30점 만점으로 25점 이상일 때 PASS할 수 있어 학생들의 성취 욕구를 자극할 수 있으며, PASS 기준에 미달했을 때는 다시 앞부분을 복습하도록 합니다.

높은 난이도의 다양한 내신 유형 문제로 구성되어 있으며, 문제가 모두 영어 지시문으로 제시됩니다. 최신 유형도 포함되어 있어 내신 시험에 철저히 대비할 수 있습니다.

My score is

50점 만점으로 41점 이상일 때 PASS할 수 있습니다.

Challenge! 주관식 서술형

주관식 서술형 문제의 비중이 30퍼센트 정도로 구성되어 있습니다.

Review Test

각 챕터의 내용을 통합적으로 다룬 문제들을 통해 응용력과 실전 감각을 키울 수 있습니다. 객관식과 주관식 서술형이 50% 정도로 구성되어 있습니다.

My score is

70점 만점으로 60점 이상일 때 PASS할 수 있습니다. Review Test를 PASS하면 해당 문법 개념을 마스터했다는 성취감과 자신감을 가지고 다음 챕터로 넘어갑니다.

인덱스 번호

문제에 대한 문법 개념이 어디에 나왔는지 알려주는 번호입니다. 인덱스 번호는 개념이해 책 기준입니다.

U01_1+3+GP
유닛 번호 개념 번호 Grammar Point

독해형 어법 문제

독해 지문에서 어법 문제가 출제되는 내신 시험에 대비할 수 있도록, Review Test의 마지막 2문제는 독해형으로 제시됩니다.

★ 고난도 — 특히 어렵거나 최신 유형이라 익숙하지 않은 문제

 한눈에 쏙 — 여러 문법 개념이 한 문제 속에 들어가 있는 문제

 함정 — 학생들이 잘 헷갈리는 문법 항목이거나 부주의하면 틀릴 수 있는 문제

차례

내공 중학영문법을 써본
독자들의 추천!

꼼꼼한 개념 정리와 바로 적용 가능한 예제들, 그리고 깔끔한 단원 정리 리뷰 문제들까지, 학생들은 물론이고 가르치는 선생님의 마음까지 꿰뚫은 너의 이름은, 내공 중학영문법! 5년째 제 특강 교재로 pick 중입니다.

잠실 이은재 어학원 강사 김한나

이 책을 만난 초등학교 때부터 실질적인 대학 입시에 치중하였던 고교 시절 내내 가장 많이 열어본 영어 과목의 교재이다. 어려운 문법 용어로 힘들어하고 탄탄한 구조와 내용에 목말라했을 때 나를 극복하게 하고 탄탄한 기본기를 유지하게 해줄 수 있는 독보적인 능력을 가진 교본이었다.

분당 대진고 졸업 고려대학교(본캠) 20학번 김주현

최근 실제 시험 유형을 상세히 검토 분석한 정성이 돋보이는 교재이다. 문법 개념을 스스로 말로 풀어 정리할 수 있게 하여 기본기를 정확히 다질 수 있게 해준 부분이 특히 인상적이다.

경기도 일산 원장 강선혜

처음 나왔을 때부터 몇 년째 내 수업 메인 교재로 쓰고 있는 대한민국 최고의 문법책. 재치 있는 예문과 삽화도 좋지만 문법의 기본 개념을 깊게 생각해 볼 수 있는 문제들은 타의 추종을 불허한다. 문제풀이책의 학생들을 위한 개념 리뷰 페이지에서도 학생들에 대한 배려가 묻어 나온다.

대치동 강사 최성실(레이첼)

내공은 다른 문법책처럼 문제만 쓸데없이 많지 않고, 꼭 필요한 개념과 개념 복습을 위한 빈칸이 마련되어 있어서 내가 이해했는지 체크하고 구조를 한 번 더 정리할 수 있었다.

도곡중 1학년 최준혁

내공 중학영문법은 제목만 보면 중등을 위한 교재 같지만 초등 고학년부터 고2 기초반까지 다양하게 쓸 수 있으며, 무엇보다도 톡톡 튀는 예문과 문제풀이책 구성이 좋아서 학생과 선생님 모두에게 유익한 책입니다. 실제 영어를 포기했던 중3(현 고1)의 기초를 잡으며 내신 준비를 완벽하게 해줄 수 있었던 교재입니다.

청주 리드인 잉글리쉬 원장 최서린

내공 중학영문법… 처음 보는 책이라 어색하고 문제풀이책은 개념이해책을 다 이해하지 못하면 풀 수 없어서 처음엔 공부하기 힘들었는데 점점 아는 것이 늘어나고 숙제 양도 익숙해지니 문제 풀기가 재밌어지고 처음으로 최고의 영어 점수를 맞고 나니 자신감이 생기게 되었습니다.

청주 율량중 3학년 김태연

한국에서 중2까지 신영주 선생님이랑 영어 공부하고 미국으로 유학 갔을 때 처음으로 간절히 생각 났던 책이다. 다시 한국에 있는 선생님께 미국으로 책을 보내 달라고 했다. 미국에서도 이렇게 쉽게 잘 정리되어 있는 책은 없었다. 이 책으로 배운 내용들은 오랫동안 기억에 남을 정도로 쉽고 확실하다.

Chaminade College Preparatory School sophomore 황인산

개념이해책으로 개념을 익히고 간단한 점검을 한 뒤, 문제풀이책의 난이도별 문제들로 그 개념을 탄탄히 정리할 수 있었다. 익혀야 하는 개념은 자주 문제에서 접할 수 있어 금방 암기하였고 간단한 개념은 생각해서 논리적으로 풀어내는 문제를 통하여 더 확실히 감을 잡을 수 있었다. 문제들이 실제로 중학교 내신에서 자주 출제되는 유형들이라서 시험 전에 몇 번 더 펼쳐보며 참고하기 좋았다.

늘푸른중학교 김혜준

교재 속의 문제들은 무의미한 단순 반복 연습을 하게 하는 것이 아니라 원리를 터득하고 문제에 따라 적합하게 반응하고 사고하게 만들어 주는 교재임에 틀림없다. 오랜 기간 동안 영어 교육의 길을 함께 걸어온 교육자로서 내공 중학영문법은 문법적 정확성을 높여 궁극적으로 의사소통의 유창성까지 길러줄 것이다.

블레싱 아카데미 원장 이봉주

CHAPTER 01

문장의 형식

개념이해책
12쪽 함께 보기

■ 아래 표의 빈칸에 알맞은 내용을 써 넣으세요. ››› 정답 02쪽

① 1형식

1)_____ +2)_____ +(부사/부사구)		He runs (fast).
There/Here+3)_____ +4)_____ +(부사/부사구)		There is a festival (at my school).

② 2형식

주어+be동사+주격 보어(5)_____ /6)_____)	He is handsome. / He is a teacher.
주어+감각동사+주격 보어(7)_____)	It may sound strange.
주어+상태동사+주격 보어(8)_____)	The city became famous.

③ 3형식

주어+동사+목적어(9)_____)	She loved the book.
주어+동사+목적어(10)_____)	I honestly didn't understand that.
주어+동사+목적어(11)_____)	We want to watch TV.
주어+동사+목적어(12)_____)	They enjoyed talking to each other.

Level 1 Test

››› 정답 02쪽

A 문장에 주어(S)와 동사(V), 보어(C)를 표시하시오. (보어는 있을 경우에만 표시할 것)

1 There was a portable computer on the desk.

2 My little brother walks to school.

3 He is becoming nervous.

4 She didn't look intelligent.

5 She was frightened of him.

B [ ]에서 알맞은 것을 고르시오.

1 The little boy ran [brave / bravely].

2 The bank doesn't look [safe / safely].

3 The party was [surprising / surprised].

4 My mom became [healthy / health].

5 This blanket feels [soft / softly].

C 문장이 1형식인지 2형식인지 구분하시오.

1 Is dinner ready yet? ➡ _____

2 Is there a bus to the airport?

　➡ _____

3 He felt really hungry. ➡ _____

4 The baby is sleeping peacefully.

　➡ _____

D 주어진 단어를 빈칸에 알맞은 형태로 쓰시오.

1 My dad enjoys _____ chess. (play)

2 Time flies _____. (quick)

3 The leaves turned _____. (yellow)

4 We hate _____ the homework. (do)

VOCA portable 휴대할 수 있는 | nervous 초조한, 긴장한 | intelligent 총명한, 똑똑한 | frightened 무서워하는 | brave 용감한 | safe 안전한 | health 건강
| healthy 건강한 | blanket 담요 | peacefully 평화롭게

01 빈칸에 들어갈 말로 알맞지 <u>않은</u> 것은? 2점

> They _____ to talk with the singer.

① wanted　　　　② enjoyed
③ wished　　　　④ hoped
⑤ decided

02 다음 문장을 바르게 설명한 학생을 <u>모두</u> 고르시오. 3점

> Sora got angrily over the late delivery of the pizza.

① 민서: 3형식 문장이다.
② 병서: 문법적으로 틀린 부분이 없다.
③ 진현: got 뒤의 부사 angrily가 보어 역할을 한다.
④ 승현: 이 문장에서 got은 2형식 동사로 사용되었다.
⑤ 희석: angrily는 angry가 되어야 한다.

03 다음 중 어법상 <u>어색한</u> 것은? 2점

① My grandma appears healthy.
② Her brother seems friendly.
③ Your puppy looks lovely.
④ This food smells nice.
⑤ Her trip sounded perfectly.

04 다음 밑줄 친 @~ⓔ 중에서 어법상 <u>어색한</u> 것은? 2점

> @ <u>The plan</u> ⓑ <u>sounds</u> ⓒ <u>well</u> and ⓓ <u>quite</u> ⓔ <u>doable</u>.

① @　　　　② ⓑ
③ ⓒ　　　　④ ⓓ
⑤ ⓔ

05 우리말과 같은 뜻이 되도록 주어진 조건에 맞게 영작하시오. 6점
서술형

> 그 계획은 잘 실행될 것이다.
> ・조건 1　work 동사를 활용할 것
> ・조건 2　미래 시제로 쓸 것
> ・조건 3　5단어로 완성할 것

→ _____

06 다음 문장에서 happy의 알맞은 형태를 쓰시오. 4점
서술형

> ・They lived ____(A)____ .
> ・They look ____(B)____ .
> ・He wanted to live a ____(C)____ life.

(A) _____
(B) _____
(C) _____

07 우리말과 같은 뜻이 되도록 주어진 단어를 이용해서 영작하시오. 5점
서술형

> 그는 유명한 음악가가 되었다.
> become, famous, musician

→ _____

08 그림을 보고 우리말과 같은 뜻이 되도록 주어진 조건에 맞게 영작하시오. 6점
서술형

> 그는 어린 남동생을 돌봐야 한다.
> ・조건 1　어휘 – have to, look after
> ・조건 2　8단어로 완성할 것

→ _____

VOCA　delivery 배달 | appear 나타나다 | lovely 사랑스러운 | doable 행할 수 있는 | work 실행되다, 작동하다 | musician 음악가 | look after ~을 돌보다

01 Which is a different sentence form? 2점

① She drove dangerously.
② He died last year at the age of 50.
③ There are ten singers on the stage.
④ She goes to school by car every day.
⑤ He is a hair designer.

02 Which cannot make a grammatically correct sentence? 2점

① need / more / I / . / time
② hi / She / . / said / to / me
③ comes / Here / Santa Claus / .
④ at /They / the / were / . / line / starting
⑤ looks / . / monster / very / angrily /The

03 Among the following sentences, choose the parts that are grammatically incorrect. 3점

ⓐ It may sound ridiculously.
ⓑ The students danced to the music.
ⓒ I didn't answer the question good.
ⓓ Mina and Jina like swimming.

① ⓑ to the music, ⓒ good
② ⓐ ridiculously, ⓒ good
③ ⓐ ridiculously, ⓓ swimming
④ ⓒ good
⑤ ⓓ swimming

04 Which is NOT proper for the blank? 3점

They _____ lonely.

① look   ② got
③ felt   ④ live
⑤ are

[05~06] Which is proper for each blank? 각 2점

05
They want to move to a new house. So they're _____ a new house.

① looking after   ② looking up
③ looking for   ④ looking
⑤ looking at

06
At that time, we were _____.

① satisfy   ② run
③ happily   ④ sadly
⑤ interested

07 Which of the following is grammatically correct? 2점

① My shoes got wet in the rain.
② The baby looked so peacefully.
③ This egg smells badly.
④ There was a lot of people in the stadium.
⑤ He seems very patiently.

08 How many sentences are grammatically incorrect? 3점

ⓐ Do you like to eat *jajangmyeon*?
ⓑ I grow vegetables in my yard.
ⓒ I decided to save my pocket money.
ⓓ Did you enjoy to participate in the discussion?
ⓔ I practiced to play the piano.

① zero   ② one
③ two   ④ three
⑤ four

VOCA stage 무대 | hair designer 미용사 | ridiculously 우스꽝스럽게, 터무니없이 | lonely 외로운 | at that time 그때에, 당시에 | satisfy 만족시키다 | interested 관심 있는 | peacefully 평화롭게 | stadium 경기장 | patiently 참을성 있게 | vegetable 야채 | pocket money 용돈 | participate 참여하다 | discussion 토론 | practice 연습하다

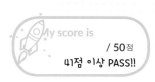
09 Which is grammatically <u>incorrect</u>? 3점

> She ⓐ <u>could solve</u> ⓑ <u>the problem</u> ⓒ <u>easy</u>. So she ⓓ <u>looked</u> ⓔ <u>confident</u>.

① ⓐ   ② ⓑ
③ ⓒ   ④ ⓓ
⑤ ⓔ

10 Choose ALL of the grammatically <u>incorrect</u> sentences. 3점

① There was few fish in the fishbowl.
② Here comes the teachers.
③ He seems happily.
④ I don't mind working on weekends.
⑤ Did she begin doing her homework?

11 Which are the correct words for the blanks? 3점

> • I promise _____ you a souvenir.
> • Why do you keep _____ me?

① bring – bothering   ② bringing – bothering
③ to bring – to bother   ④ to bring – bothering
⑤ bringing – to bother

Challenge! 주관식 서술형

12 Look at the picture and fill in the blanks by using the given words. 4점

> It rained ___(A)___ last night. (heavy)
> It sounded ___(B)___. (noise)

(A) _____

(B) _____

13 Find the sentence that has an error and correct it. 4점

> ⓐ The sun rises early.
> ⓑ We had fun at the party.
> ⓒ She enjoyed to listen to other people's adventures.

(   ) _____ ➡ _____

14 Choose the <u>necessary words</u> to complete the sentence. You may use a word more than one time. 4점

> Susan은 인형처럼 생겼지만 슬퍼 보인다.
> look, looks, like, a doll, but, sad, sadly

➡ Susan _____ .

15 Find an error and correct them. 4점

> When you come in, take off your shoes. Please put on slippers. You can take any of the books from the shelf. Read the books quiet. After reading, put the books back on the shelf.

_____ ➡ _____

16 Translate the Korean sentence according to the conditions. 6점

> 그 새로운 스마트폰은 좋아 보였고 잘 팔렸다.
>
> • Condition 1   어휘 – smartphone, look, good
> • Condition 2   과거 시제로 쓸 것
> • Condition 3   8단어로 쓸 것

➡ _____

VOCA   confident 자신감 있는 | souvenir 기념품 | bother 괴롭히다 | adventure 모험(담) | shelf 선반

4형식, 5형식

개념이해책
15쪽 함께 보기

■ 아래 표의 빈칸에 알맞은 내용을 써 넣으세요. 》》정답 03쪽

① 4형식

주어	동사	간접 목적어	직접 목적어
I	gave	him	a present.
She	made	me	a cake.
We	asked	her	a question.

주어	동사	직접 목적어	전치사	간접 목적어
I	gave	a present	1)	him.
She	made	a cake	2)	me.
We	asked	a question	3)	her.

② 5형식

주어	동사	목적어	목적격 보어
Mom	calls	me	a pig. 4)
I	found	this story	interesting. 5)

 Level 1 Test

》》 정답 03쪽

A 문장에서 목적어(O), 간접 목적어(IO), 직접 목적어(DO), 목적격 보어(OC)를 표시하시오.

1 I wrote her an email.

2 We made a birthday cake for Mom.

3 I named my hedgehog Ddochi.

4 The results of the test made me disappointed.

B 우리말과 같은 뜻이 되도록 주어진 단어를 배열해서 영작하시오.

1 그들은 우리에게 그들의 텐트를 빌려줬다.
(their tent, us, lent, they, to)

→ _____

2 나는 그녀에게 꽃 한 송이를 사주었다.
(a flower, her, bought, I)

→ _____

3 매일 운동하는 것은 너를 건강하게 만든다.
(exercising, makes, every day, healthy, you)

→ _____

C 4형식 문장을 3형식으로 바꿔 쓰시오.

1 My uncle sent me a box of apples.

→ _____

2 He made them colorful kites.

→ _____

3 She asked me a personal question.

→ _____

4 The rabbit found us a secret key.

→ _____

VOCA hedgehog 고슴도치 | result 결과 | disappointed 실망한 | kite 연 | personal 개인적인, 사적인 | rabbit 토끼

01 빈칸에 들어갈 말이 바르게 짝지어진 것은? 2점

> · She gave some fruit _____ us.
> · He bought a necklace _____ his wife.

① to – for
② to – to
③ for – to
④ for – for
⑤ for – of

02 다음 중 어색한 부분을 모두 적은 것은? 3점

> ⓐ He told me the truth.
> ⓑ Tony lent 10 dollars for me.
> ⓒ My mom asked many questions to my boyfriend.
> ⓓ You should keep the room clean.

① ⓐ the truth
② ⓑ for me, ⓓ clean
③ ⓑ for me, ⓒ to my boyfriend
④ ⓒ to my boyfriend
⑤ ⓓ clean

03 다음 중 문장의 형식이 나머지와 다른 하나는? 2점

① Could you tell me your name?
② The librarian found me the book.
③ I didn't found her polite.
④ I made him a kite.
⑤ I sent him an invitation card.

04 다음 중 어법상 어색한 것을 모두 고르시오. 3점

① Jane wrote a card for Mike.
② Did she teach history for you?
③ Spinach made Popeye strongly.
④ He inquired her interest of her.
⑤ We should keep the desk tidy.

05 두 문장이 같은 뜻이 되도록 빈칸에 알맞은 말을 쓰시오.
서술형 5점

> The flight attendant cooked the CEO ramen.

→ The flight attendant _____ the CEO.

06 다음 문장에서 어색한 부분을 찾아 바르게 고치시오. 4점
서술형

> This project has kept me busily for the last few weeks.

_____ → _____

07 우리말과 같은 뜻이 되도록 문장을 완성하시오. 5점
서술형

> 그녀의 행동이 나를 화나게 만들었다.

→ Her behavior _____ me _____.

08 그림을 보고 주어진 단어를 배열해서 영작하시오. 6점
서술형

> a diamond bracelet, the millionaire, gave, her

→ _____

VOCA necklace 목걸이 | truth 사실 | librarian 도서관 사서 | polite 예의 바른 | invitation card 초대장 | spinach 시금치 | Popeye 뽀빠이 | inquire 묻다 | interest 관심 | tidy 단정한 | flight attendant 항공 승무원 | CEO 최고 경영자, 회장 | behavior 행동 | millionaire 백만장자 | bracelet 팔찌

01 How many sentences are <u>incorrect</u>? 3점

ⓐ The students gave candy to the elderly.
ⓑ We sent the orphans some clothes.
ⓒ The refrigerator keeps food freshly.
ⓓ I inquired your address for him.
ⓔ Everybody found him honest.

① one　　　　② two
③ three　　　④ four
⑤ five

02 Which are the correct words for the blanks? 2점

• Leo gave brilliant answers _____ me at the interview.
• Dad cooked ham and eggs _____ us.

① to – to　　　② to – for
③ for – for　　④ to – of
⑤ of – to

03 Which word CANNOT be used when translating the sentence? 2점

엄마는 우리에게 파이를 만들어 주셨다.

① mom　　　　② made
③ us　　　　　④ for
⑤ to

04 Which is the same sentence form as the given sentence? 2점

Jessica wrote her grandmother a letter.

① The coffee tasted bitter.
② The seats in this car feel smooth.
③ Mom showed me old pictures from her past.
④ They knew nothing about her wedding.
⑤ There were no birds in the cage.

05 Which is the common word for the blanks? 3점

• She _____ her own clothes.
• My dad _____ lunch for me.
• My good luck _____ me rich.

① has　　　　② let
③ made　　　④ did
⑤ gets

06 Which is NOT suitable for the blank? 2점

He didn't _____ the drawing to her.

① show　　　② bring
③ give　　　④ buy
⑤ send

07 Who finds the error and corrects it properly? 3점

On Christmas Day, Santa gave to me a present. I know my parents actually bought the present for me, but I pretended not to know.

① 현영: a present → to a present
② 승훈: to me → me
③ 민서: for me → to me
④ 미나: to me → for me
⑤ 현서: for me → of me

08 Choose ALL of the <u>incorrect</u> sentences. 3점

① She didn't ask me it.
② My friends called me a genius.
③ His habit made him successfully.
④ Tell me another funny story.
⑤ We found the place interesting.

VOCA　elderly 나이 든 | orphan 고아 | refrigerator 냉장고 | address 주소 | brilliant 훌륭한 | bitter 쓴 | smooth 부드러운 | past 과거 | cage 새장 | own 자신의 | drawing 그림 | present 선물 | pretend ～인 척 하다 | genius 천재 | habit 습관

09 Which translation is correct? 2점

> 많은 사람들이 네 충고가 유용하다고 생각할 거야.

① Many people will find your advice useful.
② Many people will find useful your advice.
③ Many people will find your advice usefully.
④ Many people will find of your advice useful.
⑤ Many people will find for your advice usefully.

10 Which sentence is grammatically correct? 2점

① I gave him it.
② She sent her it.
③ We sold her them.
④ They gave us them.
⑤ She showed them to us.

11 Which is NOT proper for the blank? 2점

> My grandma _____ me happy.

① made   ② found
③ kept   ④ got
⑤ gave

Challenge! 주관식 서술형

12 Complete the sentence by rearranging the given words. 4점

> for, buy, my sister, a new CD

→ I'm going to _____
for her birthday.

13 Find the sentence that has an error and correct it. 4점

> ⓐ I'll buy her a book with my savings.
> ⓑ We call him to a scholar.
> ⓒ Competition made their relationship worse.

(   ) _____ → _____

14 Rewrite the sentence correctly. 5점

> My science teacher asked us it.

→ _____

15 Write a sentence describing the picture by using the given words. Change the verb form if necessary. (*Present Tense*) 5점

> the park, the trash, make, messy

→ _____

16 Translate the sentence according to the conditions. 6점

> 이 향기는 나를 하루 종일 신선하게 유지해 준다.
>
> · Condition 1   scent, fresh, all day
> · Condition 2   k로 시작하는 단어를 추가할 것
> · Condition 3   7단어로 쓸 것

→ _____

VOCA   useful 유용한 | savings 지금, 저축 | scholar 학자 | competition 경쟁 | relationship 관계 | worse 더 나쁜 | trash 쓰레기 | messy 지저분한, 엉망인

03 5형식

개념이해책
18쪽 함께 보기

■ 아래 표의 빈칸에 알맞은 내용을 써 넣으세요. ››› 정답 04쪽

1 목적격 보어로 1)＿＿＿＿＿＿＿ 가 오는 경우

주어	동사	목적어	목적격 보어(2)＿＿＿＿＿＿)
I	want	you	to come back.

2 목적격 보어로 3)＿＿＿＿＿ 이 오는 경우: 사역동사, 지각동사

주어	동사	목적어	목적격 보어(4)＿＿＿＿＿)
Our teacher	made	us	study hard.
Mom	had	me	do the dishes.
I	heard	the monsters	scream loudly.

3 준사역동사: help, get

주어＋help＋목적어＋(5)＿＿＿＿＿＿)＋6)＿＿＿＿＿	I helped him (to) repair the car.
주어＋get＋목적어＋7)＿＿＿＿＿＿＋8)＿＿＿＿＿	I will get her to water the plants.

4 목적격 보어가 과거분사인 경우

주어＋9)＿＿＿/10)＿＿＿ 동사＋목적어＋11)＿＿＿	She heard her name called.

 Level 1 Test

››› 정답 04쪽

A 문장에서 목적격 보어를 찾아 밑줄을 치시오.

1 The audience found the performance funny.

2 The referee allowed him to join the game.

3 Mr. Lee saw his son go into the Internet café.

4 His mean words made her angry.

B [ ]에서 알맞은 것을 고르시오.

1 She got me [clean / to clean] the floor.

2 He advised me [keep / to keep] my promise.

3 I had my brother [prepare / to prepare] dinner for me.

4 I felt something [flying / to fly] over my head.

5 They made us [get / to get] in line.

C 주어진 단어들 중 필요한 것만 골라 영작하시오.

1 나를 웃기지 좀 마. (make, laugh, let, me, don't)

→ ＿＿＿＿＿＿＿＿＿＿＿＿

2 우리는 그녀에게 거짓말하지 말라고 말했다.
(told, to, not, tell a lie, say)

→ ＿＿＿＿＿＿＿＿＿＿＿＿

3 나는 그 아이가 지갑을 훔치는 것을 보지 못했다.
(see, the kid, to, steal, the wallet)

→ ＿＿＿＿＿＿＿＿＿＿＿＿

VOCA audience 관객 | performance 공연 | referee 심판 | floor 바닥 | advise 충고하다 | promise 약속 | prepare 준비하다 | get in line 줄을 서다 | wallet 지갑

My score is
/ 30점
25점 이상 PASS!!

01 다음 문장들 중 어법상 <u>어색한</u> 부분을 <u>모두</u> 고른 것은? 3점

ⓐ We heard the bird singing.
ⓑ Dorothy saw the lion cross the street.
ⓒ I felt the sweat to run down my back.
ⓓ They watched her laughing a lot.
ⓔ The chef smelled something burning in the kitchen.

① ⓐ singing, ⓒ to run
② ⓒ to run
③ ⓑ cross, ⓓ laughing
④ ⓐ singing, ⓓ laughing
⑤ ⓔ burning

02 빈칸에 들어갈 말로 알맞은 것을 <u>2개</u> 고르면? 2점

They watched their children _____ baseball.

① play   ② to play
③ played   ④ playing
⑤ to playing

03 빈칸에 공통으로 들어갈 말로 알맞은 것은? 2점

· I wanted _____ today.
· I wanted him _____ for a minute.

① rest   ② resting
③ rested   ④ to rest
⑤ to resting

04 다음 중 어법상 올바른 문장을 <u>모두</u> 고르시오. 3점

① I made her wiping the floor.
② She asked me to correct the errors.
③ Did he help her go up to the roof?
④ He wants you to build your career.
⑤ They have helped my son going to college.

05 우리말과 같은 뜻이 되도록 주어진 단어를 배열해서 문장을 완성하시오. 5점
서술형

나는 어젯밤에 이웃들이 싸우는 소리를 들었다.
I, neighbors, my, heard, argue

→ _____

   last night.

06 다음 두 문장을 한 문장으로 만들 때 빈칸에 알맞은 말을 쓰시오. 5점
서술형

I watched some children. + The children were playing basketball.

→ I watched some children _____.

07 다음 문장에서 어법상 <u>어색한</u> 부분을 찾아 바르게 고치시오. 4점
서술형

I had my watch repair.
나는 시계 수리를 맡겼다.

_____ → _____

08 우리말과 같은 뜻이 되도록 주어진 조건에 맞게 영작하시오. 6점
서술형

아빠는 내가 아침마다 신문을 읽게 하셨다.

· 조건 1   어휘 – Dad, read, the newspaper
· 조건 2   과거 시제로 쓸 것
· 조건 3   8단어로 쓸 것

→ _____

VOCA   cross 가로지르다 | sweat 땀 | back 등, 뒤 | burn 타다 | rest 휴식을 취하다 | wipe 닦다 | correct 고치다 | error 실수 | roof 지붕 | career 직업,
진로, 경력 | neighbor 이웃 | argue 싸우다, 논쟁하다 | repair 수리하다

Level 3 Test

>>> 정답 04쪽

01 Choose ALL of the <u>incorrect</u> words from the following sentences. 3점

> ⓐ Susie watched him had dinner.
> ⓑ They heard someone yelling at them.
> ⓒ I saw your dog biting your shoes.
> ⓓ We didn't hear her say, "Thank you."
> ⓔ John felt someone push him forward.
> ⓕ We encouraged them work harder.

① ⓐ had, ⓕ work
② ⓐ had, ⓓ say
③ ⓑ yelling, ⓒ biting, ⓓ say
④ ⓔ push
⑤ ⓕ work

02 Which is grammatically <u>incorrect</u>? 2점

> Did you ① <u>hear</u> ② <u>her</u> ③ <u>made</u> ④ <u>any</u>
> ⑤ <u>strange</u> sounds?

03 Choose ALL of the correct choices for the blank. 2점

> We watched the man _____ the lollipop in the store.

① steal   ② stealing
③ to steal   ④ stole
⑤ to stealing

04 Which is the common word for the blanks? 2점

> • I helped my dad _____ the lawn.
> • My dad made me _____ the grass.

① mow   ② to mow
③ mowing   ④ mowed
⑤ to mowing

05 Choose ALL of the correct sentences. 3점

① She had her hair cut.
② He had her change the color of her hair.
③ We had the roof fixed.
④ They had me to bake some cookies.
⑤ He told me cleaning all of the stuff.

06 Which is proper for the blank? 2점

> Her parents let her _____ to the musical.

① go   ② went
③ goes   ④ to go
⑤ going

07 Which is a <u>different</u> sentence form? 2점

① I kept the window open.
② His accuracy made him a good referee.
③ He saw koalas eating leaves.
④ I had him change his password.
⑤ I made him a sandwich for breakfast.

08 Choose the common word for the blanks. 2점

> • She got the maid _____ the chandelier.
> • He told me _____ my feet on the mat.

① wipe   ② to wipe
③ wiping   ④ wiped
⑤ to wiping

VOCA yell 소리 지르다 | bite 물다 | push 밀다 | forward 앞으로 | encourage 용기를 북돋아주다 | lollipop 막대사탕 | mow the lawn 잔디를 깎다 | stuff 잡동사니, 물건 | accuracy 정확성 | referee 심판 | password 비밀번호 | maid 가정부 | wipe 닦다 | chandelier 샹들리에 | mat 매트(깔개)

09 Which is NOT proper for any of the blanks? 3점

> ⓐ The accident made her _____.
> ⓑ I helped Jane _____.

① shocked   ② sad
③ thinking   ④ study
⑤ to cook

10 Which are the correct words for the blanks? 2점

> • Who left the door _____?
> • The owner got him _____ the contract.

① open – sign   ② to open – signed
③ open – to sign   ④ to open – to sign
⑤ open – signed

Challenge! 주관식 서술형

11 Complete the sentence by rearranging the given words. 3점

> My parents don't _____ at night.
> (let, go, me, outside)

→ _____

12 Combine the two given sentences into one. 5점

> 보기   I saw her. + She was dancing.
> → I saw her dancing.
> ----
> I heard him. + He mumbled to himself.

→ _____

13 Translate the sentence according to the conditions. 6점

> 그녀의 충고는 내가 올바른 결정을 내리도록 도왔다.
> ----
> • Condition 1   어휘 – advice, make the right decision
> • Condition 2   과거 시제로 쓸 것
> • Condition 3   8단어로 쓸 것

→ _____

14 Rewrite the sentence correctly. 4점

> Green tea makes the body burning fat.

→ _____

15 Find the sentence that has an error and correct it. 4점

> ⓐ We watched her take off her shoes.
> ⓑ She had her bags carry to the airport.
> ⓒ Did he ask her not to waste any money?

(   ) _____ → _____

16 Write a sentence describing the picture by using the given words. (*past tense*) 5점

> my sister, me, told, feed, the horse

→ _____

VOCA   accident 사고 | left leave(~한 상태로 두다)의 과거형 | owner 주인 | contract 계약서 | mumble 중얼거리다 | decision 결정 | burn 태우다 | fat 지방 | feed (먹이를) 먹이다

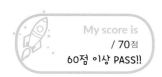

01 U01_2
다음 중 어법상 <u>어색한</u> 것은? 2점

① The story sounds sadly.
② The milk in the car tasted fine.
③ The shopkeeper looks friendly.
④ Why did you feel terrible?
⑤ Your food smells wonderful.

02 U01_2+3
빈칸에 들어갈 말로 알맞지 <u>않은</u> 것은? 2점

Early in October, it _____ cool.

① becomes   ② turns
③ is   ④ gets
⑤ changes

03 U01_2
다음 밑줄 친 ①~⑤ 중에서 어법상 <u>어색한</u> 것은? 2점

①The cookies ② in the basket ③ smelled
④ very ⑤ sweetly.

04 U02_1+GP
Which is the correct word for the blank so that the two sentences have the same meaning? 2점

The secretary got the boss a cup of coffee.
= The secretary got a cup of coffee _____ the boss.

① to   ② of
③ for   ④ with
⑤ on

05 U02_1+GP
다음 중 어법상 올바르지 <u>않은</u> 문장의 개수는? 3점

고난도

ⓐ The boy gave her a book.
ⓑ The teacher gave some advice for me.
ⓒ Can I ask a favor of you?
ⓓ She bought a present for her daughter.
ⓔ He showed the room to me.
ⓕ The company sent a box for Dad.

① one   ② two
③ three   ④ four
⑤ five

06 U02_1+GP
다음 우리말을 영어로 바르게 옮긴 것은? (답 2개) 2점

그는 나에게 자전거를 사주었다.

① He bought a bike to me.
② He bought me for a bike.
③ He bought me a bike.
④ He bought a bike me.
⑤ He bought a bike for me.

07 U03_1+2
Choose ALL of the correct sentences. 2점

고난도

① Will you have him change the plan?
② He made the dog to roll over.
③ She got me to wait for her.
④ She had the students waiting for her.
⑤ He told me buying her dinner.

08 U03_1+2+3
빈칸에 들어갈 말로 알맞지 <u>않은</u> 것은? 2점

Mike _____ me to study for the test.

① helped   ② made
③ got   ④ advised
⑤ asked

09 U03_2+GP

다음 중 어법상 어색한 문장은? 3점

고난도

① She helped me to cover the hole.

② He watched the kid ran to the park.

③ Her mother expected us to be more patient.

④ This plan will make us do extra work.

⑤ Thanks for letting me know where I can get it.

10 U03_4

빈칸에 들어갈 말이 바르게 짝지어진 것은? 3점

함정

> The director had the staff _____ the stage lighting.
> = The director had the stage lighting _____ by the staff.

① carry – to carry

② to carry – to carry

③ carry – carried

④ carried – carry

⑤ to carry – carry

11 U01_1

우리말과 같은 뜻이 되도록 빈칸에 알맞은 말을 쓰시오. 3점

> 병에 물이 거의 없다.

→ _____ little water in the bottle.

12 U01_1+U02_2

Look at the picture and fill in the blanks by using the given word. 4점

(1) The sun shines _____. (bright)

(2) The sun makes the world _____.
  (bright)

13 U01_2

다음 문장에서 어법상 어색한 부분을 찾아 바르게 고치시오. 3점

> The new baked bread looked so freshly and tasted good.

_____ → _____

14 U03_4

다음 글에서 어법상 어색한 부분을 찾아 바르게 고치시오.

고난도 4점

> When my mom asked me to put the laundry in the washing machine. I just put my jacket in after taking it off. Later, I saw my cellphone wash in the washing machine. Oh, my God! I didn't check my pocket. It was all my fault.

_____ → _____

15 U03_1

주어진 단어들 중 필요한 것만 골라 배열해서 영작하시오. 4점

함정

> 그는 나에게 그를 혼자 내버려두라고 말했다.
> leave, him, alone, told, he, me, to, for

→ _____

16 U03_1

Find the sentence that has an error and correct it. 4점

> ⓐ I know why you look so depressed.
> ⓑ The doctor advised me walk for an hour a day.
> ⓒ Did he ask her to speak quietly?

( ) _____ → _____

17 다음 문장에서 어법상 <u>어색한</u> 부분을 찾아 바르게 고치시오. 3점

> I saw he change into a wolf.

_____ ➡ _____

18 [보기]처럼 주어진 두 문장을 한 문장으로 쓰시오. 4점

> I watched the boy. + He ran down the hallway.
> ➡ I watched the boy run down the hallway.
>
> I listened to her. + She spoke in public.

➡ _____

19 우리말과 같은 뜻이 되도록 주어진 단어를 이용해서 영작하시오. 4점

> 그는 내가 수학 문제 푸는 것을 도와주었다.
> solve, the math problem

➡ _____

20 Translate the sentence according to the conditions. 6점

> 그 군인들은 그들이 국경선을 건너는 것을 허락하지 않았다.
> cross the border
>
> ·Condition 1   Use the word below.
>   l_____ : to give somebody permission to do something
> ·Condition 2   Write with 8 words.

➡ _____

[21~22] 다음 글을 읽고 물음에 답하시오.

ⓐ**Become** the best at something in one day is not possible. For instance, if you want ⓑ**to play** basketball well, you should watch experienced players ⓒ**play** the game and learn the basic skills. However, this alone (A)<u>너를 좋은 선수로 만들지 않을 것이다.</u> Practice every day. It'll give ⓓ**to you** a chance to be a better player. You cannot just pick up a basketball, bounce it a bit, and ⓔ**hope** to become a champion in a month or two. You need to put in a lot of time and energy to be an excellent player. As the old saying goes, "Practice makes perfect."

21 윗글의 밑줄 친 ⓐ~ⓔ 중 어법상 옳은 것의 개수는? 3점

고난도

① 1개
② 2개
③ 3개
④ 4개
⑤ 5개

22 밑줄 친 (A)와 같은 뜻이 되도록 주어진 단어를 배열하시오. (한 단어를 추가할 것) 5점

 한눈에 쏙

> good, you, a, won't, player

➡ _____

CHAPTER 02

to부정사

04 명사적, 형용사적, 부사적 용법

개념이해책
26쪽 함께 보기

■ 아래 표의 빈칸에 알맞은 내용을 써 넣으세요. >>> 정답 05쪽

CONCEPT 1 명사적 용법

역할	뜻	예문
1)	2)	To finish the work now is necessary.
3)	4)	His job was to repair toy cars.
5)	6)	I want to ride my bicycle.

CONCEPT 2 형용사적 용법

역할		뜻	예문
7)	수식	9)	He's not a person to tell lies.
8)	수식		I have something important to tell you.

CONCEPT 3 부사적 용법

역할	뜻	예문
10)	11)	The children ran to catch the rabbit.
12)	13)	We were very surprised to hear that.
14)	15)	Your son must be crazy to say that.
16)	17)	The boy grew up to be a race car driver.
18)	19)	Your handwriting is hard to read.

Level 1 Test

>>> 정답 05쪽

A 밑줄 친 부분의 의미를 [보기]에서 고르시오.

> 보기
> ⓐ ~하는 것　　ⓑ ~하는, ~할
> ⓒ ~하기 위해　ⓓ ~해서
> ⓔ ~하다니　　ⓕ ~해서 (결과) …하다
> ⓖ ~하기에

1 I have some pictures to draw. → _____

2 He must be silly to do such a thing. → _____

3 Swimming in the sea is hard to do. → _____

4 She woke up to find herself alone. → _____

5 They went to save the children. → _____

6 I am sorry to hear that. → _____

7 It's always a bad thing to tell a lie. → _____

B 우리말과 일치하도록 빈칸을 채우시오.

1 나는 고장 난 마우스를 사서 화가 났다.

→ I was angry _____ a broken mouse.

2 엄마는 비빔밥을 드시러 그 식당에 가셨어.

→ Mom went to the restaurant _____ bibimbap.

3 나는 쓸 종이 한 장이 필요해.

→ I need a piece of paper _____.

4 한국어를 말하는 것은 내게 쉬워.

→ _____ Korean is easy for me.

VOCA tell a lie 거짓말하다

 **Level 2 Test**

>>> 정답 06쪽

My score is
/ 30점
25점 이상 PASS!!

---

01 다음 빈칸에 들어갈 말로 알맞은 것은? 2점

> A: Can you tell me _____ print a card?
> B: Sure. It's easy. First, turn on the printer.

① how to
② when to
③ what to
④ where to
⑤ whom to

02 다음 중 밑줄 친 to부정사의 용법이 <u>다른</u> 하나는? 3점

① To respect others is always right.
② We decided to take the cable car.
③ I saved money to buy the sneakers.
④ My dream is to teach kids at kindergarten.
⑤ She wanted to know your phone number.

03 [보기]와 to부정사의 용법이 같은 예문을 쓴 학생은? 3점

> 보기   There was no place to go to.

① 미연: Your handwriting isn't easy to copy.
② 경일: I have some work to finish by 10.
③ 재민: It's important to work out regularly.
④ 현준: Your baby must be clever to do that.
⑤ 민지: Are you surprised to see me here?

04 다음 중 어법상 <u>어색한</u> 문장의 개수는? 3점

> ⓐ My dog jumped to catching the ball.
> ⓑ He needs somebody for fix his flashlight.
> ⓒ This is fun to follow her movements.
> ⓓ It was necessary for the villagers to protect the hill.
> ⓔ I turned on my computer in order to find some information.

① 1개
② 2개
③ 3개
④ 4개
⑤ 5개

---

05 그림을 보고, 주어진 단어 중 필요한 **5단어**를 골라 문장을 완성하시오. 4점

> it, that, dangerous, happy, riding, to, ride, is, be

→ _____ a bike on ice.

06 다음 두 문장이 같은 뜻이 되도록 빈칸을 채우시오. 5점

> She told me what to do next.

→ She told me _____
next.

07 그림을 보고 조건에 맞게 문장을 완성하시오. 5점

• 15 years ago	• Now

> 조건 1 to부정사의 부사적 용법을 이용할 것
> 조건 2 빈칸에 4단어로 쓸 것
> 조건 3 어휘 – grow up

→ The cute boy _____
a rocker.

08 주어진 단어를 배열하여 문장을 완성하시오. (번호를 쓸 것) 5점

> I took 11th Street _____.
> ⓐ avoid   ⓑ so   ⓒ to
> ⓓ traffic   ⓔ the   ⓕ as

→ _____

VOCA print 인쇄하다 | respect 존중하다 | kindergarten 유치원 | handwriting 필체 | copy 베끼다 | work out 운동하다 | regularly 규칙적으로 |
flashlight 손전등 | villager 마을 사람 | protect 보호하다 | avoid 피하다 | traffic 교통량

01 Which translation is <u>incorrect</u>? 2점

① Mr. Gonzales didn't know what to say.
→ Gonzales씨는 뭐라고 얘기해야 할지 몰랐다.

② I don't know when to stop.
→ 언제 멈춰야 할지 모르겠어요.

③ Ask him where to put the box.
→ 그에게 그 상자를 어디다 두었는지 물어봐.

④ I found out how to turn on this machine.
→ 이 기계를 어떻게 켜는지 알아냈어.

⑤ Can you tell me how to get there?
→ 거기에 어떻게 가는지 알려주실 수 있나요?

02 Which correction is right? 2점

> Julie wants to travel around the world and takes pictures of nature.

① wants → want   ② to → or
③ travel → traveling   ④ and → but
⑤ takes → take

03 Which underlined phrase is used <u>differently</u>? 2점

① I use voice commands <u>to set</u> my alarm.
② The man needed a pen <u>to write</u> with.
③ She stayed at home <u>to keep</u> house.
④ He went to the store <u>to buy</u> a jacket.
⑤ I'm going to New York <u>to study</u> music.

04 Which is suitable for the blank? (2 answers) 2점

> I don't know _____.

① which one choose
② which one to choose
③ which should choose
④ which one I to choose
⑤ which one I should choose

05 Which usage is NOT the same as the given sentence? 3점

> Every morning, he comes to school early <u>to sit</u> beside her.

① Roy went to the restroom <u>to wash</u> his hands.
② I ran to the market <u>to buy</u> some spaghetti.
③ The players were very glad <u>to see</u> their hero.
④ Minju went to the park <u>to look</u> for signs of autumn.
⑤ Sora turned on the light <u>to find</u> the mosquito.

06 Which of the underlined "It[it]" is used <u>differently</u> than the others? 2점

① <u>It</u> isn't possible to carry all of the books.
② <u>It</u> was very easy to understand the movie.
③ <u>It</u> is a really wonderful idea to me.
④ <u>It</u> is important to be polite to others.
⑤ Is <u>it</u> easy to make a lot of money?

07 Which sentences have the same usage for the underlined parts? 3점

> ⓐ I need to buy something <u>to wear</u>.
> ⓑ I tried everything <u>to get</u> closer to her.
> ⓒ Give me some water <u>to drink</u>.
> ⓓ <u>To drink</u> a lot of water is good for your health.
> ⓔ He used the Internet <u>to do</u> his homework.
> ⓕ I plan <u>to visit</u> Dicie in England next week.

① ⓐ, ⓒ   ② ⓑ, ⓕ
③ ⓒ, ⓔ   ④ ⓓ, ⓔ
⑤ ⓔ, ⓕ

08 Which TWO words are not necessary when translating the given sentence? 2점

> 나는 깨어나서 내 자신이 병원에 있는 것을 발견했다.
> I _____ in the hospital.

① not   ② find
③ myself   ④ woke up
⑤ in order to

VOCA take a picture 사진을 찍다 | voice command 음성 명령 | keep house 집안일을 하다 | beside ~ 옆에 | hero 영웅 | sign 기미, 징조 | mosquito 모기 | polite 예의 바른

30

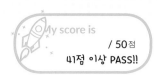

09 How many sentences have the same usage as the example? 3점

> 보기 We went to Kim's Computer together to buy a 16 gigabyte flash drive.
>
> ⓐ I'm sorry to hear that.
> ⓑ Would you like something to drink?
> ⓒ She has many friends to help her.
> ⓓ He went to Boeun to meet his sister.
> ⓔ It is not right to judge people by their clothes.

① one   ② two
③ three   ④ four
⑤ five

10 Who analyzes the given sentences correctly? 3점

> ⓐ They have no children to take care of.
> ⓑ It is important to keep calm in an emergency.

① 수하: ⓐ to take care of는 명사적 용법이야.
② 시현: ⓐ 마지막의 of를 지워야 해.
③ 찬윤: ⓑ to keep 이하가 진짜 주어야.
④ 예원: ⓑ It은 비인칭 주어야.
⑤ 세웅: ⓑ to keep calm은 형용사적 용법이야.

11 Which is NOT necessary when translating the given sentence? (2 answers) 2점

> Kate와 Edward는 다음 파티에 누구를 초대해야 할지 토론하고 있는 중이다.

① for   ② whom
③ should   ④ inviting
⑤ debating

Challenge! 주관식 서술형

12 Rewrite the sentence by using "to." 4점

> The girl grew up and became a governor.

→ The girl grew up _____.

13 Look at the picture and fill in the blanks with 4 words. Use the given words. 5점

→ He doesn't know _____

_____ _____

_____. (way, go)

14 Complete the sentence by filling in the blanks. 5점

> Click on the "send" button _____
> _____ _____ _____ _____
> _____.
> (그 메시지를 보내기 위해)

15 Find the sentence that has an error and correct it. 4점

> ⓐ She has nothing to do it today.
> ⓑ Everybody knew how to make a cake.
> ⓒ He has no friends to go to the concert with.

( ) _____ → _____

16 Find TWO errors and correct them. 6점

> Ryder is interested in too ⓐ many things. He likes singing, dancing, cooking, and even ⓑ make party music. But he doesn't have ⓒ any special plans for his future. He doesn't know ⓓ where to do in the future.

( ) _____ → _____
( ) _____ → _____

VOCA   emergency 비상 사태 | debate 토론하다 | governor 주지사 | plan 계획

의미상의 주어, 부정, 기타 용법

■ 아래 표의 빈칸에 알맞은 내용을 써 넣으세요. >>> 정답 06쪽

개념이해책
29쪽 함께 보기

CONCEPT 1 의미상의 주어

| 일반 형용사 | easy, difficult, hard, necessary, possible, impossible, interesting | 1)_____ +목적격 |
| 성품 형용사 | kind, nice, foolish, stupid, polite, rude, careful, careless, brave, wise | 2)_____ +목적격 |

CONCEPT 2 to부정사의 부정

| 3)_____ [never] 4)_____ +동사원형 |

CONCEPT 3 too ~ to...와 enough to...

| too ~ to... | so ~ 5)_____ +주어+ 6) | 너무 ~해서 …할 수 없는 |
| ~ enough to... | so ~ 7)_____ +주어+ 8) | ~할 정도로 충분히 …한 |

Level 1 Test

>>> 정답 06쪽

A 주어진 단어를 to부정사의 의미상의 주어로 쓰시오.

1 It is easy _____ _____ to find his house. (we)

2 It was kind _____ _____ to help us. (Ryan)

3 Is it safe _____ _____ to cross this bridge? (I)

4 It is selfish _____ _____ to eat the cake alone. (he)

B 우리말과 일치하도록 빈칸을 채우시오.

1 그들은 나에게 강에서 낚시하지 말라고 말했다.

→ They told me _____ _____ _____ in the river.

2 네가 문을 잠그지 않은 것은 부주의했다.

→ It was careless _____ _____ _____ _____ _____ the door.

C 밑줄 친 부분이 어색하면 고치시오.

1 He is enough generous to forgive my brother.

→ _____

2 He is so scared to make a move.

→ _____

3 He was very funny that I couldn't stop laughing.

→ _____

4 It was so dark that I couldn't see anything.

→ _____

D 두 문장의 뜻이 같도록 빈칸에 알맞은 말을 쓰시오.

1 I was too sleepy to stay awake.

→ I was _____ sleepy _____ I _____ _____ awake.

2 He was lucky enough to survive the accident.

→ He was _____ lucky _____ he _____ the accident.

VOCA selfish 이기적인 | careless 부주의한 | generous 관대한, 너그러운 | forgive 용서하다 | scared 겁먹은 | stay ~인 상태로 있다 | awake 깨어 있는 | survive 살아남다 | accident 사고

>>> 정답 06쪽

01 다음 빈칸에 들어갈 말이 바르게 짝지어진 것은? 2점

> • It's hard _____ her to drive on the highway.
> • It's nice _____ you to remember my birthday.

① for – of
② of – of
③ for – for
④ for – to
⑤ to – of

02 다음을 영작할 때 3번째 올 단어로 적절한 것은? 2점

> Cathy는 다시는 내 폴더를 지우지 않기로 약속했다.

① again
② promised
③ not
④ to
⑤ delete

03 다음 중 의미가 다른 하나는? 3점

① You are too young to see this movie.
② You are very young, so you can't see this movie.
③ You are so young that you can't see this movie.
④ You are so young that you can see this movie.
⑤ Because you are very young, you can't see this movie.

04 다음 문장에서 어법상 어색한 것을 찾아 바르게 고친 학생은? 3점

> Today, Olga got up so late that she can't get on the school bus.

① 창훈: so를 enough로 바꿔야 해.
② 시하: that은 who로 바꿔 쓸 수 있어.
③ 하준: so 대신 too를 써도 같은 의미야.
④ 연수: 과거 시제니까 can't를 couldn't로 써야 해.
⑤ 지윤: get on도 되고 got on으로 써도 돼.

05 그림을 보고 '표백제 사용하지 말랬지'라는 말이 되도록 문장을 완성하시오. 4점 〔서술형〕

→ I told you _____ _____
_____ bleach.

06 enough를 사용하여 같은 의미의 문장을 쓰시오. 5점 〔서술형〕

> He was so diligent that he could go swimming every morning.

→ _____

07 우리말과 같은 뜻이 되도록 주어진 조건에 맞게 영작하시오. 6점 〔서술형〕

> 그 공주는 용과 싸울 만큼 용감했다.
>
> · 조건 1 so ~ that 구문을 쓰지 말 것
> · 조건 2 어휘 – brave, fight
> · 조건 3 9단어로 쓸 것

→ _____

08 우리말과 같은 뜻이 되도록 주어진 단어를 배열하여 문장을 완성하시오. 5점 〔서술형〕

> 이 시계는 내가 사기에 너무 비싸요.
> me, expensive, buy, too, for, to

→ This watch is _____ .

VOCA highway 고속도로 | delete 지우다 | bleach 표백제 | brave 용감한 | fight 싸우다

01 Which TWO words for the blanks are <u>different</u> from the others? 3점

① Is it easy _____ me to see pine trees here?

② It's dangerous _____ children to go there alone.

③ It was very thoughtless _____ him to say that.

④ It isn't too heavy _____ you to move.

⑤ It's so foolish _____ them to believe in the Devil.

02 Who finds the <u>incorrect</u> sentence and corrects the error properly? 3점

> ⓐ It is not easy for me to dive from here.
> ⓑ She told me not talk in class.

① 혜진: ⓐ It is not easy of me to dive from here.

② 서희: ⓐ It is not easy for me dive from here.

③ 민주: ⓑ She told me to not talk in class.

④ 은정A: ⓑ She telled me talk in class.

⑤ 은정B: ⓑ She told me not to talk in class.

03 Which is suitable for the blank? (Find ALL.) 2점

> I told my students _____.

① not to waste money ② respect each other

③ never tell a lie ④ to do their best

⑤ never to give up

04 Which has a <u>different</u> meaning than the others? 2점

① The man was too young to get the job.

② The man was young enough to get the job.

③ The man was so young that he couldn't get the job.

④ The man was too young, so he couldn't get the job.

⑤ The man couldn't get the job because he was too young.

05 Which translation is correct? 2점

> 할아버지는 등산을 즐기실 정도로 건강하시다.

① Grandpa is healthy too to enjoy hiking.

② Grandpa is enough healthy to enjoy hiking.

③ Grandpa is too healthy to enjoy hiking.

④ Grandpa is healthy enough to enjoy hiking.

⑤ Grandpa is healthy enough enjoying hiking.

06 Whose correction is right? 2점

> The green tea is too hot for me to drink it.

① 희섭: too → enough

② 성환: for → of

③ 종식: to → too

④ 종화: me → mine

⑤ 민준: drink it → drink

07 Which word CANNOT be used when translating the sentence? 2점

> 그는 너무 빨리 말해서 나는 그의 말을 알아들을 수 없다.

① speaks

② too

③ enough

④ can't

⑤ him

08 Which is grammatically <u>incorrect</u>? (2 answers) 3점

① She was enough smart to do that.

② The ice cream was too expensive to buy.

③ I was fast enough to catch the robber.

④ This machine was too old to use it.

⑤ He was handsome enough to get a lot of attention.

VOCA pine tree 소나무 | thoughtless 생각 없는, 경솔한 | Devil 악마 | dive 다이빙하다 | do one's best 최선을 다하다 | robber 도둑, 강도 | attention 주의, 주목

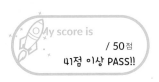

09 How many sentences are correct? 3점

ⓐ You are young too to join the army.
ⓑ It was too hard for us to finish the race.
ⓒ He was too angry to think of it as a joke.
ⓓ The uniform isn't enough warm to wear in winter.
ⓔ He advised me not to drink too much coffee.
ⓕ The milk was very bad that we couldn't drink it.
---

① one   ② two
③ three   ④ four
⑤ five

10 Which CANNOT make a grammatically correct sentence? 4점

① tired / to / was / cook / . / too / Everybody
② know / . / next / what / He / do / to / didn't
③ the / Is / enough / ice / ? / thick / on / walk / to
④ It / to / was / come / him / alone / careless / . / for
⑤ as / performance / not / . / miss / to / ran / first / his / so / We

11 Which is grammatically <u>wrong</u>? (3 answers) 3점

① The keyboard is so small that he can't use it.
   → The keyboard is too small for him to use it.
② She's tall enough to change the bulb.
   → She is so tall that she can change the bulb.
③ You were too late to buy a ticket.
   → You were so late that you can't buy a ticket.
④ He spoke so fast that I couldn't understand him.
   → He spoke too fast for me to understand.
⑤ I was lucky enough to become friends with her.
   → I was too lucky that I could become friends with her.

Challenge! 주관식 서술형

12 Translate the sentence according to the conditions. 6점

그 피자는 너무 식어서 내가 먹을 수 없었다.

· Condition 1   to부정사의 의미상의 주어를 이용할 것
· Condition 2   The pizza로 시작할 것
· Condition 3   어휘 – cold, eat

→ _____

13 In the two sentences, find TWO errors and correct them. 5점

ⓐ The book was too boring to keep reading.
ⓑ The question is enough simple to solve it.

(   ) _____ → _____
(   ) _____ → _____

14 Find the error and correct it. 5점

I really want to go to a concert this Friday. It starts at 9 p.m. However, my mom won't let me go there. She says I am too young that I can't stay out late.

_____ → _____

15 Complete the sentence describing the picture by using the given words. 5점

→ These jeans are _____ _____ _____ _____!

(too, tight)

VOCA   advise 충고하다 | bulb 전구 | boring 지루한 | tight 꽉 끼는

U04_3

01 다음 문장의 빈칸에 가장 알맞은 것은? 2점

> Erica went to the restaurant with her friends _____.

① to wash her hair
② to play football
③ to have T-bone steaks
④ to buy some milk
⑤ to return a book

U04_2+3

02 다음 중 밑줄 친 부분의 쓰임이 다른 하나는? 2점

 한눈에 쏙

① I went to the library to check out a book.
② She has lots of things to do today.
③ We studied hard to pass the exam.
④ I'm very pleased to hear that.
⑤ They grew up to be fine young men.

U04_1+GP

03 다음 우리말을 바르게 영작한 학생 2명은? 2점

> 무엇을 팔아야 할지 모르겠어.

① 준호: I don't know what to sell.
② 창모: I don't know where to sell.
③ 재교: I'm not sure where I should sell.
④ 은일: I'm not sure which should I sell.
⑤ 요셉: I'm not sure what I should sell.

U04_GP

04 밑줄 친 'It[it]'의 쓰임이 다른 하나는? 2점

① It is not hard to make.
② It isn't possible to join the club.
③ It is not easy to change the plan.
④ It is dangerous to drive a car that way.
⑤ It is simple to unlock the door.

U05_1

05 Which word for the blank is different from the others? 2점

 한눈에 쏙

① It's easy _____ you to see koalas there.
② It's dangerous _____ children to go there.
③ It's very kind _____ you to say that.
④ It's too heavy _____ you to carry.
⑤ That's a little difficult _____ me to explain.

U05_GP

06 다음 문장을 바르게 분석한 학생은? 3점

함정

> This dictionary app is easy for me to use it.

① 미선: to use는 주어를 꾸며주는 형용사적 용법이야.
② 혁진: 여기서 to는 전치사로 쓰인 거야.
③ 현주: easy가 성품 형용사라서 for가 쓰인 거야.
④ 신아: to부정사의 목적어가 주어니까 it을 지워야 해.
⑤ 효진: 틀린 부분이 없는 완벽한 문장이야.

U05_3

07 다음 주어진 문장과 의미가 같은 것은? 2점

> We were so late that we couldn't see the show.

① We were late to see the show.
② We were too late to see the show.
③ We were late, but we saw the show.
④ We were late enough to see the show.
⑤ We were enough late to see the show.

U05_1

08 다음 중 어법상 어색한 문장은? 2점

고난도

① She worked hard to be a good teacher.
② I saved some money to buy the keychain.
③ She must really like him to be that shy.
④ It was really fun to swim in the lake.
⑤ The lecture was difficult of me to understand.

09 U05_3
Where does the word "enough" best fit? 2점

Your explanation was (①) not (②) clear (③) for (④) the class (⑤) to understand.

10 U04_1+2+GP
★
고난도
다음 문장에서 어색한 곳을 모두 찾아 바르게 고친 학생은? 3점

ⓐ He is strong enough to carry it.
ⓑ I need someone to talk.
ⓒ She didn't know what to do first.
ⓓ That is hard to say sorry.

① 기태: ⓐ it 삭제, ⓑ talk → talk to
② 은주: ⓒ what → where, ⓓ That → It
③ 치현: ⓓ That → It
④ 혜림: ⓐ it 삭제, ⓓ That → It
⑤ 은지: ⓑ talk → talk to, ⓓ That → It

11 U04_GP
Write the common word for the blanks. 3점

· Do you have a friend to rely _____ ?
· He needed some paper to write _____ .

→ _____

12 U04_3
그림을 보고 주어진 조건에 맞게 문장을 완성하시오. 4점

· 조건 1   to부정사를 이용할 것
· 조건 2   어휘 – pleased, a gold medal
· 조건 3   주어진 어휘를 포함하여 빈칸에 6단어로 쓸 것

→ Jangmi was _____ _____ _____ _____
_____ _____ .

13 U05_1+3
두 문장의 뜻이 같도록 빈칸에 알맞은 말을 쓰시오. 4점

The classroom was so noisy that I couldn't study.

→ The classroom was _____ _____ _____
_____ _____ _____ .

14 U04_1
우리말과 같은 뜻이 되도록 주어진 단어를 이용해서 문장을 완성하시오. 4점

부모님은 내가 의사가 되길 원하시지만, 나는 간호사가 되길 바란다.

→ My parents want me to be a doctor, but I
_____ . (hope)

15 U05_1
다음 두 문장 중 어법상 어색한 것을 찾아 고치시오. 3점

ⓐ Was it easy of you to describe your feelings?
ⓑ It was foolish of me to tell him the truth.

(   ) _____ → _____

16 U04_3+U05_2
👁
한눈에
쏙
다음은 해병대 캠프에 참가한 학생들의 훈련 모습이다. 우리말과 같은 뜻이 되도록 주어진 단어를 이용해서 교관의 말을 완성하시오. 4점

여러분들은 여기 놀러 온 게 아니라 훈련하러 온 겁니다! 알겠습니까? (train, play)

→ You guys are here _____ _____ , _____
_____ _____ ! Got that?

17 [보기]와 같이 주어진 문장을 전환하시오. 5점

> 보기 You can't beat me.
> → It is impossible for you to beat me.
>
> Freshmen can join our club.

→ _____

18 그림을 보고 주어진 단어를 이용해서 문장을 완성하시오. 4점

함정

> too ~ to..., small, the man, ride

→ The bike is _____.

19 우리말과 같은 뜻이 되도록 조건에 맞게 영작하시오. 6점

> 나는 언제 그녀의 전화번호를 물어야 할지 몰랐다.
>
> · 조건 1 의문사를 포함할 것
> · 조건 2 should를 쓰지 말 것
> · 조건 3 her phone number를 포함할 것
> · 힌트 ask for ~ ~을 달라고 묻다

→ _____

_____

20 Rearrange the given words correctly. 4점

> isn't, handle, he, enough, strong, hatred, to

→ _____

[21~22] 다음 글을 읽고 물음에 답하시오.

Vulcan was the god of fire and the forge. He was an expert in dealing with metals, and he used fire ⓐto heat metal. (A)(people, want, didn't, Vulcan, him, bother), so he liked ⓑto work alone in the mountains. Every time he worked, sparks ⓒflew out of the mountain. When people saw a mountain ⓓexploded with smoke and sparks, they thought ⓔthat Vulcan was working. So they called an exploding mountain a volcano.

*forge: 대장간

21 윗글의 밑줄 친 ⓐ~ⓔ 중 어법상 옳은 것의 개수는? 3점

고난도

① 1개
② 2개
③ 3개
④ 4개
⑤ 5개

22 윗글의 밑줄 친 (A)에 주어진 단어를 이용해서 조건에 맞게 영작하시오. 4점

> · 조건 1 주어진 어휘를 그대로 쓸 것
> · 조건 2 한 단어를 추가할 것

→ _____

CHAPTER 03

동명사

06 동명사의 쓰임, 동명사와 to부정사

개념이해책
36쪽 함께 보기

■ 아래 표의 빈칸에 알맞은 내용을 써 넣으세요. ››› 정답 08쪽

CONCEPT 1 동명사의 역할

역할	예문
1)	Saving money is good for your future.
2)	Her hobby is collecting old toys.
3)	He enjoys traveling alone.
4)	Are you poor at singing?

CONCEPT 2 동명사와 to부정사

enjoy, mind, dislike, stop, quit, avoid, practice, finish, imagine, deny, keep (on)	5)
want, plan, hope, promise, expect, wish, decide, would like, need	6)
like, begin, start, continue, love, hate	7)

CONCEPT 3 뒤에 오는 말의 형태에 따라 의미가 달라지는 경우

forget	+ 동명사	8)	try	+ 동명사	12)
	+ to부정사	9)		+ to부정사	13)
remember	+ 동명사	10)	stop	+ 동명사	14)
	+ to부정사	11)		+ to부정사	15)

Level 1 Test

››› 정답 08쪽

A 문장에서 동명사에 밑줄을 치고, 그 역할을 [보기]에서 고르시오.

> 보기
> ⓐ 주어　　　ⓑ 보어
> ⓒ 동사의 목적어　ⓓ 전치사의 목적어

1 Listening to others is important. → _____

2 He didn't mind waiting for her. → _____

3 I can't sing. I am poor at singing. → _____

B 밑줄 친 부분이 어색하면 바꿔 쓰시오.

1 She continued to use her credit card.

　→ _____

2 The boss disliked to walk even three steps.

　→ _____

3 I would like traveling around Latin America.

　→ _____

C [ ]에서 알맞은 것을 고르시오.

1 We want [to take / taking] a break, sir.

2 The elevator stopped [to work / working].

3 Why do you avoid [to meet / meeting] him?

4 Do you promise [to tell / telling] the truth?

VOCA　be poor at ~을 못하다 | dislike 싫어하다 | take a break 잠깐 쉬다 | work 작동하다 | truth 진실

01 다음 빈칸에 알맞지 <u>않은</u> 것은? 2점

He _____ playing the harp for us.

① minds
② enjoyed
③ finished
④ planned
⑤ will give up

02 다음 문장에서 <u>어색한</u> 부분을 찾아 바르게 고친 것은? 2점

Printing 100 pages take a lot of time.

① Printing → Print
② pages → page
③ take → takes
④ a lot of → many
⑤ time → times

03 밑줄 친 부분이 [보기]와 같은 용법으로 사용된 것은? 2점

 My favorite thing to do is <u>playing</u> with my pets.

① He kept on <u>waving</u> to his son.
② My bad habit is <u>shaking</u> my legs.
③ He gave up <u>running</u> the marathon.
④ Are you interested in <u>helping</u> old people?
⑤ <u>Understanding</u> your friends is not always easy.

04 다음 중 어법상 <u>어색한</u> 것끼리 짝지어진 것은? 3점

ⓐ Clare isn't good at to catch a ball.
ⓑ Would you mind opening the window?
ⓒ When do you plan going back to school?
ⓓ Lucy likes to watch the stars at night.
ⓔ He imagined to fly high in the sky.

① ⓐ, ⓒ
② ⓑ, ⓓ
③ ⓒ, ⓔ
④ ⓐ, ⓒ, ⓓ
⑤ ⓐ, ⓒ, ⓔ

05 다음 우리말을 조건에 맞도록 영작하시오. 6점

서술형

그녀의 취미는 로맨스 소설을 읽는 것이다.

· 조건 1   동명사를 사용할 것
· 조건 2   어휘 – romance novels

→ _____

06 우리말과 같은 뜻이 되도록 주어진 단어를 배열하시오. 5점

서술형

그는 그 동굴 안으로 들어가는 것이 두려웠다.
afraid, cave, going, he, the, was, of, into

→ _____

07 ⓐ~ⓓ 중 어법상 <u>어색한</u> 것을 2개 찾아 고치시오. 5점

서술형

I played a soccer game today. I think I played very ⓐ <u>good</u>. ⓑ <u>Play</u> soccer means everything to me. I hope ⓒ <u>to be</u> like H.M. Son. But my parents don't want me ⓓ <u>to be</u> a soccer player.

( ) _____ → _____
( ) _____ → _____

08 그림을 보고 주어진 동사를 이용해서 대화를 완성하시오. 5점

서술형

A: I can't open the door. It's stuck! What should I do?
B: Stop ___(A)___ it. Try ___(B)___ it!
(pull, push)

(A) _____   (B) _____

01 Which is NOT suitable for the blank? (Find ALL.) 2점

> We _____ watching TV at night.

① enjoy   ② finished
③ wanted   ④ expect
⑤ stopped

02 Which underlined choice is used differently than the example? (2 answers) 2점

> We must finish reading this book by next Sunday.

① Taking notes in class is boring.
② The man began talking about his life.
③ Would you mind using your phone?
④ He continued drawing pictures of her.
⑤ Her job is teaching P.E. in kindergarten.

03 Which of the following best fits in the blank? 2점

> When she saw me walking on the street, she stopped _____ me a ride.

① give   ② gave
③ giving   ④ to give
⑤ to giving

04 Which is NOT suitable for the blanks? 2점

> • My nephew _____ to study science.
> • My sister _____ reading short stories.

① imagined   ② started
③ hates   ④ loves
⑤ continued

05 Which pair is correct for the blanks? 3점

> Jennifer decided _____ _____ the MTB class because _____ the class was too hard for her.

① giving up – take – to take
② giving up – taking – to take
③ to give up – to take – taking
④ to give up – to take – to take
⑤ to give up – taking – taking

06 Find ALL of the proper expressions for the blank. 3점

> Do you like _____?

① the band's first album
② to read comic books
③ buying instant food online
④ took the roller coaster
⑤ going to the movies in the morning

07 Which correction is correct? 3점

> Sometimes having angry is good for your mental health.

① Sometimes → Sometime
② having → being
③ is → are
④ good → well
⑤ mental → mentally

08 Which word CANNOT be used when translating the sentence? 2점

> 내 고양이는 상자 속에 숨는 것을 좋아해.

① likes   ② boxes
③ hide   ④ hiding
⑤ hid

VOCA take notes 필기하다 | P.E. 체육 | give A a ride A를 태워 주다 | nephew 남자 조카 | short story 단편 소설 | MTB (= mountain bike) 산악자전거 | comic book 만화책 | mental health 정신 건강

09 Which is grammatically correct? 2점

① Do you mind to hold the door for me?
② I didn't finish to do my homework.
③ I decided going to the local college.
④ The strange man began to shout at her.
⑤ Laika planned studying Korean and Japanese.

10 Which sentences are grammatically correct? 3점

> ⓐ Taking pictures of flowers are my hobby.
> ⓑ He loves having pasta at the restaurant.
> ⓒ I really don't want to change my plans, now.
> ⓓ I'll never forget to buy my first car a few years ago.

① ⓐ, ⓓ   ② ⓑ, ⓒ
③ ⓑ, ⓓ   ④ ⓐ, ⓑ, ⓓ
⑤ ⓐ, ⓒ, ⓓ

Challenge! 주관식 서술형

11 Find the sentence that has an error and correct it. 3점

> ⓐ Why do you keep to avoid my eyes?
> ⓑ I didn't expect to see my homeroom teacher at the Internet café.

(   ) _____ → _____

12 Translate the sentence according to the conditions. 6점

> 아이들을 돌보는 것은 쉽지 않다.
>
> · Condition 1   동명사를 사용할 것
> · Condition 2   어휘 – take care of
> · Condition 3   주어진 어휘를 포함해 빈칸에 5단어로 쓸 것

→ _____ not easy.

13 Summarize the dialog as shown in the example. 4점

> Mom: Why did you hit your brother?
> Ken: I didn't hit him.
> → Ken denies hitting his brother.
> ---
> Anna: Can you do your homework first?
> Minhee: I already did it.

→ Minhee _____. (finish)

14 Rearrange the given words. 5점

> 월요일 아침에 연습에 참석하는 것을 잊지 마.
>
> attend, to, on Monday morning, don't, the practice, forget

→ _____

_____

15 Look at the picture and complete the dialog. 4점

> A: Shhh. Please _____
> _____ _____ ___. The baby is sleeping. (stop, make noise)
> B: Okey-doke!

16 Find the error and correct it. 4점

> Shutaro likes stars. He wants to be an astronomer in the future. He likes hanging out with his friends and meet new people.

_____ → _____

VOCA local 지역의 | college 대학 | shout at ~에게 소리를 지르다 | avoid 피하다 | homeroom teacher 담임 선생님 | take care of ~을 돌보다 |
deny 부인하다 | attend 참석하다 | shhh 쉿 | okey-doke OK의 구어 | astronomer 천문학자 | hang out with ~와 어울리다, ~와 시간을 보내다

UNIT 07 동명사와 현재분사, 관용적 표현

■ 아래 표의 빈칸에 알맞은 내용을 써 넣으세요. ››› 정답 09쪽

개념이해책
39쪽 함께 보기

CONCEPT 1 동명사와 현재분사

	형태	기능		표현	의미
동명사	1)	3)	(주어, 목적어, 보어)	용도, 목적	4)
현재분사	+2)	5) , 6)		동작, 상태	7)

Miki is swimming in the pool. (→ 8) _____)
She wants to buy a house with a swimming pool. (→ 9) _____)

CONCEPT 2 동명사의 관용적 표현

표현	뜻	표현	뜻
go+-ing	10)	How[What] about -ing ~?	15)
be busy+-ing	11)	spend[waste] 시간[돈]+-ing	16)
be tired of+-ing	12)	look forward to+-ing	17)
be worth+-ing	13)	have difficulty[a hard time]+-ing	18)
feel like+-ing	14)		

Level 1 Test

››› 정답 09쪽

A 밑줄 친 단어를 바르게 고치시오.

1 I want to buy a house with a <u>swim</u> pool.

→ _____

2 <u>Sing</u> to herself is her hobby. → _____

3 What are you <u>drink</u>, John? → _____

B 밑줄 친 부분이 동명사면 G, 현재분사면 P를 쓰시오.

1 <u>Succeeding</u> is not enough.

→ _____

2 The <u>barking</u> dog next door drives me crazy.

→ _____

3 The soldiers were <u>fighting</u> for their country.

→ _____

C [ ]에서 알맞은 것을 고르시오.

1 I am tired of [wait / waiting] for you.

2 Will you go [camp / camping] alone?

3 What would you like [to have / having]?

D 괄호 안의 표현을 사용하여 우리말과 일치하도록 빈칸을 채우시오.

1 나는 하루 종일 자고 싶다. (feel like+-ing)

→ I _____ all day long.

2 이 앱은 다운로드할 만한 가치가 없어. (be worth+-ing)

→ This app _____ .

3 그는 음악을 들으며 여가를 보낸다. (spend ~+-ing)

→ He _____ to music.

VOCA drive A crazy A를 미치게 하다 | soldier 군인 | app (= application) 앱 | free time 여가

Level 2 Test

>>> 정답 09쪽

My score is
/ 30점
25점 이상 PASS!!

01 다음 중 동명사가 쓰인 것의 개수는? 2점

> ⓐ swimming pool　　ⓑ sleeping car
> ⓒ running man　　　ⓓ exciting game
> ⓔ dancing room　　 ⓕ cooking class

① 1개　　　　　　② 2개
③ 3개　　　　　　④ 4개
⑤ 5개

02 밑줄 친 부분의 쓰임이 [보기]와 같은 것은? 2점

> (보기)　His hobby is <u>cooking</u> Korean food.

① Don't wake up the <u>sleeping</u> tiger.
② What an <u>interesting</u> game!
③ Is the man <u>wearing</u> a shirt?
④ <u>Taking</u> too many showers is bad for your skin.
⑤ She is <u>typing</u> a report.

03 다음 문장을 바르게 분석한 학생은? 2점

> He was smoking in the smoking room.

① 소율: 앞의 smoking은 동명사야.
② 아미: 위에 쓰인 smoking은 둘 다 현재분사야.
③ 지유: 뒤의 smoking은 용도를 나타내는 동명사야.
④ 채은: 앞의 smoking은 동명사, 뒤는 현재분사야.
⑤ 하영: 뒤의 smoking은 smoke로 바꿔야 해.

04 다음 빈칸에 알맞은 것으로 짝지어진 것은? 2점

> • The news is not worth _____.
> • I don't feel like _____ now.

① watch – studying　　② to watch – studying
③ to watch – to study　④ watching – studying
⑤ watching – to study

05 밑줄 친 단어의 쓰임이 [보기]와 같은 것을 고르고, 동명사인지 현재분사인지 구분하시오. 5점

서술형

> (보기)　I bought a <u>sleeping</u> bag.
>
> ⓐ A drunken man is <u>sleeping</u> on the bench.
> ⓑ Their solution was <u>leaving</u> the town.

(　　　) _____

06 다음 두 문장을 배열할 때 ⓐ의 마지막 단어와 ⓑ의 3번째 단어를 연결하여 쓰시오. 6점

서술형

> ⓐ ramen, is, hobby, cooking, Her
> ⓑ about, The, time, five, is, cooking, minutes

→ _____　_____

07 그림을 보고 주어진 단어를 이용해서 문장을 완성하시오. 5점

서술형

> The kid _____ _____
> _____ a butterfly. (busy, catch)

08 다음 우리말을 조건에 맞도록 영작하시오. 6점

서술형

> 나는 그를 설득하는 데 어려움을 겪었다.
>
> • 조건 1　동명사를 이용할 것
> • 조건 2　어휘 – hard, time, persuade
> • 조건 3　주어진 단어를 포함하여 7단어로 쓸 것

→ _____

VOCA　drunk 술 취한 | solution 해결책 | ramen 라면 | persuade 설득하다

UNIT **07**　45

01 Which is NOT suitable for the blank? 2점

My son _____ doing the dishes.

① gave up   ② loves
③ finished   ④ hoped
⑤ minds

02 How many have a gerund, and how many have a present participle? 3점

ⓐ clapping boy   ⓑ boiling point
ⓒ waiting room   ⓓ sleeping bag
ⓔ frying pan   ⓕ shocking scene

	Gerund	Present Participle
①	one	five
②	two	four
③	three	three
④	four	two
⑤	five	one

03 Which of the underlined choices is used in the same way as the example? (Find ALL.) 2점

보기 Her dream is becoming a nightmare.

① They are playing soccer in the park.
② Do you know the dancing girl over there?
③ They went to the singing room together.
④ My grandpa bought a new walking stick.
⑤ The baby is sleeping in her mom's arms.

04 Which translation is correct? (2 answers) 2점

난 어제 종일 자장면을 먹고 싶었어.

① I felt like had *jajangmyeon* all day yesterday.
② I felt like ate *jajangmyeon* all day yesterday.
③ I felt like having *jajangmyeon* all day yesterday.
④ I felt like to eat *jajangmyeon* all day yesterday.
⑤ I felt like eating *jajangmyeon* all day yesterday.

05 When translating the two sentences, which words are used in both of the sentences? (Find ALL.) 3점

ⓐ 그는 야구를 하는 중이다.
ⓑ 그의 취미는 야구를 하는 것이다.

① is   ② playing
③ he   ④ his
⑤ baseball

06 Which TWO analyses are correct? 3점

Some people were watching TV in the waiting room.

① some은 셀 수 있는 명사에만 쓴다.
② people은 '사람'이란 뜻으로 단수이다.
③ were watching에서 watching은 현재분사이다.
④ waiting room은 room for waiting으로 이해한다.
⑤ waiting은 he's waiting의 waiting과 같은 역할이다.

07 Which pair is correct for each blank? 2점

· We could enjoy nature by _____.
· The man is _____ mismatched socks.

① walk – wear   ② walk – wore
③ walking – wear   ④ walking – wearing
⑤ walking – wore

08 Whose analysis is incorrect? (G = gerund, P = present participle) 3점

① 현주: She is looking at you. → P
② 세나: His habit is drinking milk every day. → P
③ 은경: My father likes visiting castles. → G
④ 우연: She bought new running shoes. → G
⑤ 희선: We watched the rising sun. → P

09 Which sentence is grammatically correct? 2점

① She was proud of passing the test.

② I feel like to have brunch now.

③ We had difficulty to read this poem.

④ Don't waste your money to buy clothes.

⑤ How about meet me in Las Vegas?

10 How many sentences have a gerund? 3점

> ⓐ Let's go skiing tomorrow.
> ⓑ Is wearing all black okay?
> ⓒ Training cats is not easy at all.
> ⓓ Did you bring your sleeping pill?

① none   ② one

③ two   ④ three

⑤ four

Challenge! 주관식 서술형

11 This sign is a gym's advertisement. Fill in the blank by using a word from the advertisement. 4점

TIRED OF _____ FAT & UGLY?

JUST BE UGLY! GYM

TEL: 555-9876

→ Tired of _____ fat and ugly?

12 Decide if each underlined word is a gerund[G] or a present participle[P]. 3점

(1) Kate enjoys swimming in the winter.

→ _____

(2) The swimming man is Kate's father.

→ _____

(3) I look forward to swimming in the sea.

→ _____

13 Group the underlined words as gerund or present participle. 4점

> I went ⓐ camping with my friends. We made lunch together. Hansu was ⓑ collecting wood, Gichan was ⓒ building a fire, and I was ⓓ cooking rice. ⓔ Making food wasn't easy at all, but we all had a great time.

(1) Gerund: _____

(2) Present Participle: _____

14 Find ALL of the errors and correct them. 4점

> My family will go to Egypt this autumn. Mom is busy to plan the trip. Dad wants to go sandboarding there. I'm really looking forward to visit the Giza pyramids.
>
> *sandboarding: 모래에서 보드 타기

→ _____

15 Choose the necessary words and rearrange them to make a question. 5점

> is, movie, to see, watching, worth, be, which

→ _____

16 우리말과 같은 뜻이 되도록 주어진 단어를 이용해서 영작하시오. 5점

> 나는 그 노래를 다운받느라 500원을 썼다.
> spend, download

→ _____

Review Test

U06_2A+2B

01 빈칸에 공통으로 들어갈 수 <u>없는</u> 것은? 2점

> • They _____ to learn Muay Thai.
> • Jinwoo _____ dancing the cha-cha.

① practiced   ② started

③ liked   ④ hated

⑤ continued

U06_2A

02 In which of the blanks can you NOT put "taking"? 2점

 한눈에 쏙

① He decided _____ a walk.

② _____ a test for 3 hours made me tired.

③ They enjoy _____ a nap every day.

④ She is _____ notes of his speech.

⑤ I feel like _____ you home.

U06_2A

03 다음 빈칸에 들어갈 단어가 바르게 짝지어진 것은? 2점

> • Do you mind _____ the window?
> • She wanted _____ a house for herself.

① closing – buying   ② to close – buying

③ closing – to buy   ④ to close – to buy

⑤ close – buy

U06_1

04 다음 두 문장 중 <u>어색한</u> 것을 찾아 바르게 고친 학생은? 2점

> ⓐ Please take a shower before go to bed.
> ⓑ Being rich doesn't make you happy.

① 서아: ⓐ take → takes

② 서진: ⓐ go → going

③ 세은: ⓐ bed → the bed

④ 수정: ⓑ Being → Be

⑤ 신비: ⓑ happy → happily

U07_1+GP

05 밑줄 친 부분의 쓰임이 <u>다른</u> 것은? 2점

 한눈에 쏙

① Where is the <u>smoking</u> room?

② I finished <u>making</u> a cake for my family.

③ My hobby is <u>fixing</u> computers.

④ The man <u>standing</u> at the door is my boyfriend.

⑤ Are you worried about <u>diving</u> from here?

U06_2C

06 다음 중 짝지어진 문장의 의미가 <u>다른</u> 것은? 2점

① He is good at speaking Chinese.

  = He speaks Chinese well.

② How about stopping by?

  = Why don't you stop by?

③ He went to the lake to fish.

  = He went fishing at the lake.

④ He stopped to talk to the lady.

  = He stopped talking at the lady.

⑤ Telling lies is sometimes necessary.

  = It is sometimes necessary to tell lies.

U06_2C

07 다음 문장을 바르게 해석하지 <u>못한</u> 학생은? 2점

 함정

① Suddenly, my father stopped dancing.

  → 소사: 갑자기 아빠는 춤을 멈추셨어.

② I started to buy things online.

  → 막비: 나는 온라인으로 물건을 사기 시작했어.

③ I remember to pay the money back.

  → 산비: 저는 돈을 갚은 걸로 기억하는데요.

④ He forgot to bring his credit card.

  → 선녀: 그는 신용카드를 갖고 오는 것을 잊었어.

⑤ She tried turning off all of the lights.

  → 현비: 그녀는 시험 삼아 모든 불을 꺼봤어.

08

U07_1+GP

다음 예문에서 동명사를 <u>모두</u> 찾은 학생은? 3점

> ⓐ Becoming a teacher was her dream.
> ⓑ How do you like the dancing bear toy?
> ⓒ Dad is baking cookies in the kitchen.
> ⓓ Excuse me. Where is the changing room?

① 아름: ⓐ Becoming, ⓑ dancing
② 주은: ⓐ Becoming, ⓒ baking
③ 이슬: ⓐ Becoming, ⓓ changing
④ 현민: ⓑ dancing, ⓒ baking
⑤ 두환: ⓑ dancing, ⓓ changing

09

U06_2A

고난도

다음 중 어법상 어색한 문장의 개수는? 2점

> ⓐ Everybody hopes seeing you.
> ⓑ Jamila loves listening to K-pop.
> ⓒ I hated studying math back in school.
> ⓓ You need to start over again.
> ⓔ The hunter gave up to chase the wolf.

① 1개　　　　　② 2개
③ 3개　　　　　④ 4개
⑤ 5개

10

U07_2+GP

Which is grammatically <u>incorrect</u>? 2점

① Do you feel like riding on my yacht?
② I had a hard time finishing the job.
③ How about going to a movie tonight?
④ Why don't we go to hiking this weekend?
⑤ I am tired of taking care of your son, ma'am.

11

U06_1

다음 주어진 문장을 [보기]와 같이 바꿔 쓰시오. 5점

> Travel by train. It is exciting.
> → Traveling by train is exciting.
>
> Drink a lot of water. It makes you healthy.

→ _____

12

U06_1

Find the sentence that has an error and correct it. 3점

> ⓐ The girl from Lithuania continued to study Korean.
> ⓑ Ken likes to take a walk after to have dinner.

(　　) _____ → _____

13

U06_2A

우리말과 같은 뜻이 되도록 주어진 단어를 배열하시오. 4점

> 나는 그 영화를 다시 봐도 상관없어.
> I, the, mind, again, movie, don't, watching

→ _____

14

U06_GP

다음 문장에서 어법상 어색한 것을 찾아 고치시오. 3점

> Spending your summer holidays in the Virgin Islands are a good idea.

_____ → _____

15

U06_1

Rearrange the given words. 4점

> of, mistakes, afraid, was, making, she

→ _____

16

U06_1

그림을 보고 주어진 조건에 맞게 문장을 완성하시오. 4점

> · 조건 1　현재형으로 쓸 것
> · 조건 2　동명사를 포함할 것
> · 조건 3　어휘 – be tired of, drink

→ _____ you _____ white milk? So am I.

17 다음 주어진 단어를 흐름에 맞게 고쳐 쓰시오. 4점

함정

I remembered _____ the door when I left, but I forgot _____ the windows. (lock, shut)

18 주어진 단어를 배열하여 문장을 완성하시오. (번호를 쓸 것) 4점

The poor guy _____.

ⓐ all his money   ⓑ presents
ⓒ spent   ⓓ buying
ⓔ his girlfriend   ⓕ for

→ _____

19 다음은 가람이의 영작 숙제이다. 어색한 부분을 모두 고쳐 문장을 다시 쓰시오. 4점

제발 말 좀 그만하고 내 말 좀 들어봐.
→ Please stop to talk and listening to me.

→ _____
_____

20 다음 우리말을 조건에 맞게 영작하시오. 6점

나의 첫 번째 일은 대통령을 보호하는 것이었지.
job, protect, the

· 조건1   동명사를 사용할 것
· 조건2   모두 7단어로 쓸 것

→ _____

[21~22] 다음 글을 읽고 물음에 답하시오.

(A)자전거를 타는 것은 재미있을 수 있다, but ⓐ**learning** safety guidelines is important. Here are some tips for safe bike riding. Always wear a bicycle helmet ⓑ**to protect** your head. When you ride a bike in the street, you have to follow the traffic rules. Remember ⓒ**wearing** bright-colored clothes so that drivers and pedestrians can see you easily. Check your brakes and tires to help you ⓓ**slow** down and stop safely. Keep these tips in mind and enjoy ⓔ**to ride** your bike.

21 윗글의 밑줄 친 ⓐ~ⓔ 중 어법상 옳은 것으로 짝지어진 것은? 3점

고난도

① ⓐ ⓒ
② ⓐ ⓑ
③ ⓒ ⓔ
④ ⓐ ⓑ ⓓ
⑤ ⓐ ⓒ ⓔ

22 윗글의 밑줄 친 (A)와 같은 뜻이 되도록 주어진 조건에 맞게 영작하시오. 5점

· 조건1   어휘 – ride, a, can, fun
· 조건2   필요시 어형 변화할 것
· 조건3   6단어로 쓸 것

→ _____

CHAPTER 04
현재완료

현재완료의 의미와 용법

개념이해책
46쪽 함께 보기

■ 아래 표의 빈칸에 알맞은 내용을 써 넣으세요. **›››** 정답 10쪽

1 현재완료의 기본 형태: have+p.p.

> The cat began to live in the attic. (과거) The cat still lives in the attic. (현재)
> → The cat has lived in the attic. (현재완료)

2 현재완료 부정문과 의문문

부정문	1)_____ /2)_____ +3)_____ /4)_____ +5)_____
의문문	6)_____ /7)_____ +주어+8)_____ ~? – Yes, 주어+9)_____ /10)_____ . / No, 주어+11)_____ /12)_____ .

3 현재완료의 용법

	의미	함께 자주 쓰이는 표현
완료	13)_____	just, already, yet
경험	14)_____	ever, never, before, once, twice
계속	15)_____	for, since, how long
결과	16)_____	go, come, leave, lose, buy

Level 1 Test

››› 정답 10쪽

A [ ]에서 알맞은 것을 고르시오.

1 I've [thought / thought] about my future.

2 She [hasn't / doesn't] opened the box yet.

3 What have you [did / done] all day?

4 I haven't eaten anything [since / for] 8 o'clock.

B 문장을 괄호 안의 지시대로 고치시오.

1 She has volunteered many times. (의문문)

→ _____ _____ _____ many times?

2 They have tasted the food. (부정문)

→ They _____ _____ the food.

3 Have you ever touched a spider? (부정의 대답)

→ _____, _____ _____.

C 주어진 단어를 현재완료로 쓰고, 그 용법을 쓰시오.

1 The train _____ _____ yet.
(not, arrive) → _____

2 Rahee _____ _____ interest
in math, too. (lose) → _____

3 My aunt _____ _____ in Brazil
for a month. (stay) → _____

4 We _____ _____ an elephant in
Thailand. (ride) → _____

5 She _____ _____ his phone
number. (forget) → _____

6 _____ she _____ to my email
yet? (reply) → _____

VOCA volunteer 자원봉사하다 | taste 맛보다

01 다음 빈칸에 가장 적절한 것은? 2점

> We _____ in the same house since I was six.

① live
② lived
③ were living
④ are living
⑤ have lived

02 두 문장의 뜻이 같도록 할 때, 빈칸에 알맞은 것은? 3점

> My cat drank my milk, so she's not hungry now.
> = My cat _____ my milk.

① was drinking
② was drunk
③ has drinking
④ has drunk
⑤ has drank

03 밑줄 친 부분의 용법이 [보기]와 같은 것은? 2점

> [보기] Others have experienced similar problems.

① I've never had a headache.
② She hasn't bought the ticket yet.
③ They have just arrived in Korea.
④ Mom has been sick for about a week.
⑤ We have lived in this town since 2009.

04 다음 중 어법상 어색한 문장의 개수는? 2점

> ⓐ Where did my bike gone?
> ⓑ She has read the book three times.
> ⓒ Lao hasn't finished his homework yet.
> ⓓ Have you ever seen any of these movies?
> ⓔ I've worked with him since a year.

① 1개
② 2개
③ 3개
④ 4개
⑤ 5개

05 두 문장이 같은 뜻이 되도록 빈칸에 알맞은 말을 쓰시오. 5점

 서술형

> Tiffany started teaching zumba in 2015. She still teaches it.

→ Tiffany _____ _____ zumba _____ 2015.

06 다음 문장을 지시대로 바꾸시오. 6점

 서술형

> All the players did their best.

(1) 현재완료 부정문 _____
(2) 현재완료 의문문 _____
(3) 긍정의 대답 _____

07 주어진 조건에 맞게 대화를 완성하시오. 5점

 서술형

> · 조건 1 현재완료를 사용할 것
> · 조건 2 just를 넣어 5단어로 완성할 것
> · 힌트 step out: to leave a place for a short time

A: Hello. This is Fred Rogers. Can I talk to Amy Jung?

B: Oh, _____.

08 그림을 보고 주어진 단어를 이용해서 문장을 완성하시오. 5점

서술형

> Mr. Watt _____ for the elevator _____ ten minutes. (wait)

01 How many of the following past participle forms are correct? 2점

ⓐ run	ⓑ fought	ⓒ put
ⓓ swam	ⓔ sung	ⓕ founded
ⓖ denied	ⓗ rosed	ⓘ shaken

① three
② four
③ five
④ six
⑤ seven

[02~03] Which pair is correct for each blank? 각 2점

02
> He bought the statue in 2018, and he still has it.
> = He _____ the statue _____ 2020.

① has been – since
② has been – for
③ has had – since
④ has had – for
⑤ is having – in

03
> Hana has _____ eaten two hotdogs, but Duri hasn't even eaten one _____.

① just – once
② never – yet
③ ever – before
④ yet – already
⑤ already – yet

04 Which dialog has a grammatical error? 3점

① A: Have we met before?
  B: No, we have never met before.
② A: Has she done her work well?
  B: Yes, she has. She's a good worker.
③ A: Who has had lunch already?
  B: I don't know. Maybe Paolo has.
④ A: Somebody has taken my jacket.
  B: Really? I hope you find it soon.
⑤ A: Have you ever thought about being an actor?
  B: No, I haven't. Why?

05 Which sentence has the same usage of the present perfect tense as the example? (2 answers) 3점

> He has written books about deep-sea animals for a long time.

① My dad has changed cars many times.
② How long have you owned your dog?
③ He has just broken your computer.
④ My wife has boxed for 10 years.
⑤ She has memorized the whole paragraph.

06 Who groups the sentences with the same usage? 3점

> ⓐ It has snowed since yesterday.
> ⓑ Have you ever seen a ghost?
> ⓒ They have already bought the house.
> ⓓ I'm sorry that I've sold your car.
> ⓔ Have you called your brother yet?
> ⓕ How many times have you gone swimming this summer?

① 상하: ⓐ, ⓔ
② 서원: ⓑ, ⓓ
③ 은구: ⓒ, ⓓ
④ 정아: ⓔ, ⓕ
⑤ 서연: ⓒ, ⓔ

07 Which pair has the <u>different</u> usage? 3점

① Kyle has just finished his homework.
  Has the man read the book yet?
② Julie and Rachel have lost their key.
  Suddenly, my car has stopped.
③ They have been in Korea for 9 months.
  We have known each other since I was a kid.
④ I have met him several times.
  Have you tried Mexican food before?
⑤ We have already prepared for the party.
  Blanka has visited the castle once.

VOCA **found** 설립하다 | **shake** 흔들다 | **statue** 조각상 | **actor** 배우 | **deep-sea** 심해의 | **own** 소유하다 | **memorize** 암기하다 | **whole** 전체의 | **paragraph** 단락 | **ghost** 유령, 귀신

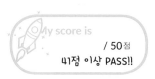

08 How many sentences are grammatically incorrect? 3점

> ⓐ It doesn't rained a lot lately.
> ⓑ She hasn't eatten breakfast yet.
> ⓒ We have worked since 10 hours, sir.
> ⓓ They haven't broken the record yet.
> ⓔ Have your brother lost his umbrella again?

① one   ② two
③ three   ④ four
⑤ five

09 Which of the following CANNOT make a grammatically correct sentence? 4점

① her / you / ? / have / today / seen
② yet / I / . / have / not / him / to / spoken
③ caught / a / ever / ? / her / has / cat / mouse
④ 2018 / Ellie / . / played / for / the / guitar / has
⑤ Day / ? / they / Children's / received / have / presents / their

10 Look at the picture and complete the sentence in the present perfect tense. 4점

A dog _____ _____ the boy's arm. (bite)

Challenge! 주관식 서술형

11 Combine the two sentences to make one sentence by using the proper words. 4점

Charlie was interested in movies when he was a kid. + He is still interested in movies.

→ Charlie _____ _____ _____ _____ movies _____ he was a kid.

12 Read the situation and complete the dialog. 6점

My father bought me a bike a week ago. I parked it in front of the door last night. But the next morning, it wasn't there.

Father: Where is your bike, son?
Son: I don't know. Maybe _____
_____ _____
_____ . (somebody, take)

13 Look at the table and make a complete sentence as shown in the example. 6점

	Lucy	I
To lose her/his smartphone	Yes	No
To download the app	No	Yes

> 보기   To lose her/his smartphone
> → Lucy has lost her smartphone, but I haven't lost my smartphone.
>
> To download the app

→ _____
_____

14 Translate the Korean by using the given words. 5점

너는 덥고 맑은 날에 태양을 바라본 적이 있니?
ever, look at, a hot and clear day

→ _____

UNIT 09 주의해야 할 현재완료

개념이해책
49쪽 함께 보기

■ 아래 표의 빈칸에 알맞은 내용을 써 넣으세요. 〉〉〉 정답 11쪽

 1 주의해야 할 현재완료

A 현재완료와 함께 쓸 수 없는 어구

과거 시점 표현	yesterday, last, ago, then, just now, in+연도
특정한 때	what time, when

B have been to와 have gone to

have been to	경험	～에 1)
have gone to	결과	～에 2)

 2 과거와 현재완료

과거	특정한 과거에 발생	현재의 정보를 알 수 3)
현재완료	불확실한 과거에 발생	현재의 정보를 알 수 4)

Level 1 Test

〉〉〉 정답 11쪽

A [ ]에서 알맞은 것을 고르시오.

1 He [arrived / has arrived] in Vietnam last week.

2 My uncle has painted pictures [since / in] 2002.

3 [When / How long] have they lived here?

4 What time [did he meet / has he met] you?

5 She has visited the museum [twice / yesterday].

B 빈칸에 been과 gone 중 알맞은 것을 쓰시오.

1 I know you haven't _____ to Sydney.

2 He has _____ to the North Pole three times.

3 Sarah has _____ to the store. She'll be back soon.

4 A: Has he _____ back to his country?

B: No, he hasn't. He has just _____ to his country.

C 빈칸에 알맞은 말을 [보기]에서 골라 쓰시오.

> 보기   have   has   stayed   went   gone
> did   done   in   for   since

1 After lunch, we _____ for a walk.

2 Carmen and Lou got married _____ 2008.

3 I _____ practiced skating _____ 2015.

4 How long _____ she _____ there?

D 빈칸에 알맞은 말을 써 넣으시오.

1 그녀는 프랑스로 돌아가 버렸다.

→ She _____ _____ back to France.

2 그는 18년 동안 제주도에 살고 있다.

→ He _____ _____ in Jeju _____ 18 years.

3 난 어릴 때부터 키가 컸어.

→ I _____ _____ tall _____ I was little.

VOCA   Vietnam 베트남(나라 이름) | North Pole 북극 | go for a walk 산책 가다

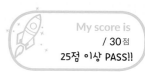

01 다음 빈칸에 알맞지 <u>않은</u> 것은? (답 2개) 2점

> It has rained _____.

① two days ago
② a lot this week
③ since yesterday
④ for three days
⑤ last night

02 다음 빈칸에 알맞은 것은? (답 2개) 2점

> Pam _____ to Seoul, but she will go there next year.

① hasn't been
② has been
③ hasn't gone
④ has gone
⑤ has never been

03 다음 중 어색한 문장을 찾아 바르게 고친 학생은? (답 2개) 3점

> ⓐ He was the best player since 2020.
> ⓑ I arrived from Italy this morning.

① 송현: ⓐ He is the best player since 2020.
② 혜진: ⓐ He was the best player in 2020.
③ 진아: ⓐ He has been the best player since 2020.
④ 성택: ⓑ I have arrived from Italy this morning.
⑤ 정욱: ⓑ I arrive from Italy this morning.

04 다음 중 어법상 <u>어색한</u> 문장을 <u>모두</u> 고르면? 2점

① I haven't visited my grandparents yet.
② She has lived with me since three years.
③ He has been sick in bed yesterday.
④ When has he come back home?
⑤ Who has taken my science notebook?

05 주어진 문장과 같은 뜻이 되도록 문장을 완성하시오. 4점

서술형

> My best friend went to Busan last month, and he is still there.

→ My best friend _____
_____ _____ Busan.

06 어법상 <u>어색한</u> 부분을 바르게 고쳐 쓰시오. 5점

서술형

> I have lost your backpack two days ago.

→ _____ two days ago.

07 우리말과 같은 뜻이 되도록 주어진 조건에 맞게 대화를 완성하시오. 6점

서술형

> Do you know my friend Charlie?
>
> (A) 아니, 우린 아직 만나지 않았어.
>
> · 조건 1 줄임말을 사용하여 5단어로 쓸 것
> · 조건 2 어휘 – meet, yet

(A) _____

08 단어 조각 중에서 필요한 것만 골라 질문을 완성하시오. 6점

서술형

> A: _____ ?
> B: For about 6 years, I guess.
>
> the   when   ran   did   run
> how   company   has   long   she

01 Which is proper for the blank? (Find ALL.) 2점

> Hernandez has played the violin _____ .

① then　　　　　　② before

③ since 2000　　　④ for one year

⑤ since he was young

02 Which are the suitable words for the blanks? 2점

> • We _____ camping last weekend.
> • I've _____ to London twice.
> • Where is Tom? Has he _____ to the bank?

① have gone – gone – been

② have gone – been – gone

③ have been – gone – been

④ went – been – gone

⑤ went – been – been

03 Which correction is correct? 2점

> He didn't get out of bed yet because he went to bed too late last night.

① didn't get → hasn't gotten

② yet → already

③ because → so

④ went → has gone

⑤ late → lately

04 Which dialog has a grammatical error? 2점

① A: Have you ever been to Mt. Everest?

　B: Yes, I have. I have been there twice.

② A: Have you ever spoken to a foreigner?

　B: No, I haven't. You know I'm very shy.

③ A: When did you visit the museum?

　B: I've visited it last weekend.

④ A: Has your father found his car yet?

　B: I'm afraid he hasn't.

⑤ A: I haven't seen you for a long time. How have you been?

　B: I've been fine. How about you?

05 Which pair is correct for the blanks? 2점

> Terry _____ the rap club last semester, but this semester, he _____ time to attend any meetings.

① joined – has had　　② joined – hasn't had

③ joins – had　　　　④ have joined – has had

⑤ have joined – hasn't had

06 Who finds the error and corrects it properly? 2점

> ⓐ When I was a kid, I didn't like spinach.
> ⓑ When has she left the classroom?

① 주연: ⓐ didn't like → haven't liked

② 서이: ⓐ was → have been

③ 미경: ⓑ When → What time

④ 지윤: ⓑ has → did

⑤ 소을: ⓑ has she left → did she leave

07 Which correction is correct? (2 answers) 2점

> I have received many invitations yesterday.

① I has received many invitations yesterday.

② I received many invitations yesterday.

③ I received many invitations since yesterday.

④ I have received many invitations for yesterday.

⑤ I've received many invitations since yesterday.

08 Among ①~⑤, which is incorrect? 3점

> Mrs. Kimberly called to ask, "Is Lily with you?" Lily, her dog, spends lots of time ① playing with my son, so whenever she is not able ② to find Lily, she calls. "I'm afraid I ③ haven't seen her today," I said. "But my son ④ has gone to the beach this morning and ⑤ hasn't come back yet. Perhaps she went with him."
>
> *whenever: ~할 때마다

VOCA　Mt. Everest 에베레스트 산 | foreigner 외국인 | shy 수줍은 | spinach 시금치 | receive 받다 | invitation 초대(장) | perhaps 아마

09 Which is grammatically <u>wrong</u>? (up to 3 answers) 2점

① A: Have you ever seen an alien?
② B: Sure, I did... many times.
③ A: Oh, really? When did you see one?
④ B: I've seen one yesterday. Actually, he lives with me.
⑤ A: And he rides a bike, too, doesn't he?

10 Which of the following CANNOT make a grammatically correct sentence? 4점

① has / the / ? / gone / Where / kid
② to / Quebec / Have / been / ? / you / ever
③ a / you / When / citizen / become / have / ? / U.S.
④ very / late / home / got / night / We / . / last
⑤ eaten / . / yesterday / She / hasn't / since / anything

Challenge! 주관식 서술형

11 Translate the Korean sentences by using the given words. 5점

A: I'm looking for Sally. (A) 그녀를 본 적 있나요?
B: Well, (B) 그녀는 막 캐나다로 갔어요.

(A) _____ (see)
(B) _____ (just, go)

12 In the two sentences, find TWO errors and correct them. 4점

ⓐ John lived in New York for ten years. Now, he has lived in Los Angles.
ⓑ John lives in Los Angeles. He lived there for seven years.

( ) _____ → _____
( ) _____ → _____

13 Find the error and correct it. 3점

 What time has the delivery person visited your house?

 Before my house got robbed!

*get robbed: 도둑 맞다

_____ → _____

14 Fill in the blanks by using one of the two given words. 4점

Keith knows Istanbul very well. He _____ _____ there many times. (be, go)

15 Read the situation and dialog and fill in the blanks. 6점

Suppose you started teaching English five years ago, and you still teach it. One of your new students asks the following questions. Answer each question with a complete sentence.

Student: What do you teach?
You: (A) _____

Student: How long have you taught it?
You: (B) _____

16 Choose the <u>necessary words</u> to complete the sentence. 5점

He _____. (8 words)
for, taken, has, have, shower, a, a, since, not, month

→ _____

VOCA delivery person 택배 기사

CHAPTER 04
Review Test

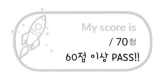

U08_1+GP

01 다음 중 과거분사형이 <u>잘못된</u> 것의 개수는? 2점

ⓐ thought	ⓑ swam	ⓒ understood
ⓓ forgotten	ⓔ taken	ⓕ drew
ⓖ chosen	ⓗ hided	ⓘ caught

① 2개　　　　　② 3개
③ 4개　　　　　④ 5개
⑤ 6개

U08_1+U07_2

02 Which is suitable for the blank? 2점

I have _____ skydiving many times.

① were　　　　　② goes
③ gone　　　　　④ went
⑤ been

U08_3

03 다음 문장을 보고 대답할 수 <u>없는</u> 질문은? 2점

 한눈에 쏙

He has learned Confucianism for five years.
*Confucianism: 유교

① Is he still learning Confucianism?
② When did he start learning Confucianism?
③ What has he learned for five years?
④ How long has he learned Confucianism?
⑤ How often does he learn Confucianism?

U09_1A+U08_3

04 빈칸에 알맞은 말이 바르게 짝지어진 것은? 2점

David started to watch a movie two hours
_____. He is still watching it.
= David has watched a movie _____ two
hours.

① ago – for　　　　② for – since
③ since – ago　　　④ by – since
⑤ for – ago

U06_2A+U08_2

05 다음 문장의 <u>어색한</u> 부분을 바르게 고치고 의문문으로 바꾼 학생은? 3점

She has finished to read the fairy tale.

① 아라: Does she have finished reading the fairy tale?
② 영은: Has she finished reading the fairy tale?
③ 혜지: Did she finish reading the fairy tale?
④ 민채: Has she finished to read the fairy tale?
⑤ 예지: Is she finished reading the fairy tale?

U09_1B

06 다음 두 문장을 한 문장으로 만들 때 빈칸에 알맞은 것은? 2점

Mr. Cha went to Columbia to visit his friends.
+ He isn't here now.
= Mr. Cha _____ to Columbia to visit his friends.

① is coming
② has come
③ has gone
④ has been
⑤ has came

U08_3

07 [보기]와 현재완료의 쓰임이 같은 것을 <u>모두</u> 고르면? 2점

 한눈에 쏙

보기　I have never fought with my girlfriend.

ⓐ I have lost my watch on the bus.
ⓑ I haven't finished my work yet.
ⓒ I have been to a few foreign countries.
ⓓ I have played tennis once.
ⓔ I have worked in Texas for three years.

① ⓐ, ⓑ　　　　　② ⓑ, ⓓ
③ ⓒ, ⓓ　　　　　④ ⓓ, ⓔ
⑤ ⓔ

U08_1+GP

08 Which sentence is grammatically correct? 2점

① She has just finish planting a flower.
② He have lived in Jeju all his life.
③ They have already saw the movie.
④ I have never been to Busan before.
⑤ She has been away from home since a year.

U09_1B

09 다음 중 어법상 어색한 문장을 찾아 바르게 고친 학생은? 2점

> ⓐ She has studied Spanish for five years.
> ⓑ I have gone to Vienna many times.

① 은율: ⓐ has → have   ② 율희: ⓐ for → since
③ 희라: ⓑ have → did   ④ 라미: ⓑ gone → been
⑤ 미은: ⓑ gone → go

U09_1A

10 다음 중 어법상 옳은 것을 모두 고르시오. 3점

① He has invented this wheel monitor in 1984.
② Roy has been on a TV program.
③ Mika has been to Taiwan with me before.
④ He has just broken the window a little ago.
⑤ Have you ever played soccer in a classroom?

U08_2

11 다음 문장을 지시대로 고쳐 쓰시오. 4점

> You have had a hamster.

(1) 현재완료 부정문 _____
(2) 현재완료 의문문 _____
(3) 부정의 대답 _____

U08_1

12 다음 두 문장을 하나의 현재완료 문장으로 쓰시오. 4점

> The printer broke down. + It still doesn't work.

→ _____

U08_1

13 Fill in the blanks by using the given verb. 3점

> I _____ _____ one centimeter in a year.
> (grow)

U08_2

14 다음은 Ally가 한국 생활에서 경험한 일과 경험하지 않은 일을 나타낸 것이다. [보기]처럼 문장을 완성하시오. 5점

| To have *tteokbokki* | experienced |
| To wear *hanbok* | not experienced |

> 보기   To have *tteokbokki*
> → Ally has had *tteokbokki*.
>
> To wear *hanbok*

→ _____

U08_GP

15 우리말과 같은 뜻이 되도록 주어진 조건에 맞게 영작하시오. 6점

> 나는 친구들과 이미 점심을 먹었어.
>
> · 조건 1 현재완료를 사용할 것
> · 조건 2 already와 yet 중에서 필요한 단어를 쓸 것
> · 조건 3 관사의 유무에 주의할 것

→ _____

U08_1+U09_1A

16 다음 문장들에서 어색한 것을 모두 찾아 고치시오. 3점

> ⓐ Have you ever thought about your future?
> ⓑ What time has she knocked on your door?

( ) _____ → _____
( ) _____ → _____

17 B의 대답을 보고 A의 질문을 6단어로 영작하시오. 4점

> A: _____ ?
> B: I have lived here for two years.

18 Find TWO errors and correct them. 3점

> A: He has come back last night.
> B: Really? I didn't see him yet.

(   ) _____ → _____

(   ) _____ → _____

19 다음 중 '결과'를 나타내는 문장들의 첫 번째 글자를 알맞은 칸에 써서 주어진 단어 퍼즐을 완성하시오. 3점

★ 고난도

> ⓐ Claudia has lost her bag.
> ⓑ Bart has broken the window.
> ⓒ Ian and I have washed the car.
> ⓓ Have you ever driven a motorboat?
> ⓔ Yurim has gone to the forest.
> ⓕ Miguel has lived in Daejeon for 10 years.

	R	A		N	

20 다음은 been과 gone의 차이점에 대한 영영사전의 설명이다. 빈칸에 알맞은 말을 써 넣으시오. 4점

> **Been or Gone?**
>
> With the present perfect tense, we can use both *been* and *gone*.
> (A) _____ is the past participle of *be*. *Gone* is the past participle of (B) _____. Use *been* to describe completed visits. If you have visited a place on holiday and then returned, you have (C) _____ there. If someone visits a place but has not come home, that person has (D) _____ there.

[21~22] 다음 글을 읽고 물음에 답하시오.

　(A)너는 나무를 타는 염소들에 대해 들어본 적이 있니? The goats in Morocco's argan forest ⓐ**has** a special skill. They climb trees ⓑ**to eat** berries. The berries are similar to olives. The berries have nuts inside, and people use ⓒ**them** to make cooking oil. Farmers follow these special goats because the goats spit out the nuts after ⓓ**to eat** the berries. The farmers can collect them with ease without climbing the trees. They ⓔ**have made** argan oil with the argan nuts for centuries.

*argan: 아르간(모로코 산의 상록수)

21 윗글의 밑줄 친 ⓐ~ⓔ 중 어법상 옳은 것의 개수는? 3점

★ 고난도

① 1개
② 2개
③ 3개
④ 4개
⑤ 5개

22 윗글의 밑줄 친 (A)와 같은 뜻이 되도록 주어진 조건에 맞게 영작하시오. 6점

> · 조건1 　어휘 – ever, hear of, tree-climbing
> · 조건2 　현재완료 구문을 이용할 것
> · 조건3 　주어진 단어를 포함하여 7단어로 쓸 것

→ _____

CHAPTER 05
조동사

10 can, may, will

■ 아래 표의 빈칸에 알맞은 내용을 써 넣으세요. ▶▶▶ 정답 13쪽

개념이해책
56쪽 함께 보기

CONCEPT 1 can

조동사	의미	긍정	부정
can could	형태	can + 1) _____	2) _____ [3) _____] + 4) _____
	능력, 가능	~할 수 있다 (= 5) _____)	~할 수 있다 (= 6) _____)
	허락	~해도 된다 (= 7) _____)	~하면 안 된다 (= 8) _____)

CONCEPT 2 may

조동사	의미	긍정	부정
may might	형태	may + 9) _____	10) _____ + 11) _____
	약한 추측	~일지도 모른다	~이 아닐지도 모른다
	허락	~해도 된다 (= 12) _____)	~하면 안 된다 (= 13) _____)

CONCEPT 3 will

조동사	의미	긍정	부정
will would	형태	will + 14) _____	15) _____ [16) _____] + 17) _____
	미래	~할 것이다 (= 18) _____)	~하지 않을 것이다 (= 19) _____)

Level 1 Test

▶▶▶ 정답 13쪽

A can, may, will 중 하나를 활용하여 우리말과 같은 뜻이 되도록 빈칸을 채우시오.

1 나는 그때 장학금을 받을 수 있었다.

→ I _____ get a scholarship then.

2 내일 날씨가 맑지 않을지도 모른다.

→ It _____ _____ be fine tomorrow.

3 너는 그 벤치에 앉으면 안 된다.

→ You _____ _____ sit on the bench.

4 우리는 그 시험에 합격할 수 있을 것이다.

→ We _____ _____ _____ _____ pass the test.

B 문장에서 어색한 부분이 있으면 밑줄을 치고 바르게 고치시오.

1 She may have not enough money.

_____ → _____

2 He can't visit us the day before yesterday.

_____ → _____

3 She may not late for the meeting.

_____ → _____

4 She is able to help you tomorrow.

_____ → _____

5 Can he speaks French?

_____ → _____

VOCA scholarship 장학금 | pass a test 시험에 합격하다 | the day before yesterday 그저께 | be late for ~에 늦다 | French 프랑스어

01 밑줄 친 부분의 쓰임이 같은 것끼리 묶인 것은? 3점

> ⓐ The news may not be true.
> ⓑ My father may not be forever young.
> ⓒ Kathy may buy a gift for you.
> ⓓ You may go out when she comes here.
> ⓔ May I take your order?

① ⓐ, ⓑ, ⓔ   ② ⓑ, ⓒ, ⓓ
③ ⓑ, ⓔ   ④ ⓒ, ⓓ, ⓔ
⑤ ⓓ, ⓔ

02 Which of the underlined words have the same meaning? 2점

> ⓐ He can sing as well as you.
> ⓑ Can frogs live both in water and on land?
> ⓒ If you want, you can look around.
> ⓓ Can I buy duty-free stuff on credit?
> ⓔ Can you read Japanese?
> ⓕ Can I ask you something?

① ⓐ, ⓑ, ⓓ   ② ⓒ, ⓓ, ⓔ
③ ⓒ, ⓓ, ⓕ   ④ ⓑ, ⓒ, ⓕ
⑤ ⓒ, ⓔ, ⓕ

03 빈칸에 들어갈 말로 알맞은 것을 모두 고르면? 2점

> My school will have a big festival tomorrow.
> A lot of guests _____ come.

① will   ② are going to
③ may not   ④ is going to
⑤ will be

04 빈칸에 공통으로 들어갈 말로 알맞은 것은? 2점

> • It's hot in here. _____ turn on the air conditioner?
> • I baked some pies. _____ like some?

① Will I   ② Can you
③ May I   ④ Would you
⑤ Can't you

05 주어진 단어를 배열해서 대화를 완성하시오. 6점

서술형

> A: Hurry up! _____
>   (we're, to, going, be, for, the concert, late)
> B: Okay. I don't want to be late.

→ _____

06 우리말과 같은 뜻이 되도록 빈칸에 알맞은 말을 2개 쓰시오. 5점

서술형

> 보안 구역에 들어가면 안 됩니다.

(1) You _____ enter the security area.
(2) You _____ enter the security area.

07 다음 문장에서 어색한 곳을 찾아 바르게 고치시오. 4점

서술형

> The workers may very tired by now.

_____ → _____

08 우리말과 같은 뜻이 되도록 주어진 조건에 맞게 영작하시오. 6점

서술형

> 나는 그 실수를 다시 하지 않겠다.
>
> ·조건 1   어휘 – make that mistake
> ·조건 2   6단어로 쓸 것

→ _____

VOCA   duty-free stuff 면세품 | credit 신용, 외상 | festival 축제 | guest 손님 | air conditioner 에어컨 | bake 굽다 | security area 보안 구역 | mistake 실수

01 Which of the underlined words has a different meaning? 2점

① His story <u>may</u> be false.

② It <u>may</u> be foggy near the river.

③ You <u>may</u> come here anytime.

④ Smoking <u>may</u> cause lung cancer.

⑤ She <u>may</u> not be sick.

02 Which of the underlined words have the same meaning? 3점

> ⓐ Mina <u>can</u> calculate like a calculator.
> ⓑ <u>Can</u> she understand humans?
> ⓒ The rumor <u>cannot</u> be true.
> ⓓ <u>Can</u> I come in your room?
> ⓔ How many sit-ups <u>can</u> you do?
> ⓕ <u>Can</u> I read your book?

① ⓐ, ⓑ, ⓓ   ② ⓒ, ⓓ, ⓔ

③ ⓒ, ⓔ, ⓕ   ④ ⓑ, ⓒ, ⓓ, ⓕ

⑤ ⓓ, ⓕ

03 How many sentences are grammatically <u>incorrect</u>? 3점

> ⓐ Were they able to taking the bus?
> ⓑ She isn't going to reject your request.
> ⓒ Could you videotape me, please?
> ⓓ When will we be able to travel again?
> ⓔ She may in the yard.

① one   ② two

③ three   ④ four

⑤ five

04 Which is suitable for the blank? (2 answers) 2점

> A: _____ I sleep over at Jane's house?
> B: Sure. It's up to you.

① Can   ② Do

③ May   ④ Will

⑤ Am

05 Choose the best pair for the blanks. 2점

> • Leo isn't tall, but he _____ play basketball well.
> • The sneakers look nice, but I _____ buy them.

① may – will   ② can – won't

③ has to – may   ④ may not – can

⑤ don't – won't

06 Which sentence has the same meaning as the one in the box? 3점

> 보기   It <u>can't</u> be a big problem.

① I <u>can't</u> do it alone.

② You <u>can't</u> ride my bike.

③ Sumi <u>can't</u> be sleepy now.

④ We <u>can't</u> accept all of your suggestions.

⑤ I <u>can't</u> see well in the dark.

07 Which is suitable for the blank? 2점

> He _____ be right, but I can't understand him.

① can't   ② is able to

③ may   ④ will

⑤ doesn't

08 Which is NOT suitable for the answer? 2점

> A: May I reserve a table by the window?
> B: _____

① Of course.

② Yes, you may.

③ No, you may not.

④ I'm sorry, but you can't.

⑤ No, you won't.

VOCA false 잘못된 | anytime 언제든지 | cause ~의 원인이 되다 | lung cancer 폐암 | calculate 계산하다 | rumor 헛소문 | sit-up 윗몸 일으키기 | reject 거절하다 | request 요구 | sleep over (친구 집에서) 함께 자며 놀다 | sneakers 운동화 | accept 받아들이다 | suggestion 제안, 의견 | reserve 예약하다

09 Which word is suitable for the blank? 2점

> I asked Tom to help me with the report. He said he _____ help me the next day. I was glad to hear that.

① will   ② wouldn't

③ would   ④ couldn't

⑤ won't

10 Which word is NOT suitable for the blank? (2 answers) 2점

> A: Ms. Shin, _____ I ask a simple question?
> B: Sure. Go ahead.

① would   ② can

③ may   ④ will

⑤ could

Challenge! 주관식 서술형

11 Translate the sentence according to the conditions. 6점

> 그의 의견이 옳을 리가 없다.
>
> · Condition 1   어휘 – opinion, right
> · Condition 2   5단어로 쓸 것

→ _____

12 Complete the sentence so that it has the same meaning as the given one. 4점

> He wouldn't tell the truth.

→ He _____ _____ to tell the truth.

13 Rearrange the words correctly. 5점

> not, found, be, the bag, may

→ _____

14 Find the error in the dialog and correct it. 4점

> A: Good afternoon. How may I help you?
> B: Well, that sweater looks cool. Will I try it on?
> A: Sure. The fitting room is over there.

(   ) _____ → _____

15 Write the common word for the blanks. 4점

> · This is too much. I _____ do it all by myself.
> · You had lunch just now, so you _____ be hungry.

→ _____

16 Find the sentence that has an error and correct it. 4점

> ⓐ Can you ask him to call me back?
> ⓑ We may get to the airport on time because of heavy traffic.

(   ) _____ → _____

VOCA   report 보고서 | simple 간단한, 단순한 | opinion 의견 | tell the truth 사실대로 말하다 | sweater 스웨터 | fitting room 탈의실 | by oneself 혼자 | on time 제시간에

11 must, have to, should, ought to

■ 아래 표의 빈칸에 알맞은 내용을 써 넣으세요. ››› 정답 14쪽

개념이해책
59쪽 함께 보기

CONCEPT 1 must, have to

조동사	의미	긍정	부정
must have to	의무	must+동사원형: ~해야 한다 (= 1)) Must I come early? (= Do I have to come early?) –Yes, you must. (의무) (=Yes, you do.) – No, you don't have to. (불필요)	2) +동사원형: ~할 필요가 없다 (= 3) +동사원형 = 4) +동사원형) 5) +동사원형: ~해서는 안 된다 (= 6))
must	강한 추측 (확신)	must+동사원형: ~임에 틀림없다	7) +동사원형: ~일 리가 없다

CONCEPT 2 should, ought to

	긍정	부정
충고, 조언	should+동사원형: ~해야 한다 (= 8))	9) [10)]+11) : ~해서는 안 된다 (= 12))

Level 1 Test

››› 정답 14쪽

A [ ]에서 알맞은 것을 고르시오.

1 What [do I have to / I have to] do now?

2 He doesn't [must / have to] go to the market.

3 You should not [go / to go] to bed so late.

4 She [has to / had to] wash the dishes yesterday.

B 우리말과 같은 뜻이 되도록 빈칸을 채우시오.

1 나는 공부를 더 열심히 해야 한다.

→ I _____ to study harder.

2 그 소녀는 울고 있는 것이 틀림없다.

→ The girl _____ _____ crying.

3 너는 새치기를 하면 안 된다.

→ You _____ _____ cut in line.

C 주어진 문장에 조동사를 넣어 영작하시오.

1 그는 사복 경찰관임에 틀림없다.

He is a plainclothes police officer.

→ _____

2 그는 어제 치과에 가야 했다.

He goes to the dentist.

→ _____

3 어린이들은 낯선 이에게 말하면 안 된다.

Children don't talk to strangers.

→ _____

4 우리는 인터넷으로 표들을 예약해야 한다.

We book the tickets online.

→ _____

VOCA cut in line 새치기하다 | plainclothes police officer 사복 경찰 | dentist 치과(의사) | book a ticket 표를 예약하다 | online 인터넷으로

My score is
/ 30점
25점 이상 PASS!!

01 빈칸에 들어갈 말로 알맞은 것은? 2점

> A: Mom, this medicine tastes bitter.
> B: Yes, but you _____ it to get healthy again.

① didn't take   ② will not take

③ must take   ④ must not take

⑤ had to take

02 다음 대화의 밑줄 친 ①~⑤ 중에서 어법상 어색한 것은? 2점

> A: We ① shouldn't eat fast food ② too often.
> B: I agree. Young people ③ ought ④ to not have ⑤ too much junk food.

03 우리말과 같은 뜻이 되도록 할 때 빈칸에 들어갈 말로 알맞은 것은? 2점

> 너는 그녀에게 그 계획에 대해 말할 필요가 없다.
> = You _____ tell her about the plan.

① must not   ② don't have to

③ may not   ④ can't

⑤ have not to

04 다음 중 문법적으로 어색한 문장을 모두 고른 것은? 2점

> ⓐ She must sad and lonely now.
> ⓑ We have to wait for her yesterday.
> ⓒ You shouldn't underestimate his ability.
> ⓓ He need not hurry up.
> ⓔ The students ought not to cheat on the test.

① ⓐ, ⓑ   ② ⓐ, ⓒ

③ ⓑ, ⓔ   ④ ⓒ, ⓓ

⑤ ⓓ, ⓔ

05 주어진 조건에 맞게 영작하시오. 6점

서술형

> · 조건 1   다음 문장과 같은 의미로 쓸 것
>   I'm sure Harry is excited.
> · 조건 2   조동사를 쓸 것
> · 조건 3   4단어로 쓸 것

→ _____

06 그림을 보고 주어진 문장을 must를 이용해서 금지를 나타내는 문장으로 바꾸어 쓰시오. 5점

서술형

Violence merely increases hate
Martin Luther King, Jr.

> We use violence.

→ _____

07 다음 문장에서 어색한 부분을 고쳐 문장을 다시 쓰시오. 5점

서술형

> You ought to not eat food too fast.

→ _____

08 우리말과 같은 뜻이 되도록 주어진 조건에 맞게 영작하시오. 6점

서술형

> 그녀는 어제 그 모임에 참석할 필요가 없었다.
>
> · 조건 1   어휘 – attend, the meeting
> · 조건 2   8단어로 쓸 것

→ _____

VOCA   medicine 약 | taste ~한 맛이 나다 | bitter 쓴 | underestimate 과소평가하다 | ability 능력 | junk food 정크 푸드(건강에 좋지 않은 패스트 푸드나 인스턴트 음식) | lonely 외로운 | violence 폭력 | merely 단지 | increase 증가시키다 | hate 증오 | attend 참석하다

01 Which of the following is best for the blank? 2점

> The hot chocolate is too hot. You _____ drink it yet. Wait for it to cool.

① must not   ② will

③ can   ④ ought to

⑤ will not

02 Which sentence has the same meaning as the one in the box? 2점

> You need not wear a swimming cap in the sea.

① You may not wear a swimming cap in the sea.

② You cannot wear a swimming cap in the sea.

③ You don't have to wear a swimming cap in the sea.

④ You will not wear a swimming cap in the sea.

⑤ You must not wear a swimming cap in the sea.

[03~04] Choose the best expression for the blank. 각 2점

03

> A: Hey, look at the man climbing over the wall.
> B: Oh, he _____.
> A: I think so, too. Let's call the police.

① must be tired   ② can be brave

③ can't be a liar   ④ must be a thief

⑤ must not be safe

04

> A: I want to lose weight.
> B: I think you _____ exercise regularly.

① may   ② were able to

③ should   ④ shouldn't

⑤ don't have to

05 Which sentences are grammatically incorrect? 3점

> ⓐ Jane must be very pleased.
> ⓑ Should we sing the school song again?
> ⓒ He has to leave Seattle a few days ago.
> ⓓ You ought to not accept her offer.
> ⓔ He don't have to go shopping now.

① ⓐ, ⓒ   ② ⓒ, ⓓ

③ ⓒ, ⓓ, ⓔ   ④ ⓑ, ⓓ

⑤ ⓓ, ⓔ

06 Among ①~⑤, which is grammatically incorrect? 2점

> A: Why ① don't we ② invite Tom to our party?
> B: That's ③ a good idea. He ④ has to be very ⑤ lonely all alone at his house.

07 Which is grammatically incorrect? 2점

① Mina has to take care of her sisters.

② You need not to come tomorrow.

③ She will have to work even on the holiday.

④ Why do I have to do all the work?

⑤ What time should we meet tonight?

08 Which of the underlined words has a different meaning? 3점

① I must arrange my room by myself.

② You must go to school on foot every day.

③ That must be Ann. They said she has red hair.

④ You must not run in the classroom.

⑤ A teacher has to be patient.

VOCA   cool 식다 | swimming cap 수영 모자 | climb 오르다 | liar 거짓말쟁이 | thief 도둑 | lose weight 살을 빼다 | regularly 규칙적으로 | accept 받아들이다 | offer 제안 | lonely 외로운(형용사) | alone 혼자(형용사, 부사) | even 심지어, 조차 | by oneself 혼자 | patient 참을성 있는

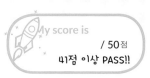
09 Which word is common for the blanks? 2점

> • Danny ran for an hour. He _____ be thirsty.
> • You _____ not drive without a license.

① must
② can
③ be able to
④ have to
⑤ should

10 Which sentence has a <u>different</u> meaning? 3점

① Don't be noisy during class.
② You should be noisy during class.
③ You must not be noisy during class.
④ You ought to be quiet during class.
⑤ You have to be quiet during class.

11 Choose ALL of the grammatically <u>incorrect</u> sentences. 3점

① You must not park in spaces for the disabled.
② You shouldn't forget your password.
③ He doesn't have to do it yesterday.
④ You ought to learn more about yourself.
⑤ We ought to not speak so loudly.

Challenge! 주관식 서술형

12 Translate the sentence according to the conditions. 6점

> 여기서 종이컵을 사용하면 안 됩니다.
>
> · Condition 1   어휘 – paper cups, use
> · Condition 2   You로 시작할 것
> · Condition 3   to를 포함할 것
> · Condition 4   8단어로 쓸 것

→ _____

13 Rearrange the words correctly. 5점

> should, when, are sneezing, your mouth, cover, you

→ You _____
_____ .

14 Rewrite the sentence correctly. 4점

> You don't need write it down.

→ _____

15 Write the proper answer with <u>five</u> words. 5점

> A: Must I accept the offer?
> B: _____ You can accept the other one.

16 Complete the sentences by using the proper expressions in the box. 4점

> 보기   should not   don't have to

(1) You _____ talk with your mouth full.

(2) You _____ serve yourself food at that luxurious restaurant.

VOCA   license 자격증, 면허증 | noisy 시끄러운 | disabled 장애가 있는 | cover 가리다 | sneeze 재채기하다 | accept 받아들이다 | offer 제안 | luxurious 호화스러운, 고급스러운

UNIT 11   71

UNIT 12 would like to, had better, used to

개념이해책
62쪽 함께 보기

■ 아래 표의 빈칸에 알맞은 내용을 써 넣으세요. >>> 정답 15쪽

CONCEPT 1 would like to

긍정	부정
1)_____ +동사원형: ~하고 싶다	2)_____ +동사원형: ~하고 싶지 않다

CONCEPT 2 had better

긍정	부정
3)_____ +동사원형: ~하는 것이 좋다	4)_____ +동사원형: ~하지 않는 것이 좋겠다

CONCEPT 3 used to

	긍정	부정	의문
형태	5)_____ +동사원형	6)_____ +동사원형	7)_____ +주어+ 8)_____ +동사원형 ~?
과거의 습관 (9)_____)	On weekends, we 10)_____ climb the mountain.	We 11)_____ [12)_____] go camping.	13)_____ you 14)_____ drink river water?
상태 (15)_____)	There 16)_____ be a pond in the yard, but now there isn't.	There 17)_____ [18)_____] be a pond, but now there is.	19)_____ there 20)_____ be owls here?

Level 1 Test

>>> 정답 15쪽

A 우리말과 같은 뜻이 되도록 주어진 단어를 배열해서 문장을 완성하시오.

1 너는 빨간 모자를 쓰는 것이 낫겠다.
(had, put, better, on)
→ You _____ the red cap.

2 그녀의 정원에는 꽃들이 있었다.
(used, there, be, to, flowers)
→ _____ in her garden.

3 나는 다시는 거기에 가고 싶지 않다.
(not, like, would, to, go)
→ I _____ there again.

4 너는 지금 자지 않는 게 낫겠다.
(had, you, better, not, sleep)
→ _____ now.

B 주어진 문장에 조동사를 넣어 영작하시오.

1 나는 방과 후에 쉬고 싶다.
I rest after school.
→ _____

2 나의 조부모님들은 아침 식사 후에 커피를 마시곤 했다.
My grandparents drink coffee after breakfast.
→ _____

3 너는 콩류를 너무 많이 먹지 않는 게 좋겠다.
You eat too many beans.
→ _____

VOCA rest 휴식을 취하다 | grandparents 조부모 | bean 콩

>>> 정답 15쪽

01 빈칸에 들어갈 말로 알맞은 것은? 2점

> You _____ wear a muffler. It is very cold outside.

① could
② would
③ had better
④ would rather
⑤ used to

02 빈칸에 들어갈 말이 바르게 짝지어진 것은? 2점

> • My grandmother used to _____ me interesting stories at night.
> • She was used to _____ his boring jokes.

① told – hear
② tell – hearing
③ tell – hear
④ told – hearing
⑤ telling – hear

03 다음 우리말을 영어로 바르게 옮긴 것은? 2점

> 그들은 그 벤치에 앉아서 해가 지는 것을 보곤 했다.

① They used to sit and watch the sun set on the bench.
② They could sit and watch the sun set on the bench.
③ They might sit and watch the sun set on the bench.
④ They would like to sit and watch the sun set on the bench.
⑤ They were used to sitting and watching the sun set on the bench.

04 다음 문장을 바르게 설명한 학생은? 3점

> You had better not talk to her about it.

① 선희: had better not은 had not better가 되어야 한다.
② 경용: had better는 had to better가 되어야 한다.
③ 민진: talk는 to talk가 되어야 한다.
④ 인식: talk to는 to talk가 되어야 한다.
⑤ 윤혜: 틀린 곳을 찾을 수 없다.

05 주어진 조건에 맞게 영작하시오. 6점

서술형

> There was a statue here. There isn't a statue here now.
>
> · 조건 1 위 두 문장의 의미를 포함하는 한 문장으로 쓸 것
> · 조건 2 조동사를 쓸 것
> · 조건 3 7단어로 쓸 것

→ _____

06 두 문장이 같은 뜻이 되도록 빈칸에 알맞은 말을 쓰시오. 5점

서술형

> I want to be a generous parent.

→ I _____ _____ _____

_____ a generous parent.

07 다음 글에서 어색한 문장을 찾아 바르게 고쳐 쓰시오. 5점

서술형

> Dana's father is a diplomat. So she has lived in many countries. She is used to mix with foreigners.

→ _____

08 다음 그림을 보고 대화를 완성하시오. 5점

서술형

> Customer: I want to have a cute hairstyle.
> Hairdresser: Then you _____ _____ have your bangs cut.
>
> *bangs: 앞머리

VOCA muffler 목도리 | joke 농담 | set (해가) 지다 | statue 조각상 | generous 관대한 | diplomat 외교관 | mix with ～와 어울리다

01 Which of the underlined choices has a similar meaning as the given sentence? 2점

> He <u>used to</u> eat a lot when he was stressed.

① She <u>would</u> take a nap after lunch.
② He <u>had better</u> be there on time.
③ I <u>would like to</u> start right now.
④ He <u>had to</u> take some medicine.
⑤ We <u>ought to</u> tell the truth.

02 Which of the following is not proper for the blanks? (up to 3 answers) 2점

> • I would like _____.
> • You'd better _____.

① nice to her
② not touching the files
③ to teach the world to sing
④ check out early in the morning
⑤ to have a second chance at my first love

03 Choose the best expression for the blank. 2점

> A: I want many people to like me.
> B: You _____.

① had better be kinder and more sociable
② would rather talk to your old friends
③ must not study hard
④ used to get along with your friends
⑤ shouldn't behave politely

04 Which word is NOT necessary when translating the following sentence? 2점

> 원자력은 전기를 생산하기 위해 사용된다.

① nuclear energy   ② is
③ used to   ④ electricity
⑤ producing

05 Which sentences are grammatically <u>incorrect</u>? 2점

> ⓐ We used to going to see fireworks.
> ⓑ You ought to not lie to your friends.
> ⓒ You had better not talk to her now.
> ⓓ I would rather fail than cheat.
> ⓔ I wouldn't like to meet her.

① ⓐ, ⓑ   ② ⓐ, ⓑ, ⓒ
③ ⓑ, ⓒ, ⓓ   ④ ⓒ, ⓓ
⑤ ⓓ, ⓔ

06 Which phrase is the most appropriate for the blank? 3점

> A: I'm thinking of going to the Coco Mall with my son this Sunday.
> B: I think you _____ there. The mall is huge, crowded, and confusing. Going there with children is especially dangerous. It is easy to get lost.

① should go   ② would rather go
③ had better not go   ④ had better go
⑤ would not like to go

07 Which correction is correct? 2점

> Did Bryant use to live in that place?

① use → used   ② to live → living
③ Did → Does   ④ use to → used
⑤ The sentence is correct.

08 Which is grammatically <u>incorrect</u>? 2점

① We would visit the farm when we were little.
② Mina didn't use to speak English fluently.
③ She is not used to draw cartoons.
④ A ruler is used to measure length.
⑤ I would like to invite Mary to my party.

VOCA stressed 스트레스 받는 | take a nap 낮잠을 자다 | take medicine 약을 먹다 | sociable 사교적인 | behave 행동하다 | nuclear 원자력의, 핵의 | electricity 전기 | produce 생산하다 | firework 불꽃놀이 | fail 실패하다, 낙제하다 | cheat 부정행위를 하다 | huge 거대한 | crowded 붐비는 | especially 특히 | fluently 능숙하게, 유창하게 | cartoon 만화 | ruler 자 | measure 측정하다 | length 길이

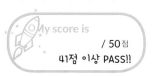

09 Which CANNOT make a grammatically correct sentence? 4점

① she / to / be / healthy / . / used

② would / . / rather / home / stay / I / than / go out

③ to / went / used / he / . / to / library / the

④ you / to / like / would / message / leave / ? / a

⑤ better / not / had / . / you / go / out

10 Which is grammatically <u>wrong</u>? (up to 3 answers) 2점

① She had better not to use my computer.

② Are you used to staying up late?

③ I used to being thin.

④ I would rather not take off the mask.

⑤ I wouldn't like be in your shoes.

Challenge! 주관식 서술형

11 Find the sentence that has an error and correct it. 3점

ⓐ You had not better go fishing tomorrow.
ⓑ I would not like to talk to him.

(   ) _____ → _____

12 Change the sentence into a negative one. 4점

I would like to see you become a pianist.

→ _____

13 Translate the sentence according to the conditions. 6점

나는 그것을 하는 것보다는 죽는 것이 낫겠다.

· Condition 1   어휘 – die, do it, than
· Condition 2   조동사 would를 쓸 것
· Condition 3   7단어로 쓸 것

→ _____

14 Rearrange the given words. (Add one word.) 4점

after, organs, donate, my, all, like, I'd, death

→ _____

15 Change the sentence into a negative one. 5점

There used to be a bookstore on the corner.

→ _____

16 Complete the sentence that summarizes the given situation. 5점

· before	· now

My brother had a lizard.	My brother doesn't have a lizard any longer. He has a hamster.

→ My brother _____ _____

_____ a lizard.

VOCA   organ 장기 | death 사망 | on the corner 모퉁이에 | lizard 도마뱀

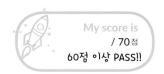

01 U10_2
다음 밑줄 친 부분의 쓰임이 <u>다른</u> 하나는? 2점

① <u>Can</u> you understand the situation?

② <u>Can't</u> you stay a little longer?

③ The story <u>cannot</u> be true.

④ I <u>cannot</u> wrap the gift well.

⑤ <u>Can</u> the boy understand your request?

02 U10_2+3
Choose the best pair for the blanks. 2점

• Mary is very good at singing, but she _____ dance well.

• I'm not sure, but he _____ be hungry.

① can't – will

② can – may

③ can – might

④ can't – might

⑤ will – may

03 U10_1+GP
다음 중 어법상 어색한 것은? 2점

① You may go home now.

② Ms. White is able to work from home.

③ What are you going to wear today?

④ He may be waiting for us.

⑤ Will she able to break the record?

04 U10_2
[보기]와 의미가 같은 문장은? 2점

> 보기 Mina can't beat Lucy at swimming.

① Mina isn't able to beat Lucy at swimming.

② Mina won't beat Lucy at swimming.

③ Mina is not going to beat Lucy at swimming.

④ Mina wouldn't beat Lucy at swimming.

⑤ Mina must not beat Lucy at swimming.

05 U11_1
대화의 빈칸에 들어갈 말로 알맞은 것은? 2점

A: Excuse me. You _____ park here.

B: Oh, I'm sorry. I'll move my car right away.

① must

② don't have to

③ must not

④ ought to

⑤ used to

06 U11_1+U12_2
빈칸에 공통으로 들어갈 말로 알맞은 것은? 2점

• I _____ to leave my hometown during the Korean War.

• You _____ better accept his offer.

① would

② used

③ must

④ had

⑤ should

07 U11_1+GP+U12_2
Which sentences are grammatically <u>incorrect</u>? 2점

고난도

ⓐ Would you like to try this?

ⓑ She will can clean her room.

ⓒ Daniel must be very pleased.

ⓓ You need not to read all the books.

ⓔ You'd better to bring the bag.

① ⓑ, ⓒ

② ⓑ, ⓓ

③ ⓒ, ⓓ

④ ⓑ, ⓓ, ⓔ

⑤ ⓔ

08 U12_GP
대화의 빈칸에 들어갈 말로 알맞은 것은? 2점

A: It takes a long time for me to type.

B: I can help you. I _____.

① am used to typing

② used to type

③ used to typing

④ am used to type

⑤ am used type

09 다음 대화에서 질문에 대한 대답으로 바르지 <u>않은</u> 것은? 2점

U10_3+U11_1

> A: May I take a photo here?
> B: _____

① Yes, you may.

② No, you may not.

③ No, you must not.

④ No, you don't have to.

⑤ Yes, you can.

10 Which cannot make a grammatically correct sentence? 4점

U11_1

★ 고난도

① better / You / think / had / it / . / over

② like / you / would / Where / ? / go / to

③ better / You'd / . / looking / not / back

④ like / didn't / . / I / food / to / Indian / use

⑤ used / a / to / theater / be / There / . / here

11 빈칸에 공통으로 들어갈 수 있는 조동사를 쓰시오. 3점

U10_2+U11_1

> • I _____ hang out because I have a science quiz tomorrow.
> • You woke up just now, so you _____ be sleepy.

→ _____

12 우리말과 같은 뜻이 되도록 빈칸에 알맞은 단어를 쓰시오. 3점

U10_3

> Chris는 어린이 센터에서 자원봉사 활동을 할지도 모른다.

→ Chris _____ volunteer at the children's center.

13 주어진 단어들 외에 필요한 단어 하나를 <u>더</u> 사용해서 문장을 완성하시오. 4점

U11_2

> When you are bored with your life,
> _____.
> (ought, something, find, you, exciting)

14 다음 두 문장 중 <u>어색한</u> 것을 찾아 바르게 고치시오. 3점

U11_2

> ⓐ You'd better not do that again.
> ⓑ People ought to not behave cruelly to animals.

( ) _____ → _____

15 우리말과 같은 뜻이 되도록 주어진 조건에 맞게 영작하시오. 5점

U12_2

> 너는 휴식을 좀 취하는 것이 좋겠다.
>
> ·조건1 어휘 – get some rest
> ·조건2 6단어로 쓸 것

→ _____

16 Write the proper word for the blank so that the two sentences have the same meaning. 3점

U10_4

> He said he wasn't going to leave her.

→ He said he _____ leave her.

17

U12_3

적절한 조동사를 사용해서 다음 두 문장을 한 문장으로 만들 때 빈칸에 알맞은 말을 쓰시오. 4점

> My mom often compared me with my brother. + My mom doesn't compare me with my brother now.

→ My mom _____ _____

_____ me with my brother.

18

U12_GP

Rewrite the sentence correctly. 5점

> Children would like watch YouTube than read books.

→ _____

19

U11_1+U12_2

Complete each sentence by using one of the given phrases. 3점

| 보기 | must not | had better |

(1) You _____ cross the street when the traffic light is red.

(2) You _____ wait for a few seconds before you cross the road.

20

U11_1

그림을 보고 우리말과 같은 뜻이 되도록 주어진 조건에 맞게 영작하시오. 6점

> 그가 모델일 리 없다. 그는 거지임에 틀림없다.
>
> · 조건 1   어휘 – a model, a beggar
> · 조건 2   조동사를 포함시킬 것

→ He _____ .

He _____ .

[21~22] 다음 글을 읽고 물음에 답하시오.

Unlike any other sand, quicksand is very dangerous. If you walk into it, you will sink down and down and finally _____(A)_____. In quicksand, however, ⓐ**it** is possible to float just like a human floats in water. ⓑ**Keeping** your arms away from your body if you walk into quicksand. Do not try ⓒ**to move** your legs, and you will stop ⓓ**sinking** soon. Then, move your arms slowly, and you can move toward firm ground. Most importantly, remain calm. If you ⓔ**are**, it is possible that "hungry sand" will stay hungry.

*quicksand: 유사(流砂: 바람이나 물에 의해 아래로 흘러내리는 모래)

21

U04_GP+U06_1+2

★ 고난도

윗글의 밑줄 친 부분 ⓐ~ⓔ 중 어법상 옳은 것으로 짝지어진 것은? 3점

① ⓐ, ⓒ   ② ⓑ, ⓒ

③ ⓒ, ⓓ   ④ ⓐ, ⓒ, ⓓ

⑤ ⓐ, ⓒ, ⓔ

22

U10_3

★ 고난도

우리말과 같은 뜻이 되도록 주어진 조건에 맞게 영작하시오. 6점

> 너는 심지어 사라질 수도 있다.
> **even disappear**
>
> · 조건 1   주어진 어휘를 그대로 쓸 것
> · 조건 2   모두 4단어로 쓸 것
> · 조건 3   다음 영영풀이를 참고하여 한 단어를 추가할 것
>   "This" is a modal verb most commonly used to express possibility. "This" can also be used to give or request permission.
>
> *modal verb: 조동사

→ _____

CHAPTER 06
명사, 부정대명사

명사의 종류, 수량 표현, 소유격

개념이해책
70쪽 함께 보기

① 명사의 종류

셀 수 1)_____ 명사	2)_____ 명사	사람·사물의 일반적인 명칭	computer, son, nurse
	3)_____ 명사	개체가 모인 하나의 집합체	class, family, team
	4)_____ 명사	유일한 사람·사물의 이름	Brian, Tokyo, Christmas
셀 수 5)_____ 명사	6)_____ 명사	특정한 형태가 없는 명사	paper, air, water
	7)_____ 명사	오감으로 감지할 수 없는 명사	beauty, health, hope

② 명사의 수량 표현

많은	약간의	거의 없는	종류
a lot of, lots of, plenty of	8)_____	9)_____	10)_____	셀 수 있는 명사
	11)_____	12)_____	13)_____	셀 수 없는 명사

③ 물질명사의 수량 표현

수사/지시사+단위 명사+of+물질명사

a 14)_____ of coffee	two 15)_____ of water	three 16)_____ of cheese
that 17)_____ of juice	two 18)_____ of pizza	three 19)_____ of meat
this 20)_____ of paper	two 21)_____ of sugar	three 22)_____ of soup
those 23)_____ of ice	two 24)_____ of bread	three 25)_____ of chocolate

④ 명사의 소유격

생물	명사+26)_____	the cat's tail	무생물	27)_____ +명사	the title of the movie

 Level 1 Test

〉〉〉정답 17쪽

A 밑줄 친 표현을 바르게 고쳐 쓰시오.

1 A little people were interested in the exhibition.

→ _____

2 A: How much oranges do you want?

B: Six, please.

→ _____

3 I can't pay for your lunch. I have few money.

→ _____

B 빈칸에 알맞은 말을 [보기]에서 고르시오. (중복 가능)

보기	bar	glass	pair	bottle
	bowl	spoonful	piece	slice

1 How many _____ of soup do you need?

2 I want two _____ of chocolate, please.

3 He drinks ten _____ of water every day.

4 I used to eat five _____ of pizza.

VOCA be interested in ~에 관심이 있다 | exhibition 전시회

01 밑줄 친 단어들 중 복수형으로 만들 수 있는 것끼리 짝지어진 것은? 2점

> My mom prepared <u>sugar</u>, <u>butter</u>, <u>flour</u>, <u>baking soda</u>, <u>egg</u>, and <u>milk</u>. But she didn't have any <u>strawberry</u>.

① flour, baking soda ② sugar, butter
③ flour, egg ④ milk, strawberry
⑤ egg, strawberry

02 다음 문장을 바르게 분석한 학생은? 3점

> Her students have had lots of math homework lately.

① 하늬: Her가 단수니까 have를 has로 써야 해.
② 길찬: have had는 현재진행형이야.
③ 누리: lots 대신에 plenty를 써도 돼.
④ 루다: homework을 homeworks로 써야 해.
⑤ 나래: lately는 late의 비교급이야.

03 다음을 영작할 때 사용될 수 없는 단어는? 2점

> 언니는 나에게 매주 약간의 용돈을 준다.

① older ② gives
③ to ④ few
⑤ week

04 다음 중 어법상 어색한 것은? 3점

① The tapeline is 300 centimeters long.
② When can I have a one-month vacation?
③ *Shut Up* is the name of the movie.
④ Alanis' clothes are too tight for me.
⑤ Oh, you still have a 5-inch floppy disk.

05 다음 각 [ ]에서 알맞은 것을 고르시오. 4점

서술형

> Sena bought a ① [pairs / pair] of brown boots for her grandmother. She paid only 5 ② [dollar / dollars] for ③ [it / them].

06 다음 문장에서 어색한 부분을 찾아 고치시오. 5점

서술형

> Michael isn't very popular at school. He has little friends.

_____ ➡ _____

07 그림을 보고 대화를 완성하시오. 5점

서술형

> A: Look! There is a _____ bill under the door! What a lucky day!
> B: C'mon. It's a fake. It's just a flyer.
>
> *bill: a piece of paper money

08 우리말과 같은 뜻이 되도록 주어진 조건에 맞게 영작하시오. 6점

서술형

> 나라(Nara)의 고양이는 매일 5분 동안의 낮잠을 자.
>
> ·조건 1 하이픈(-)을 이용할 것
> ·조건 2 소유격과 단·복수에 유의할 것
> ·조건 3 아라비아 숫자를 쓰지 말 것
> ·조건 4 take a nap을 활용할 것

➡ _____

VOCA **prepare** 준비하다 | **flour** 밀가루 | **lately** 최근에 | **tapeline** 줄자 | **floppy disk** 플로피 디스크 | **bill** 지폐 | **C'mon.** (= Come on.) 그러지 마. |
fake 가짜 | **flyer** 전단지 | **take a nap** 낮잠을 자다

01 다음 밑줄 친 부분 중 올바른 것은? 2점

① Where did you buy these bottle of water?

② Pass two pieces of cakes to the back.

③ She bought two pair of red socks for me.

④ He has just eaten three loaves of bread.

⑤ I need a few piece of paper to make a paper boat.

02 Which of the following is grammatically incorrect? 2점

① We have no furniture. We don't even have a bed or a table.

② I don't have much luggage. I have just two small bags.

③ He has a long beard and a very short hair.

④ Justin is unemployed. He's looking for a job.

⑤ The farmer loaded his cart with fresh vegetables.

03 Who finds ALL of the errors? 3점

ⓐ The exercises in this book is interesting.
ⓑ We need some glue to fix these vase.
ⓒ Some policemen is looking for you.

① 여혜: ⓐ is, ⓒ is

② 하영: ⓐ is, ⓑ these vase

③ 여정: ⓑ these vase, ⓒ is

④ 복길: ⓐ is, ⓑ these vase, ⓒ is

⑤ 현이: ⓐ is, ⓑ these vase, ⓒ looking

04 Which is grammatically right? (up to 3 answers) 3점

① I have a thirteen-month-old brother.

② How much is it to build a 4-bedroom house?

③ She has just finished a 15-page document.

④ The woman's nail is about 10 centimeter long.

⑤ 3,000-year-olds ginseng is common in Yenben.

05 Which TWO words are NOT necessary when translating the sentence? 2점

팬케이크를 만들기 위해 계란 몇 개와 약간의 밀가루가 필요하다.

① lot　　　　② a little

③ a few　　　④ to

⑤ plenty of

06 Which correction is right? 3점

ⓐ I missed the first scene of the movie.
ⓑ The woman in jeans is Chris' mother.

① ⓐ I missed the movie of the first scene.

② ⓐ I missed the first movie of the scene.

③ ⓑ The woman in jeans is Chris' mother.

④ ⓑ The woman in jeans is Chris's mother.

⑤ ⓑ The woman in jeans is the mother of Chris'.

07 Which word appears fourth when translating the sentence according to the conditions? 3점

나는 온라인으로 많은 아이템을 팔았다.

· Condition 1　현재완료로 쓸 것
· Condition 2　관사를 쓰지 말 것
· Condition 3　첫 단어는 I로 하고 줄임말을 쓰지 말 것

① sold　　　　② plenty

③ lot　　　　④ of

⑤ items

08 Which correction is right? (Find ALL.) 3점

Charles' two sons and a few workers ate ten pieces of breads together.

① Charles' → Charles's　② a few → a little

③ workers → worker　　④ pieces → piece

⑤ breads → bread

VOCA　luggage 수하물 | beard 턱수염 | unemployed 무직의 | load 싣다 | exercise 연습 문제 | glue 접착제 | fix 고치다 | document 서류 | scene 장면

09 Which is not suitable for the blank? (2 answers) 2점

> That sounds like a great piece of _____!

① furniture   ② advise
③ information   ④ chocolate cake
⑤ hot soup

10 Which words are NOT suitable for the blanks? 3점

> 보기 bar   pounds   lump
>   sheets   bottle   pairs

> ⓐ I'll drink that _____ of orange juice.
> ⓑ You just dropped a _____ of ice there.
> ⓒ Mom bought me two _____ of shoes.
> ⓓ How many _____ of meat do I need for 10 people?

① bar   ② bar, pounds
③ pounds, lump   ④ lump, sheets
⑤ bar, sheets

11 How many sentences are incorrect? 3점

> ⓐ No news are good news.
> ⓑ Emily's paintings were beautiful.
> ⓒ Were there rats? How much did you see?
> ⓓ We have a few light bulbs to change.
> ⓔ She wanted to buy that pair of coat.

① one   ② two
③ three   ④ four
⑤ five

Challenge! 주관식 서술형

12 Find ALL of the errors and correct them. 3점

> Your house is almost empty! You have few furnitures.

→ _____

_____

13 Write the proper word for the blank so that the two sentences have the same meaning. 4점

> This school is for girls only.

→ This is a _____ _____.

14 Rearrange the given words to translate the sentence. 5점

> 아우는 쌀이 많았지만 형은 많지 않았다.
> the older brother, but, the younger brother, have, of, a, didn't, much, rice, lot, had

→ _____

15 Look at the picture and fill in the blanks. 3점

> Would you like _____ __ _____ lemon in your Coke?

16 Translate the sentence according to the conditions. 6점

> 키가 180센티미터인 그 여자분은 Kobe의 할머니이시다.
> · Condition 1   하이픈(-)을 사용할 것
> · Condition 2   명사의 소유격을 사용할 것
> · Condition 3   약자는 풀어서 쓸 것

→ _____

VOCA drop 떨어뜨리다 | light bulb 전구 | empty 텅 빈

UNIT 14 부정대명사

■ 아래 표의 빈칸에 알맞은 내용을 써 넣으세요. ››› 정답 18쪽

개념이해책
73쪽 함께 보기

① 부정대명사

종류	의미와 쓰임	주의할 점	
one	'~한 것'이라는 의미로 막연한 단수 명사를 나타냄	복수는 1)_____ (cf. 2)_____ : 특정한 명사)	
3)_____	'각자, 각기'라는 의미로 단수 취급	4)_____ of+복수 명사+단수 동사	
every-	'모든 것' 또는 '모든 사람'이라는 의미로 항상 단수 취급	5)_____ /6)_____ /7)_____ +단수 동사	
8)_____	'모두, 모든 것'의 뜻으로 단수 또는 복수 취급	9)_____ (of)+복수 명사+복수 동사 / 10)_____ (of)+단수 명사+단수 동사	
11)_____	'둘 다'의 뜻으로 항상 복수 취급	12)_____ (of)+복수 명사+복수 동사	
13)_____	주로 긍정문에 쓰임	의문문: 권유	-one, -body, -thing은 형용사가 뒤에서 수식
14)_____	주로 부정문과 의문문에 쓰임	긍정문: ~라도	

② 부정대명사의 관용 표현

둘일 때	15)_____ ~, 16)_____ …		
셋일 때	17)_____ ~, 18)_____ …, 19)_____ ~		
넷 이상일 때	20)_____ ~, 21)_____ …, 22)_____ , ~ and 23)_____ …		
일부는 ~, 다른 일부는 …	24)_____ ~, 25)_____ …		
일부는 ~, 나머지 일부는 …	26)_____ ~, 27)_____ …		

Level 1 Test

››› 정답 18쪽

A 밑줄 친 부분이 어색하면 고치시오.

1 He bought an old camera. It was nice.

→ _____

2 Each of the boys are in his own room.

→ _____

3 Both scientist arrived at the same conclusion.

→ _____

4 Horrible something happened last night.

→ _____

B 우리말과 일치하도록 빈칸에 알맞은 말을 쓰시오.

1 각각의 참가자들은 질문을 해야 합니다.

→ _____ participant _____ to ask a question.

2 나에겐 또 다른 자동차가 하나 있어. 넌 그걸 써도 돼.

→ I have _____ car. You can use _____.

3 누구든지 오셔서 무료로 식사를 하실 수 있습니다.

→ _____ can come in and have a free meal.

VOCA conclusion 결론 | horrible 끔찍한 | participant 참가자

>>> 정답 18쪽

01 빈칸에 알맞은 말로 짝지어진 것은? 2점

> There are two men near the bus stop.
> _____ is yawning, and _____ is
> watching him.

① One – two
② One – another
③ He – he
④ The one – other
⑤ One – the other

02 다음 중 밑줄 친 부분이 어법상 어색한 것은? 2점

① All of the students <u>were</u> at school on time.
② Both of the players <u>are</u> not strong enough.
③ Each of the sneakers <u>have</u> a different shape.
④ All of the students <u>want</u> to take my class.
⑤ Every <u>evening</u>, I practice the piano.

03 주어진 표현을 활용하여 문장을 영작할 때 5번째 올 단어로 적절한 것은? 3점

> 그 회사는 뭔가 더 흥미진진한 것을 필요로 한다.
> -thing, exciting

① anything
② something
③ more
④ than
⑤ exciting

04 Which is NOT true according to the picture? 3점

① All of the babies are wearing their diapers.
② One baby is bigger than the others.
③ Two are crying, and the other is smiling.
④ One is wearing a hat, and the others are not.
⑤ One has a teddy bear, another has an
　 elephant, and the other has a duck.

05 빈칸에 공통으로 들어갈 말을 쓰시오. 5점

서술형

> • I bought a bag yesterday. But I need another
>   _____.
> • I have three friends. _____ is handsome.
>   Another is funny. The other is smart.

→ _____

06 그림을 보고 문장을 완성하시오. 6점

서술형

→ The dragon is holding a _____ in
　 _____ hand and _____ in
　 _____ _____.

07 다음 두 문장 중 어법상 어색한 것을 찾아 고치시오. 4점

서술형

> ⓐ He didn't say something useful.
> ⓑ Does anybody live in that old house?

(　) _____ → _____

08 우리말과 같은 뜻이 되도록 문장을 완성하시오. 5점

서술형

> 그 학생들은 항상 서로 돕는다.

→ The students always help e_____
　 o_____.

01 Who corrects ALL of the errors properly? 2점

> ⓐ Every koala have a unique fingerprint.
> ⓑ Each of the man wants to pass the course.

① 세연: ⓐ koala → koalas
② 서진: ⓐ have → has, a → an
③ 하린: ⓐ have → has ⓑ wants → want
④ 서율: ⓐ have → has, a → an ⓑ man → men
⑤ 지안: ⓐ have → has ⓑ man → men

02 Which is grammatically correct? 2점

① Both of his parents are not working.
② Every person wish to have a vacation.
③ Some people tries to go up the mountain.
④ We don't have some money to waste.
⑤ You have to answer each questions now.

03 Which word is correct for each blank? 2점

> A: I'm looking for a book about Mars.
> B: How about this _____?
> A: That's good. I'll take _____.

① one – ones
② ones – one
③ one – it
④ it – one
⑤ it – ones

04 Which correction is correct? (Find ALL.) 2점

> What do each of this signs mean?

① What → Which
② do → does
③ each → every
④ this → these
⑤ mean → means

05 Which set is correct for the blanks? 2점

> Sam took two oranges out of the bag. He gave _____ to Minsik and _____ to Youngmi. He took out _____ and gave _____ to me.

① one – another – the other – one
② one – the other – another – it
③ another – the other – one – one
④ the other – one – another – it
⑤ another – one – the other – it

06 Which is NOT correct for each blank? 3점

> • Here are five balls; one is green, ⓐ _____ is blue, and ⓑ _____ are white.
> • I read five storybooks last year. ⓒ _____ were interesting, but ⓓ _____ were boring.
> • There are three books on the desk; two of these are mine, and ⓔ _____ is yours.

① ⓐ another
② ⓑ the others
③ ⓒ Some
④ ⓓ the others
⑤ ⓔ the others

07 Which word is NOT necessary when translating the sentence? 2점

> 두 개 다 해서 3,000원이 아니라, 각각 3,000원입니다.

① both
② of
③ them
④ every
⑤ each

08 How many grammatical errors are there? 2점

> ⓐ Each of the man has 9 dollar.
> ⓑ Every heart have its own sorrow.

① one
② two
③ three
④ four
⑤ five

VOCA | unique 독특한 | fingerprint 지문 | course 강의, 과정 | waste 낭비하다 | Mars 화성 | sign 표지판, 기호 | storybook 이야기책 | sorrow 슬픔

86

09 Which sentences are grammatically incorrect? 3점

> ⓐ Feel the love in each children's eyes.
> ⓑ I lost my contact lens. It was expensive.
> ⓒ She takes ten subjects every semesters.
> ⓓ The market is on the other side of the street.
> ⓔ All of the people wears the same shoes and T-shirts.

① ⓐ, ⓑ   ② ⓑ, ⓒ
③ ⓒ, ⓓ   ④ ⓐ, ⓒ, ⓔ
⑤ ⓒ, ⓓ, ⓔ

10 Which TWO are not necessary for the blanks? 2점

> Lahee and Yurim are twins. _____ is a girl, and _____ a boy. But I can't tell _____ from the _____.

① one   ② another
③ other   ④ the other
⑤ it

11 Which sentence has the most errors? 3점

① Every day are a new day.
② Drill a hole in both corner.
③ Do anyone here speak French?
④ Each items has a number on them.
⑤ Let's keep in touch with each others.

Challenge! 주관식 서술형

12 Find ALL of the errors in the dialog and correct them. 4점

> A: I think I lost my Bluetooth headset. I'm going to buy the other.
> B: I borrowed one from you last week. Don't you remember?

→ _____

13 Look at the picture and fill in the blanks. 4점

> The little alien has three eyes. One eye is higher than _____ _____.

14 Among the underlined words, find TWO errors, and correct them. 5점

> Akenarin is from Thailand. She has 9 Korean ⓐ friends. Only one of them ⓑ is from Jeju, and ⓒ another are from Seoul. Four of them are girls, and ⓓ the others are boys. Everybody ⓔ are interested in Thai culture.

(   ) _____
(   ) _____

15 Choose the necessary words and rearrange them to translate the sentence. 6점

> 왜 어떤 별들은 나머지 다른 별보다 더 밝지?
> why, some, others, the others, are, stars, another, brighter, more bright, than

→ _____

16 Rearrange the given words to translate the sentence. 6점

> 일부 학생들을 독일어를 하고, 다른 일부는 네덜란드어를 하며, 나머지는 둘 다 한다.
> students, both, speak, speak, speak, Dutch, German, others, and, some, the others

→ _____

VOCA   contact lens 콘택트렌즈 | subject 과목 | semester 학기 | drill 뚫다 | alien 외계인 | Thai 태국의 | German 독일어 | Dutch 네덜란드어

01 두 문장의 의미가 비슷하도록 할 때 빈칸에 알맞은 말은?

U13_2

2점

> She is too busy to text back.
> = She _____ time to text back.

① has few
② has little
③ has much
④ doesn't have little
⑤ doesn't have few

02 Which is NOT suitable for the blank? 2점

U13_3

> I'm starving to death. Please give me _____.

① that piece of pizza
② those slices of hams
③ a big loaf of bread
④ two bowls of rice
⑤ three bars of chocolate

03 다음 밑줄 친 부분의 쓰임이 올바르지 않은 것은? 2점

U13_GP

한눈에 쏙

① Please bring me two pieces of cheese.
② How many loaves of bread do you want?
③ I put three lumps of sugar in my coffee.
④ He drank ten bottles of beer last night.
⑤ She bought a pair of new blouse on Monday.

04 빈칸에 알맞지 않은 말을 예로 든 학생 2명은? 2점

U13_2+GP

> Can you lend me a pair of _____?

① 으뜸: furniture
② 솔아: your shoes
③ 잎새: baggy pants
④ 꽃내: blue jeans
⑤ 벼리: your sister's coat

05 빈칸에 들어갈 말이 순서대로 바르게 연결된 것은? 2점

U14_1+GP

> • Each of them _____ two brothers.
> • Every student _____ the answer.

① have – know
② has – know
③ have – knew
④ have – knows
⑤ has – knows

06 어법상 어색한 부분을 찾아 바르게 고친 것은? 2점

U14_GP

> They've not had a chance to spend much time with each another for so long.

① They've → They're
② had → have
③ much → many
④ another → other
⑤ for → since

07 빈칸에 가장 알맞은 것은? 2점

U14_2

> Of these four keys, only one can open the door. _____ can't.

① Another
② Other
③ The other
④ The others
⑤ Some

08 빈칸에 알맞은 것을 모두 고르면? 2점

U14_1

★ 고난도

> _____ of the volunteers were CEOs.

① Some
② All
③ Each
④ Both
⑤ Every

09 U14_2

빈칸에 들어갈 말이 바르게 짝지어진 것은? 2점

> She texts me three times every day. _____ time is after breakfast, _____ time is after lunch, and _____ is after dinner.

① One – another – other
② One – the other – another
③ One – another – the other
④ One – some – others
⑤ One – some – the others

10 U14_1

함정

Which sentence is grammatically incorrect? 2점

① Everybody, raise your hands.
② Each guesthouse was full of tourists.
③ Both of the sisters are staying in Quebec.
④ Where are everybody? I don't see anyone.
⑤ All of the cars in the parking lot are new ones.

11 U07_2+U13_2

다음 밑줄 친 부분을 어법에 맞게 고치시오. 3점

> She wasted all of her money (1) to buy unimportant things, so she has (2) few money left now.

(1) _____
(2) _____

12 U13_3

다음 주어진 단어를 배열하시오. 5점

> the cook, cookies, of, needs, bake, cups, flour, two, to

→ _____

13 U13_2

두 문장의 뜻이 같도록 빈칸에 알맞은 말을 쓰시오. 4점

> There was almost no one at my first play.

→ There _____ _____ people at my first play.

14 U13_4

다음 두 문장 중 어법상 어색한 것을 찾아 고치시오. 4점

> ⓐ The computer of the speakers are not working.
> ⓑ My grandfather is reading yesterday's newspaper.

( ) _____

→ _____

15 U13_GP

Find the error and correct it. 3점

> Now the 18-years-old boy can get his driver's license.

_____ → _____

16 U14_1

주어진 단어를 넣어 문장을 다시 쓰시오. 4점

> They are looking for someone to work with. (intelligent)

→ _____

17 U14_1+2

한눈에 쏙

우리말과 같은 뜻이 되도록 빈칸에 알맞은 말을 쓰시오. 5점

> 어떤 사람들은 라면에 계란을 넣는 것을 좋아하고, 어떤 사람들은 치즈를 약간 넣는 것을 좋아한다.

→ _____ people like to put an _____ in their ramen, and _____ like to put _____ _____ in it.

18 Look at the picture and fill in the blanks. 4점

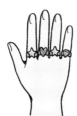

| I am wearing four rings. _____ is heart shaped, _____ is diamond shaped, and _____ _____ are star shaped. |

19 빈칸에 알맞은 말을 쓰시오. 4점

| I always have four pets with me. _____ is a tarantula, _____ is a parrot, the third is an iguana, and _____ _____ is a snake. |

20 빈칸에 들어갈 수 없는 말을 [보기]에서 모두 찾아 쓰시오. 6점

고난도

보기	one	it
	another	other
	the other	the others
	each	both
	some	any

ⓐ _____ child can solve the problem.

ⓑ _____ person has to hand in his or her own report.

ⓒ A: Do you want a car?
   B: Yes. I need _____.

ⓓ Here are five balls. One is black, _____ is purple, the third is blue, and _____ are white.

→ _____

[21~22] 다음 글을 읽고 물음에 답하시오.

Boxing is popular in ⓐ**much** countries. In boxing matches, when the bell rings, ⓑ**each** of the boxers have boxing gloves on their hands and hit each other. However, Thai boxing is different. The boxing match begins with music. While the music plays, the two fighters kneel and pray to God. Next, they begin ⓒ**to dance**. ⓓ**During** this dance, (A)각 선수는 다른 선수에게 자기가 최고라는 것을 보여주려고 노력한다. After that, the fight begins. In Thai boxing, the fighters can kick with their feet and hit ⓔ**each other** with their elbows and knees. Of course, they hit with their hands too.

21 윗글의 밑줄 친 ⓐ~ⓔ 중 어법상 옳은 것은? (정답 최대 3개)

★ 고난도 3점

① ⓐ

② ⓑ

③ ⓒ

④ ⓓ

⑤ ⓔ

22 윗글의 밑줄 친 (A)와 같은 뜻이 되도록 주어진 단어를 이용해서 문장을 완성하시오. 5점

함정

→ _____ fighter _____ _____ _____

_____ _____ that he is best (try, show)

CHAPTER 07
수동태

■ 아래 표의 빈칸에 알맞은 내용을 써 넣으세요. ››› 정답 19쪽

개념이해책
80쪽 함께 보기

CONCEPT 1 수동태의 의미와 형태

태	의미	기본 해석	기본 형태
능동태	주어가 동작을 1)	2)	동사
수동태	주어가 동작을 3)	4)	5)_____ + 6)_____ (+ 7)_____ +목적격)

CONCEPT 2 수동태 전환법

능동: She teaches math.

수동: Math is taught by her.

① 능동태의 목적어 → 수동태의 8)_____
② 능동태의 동사 → 9)_____ +10)_____
③ 능동태의 주어 → 11)_____ +행위자(목적격자)

CONCEPT 3 수동태의 시제

현재	12)_____ +p.p.	과거	13)_____ +p.p.	미래	14)_____ +p.p.

CONCEPT 4 'by+행위자'의 생략

15)_____ 행위자	Korean is spoken in Korea (by people).
16)_____ 행위자	The grass was cut yesterday (by somebody).
17)_____ 행위자	I was invited to Cindy's birthday party (by Cindy).

Level 1 Test

››› 정답 19쪽

A [ ]에서 알맞은 것을 고르시오.

1 Her lies [believed / were believed] by everybody.

2 The diamond rings [not were / were not] stolen.

3 The parcel will [delivered / be delivered] tomorrow afternoon.

4 Some people [witnessed / were witnessed] the theft.

B 문장을 수동태로 바꾸시오.

1 Someone opens the gate every day.

→ _____

2 They pay the workers in peso.

→ _____

3 The company will hire all of the applicants.

→ _____

VOCA parcel 소포 | deliver 배달하다 | witness 목격하다 | theft 절도 | gate 문 | pay 지불하다 | worker 직원 | peso 중남미 국가들과 필리핀의 화폐 단위 | hire 채용하다, 고용하다 | applicant 지원자

01 빈칸에 들어갈 말이 바르게 짝지어진 것은? 2점

> • This restaurant _____ by the man over there.
> • The thieves _____ by the police.

① runs – chased　　② runs – was chased
③ is run – chased　　④ is run – was chased
⑤ is run – were chased

02 두 문장이 같은 뜻이 되도록 할 때 빈칸에 알맞은 말은? 2점

> Jason did not forget the lessons.
> =The lessons _____ by Jason.

① were not forget　　② did not forget
③ was not forgotten　　④ were not forgotten
⑤ not forgotten

03 다음 문장들에 대해 바르게 이해하고 있는 학생은? 3점

> The hunter didn't bring his guns.
> → The guns did not brought by the hunter.

① 예다: 위 문장은 수동태고 아래 문장은 능동태야.
② 인혜: 수동태의 부정은 not을 쓰니까 아래 문장은 맞아.
③ 차진: 아래 문장에서 did not이 아니라 were not으로 써야 해.
④ 슬비: 아래 문장에서 brought 대신 bought를 써야 해.
⑤ 규로: 아래 문장에서 「be+p.p.+by+목적격」이니까 not을 빼야 해.

04 다음 중 어법상 어색한 것으로 짝지어진 것은? 3점

> ⓐ *Harry Potter* was written by J.K. Rowling.
> ⓑ The window not was broken by them.
> ⓒ I was took to the hospital by her.
> ⓓ The hamburgers made by Mrs. Watson.
> ⓔ The company was founded in 1903.

① ⓐ, ⓑ　　　　　② ⓑ, ⓔ
③ ⓑ, ⓓ, ⓔ　　　④ ⓑ, ⓒ, ⓓ
⑤ ⓑ, ⓒ, ⓔ

05 다음 영어 문장에서 어색한 것을 찾아 고치시오. 4점

서술형

> 그 불쌍한 소녀는 그 여인에게 혼나지 않았다.
> = The poor girl not scolded by the lady.

_____ → _____

06 다음 두 문장 중 어법상 어색한 것을 찾아 고치시오. 4점

서술형

> ⓐ A text message will sent to you soon.
> ⓑ The singer is loved by many teenagers.

( ) _____ → _____

07 그림을 보고 동사 paint를 이용해서 대화를 완성하시오. 6점

서술형

> A: Who (1) _____ this? (2) _____ it _____ by Picasso?
> B: No, it (3) _____ by Picasso. French painter Georges Braque (4) _____ it.

08 주어진 단어들 중 필요한 것만 골라 수동태 문장을 쓰시오. 6점

서술형

> room, she, didn't, by, the, wasn't, cleaned, her

→ _____

VOCA　run 운영하다 | thief 도둑 | chase 쫓다 | lesson 교훈 | hunter 사냥꾼 | found 설립하다 | scold 혼내다 | paint 그림을 그리다 | painter 화가

01 Which is proper for the blank? (Find ALL.) 2점

> A: What happened in Tokyo?
> B: A big earthquake hit the area last night. So a lot of people _____ .

① die ② died
③ killed ④ were killed
⑤ are killed

02 Which comes fourth when changing the sentence into the passive voice? 2점

> My cat caught two mice yesterday.

① was ② caught
③ by ④ my
⑤ yesterday

03 Which change in the sentences is incorrect? 2점

① Cathy didn't take the medicine.
→ The medicine wasn't taken by Cathy.
② She made this paper boat.
→ This paper boat was made by her.
③ My father made the pond.
→ The pond was made by my father.
④ Your son broke the car window.
→ The car window was broke by your son.
⑤ My sister draws many pictures.
→ Many pictures are drawn by my sister.

04 Which is correct for each blank in the following dialog? 2점

> A: Where did you _____ my dog?
> B: Your dog _____ in front of your car.
> A: Thank you, Jason, for _____ my dog.

① find – found – founding
② find – found – finding
③ find – was found – finding
④ found – was founded – finding
⑤ found – was found – finding

05 Which is NOT necessary when translating the sentence in 7 words? 2점

> 그리고 나서 이 와인은 병에 저장됩니다.

① the ② is
③ in ④ by
⑤ stored

06 Who does NOT understand the sentence correctly? 3점

> The houses didn't built by people in 2002.

① 윤희: didn't를 weren't로 바꿔야 해.
② 지혜: built는 build의 과거분사야.
③ 현주: 수동태로 써야 하는데 be동사가 없어.
④ 주희: by people은 꼭 필요하니까 생략하면 안 돼.
⑤ 보은: 능동태는 They didn't build the houses in 2002야.

07 Which sentence is grammatically incorrect? 2점

① The old coin was sold at a high price.
② These nuts will eaten by my squirrel.
③ The tree was moved by strong men.
④ This kind of camera isn't used these days.
⑤ This piece was composed by Beethoven.

08 How many sentences are grammatically correct? 3점

> ⓐ We are played the game.
> ⓑ This love song was singing by G7.
> ⓒ Today's dinner was prepared by my chef.
> ⓓ The treasure discovered by the explorer.
> ⓔ The washing machine wasn't repaired by him.
> ⓕ The first modern Olympic Games held in Athens in 1896.

① one ② two
③ three ④ four
⑤ five

VOCA earthquake 지진 | area 지역 | pond 연못 | store 저장하다 | coin 동전 | squirrel 다람쥐 | piece 곡 | compose 작곡하다 | Beethoven 베토벤 | chef 주방장, 요리사 | treasure 보물 | discover 발견하다 | explorer 탐험가 | repair 수리하다 | Athens 아테네

09 Among the underlined, how many can be omitted? 3점

> ⓐ I am loved by everybody.
> ⓑ French is spoken in Quebec by them.
> ⓒ America wasn't discovered by Columbus.
> ⓓ The baseball was played by the children.
> ⓔ Her clothes were made in Paris by someone.

① one   ② two
③ three   ④ four
⑤ five

10 Which of the following CANNOT make a grammatically correct sentence? 4점

① anymore / mouse / used / . / isn't / The
② printed / to / The / is / . / image / going
③ in / Korea / everywhere / Pines / . / found / are
④ helmet / was / by / worn / This / . / people / many
⑤ the / police / by / were / caught / . / The / robbers

11 Which is grammatically wrong? (up to 3 answers) 3점

① The meeting will be hold today.
② The bag was packed by his mom.
③ Last night, lots of buildings destroyed.
④ His company is not going to be sold.
⑤ Blue jeans was invented by Levi Strauss.

Challenge! 주관식 서술형

12 Rearrange the given words to make a complete sentence. 4점

> going, be, The, food, soon, is, served, to

→ _____

13 Find the sentence that has an error and correct it. 3점

> ⓐ The castles were built in England by the Normans.
> ⓑ The color of the chair will be changed by red.

(   ) _____ → _____

14 Rewrite the sentence according to the conditions. 6점

> People don't use this well anymore.
>
> · Condition 1   수동태로 전환할 것
> · Condition 2   생략 가능한 단어는 생략할 것
> · Condition 3   6단어로 쓸 것
>
> *well: 우물

→ _____

15 Translate the sentence by using the given words. 5점

> 죄송하지만 당신은 초대받지 않았습니다.
> but, invite

→ _____

16 Look at the picture and complete the dialog by using the verb "clean." 4점

> A: Do they ever (1) _____ the Statue of Liberty?
> B: I heard it (2) _____ during its restoration in 1986.

VOCA   print 인쇄하다 | pine 소나무 | robber 도둑 | hold 개최하다 | pack 싸다, 꾸리다 | destroy 파괴하다 | Norman 노르만인 | Statue of Liberty 자유의 여신상 | restoration 복원

16 여러 가지 수동태(1)

개념이해책
83쪽 함께 보기

■ 아래 표의 빈칸에 알맞은 내용을 써 넣으세요. 〉〉〉 정답 20쪽

CONCEPT 1 조동사의 수동태: 1)＿＿＿＿＿＿＿ + 2)＿＿＿＿＿＿＿ + 3)＿＿＿＿＿

CONCEPT 2 의문문 수동태

의문사가 없는 경우		4)＿＿＿＿＿ + 5)＿＿＿＿＿ + 6)＿＿＿＿＿ (+by+행위자) ~?
의문사가 있는 경우	주어가 있을 때	7)＿＿ + 8)＿＿ +주어+ 9)＿＿ (+ 10)＿＿ +행위자) ~?
	의문사가 주어일 때	11)＿＿ +의문사+ 12)＿＿ +주어+ 13)＿＿ ~?

CONCEPT 3 4형식 문장의 수동태 전환

> His mother gave me the shirt.
> 　　　　　　　간접목적어 직접목적어
> → I was given the shirt by his mother.
> → The shirt was given to me by his mother.

전치사	동사
14)＿＿＿＿＿＿＿	give, teach, send, sell, write, show, pass, bring
15)＿＿＿＿＿＿＿	sing, find, make, buy, cook, get
16)＿＿＿＿＿＿＿	ask

Level 1 Test

〉〉〉 정답 20쪽

A [ ]에서 알맞은 것을 고르시오.

1 It should [is / be] done by this weekend.

2 When [did / was] the pyramid built?

3 [Is / Does] this song sung by Nena?

4 The ball was thrown [for / to] me by him.

B 밑줄 친 부분을 바르게 고쳐 쓰시오.

1 Your clock can't fixed. → ＿＿＿＿＿＿＿

2 I am given to an allowance by my mom every week. → ＿＿＿＿＿＿＿

3 Some good advice was given for me by Mr. Green. → ＿＿＿＿＿＿＿

C 우리말과 같은 뜻이 되도록 주어진 단어를 이용해서 문장을 완성하시오.

1 그건 오늘 저녁 때까지 결정되어야 한다.
(have to, decide)

→ That ＿＿＿＿＿＿ ＿＿＿＿＿＿

＿＿＿＿＿＿ ＿＿＿＿＿＿ by this evening.

2 너의 남동생은 그 파티에 초대되었니? (invite)

→ ＿＿＿＿＿＿ your little brother ＿＿＿＿＿＿

to the party?

3 세 통의 문자가 누군가에 의해 나에게 보내졌다. (send)

→ Three texts ＿＿＿＿＿＿ ＿＿＿＿＿＿

＿＿＿＿＿＿ me by someone.

VOCA pyramid 피라미드 | fix 고치다 | allowance 용돈 | advice 충고 | decide 결정하다 | text(= text message) 문자 메시지

01 다음 문장을 수동태로 바르게 고친 것은? 2점

> Gina cannot do the work.

① The work cannot do by Gina.
② The work cannot be done by Gina.
③ The work cannot done by Gina.
④ Gina cannot be done by the work.
⑤ Gina is not done the work.

02 다음을 수동태로 바꿀 때 <u>6번째</u> 올 단어로 적절한 것은? 3점

> When did they sell the electric guitar?

① electric   ② guitar
③ sold   ④ by
⑤ them

03 다음 문장을 수동태로 바꿀 때 필요 <u>없는</u> 것은? 2점

> Will she accept my apology?

① be   ② are
③ accepted   ④ by
⑤ will

04 다음 중 어법상 <u>어색한</u> 것은? 3점

① We are taught Japanese by Akie.
② A question was asked of her by the reporter.
③ The same meal was brought of me again.
④ A big house was built for her by the men.
⑤ A song was sung for us by the Maori boys.

05 우리말과 같은 뜻이 되도록 주어진 단어를 배열해서 문장을 완성하시오. 5점 〔서술형〕

> 내일까지 그 꽃이 배달될 수 있나요?
> flowers, can, delivered, be, the

→ _____

   by tomorrow?

06 우리말과 같은 뜻이 되도록 주어진 조건에 맞게 대화를 완성하시오. 6점 〔서술형〕

> A: Is Spanish spoken here?
> B: No, it's not.
> A: (A) 그럼, 여기에선 어떤 언어가 말해지나요?
> B: German is spoken here.
>
> · 조건 1   수동태로 쓸 것
> · 조건 2   대화의 단어를 2개 이상 사용할 것
> · 조건 3   then을 포함하여 6단어로 쓸 것

(A) _____

07 다음 두 문장 중 <u>어색한</u> 것을 찾아 바르게 고치시오. 4점 〔서술형〕

> ⓐ Is cricket played in Australia?
> ⓑ Dolphins might seen around here.

(   ) _____ → _____

08 주어진 문장과 같은 뜻이 되도록 빈칸을 채우시오. 5점 〔서술형〕

> She showed us the picture.

(1) We _____ by her.

(2) The picture _____ by her.

VOCA electric 전기의 | accept 받아들이다 | apology 사과 | Japanese 일본어 | deliver 배달하다 | Spanish 스페인어 | German 독일어 | cricket 크리켓(운동 경기)

01 Which is NOT proper for the blank? 2점

> The problem _____ at the meeting.

① was mentioned
② can't be mentioned
③ must be mentioned
④ didn't mention
⑤ is going to be mentioned

02 Which translation is correct? (2 answers) 2점

> 애완동물이 그 음식점에서 허용되어서는 안 된다.

① Pets are not allowed in the restaurant.
② Pets should not allowed in the restaurant.
③ Pets ought not to be allowed in the restaurant.
④ Pets shouldn't be allowed in the restaurant.
⑤ Pets aren't must allowed in the restaurant.

03 Which comes fifth when rearranging the given words to make a question? 2점

> found, artifact, ?, Bella, where, by, was, this

① was   ② this
③ by   ④ artifact
⑤ found

04 Whose correction is correct? 2점

> My girlfriend was given a pretty doll to me yesterday.

① 정아: was → is
② 정향: given → gave
③ 현우: was given → given
④ 은정: to → for
⑤ 민재: to → by

05 Which is NOT necessary when changing the sentence into the passive voice? 2점

> Who drew this picture?

① by   ② done
③ was   ④ whom
⑤ drawn

06 Which is the active voice of the given sentence? 2점

> Where was the cap bought by her?

① Where did the cap she buy?
② Where does she buy the cap?
③ Where does she bought the cap?
④ Where did she buy the cap?
⑤ Where did she bought the cap?

07 Who finds the error and corrects it? 2점

> What was bought at that store to him?

① 은미: What → By what
② 미려: bought → did buy
③ 여진: was bought → bought
④ 진주: at → for
⑤ 주원: to → by

08 Find ALL of the grammatically incorrect sentences. 3점

① The kittens must be kept inside.
② Did the question be understood by everyone?
③ Were all the candy bars sold by the little girl?
④ His homework may not finished by tonight.
⑤ What was taught to you in the 2nd grade?

VOCA mention 언급하다 | allow 허락하다 | artifact 공예품, 유물 | kitten 새끼 고양이 | discover 발견하다 | grade 학년

09 How many sentences are grammatically correct? 2점

> ⓐ All fees must paid by Monday.
> ⓑ Was the door locked firmly?
> ⓒ By who was the window cleaned yesterday?
> ⓓ A stone was thrown for the frog by a boy.
> ⓔ 1,000 won was lent to him by his sister.

① one   ② two
③ three   ④ four
⑤ five

10 Which cannot make a grammatically correct sentence? 4점

① were / ? / this / By / whom / told / you
② grown / ? / California / in / grapes / Are
③ given / The / wasn't / money / me / to / .
④ The / video / online / . / posted / be / will
⑤ boy / . / to / made / was / plane / paper / A / the

Challenge! 주관식 서술형

11 The second sentence changes the first sentence into the passive voice. Find the error in the second sentence and correct it. 4점

> You have to use this computer carefully.
> → This computer is had to use carefully.

_____ → _____

12 Rearrange the words to make a question. 4점

> China, everything, made, in, is

→ _____

13 Fill in the blanks to make the sentences have the same meaning as the one in the box. 4점

> Sansu gave the police the information.

(1) The police _____ _____
   the information by Sansu.

(2) The information _____
   _____ _____ the police by
   Sansu.

14 Write the question according to the answer. Use the given words. 5점

> A: _____
>   (this robot cleaner)
> B: It was made in Minnesota.

15 Change the sentence into the passive voice. 4점

> My mom cooked me Vietnamese noodles.

→ _____
  _____

16 This is Louganis's profile on his instant messenger. Change the status message into the passive voice. 6점

> ☆   ✕
> Louganis
> What touched you today?
> 1:1 chat

→ _____
  _____

VOCA   fee 요금, 비용 | firmly 단단히 | lend 빌리다 | carefully 신중하게, 주의해서 | Vietnamese 베트남의 | noodle 국수 | touch 감동시키다

여러 가지 수동태(2)

개념이해책
86쪽 함께 보기

■ 아래 표의 빈칸에 알맞은 내용을 써 넣으세요. >>> 정답 21쪽

① by 이외의 전치사를 쓰는 수동태

1)	~에 관심이 있다	2)	~에 위치하다
3)	(비)를 만나다, ~에 갇히다	4)	~에 실망하다
5)	~에 놀라다	6)	~에 충격 받다
7)	~에 흥분해 있다	8)	~에 대해 걱정하다
9)	~에 놀라다	10)	~로 덮여 있다
11)	~에 만족하다	12)	~에 겁먹다
13)	~로 가득 차다	14)	~에 기뻐하다
15)	~와 결혼하다	16)	~로 붐비다
17)	~을 입고 있다	18)	~에 질리다
19)	~로 만들어져 있다 (물리적 변화)	21)	~로 유명하다
		22)	~에게 알려져 있다
20)	~로 만들어져 있다 (화학적 변화)	23)	~로 알려져 있다
		24)	~로 알 수 있다

② 동사구의 수동태

Jean takes care of the children. → The children 25)_____ by Jean.

Level 1 Test

>>> 정답 21쪽

A 밑줄 친 부분에서 어색한 것을 고치시오.

1 He was pleased in my progress.

→ _____

2 Her novel is known as its realism.

→ _____

3 She is scared from every kind of insect.

→ _____

B 빈칸을 채워 문장을 수동태로 전환하시오.

1 We ran out of gas.

→ Gas _____ _____

_____ _____ (by us).

2 She will pick you up at the airport.

→ You will _____ _____

_____ _____ her at the airport.

C 우리말과 같은 뜻이 되도록 주어진 단어를 이용해서 문장을 완성하시오.

1 코치님은 나의 기술에 절대 만족해하지 않는다.

→ The coach _____ _____ _____

_____ my skills. (satisfy)

2 치즈는 우유로 만들어진다.

→ Cheese _____ _____ _____ milk.

(make)

VOCA run out of ~을 다 쓰다 | pick up ~을 데리러 가다 | progress 발전, 진보 | realism 사실주의, 리얼리즘 | skill 기술

My score is

/ 30점

25점 이상 PASS!!

01 빈칸에 들어갈 말로 알맞은 것은? 2점

> What is the chair covered _____ ?

① to   ② for

③ at   ④ with

⑤ after

02 다음 우리말을 영어로 바르게 옮긴 것은? 2점

> 마네킹의 모자가 그녀에 의해서 씌워졌다.

① The mannequin's hat put on by her.

② The mannequin's hat was putted by her.

③ The mannequin's hat was put by her.

④ The mannequin's hat was put on by her.

⑤ The mannequin's hat did put on by her.

03 빈칸에 들어갈 말이 바르게 짝지어진 것은? 2점

> • The square was crowded _____ people.
>
> • Were you surprised _____ the joke?

① by – in   ② by – at

③ of – by   ④ with – of

⑤ with – at

04 다음 중 어법상 어색한 것으로 짝지어진 것은? 3점

> ⓐ Wait! My shoe has been taken off.
>
> ⓑ I am not disappointed in you.
>
> ⓒ The paper bag was run over a bike.
>
> ⓓ The writer is known as his unique style.
>
> ⓔ Are the judges satisfied in my performance?

① ⓑ, ⓒ   ② ⓓ, ⓔ

③ ⓐ, ⓓ, ⓔ   ④ ⓑ, ⓓ

⑤ ⓒ, ⓓ, ⓔ

05 다음을 수동태로 전환할 때 빈칸에 알맞은 말을 쓰시오. 4점

서술형

> My father had to put off the wedding.

→ The wedding _____

    my father.

06 그림을 보고 make를 이용하여 문장을 완성하시오. 5점

서술형

(1) The house _____ cookies.

(2) The cookies _____ flour.

07 우리말과 같은 뜻이 되도록 주어진 조건에 맞게 영작하시오. 6점

서술형

> 그 계획은 실행되지 않을 것이다.
>
> ·조건1   수동태로 쓸 것
>
> ·조건2   carry out을 활용할 것
>
> ·조건3   어휘 – plan, be going to

→ _____

08 주어진 단어들 중 필요한 것만 골라 배열해서 의문문을 완성하시오. 6점

서술형

> choice, she, does, by, from, is, pleased, my, with

→ _____

VOCA   mannequin 마네킹 | put on ~을 쓰다[입다] | square 광장 | joke 농담 | take off 벗다 | disappoint 실망시키다 | run over (차로) 치다 | unique 독특한 | style 문체 | judge 심사위원 | performance 공연 | put off 연기하다 | carry out 실행하다

01 Which word for the blank is the same as the blank in the example? 2점

> 보기 The hall is filled _____ people.

① I am not interested _____ music.
② This suitcase is made _____ leather.
③ He was married _____ a rich woman.
④ She was tired _____ walking.
⑤ The roof is covered _____ snow.

02 Which word comes fifth when changing the sentence into the passive voice? 2점

> The girls in my class made fun of me.

① made
② fun
③ of
④ by
⑤ the

03 Which change in the sentences is incorrect? 2점

① Did Clara drive my car?
  ➡ Was my car driven by Clara?
② He didn't lock the door.
  ➡ The door wasn't locked by him.
③ They looked after the bird.
  ➡ The bird was looked after by them.
④ Who made the box?
  ➡ By whom was the box made?
⑤ People didn't pay attention to the title.
  ➡ The title wasn't paid attention.

04 Which set of the answer is correct? 3점

> • Ice cream is made _____ milk.
> • Is the flower made _____ paper?
> • My story will be made _____ a movie.

① from – of – into
② from – by – from
③ into – of – from
④ of – from – into
⑤ of – by – from

05 Which is NOT necessary when translating the sentence? 3점

> 그는 원숭이를 조련하는 능력으로 유명하다.

① ability
② to
③ as
④ train
⑤ for

06 Which translation is incorrect? 2점

① 우리는 갑자기 소나기를 만났어요.
  ➡ Suddenly, we were caught in a shower.
② 그 낡은 집은 귀신들로 가득 차 있었어요.
  ➡ The old house was crowded of ghosts.
③ 그 오래된 우물은 거미줄로 덮여 있었어요.
  ➡ The old well was covered with webs.
④ 우리는 검은 물체에 무척 겁먹었어요.
  ➡ We were very scared of something dark.
⑤ 그것은 저승사자처럼 검은 옷을 입고 있었어요.
  ➡ It was dressed in black like the Angel of Death.

07 Who correctly changes the sentence into the active voice? 2점

> Why is he looked down on by everybody?

① 은영: Why does he look down on everybody?
② 희정: Why do everybody look down on him?
③ 주희: Why everybody is looked down on?
④ 정아: Why does everybody look down on him?
⑤ 자경: Why does everybody look down him?

08 Whose correction is correct? 2점

> The children were brought up an Indian couple.

① were → was
② brought → bought
③ up → down
④ up → up by
⑤ an → a

VOCA suitcase 여행 가방 | leather 가죽 | make fun of ~을 놀리다 | look after ~을 돌보다 | pay attention to ~에 주의를 기울이다 | train 조련하다 | shower 소나기 | web 거미줄 | Angel of Death 저승사자 | look down on ~을 깔보다, 무시하다 | bring up 키우다 | Indian 인도의

09 How many sentences are grammatically incorrect? 2점

> ⓐ I am never satisfied with myself.
> ⓑ Was the microwave turned off him?
> ⓒ The doctor was sent for by Mr. Wang.
> ⓓ The coats weren't put on by the kids.
> ⓔ Boy, you are looking for by your parents.

① one   ② two
③ three   ④ four
⑤ five

10 Which CANNOT make a grammatically correct sentence? 4점

① you / Are / with / dark / the / scared / ?
② Kathy / . / is / to / brother / married / my
③ caught / a / They / dilemma / were / . / in
④ at / shocked / his / were / accent / . / We
⑤ was / disappointed / . / the / He / at / results

11 Which is grammatically wrong? (up to 3 answers) 3점

① They were surprised from the sound.
② The gamer is known to every gamer.
③ Why was he disappointed in me?
④ We were amazed with his teaching.
⑤ Were you pleased by my instant message?

Challenge! 주관식 서술형

12 Complete the dialog by using words used in the dialog. 4점

> A: Who will take care of the dog?
> B: It _____ my vet.

13 Rewrite the sentence by using the underlined words as a subject. 4점

> The girls will take out the twin bed.

→ _____

14 Change the sentence into the passive voice. 4점

> Who looks after national parks?

→ _____

15 Read the dialog and complete Mom's line. 5점

> Son: I'm home! It was such a long trip. Where are my iguanas, Mom? Did you take good care of them?
> Mom: Not actually. Your iguanas _____ _____ _____ _____ by your grandmother.
>
> ·조건 1   수동태로 쓸 것
> ·조건 2   과거 시제를 사용할 것

16 Translate the sentence according to the conditions. 6점

> 난 런던 날씨가 지긋지긋해.
>
> ·Condition 1   tired를 포함할 것
> ·Condition 2   'the+날씨+in+지역' 형식으로 쓸 것
> ·Condition 3   8단어의 완전한 문장으로 쓸 것

→ _____

VOCA   microwave 전자레인지 | send for ～을 부르러 보내다 | dilemma 딜레마, 진퇴양난 | take care of ～을 돌보다 | vet 수의사 | national park 국립 공원

Review Test

01 U15_1

빈칸에 들어갈 말로 알맞은 것은? 2점

> The plane will _____ to New York.

① flown ② is flies
③ be flown ④ is flown
⑤ be flew

02 U16_1+2

Which is suitable for the blank? 2점

> Can the bamboo boat _____ by the little girls?

① carry ② carried
③ is carried ④ be carried
⑤ was carried

03 U16_2

다음 문장을 수동태로 바르게 전환한 것은? 2점

한눈에 쏙

> Where did he hide the gun?

① Where was he hidden the gun?
② Where was the gun hidden?
③ Where was the gun hiding?
④ Where did he hidden the gun?
⑤ Where was hidden the gun?

04 U15+1+2+GP

다음 중 문장 전환이 올바르지 <u>않은</u> 것을 <u>모두</u> 고르시오.

한눈에 쏙 3점

① Mrs. Kim teaches the students.
  → The students is taught by Mrs. Kim.
② Did Sowol write all of the poems?
  → Were all of the poems wrote by Sowol?
③ King Sejong invented Hangeul.
  → Hangeul was invented by King Sejong.
④ She read the news on the Internet.
  → The news is read by her on the Internet.
⑤ An old woman swept the floor.
  → The floor was swept by an old woman.

05 U17_1

빈칸에 공통으로 들어갈 말로 알맞은 것은? 2점

> • She was dressed _____ a green sweater and jeans.
> • Is your hometown located _____ Gangwon-do?

① with ② to
③ on ④ of
⑤ in

06 U16_3

다음 중 밑줄 친 부분이 어법상 어색한 것은? 2점

함정

① The email <u>was sent to</u> her by Eric.
② This cake <u>was bought for</u> me by her.
③ She <u>was shown to</u> our house by us.
④ Those motorcycles <u>are lent to</u> me.
⑤ Sign language <u>was taught to</u> her by Helen.

07 U17_1

Which word for the blank is <u>different</u> from the others? 2점

① I was pleased _____ your thank–you card.
② Her closet was filled _____ many shoes.
③ The park was crowded _____ visitors.
④ Is the secretary satisfied _____ her income?
⑤ Busan is known _____ its beautiful beaches.

08 U15_4

밑줄 친 부분이 생략 가능한 것끼리 짝지어진 것은? 3점

> ⓐ My door was knocked on <u>by someone</u>.
> ⓑ They were helped <u>by a rich old lady</u>.
> ⓒ She wasn't given a ring <u>by her boyfriend</u>.
> ⓓ Spanish is also spoken in Mexico <u>by Mexicans</u>.

① ⓐ, ⓒ ② ⓑ, ⓓ
③ ⓐ, ⓓ ④ ⓐ, ⓑ, ⓓ
⑤ ⓑ, ⓒ, ⓓ

09 U17_2 다음 중 <u>어색한</u> 부분을 찾아 바르게 고친 학생은? 2점

> Was the plan put off you?

① 수미: Was → Did ② 용수: the → an

③ 태만: put → putted ④ 채린: off → up

⑤ 철희: you → by you

10 U17_1+2 다음 중 어법상 옳은 것은? 2점

★ 고난도

① She was laughed by the girls.

② I was so worried in you, son.

③ He was amazed to the size of the truck.

④ My sister is interested by Japanese cartoons.

⑤ He is known as the greatest Indian warrior.

11 U15_1 주어진 단어를 이용해서 과거 시제로 문장을 완성하시오.

3점

> The chicken _____ without any Coke. (deliver)

12 U17_1 Write the common word for the blanks. 3점

> • The prince is married _____ Princess Máxima.
>
> • The author is known _____ almost everybody in Korea.

→ _____

13 U16_3 다음 문장을 능동태로 바꾸시오. 4점

> Difficult questions are always asked of me by the teacher.

→ _____

14 U15_4 그림을 보고 주어진 조건에 맞게 대화를 완성하시오. 6점

> A: Where did you hide my cell phone?
>
> B: _____
>
> · 조건 1 수동태로 답할 것
>
> · 조건 2 「by + 행위자」는 생략할 것
>
> · 조건 3 어휘 – inside, the book
>
> · 조건 4 조건 3의 어휘를 포함하여 6단어로 쓸 것

15 U17_1 빈칸에 필요하지 <u>않은</u> 말을 [보기]에서 <u>모두</u> 골라 쓰시오.

3점

> | 보기 | from | of | at |
> |---|---|---|---|
> | | with | in | about |

> (1) I am scared _____ nothing.
>
> (2) Nobody is shocked _____ your decision.
>
> (3) His desk was covered _____ lots of books.

→ _____

16 U16_1+GP 다음 영작에서 <u>어색한</u> 것을 찾아 고치시오. 3점

> 공항에서 대부분의 짐은 점검을 받아야 한다.
>
> = Most baggage ought to check at the airport.

_____ → _____

17 다음 말풍선에 알맞은 말을 영작하시오. 5점

| 미안하지만, 난 깜짝 파티에 놀라지 않아.
a surprise party |

→ I'm sorry, but _____

_____ .

U15_2

18 다음 문장 전환 중 잘못된 것을 찾아 바르게 쓰시오. 4점

함정

ⓐ We don't sell junk food here.
  → Junk food isn't sold here.
ⓑ The tourists pollute the water.
  → The water is polluted by the tourists.
ⓒ My uncle took me to the dentist.
  → The dentist was taken to me by my uncle.

(   ) _____

→ _____

U16_2

19 Rearrange the given words to translate the sentence. 5점

얼마나 오래 전에 컴퓨터가 켜졌나요?
ago, turned, the, on, long, how, was, computer

→ _____

U16_3

20 주어진 문장을 수동태로 바꿀 때 빈칸에 알맞은 말을 쓰시오. 4점

He gave me the wrong information.

(1) I _____ by him.

(2) The wrong information _____ him.

[21~22] 다음 글을 읽고 물음에 답하시오.

　(A)(filled, our lives, many, things, are, to, do, with). It's very difficult ⓐfor us to sit still and do nothing, even for a few minutes. People are not human beings any longer. We should ⓑcall human doings. As a matter of fact, we are often frightened at the thought of not ⓒto have something to do. Just ⓓlike our bodies, however, our minds need a break from time to time. After ⓔtaking a break, our minds become strong, free, and creative.

U15_1+U06_1

21 윗글의 밑줄 친 ⓐ~ⓔ 중 어법상 어색한 것을 찾아 바르게 고친 것은? (정답 2개) 3점

고난도

① ⓐ for us → of us
② ⓑ call → be called
③ ⓒ to have → having
④ ⓓ like → likes
⑤ ⓔ taking → to take

U17_1

22 다음 우리말과 같은 뜻이 되도록 윗글의 (A)에 주어진 단어를 배열하시오. 5점

우리의 삶은 해야 할 많은 것들로 가득 차 있다.

→ _____

CHAPTER 08
관계사

18 관계대명사 who, which

■ 아래 표의 빈칸에 알맞은 내용을 써 넣으세요. >>> 정답 23쪽

개념이해책
94쪽 함께 보기

CONCEPT 1 관계대명사란?

I have a friend. + My friend can speak French. → I have a friend who can speak French.
선행사   관계대명사   형용사절

CONCEPT 2 관계대명사 who: 선행사가 1)_____ 일 때

주격	2)_____	= 5)_____	I met a boy 6)_____ liked my sister.
목적격(생략 가능)	3)_____		I met the boy 7)_____ my sister loves.
소유격	4)_____	I know the man 8)_____ wallet was stolen.	

CONCEPT 3 관계대명사 which: 선행사가 9)_____ 또는 10)_____ 일 때

주격	11)_____	= 13)_____	She likes the dog 14)_____ has fluffy hair.
목적격(생략 가능)	12)_____		She likes the dog 15)_____ I have.
소유격	16)_____ (= 17)_____ 18)_____)	She likes the dog 19)_____ legs are short. (= She like the dog, the legs 20)_____ are short.)	

CONCEPT 4 관계대명사의 용법

제한적 용법	관계대명사절이 선행사를 21)_____	He has a son 22)_____ is a singer.
계속적 용법	관계대명사절이 선행사에 대한 23)_____ 앞에 24)_____ 가 있음 「25)_____ + 26)_____」로 바꾸어 쓸 수 있음	He has a son, 27)_____ (= 28)_____ 29)_____) is a singer.

Level 1 Test

>>> 정답 23쪽

A [ ]에서 알맞은 것을 고르시오. (답이 2개인 경우도 있음)

1 I have a friend [who / which] is good at swimming.

2 The man who sent me the flowers [work / works] at a bank.

3 She gave me the cake [that / which] her mother made for her.

B 두 문장을 관계대명사를 이용해서 하나의 문장으로 전환하시오.

1 The customer liked the waitress. She was very friendly.

→ _____

2 The dictionary has many new words. I'm using the dictionary now.

→ _____

3 I know the man. You respect him.

→ _____

VOCA **be good at** ~에 능숙하다 | **customer** 고객 | **dictionary** 사전 | **respect** 존경하다

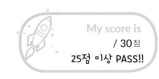

01 다음 두 문장을 한 문장으로 연결할 때 빈칸에 알맞은 것을 <u>모두</u> 고르시오. 2점

> This is the boy. He won the contest.
> = This is the boy _____ won the contest.

① who　　　　　② whom
③ which　　　　④ that
⑤ what

02 빈칸에 which가 들어갈 수 <u>없는</u> 것은? 2점

① This is the fish _____ lives in the sea.
② She has an aunt _____ runs a beauty shop.
③ He has a car _____ was made in Korea.
④ This is the book _____ is written in Korean.
⑤ Science has made many things _____ are useful.

03 다음 중 관계사가 <u>아닌</u> 것을 <u>모두</u> 고르시오. 2점

① We met the girl <u>who</u> gave us some milk.
② She told me <u>that</u> her brother lived in Seoul.
③ Do you know <u>who</u> stole my money?
④ I will tell you <u>which</u> one I will choose.
⑤ He has a cat <u>that</u> eats little.

04 다음 문장들에 대해 바르게 설명한 학생은? 3점

> ⓐ She has a friend who lives in Hong Kong.
> ⓑ I met a boy who has a nice bike.
> ⓒ Jane was wearing a hat that was too small.

① 단아: ⓐ의 who는 that으로 바꿔 써야 한다.
② 민수: ⓑ의 has는 have가 되어야 한다.
③ 진하: ⓒ의 that은 생략할 수 있다.
④ 효정: ⓑ의 who는 의문사이다.
⑤ 지수: 세 문장 모두 어법상 올바른 문장이다.

05 빈칸에 알맞은 관계대명사를 넣어 문장을 완성하시오. 5점

서술형

> The movie *Hide and Seek*, _____ we watched last Sunday, was very scary.

→ _____

06 밑줄 친 부분 대신 쓸 수 있는 말을 2개 쓰시오. 5점

서술형

> The man <u>that</u> you met yesterday is my uncle.

→ _____ , _____

07 관계대명사를 이용해 두 문장을 한 문장으로 쓰시오. 5점

서술형

> We adopted a child. + The child's parents were killed in an accident.

→ _____

_____

08 그림을 보고 우리말과 같은 뜻이 되도록 주어진 조건에 맞게 문장을 완성하시오. 6점

서술형

> 잔디밭에 앉아 있는 몇 명의 아이들이 있다.
>
> · 조건 1　어휘 – sit on the grass
> · 조건 2　시제 – 현재 진행형
> · 조건 3　관계사를 포함하여 빈칸에 6단어로 쓸 것

→ There are a few children _____

_____ .

VOCA　win 우승하다 | contest 대회 | run 운영하다 | beauty shop 미용실 | useful 유용한 | hide and seek 숨바꼭질 | scary 무서운 | adopt 양자로 삼다 | accident 사고

01 Which is grammatically underlined incorrect? 2점

> She ① knows ② a man ③ whose brothers
> ④ resembles ⑤ each other.

02 Which combines the two sentences into one? 2점

> She has a grandson. + He is an architect.

① She has a grandson that he is an architect.
② She has a grandson who he is an architect.
③ She has a grandson who is an architect.
④ She has a grandson which he is an architect.
⑤ She has a grandson which is an architect.

03 Which underlined "that" is used differently? 3점

① Roses are the flowers that I like most.
② This is the bird that can speak English.
③ This is the letter that Mike wrote to me.
④ This is the room that my sister studies in.
⑤ Pass me the magazine that you are reading.

04 Which underlined "who" is used in the same way as the example? (2 answers) 3점

> 보기 The woman who had a steak didn't give me a tip.

① Don't you know who that girl is?
② I hate people who talk during movies.
③ The man who keeps coughing looks terrible.
④ Tell me who you are going to invite.
⑤ Who borrowed your cell phone?

05 Which word can replace the underlined words? 2점

> I got a gift, and it was bought by my father.

① what   ② who
③ that   ④ which
⑤ whose

06 Choose ALL of the choices whose underlined word is a relative pronoun. 3점

① He can't believe that she is not a singer.
② She needs someone who can teach her math.
③ Is that the machine that works well?
④ I will show you which she chose.
⑤ I'm not sure who will agree with you.

07 Which sentences are incorrect? 3점

> ⓐ There are some things that all people need.
> ⓑ They are some of the people who provide services in our communities.
> ⓒ It is a great book who is very interesting.
> ⓓ She's the girl who is my best friend.
> ⓔ This is a piano which the leg has unique patterns.

① ⓐ, ⓒ   ② ⓑ, ⓒ
③ ⓒ, ⓓ   ④ ⓒ, ⓔ
⑤ ⓓ, ⓔ

08 Which words are proper for the blanks? 2점

> • Summer is the season _____ we like best.
> • She is the lady _____ I met at the party.

① that – which   ② which – whom
③ whose – who   ④ whom – which
⑤ whom – that

VOCA resemble ~와 닮다 | grandson 손자 | architect 건축가 | magazine 잡지 | steak 스테이크 | tip 팁, 봉사료 | cough 기침하다 | gift 선물 |
provide 제공하다 | community 주민, 지역사회 | unique 독특한 | pattern 문양

09 Which is the proper word for the blank? 2점

> I know a girl _____ talent in music is exceptional.

① who
② which
③ whose
④ what
⑤ that

10 Choose the word that can replace the underlined words. 2점

> She failed the test, <u>and it</u> disappointed all of us.

① what
② that
③ who
④ which
⑤ whom

Challenge! 주관식 서술형

11 Write the common word for the blanks. 4점

> • I want a robot _____ can cook for me.
> • The student _____ broke the classroom mirror ran away.
> • I know _____ he is attractive.

→ _____

12 Rewrite the sentence correctly. 4점

> The woman whom I take care of suffer from cancer.

→ _____

13 Rearrange the words and add a relative pronoun to translate the sentence. 5점

> 그녀는 어젯밤에 남겨 놓은 피자를 먹을 것이다.
> the pizza, she, eat, last night, will, left

→ She _____

_____.

14 Combine the two sentences by using the word "which." 4점

> Look at the calendar. + It is hanging on the wall.

→ _____

15 Rewrite the underlined word in TWO words. 3점

> He visited Disneyland, <u>which</u> is located in Los Angeles.

→ _____ _____

16 Translate the sentence correctly according to the conditions. 6점

> 우리는 꼭대기가 눈으로 덮여 있는 산을 올랐다.
> ·Condition 1   어휘 – top, be covered with
> ·Condition 2   관계사를 포함하여 빈칸에 6단어로 쓸 것

→ We climbed the mountain _____

_____.

VOCA   talent 재능 | exceptional 특출한, 예외적인 | disappoint 실망시키다 | attractive 매력적인 | suffer from ~을 앓고 있다 | cancer 암 | calendar 달력 | hang 걸려 있다 | top 꼭대기, 정상

관계대명사 that, what

개념이해책
97쪽 함께 보기

■ 아래 표의 빈칸에 알맞은 내용을 써 넣으세요. ≫≫ 정답 24쪽

① that을 쓸 수 없거나 that을 주로 쓰는 경우

that을 쓸 수 없는 경우	that을 주로 쓰는 경우
• 1)_____ 격이 없음	• 선행사에 형용사의 4)_____, 5)_____, the 6)_____, the 7)_____, the 8)_____ 등이 있을 때
• 2)_____ 적 용법에는 쓰이지 않음	
• 3)_____ 와 나란히 함께 쓰일 수 없음	• 선행사에 9)_____, 10)_____, 11)_____, 12)_____, ~13)_____ 등이 있을 때

② 관계대명사 what = the thing(s) which[that]

14)_____	What I have now is only water.
15)_____	This vegetable pizza is what my mom wants to eat.
16)_____	Tell me what you know.

③ 관계대명사의 생략

17)_____ 격	타동사의 18)_____ 격	He is the man (19)_____) I met yesterday.
	전치사의 20)_____ 격	This is the dog (21)_____) I am fond of.
22)_____ 격 관계대명사+23)_____		The book (24)_____) on the desk is mine.

👤⁺ Level 1 Test

≫≫ 정답 24쪽

A [ ]에서 알맞은 것을 고르시오. (답이 2개인 경우도 있음)

1 I had lunch with the man [that / whom] you introduced to me.

2 He has to give up [which / what] he wants.

3 The hobby on [which / that] he spends most of his time is collecting miniatures.

4 It's the only solution [what / that] we have.

5 There are the girls and the puppies [which / that] are sitting on the grass.

6 [What / That] is important is your safety.

7 She has everything [which / that] she wants.

B 우리말과 같은 뜻이 되도록 관계대명사를 추가하여 주어진 단어를 배열하시오.

1 나는 그가 버린 쓰레기를 주웠다.
(the trash, threw out, he, I, picked up)

→ _____

2 그는 그가 가지고 있던 것을 나에게 주었다.
(gave, he, me, had, he)

→ _____

3 나는 아빠가 운전하곤 했던 바로 그 차를 운전한다.
(my father, drive, used to, the very car)

→ I drive _____.

VOCA introduce 소개하다 | give up 포기하다 | collect 수집하다 | miniature 미니어처, 모형 | solution 해결책 | trash 쓰레기 | pick up 줍다 | throw out 버리다 | puppy 강아지 | safety 안전

112

>>> 정답 24쪽

01 빈칸에 that이 들어갈 수 <u>없는</u> 것을 <u>모두</u> 고르시오. 3점

① This is the man _____ broke your vase.

② This is the toy _____ makes me laugh.

③ I believe _____ you will succeed.

④ The boy _____ backpack is filled with cartoons is John.

⑤ This is the restaurant in _____ I met her.

02 밑줄 친 What[what]의 쓰임이 나머지와 <u>다른</u> 하나는? 2점

① This is <u>what</u> I lost at the subway station.

② I hope you are going to get <u>what</u> you need.

③ <u>What</u> does she want to do in Europe?

④ <u>What</u> makes me angry is my stupid mistake.

⑤ <u>What</u> is important is your future.

03 다음 문장들에 대해 바르게 설명한 학생은? 3점

ⓐ The house which I live in is not mine.
ⓑ The boy who she teaches him is my friend.
ⓒ The woman who called you is my mom.

① 미숙: ⓐ 전치사 in 은 which 앞으로 와야 한다.

② 영식: ⓐ which는 that으로 써야 한다.

③ 서영: ⓑ who는 주격 관계대명사이다.

④ 준식: ⓑ him은 삭제되어야 한다.

⑤ 형주: ⓒ called는 calling이 되어야 한다.

04 다음 밑줄 친 것 중 생략할 수 <u>없는</u> 것은? 2점

① I am looking for someone <u>who</u> can watch my dog.

② I spent all the money <u>that</u> I had.

③ The subject <u>which</u> I'm interested in is history.

④ Do you like the cake <u>that</u> I made for you?

⑤ I will meet someone <u>who</u> is coming from L.A.

05 다음 빈칸에 공통으로 들어갈 단어를 쓰시오. 4점

서술형

• Won Bin is the most handsome man _____ I have ever seen.
• Please tell him _____ I called.

➝ _____

06 다음 문장에서 생략 가능한 <u>두 단어</u>에 괄호로 표시하시오. 4점

서술형

Look at the girls who are dancing on the bench.

07 다음 중 어색한 문장을 찾아 바르게 고쳐 쓰시오. 6점

서술형

ⓐ This is the thing what you are looking for.
ⓑ I have the thing you want.
ⓒ I believe what he said.

( ) _____

08 그림을 보고 조건에 맞게 영작하시오. 6점

서술형

나는 그가 나를 위해 만든 것을 먹었다.

· 조건 I 어휘 – eat, for, make, me
· 조건 2 7단어로 쓸 것
· 조건 3 관계사를 포함할 것

➝ _____

VOCA backpack 배낭 | be filled with ~로 가득 차다 | cartoon 만화 | stupid 멍청한 | mistake 실수 | future 미래 | advice 충고 | subject 과목

01 Which is appropriate for the blanks? 2점

> • He gave me _____ he had found.
> • Choose the shield _____ you want to use.

① what – what   ② what – that

③ that – what   ④ that – which

⑤ that – that

02 Which of the underlined words CANNOT be replaced by "that"? 3점

① The man with <u>whom</u> you talked was my cousin.

② The cap <u>which</u> she is wearing is mine.

③ He is the man <u>whom</u> she respects.

④ I have a friend <u>who</u> wants to be a singer.

⑤ I like the suit <u>that</u> you wore for the wedding.

[03~04] Which underlined "that" is used in the same way as in the example? (Find ALL.) 각 2점

03   I like books <u>that</u> have many pictures.

① What is <u>that</u>?

② It is true <u>that</u> he likes you.

③ I know <u>that</u> he is in Seoul now.

④ She is so kind <u>that</u> everyone likes her.

⑤ I want to talk with the boy <u>that</u> has red hair.

04   The man <u>that</u> lives in the big house is very wealthy.

① It was yesterday <u>that</u> we met her.

② I think <u>that</u> you are wrong.

③ He has dogs <u>that</u> have long hair.

④ Sugar is something <u>that</u> is sweet.

⑤ Spring is the season <u>that</u> comes after winter.

05 Which of the underlined words CANNOT be omitted? (up to 3 answers) 3점

① She has a son <u>whom</u> you may like.

② This is the watch for <u>which</u> I'm looking.

③ I like the girl <u>who</u> I talked with this morning.

④ The boy <u>whom</u> you yelled at is my brother.

⑤ I took a picture of a bird <u>whose</u> head was bald.

06 Which sentences are <u>incorrect</u>? 2점

> ⓐ She sold the phone case what she made.
> ⓑ The temple which we go to every Sunday give us free lunch.
> ⓒ This is the first *songpyeon* that she made.

① ⓐ   ② ⓐ, ⓑ

③ ⓐ, ⓒ   ④ ⓑ, ⓒ

⑤ ⓐ, ⓑ, ⓒ

07 Which underlined "that" is used <u>differently</u> than the others? 2점

① This is the bike <u>that</u> I need to repair today.

② There is a big house <u>that</u> looks like a palace.

③ Is it true <u>that</u> the Earth is round?

④ The puppy <u>that</u> I found yesterday was my neighbor's dog.

⑤ This is the most comfortable sofa <u>that</u> I have ever sat on.

08 Which underlined "What[what]" is used <u>differently</u> than the others? 2점

① That's just <u>what</u> I'm looking for.

② <u>What</u> kept me busy was my work.

③ <u>What</u> made him happy was his son's success.

④ He showed me <u>what</u> Mike gave him.

⑤ Can you tell me <u>what</u> this doughnut is made from?

VOCA   shield 방패 | cousin 사촌 | wear 쓰다, 입다 | respect 존경하다 | wealthy 부유한 | season 계절 | watch 손목시계; 보다 | yell at ~에게 소리지르다 | bald 대머리의 | temple 절, 사찰 | repair 수선하다 | palace 궁전 | used to ~하곤 했다 | neighbor 이웃 | comfortable 편안한 | success 성공

09 Which blank needs a <u>different</u> word than the others? 3점

① She has the same thing _____ I have.

② This is _____ they gave up.

③ We don't know _____ he wants.

④ He lost _____ he bought yesterday.

⑤ Did you understand _____ he told you?

10 Who corrects the error(s) correctly? 3점

> Bring me the biggest potato what you have it.

① 민수: what → that

② 지형: what → the thing which

③ 현주: it 삭제

④ 효정: what 삭제

⑤ 유정: what → that, it 삭제

Challenge! 주관식 서술형

11 Write the proper word for each blank. 3점

> • I won't give my children anything ___(A)___ I have.
> • This convenience store is ___(B)___ I was looking for.

(A) _____

(B) _____

12 Rewrite the sentence by omitting the relative pronoun. 4점

> Vanilla is a flavor of which I am fond.

→ _____

13 Rewrite the sentence correctly. 4점

> She is the very person whom I want to work with.

→ _____

14 Rewrite the sentence with the omitted words. 5점

> He got the package sent by me.

→ _____

15 Choose ALL of the <u>incorrect</u> sentences and rewrite them correctly. 4점

> ⓐ He has a new car what he drives every day.
> ⓑ We told him what he had to do.
> ⓒ It is a crayon with I drew this picture.

( ) _____

( ) _____

16 Translate the sentence according to the conditions. 6점

> 그를 화나게 만든 것은 나의 실수였다.
> (내가 실수를 해서 그가 화가 났다.)
>
> • Condition 1   어휘 – him, my, angry, made, was, mistake
> • Condition 2   관계사를 포함할 것
> • Condition 3   7단어

→ _____

VOCA hand 건네주다; 손 | convenience store 편의점 | flavor 맛 | be fond of ~을 좋아하다 | package 소포, 상자, 포장물 | crayon 크레용

관계부사

■ 아래 표의 빈칸에 알맞은 내용을 써 넣으세요. >>> 정답 25쪽

개념이해책
100쪽 함께 보기

CONCEPT 1 관계부사 = 1)_____ + 2)_____

용도	선행사	관계부사	3)_____ + 4)_____	예문
장소	the place, the house	5)____	6)____ [7)____ , 8)____]which	I know the exact place. He was born in it. → I know the exact place 9)_____ he was born.
시간	the time, the year	10)____	11)____ [12)____ , 13)____]which	The time wasn't known to me. She left for America at that time. → The time 14)_____ she left for America wasn't known to me.
이유	the reason	15)____	16)____ which	Do you know the reason? He feels so good for the reason. → Do you know the reason 17)_____ he feels so good?
방법	(the way)	18)____	19)____ which	I don't know the way. She has succeeded in that way. → I don't know 20)_____ she has succeeded. → I don't know 21)_____ she has succeeded.

Level 1 Test

>>> 정답 25쪽

A 빈칸에 알맞은 말을 [보기]에서 골라 쓰시오.

보기	where	when	how	why

1 This is the park _____ I often exercise.

2 I like summer _____ we can go to the beach.

3 I know the reason _____ she hates me.

4 My math teacher asked me _____ I solved the problem.

5 He wants to go back to the city _____ he was born.

6 December is the month of the year _____ people like to have parties.

B 빈칸에 알맞은 말을 써서 다음 두 문장을 한 문장으로 만드시오.

1 The museum is far from here. + He works at the museum.

→ The museum _____ _____ he works is far from here.

→ The museum he works _____ is far from here.

→ The museum _____ he works is far from here.

2 Tell me the way. + You fixed the computer in the way.

→ Tell me the way _____ _____ you fixed the computer.

→ Tell me _____ _____ you fixed the computer.

→ Tell me _____ you fixed the computer.

VOCA exercise 운동하다 | far from ~로부터 먼 | fix 고치다

01 밑줄 친 where의 쓰임이 [보기]와 같은 것을 <u>모두</u> 고르시오. 2점

> [보기] This is the stream <u>where</u> we used to swim.

① Tell me <u>where</u> you are.

② I visited the bank <u>where</u> my mother works.

③ He didn't know <u>where</u> he was going.

④ <u>Where</u> have you been?

⑤ She wants to join a club <u>where</u> she can make friends.

02 How many sentences are <u>incorrect</u>? 3점

> ⓐ She made the cake the way I showed her.
> ⓑ I remembered the time when she arrived here.
> ⓒ How you told him about it was rude.
> ⓓ She built the house her son lives in now.
> ⓔ The reason why she likes him is because he is wise.

① zero   ② one

③ two   ④ three

⑤ four

03 다음 우리말을 영어로 옮긴 것으로 알맞지 <u>않은</u> 것은? 2점

> 이곳은 그가 저녁을 먹는 식당이다.

① This is the restaurant where he has dinner.

② This is the restaurant which he has dinner in.

③ This is the restaurant in which he has dinner.

④ This is the restaurant that he has dinner in.

⑤ This is the restaurant where he has dinner in.

04 빈칸에 공통으로 들어갈 말로 가장 적절한 것은? 3점

> • _____ did you miss the shuttle bus?
> • The reason _____ the boy is crying is that he didn't choose a good card.

① Which[which]   ② Why[why]

③ Who[who]   ④ When[when]

⑤ How[how]

05 다음 빈칸에 들어갈 말을 한 단어로 쓰시오. 4점

서술형

> A: Yes! I finally solved the riddle.
> B: Really? Please tell me _____ you did it.

→ _____

06 그림을 보고 단어 조각을 바르게 배열해서 문장을 완성하시오. 5점

서술형

| the place | I | my keys | hang | where |

→ This is _____.

07 다음 문장의 빈칸에 알맞은 말을 쓰시오. 5점

서술형

> _____ she failed was that she never studied.

→ _____

08 우리말과 같은 뜻이 되도록 주어진 조건에 맞게 영작하시오. 6점

서술형

> 그는 엄마에게 전화해야 했던 시간을 잊었다.
>
> · 조건 1 어휘 – the time, have to, call
> · 조건 2 9단어로 쓸 것
> · 조건 3 관계부사를 쓸 것

→ He forgot _____

_____.

VOCA stream 개울, 시내 | join 가입하다, 함께 하다 | miss 놓치다 | shuttle bus 정기 왕복 버스 | solve 풀다 | riddle 수수께끼 | hang 걸다 | fail 실패하다, 낙제하다

01 Which of the underlined words is used underlined differently than the others? 2점

① She was having dinner when I came home.

② April is the month when flowers bloom.

③ Do you remember the day when we first met?

④ I'll tell you the time when you should leave.

⑤ I'm waiting for the day when he will get married.

02 Which underlined "where" is used differently than in the example? 2점

> 보기   The museum is near the place where I live.

① He wanted to know where she went.

② He visited the country where he was born.

③ I grew up in a village where everybody knew everybody.

④ The company where he works is downtown.

⑤ Have you ever been to the place where the movie was shot?

03 Who corrects ALL of the errors correctly? 3점

> ⓐ The way she dresses is wonderful.
> ⓑ How she told the story was interesting.
> ⓒ There are many places where you can visit.
> ⓓ What is the reason she got fired?
> ⓔ She works in an office which she can use her skills.

① 성희: ⓐ The way → How

② 승훈: ⓑ How → The way

③ 미나: ⓒ where → which, ⓔ which → where

④ 광수: ⓒ where → which, ⓓ What → That

⑤ 수희: ⓔ which → where

04 Which CANNOT make a grammatically correct sentence? 4점

① upset / . / got / I / knew / Claudia / why

② which / live / . / beautiful / in / I / is / The / city

③ born / . / month / is / The / November / I / was / when

④ a / That's / has / . / he / which / restaurant / part-time job / the

⑤ not / my / with / . / she / hair / way / the / I'm / cut / satisfied

05 Which line is incorrect in the dialog? 2점

① A: Have you ever been to Australia?

② B: No. But I've heard the country is famous for koalas and kangaroos.

③ A: Yes, it's the country which I spent my holiday.

④ B: It is the country where I want to go.

⑤ A: The English that you learn is important there.

06 Which sentence is grammatically incorrect? 2점

① Describe a situation when you had to deal with a difficult person.

② I forgot the day when I bought this machine.

③ She checked the time when it started raining.

④ Ngannou wasn't aware of the moment when he fell asleep.

⑤ Summer is the season when people usually get lazier.

07 Which sentences are incorrect? 2점

> ⓐ He will visit the place where she was born in.
> ⓑ I will let you know the day when she will get married.
> ⓒ The house where Mozart was born in is now a museum.
> ⓓ I don't know why she broke up with him.
> ⓔ I hate the way she treats people.

① ⓐ, ⓑ   ② ⓐ, ⓒ

③ ⓒ, ⓓ, ⓔ   ④ ⓓ, ⓔ

⑤ ⓔ

VOCA   bloom 꽃이 피다 | get married 결혼하다 | village 마을 | grow up 자라다 | downtown 시내에 | shoot 촬영하다 | get fired 해고되다 | skill 기술 | be famous for ~로 유명하다 | describe 묘사하다 | situation 상황 | deal with 다루다 | check 확인하다 | be aware of ~을 알다 | break up with ~와 헤어지다 | treat 대하다

08 Which blank needs a <u>different</u> word? 3점

① This is the shop _____ I bought a doll.

② I remember the place _____ you drew on your canvas.

③ This is the station _____ I met your father for the first time.

④ Do you remember the house _____ you grew up?

⑤ Do you know the country _____ the next World Cup will be held?

Challenge! 주관식 서술형

09 Write the proper words for the blanks. 4점

> The reason ___(A)___ she got confused was ___(B)___ you explained nothing to her.

(A) _____ (B) _____

10 Rewrite the sentence correctly. 4점

> I remember the way how he looked at me.

→ _____

_____

11 Combine the two sentences to make one sentence by using the proper relative adverb. 5점

> Pyeongchang is the city in Korea. + In the city, the Winter Olympics were held in 2018.

→ _____

_____

12 Rearrange the given words and add one more word to make a sentence. (8 words) 6점

> · 조건 1 어휘 – 2005, the year, got married, was, we
> · 조건 2 2005로 시작할 것

→ _____

13 Look at the picture and translate the sentence according to the conditions. 6점

> 그가 서 있는 방은 책으로 가득 차 있다.
> · Condition 어휘 – stand, be full of
> · Condition 빈칸에 8단어로 쓸 것

→ The room _____

_____ .

14 Find the error and correct it. 5점

> A long time ago, people didn't like stripes. Why? Stripes symbolized evil things. That's the reason which prisoners wore stripes. But thanks to the French and American revolutions, stripes started to symbolize youth and health. Now, almost everybody loves stripes.
>
> *revolution: 혁명

_____ → _____

VOCA   get confused 헷갈리다 | explain 설명하다 | be held 개최되다 | stripe 줄무늬 | symbolize 상징하다

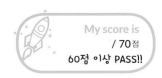

01 U18_2
다음 중 빈칸에 알맞은 관계대명사를 <u>모두</u> 고르시오. 2점

> She has a daughter _____ goes to Harvard.

① which ② who
③ whom ④ that
⑤ what

02 U18_3+GP
한눈에 쏙
Choose ALL of the grammatically <u>incorrect</u> sentences. 2점

① A chicken is a bird who can't fly.
② I live in a house that is 100 years old.
③ She proposed to a man who rejected her before.
④ Jane was wearing a hat that was too small for her.
⑤ She asked me questions that was hard to answer.

03 U18_1+2
고난도
Which sentences are grammatically <u>incorrect</u>? 2점

> ⓐ The girl who has enough money is Susie.
> ⓑ The map that shows the way is not clear.
> ⓒ The dog that often barks at me look cute.
> ⓓ The movie that made me fall asleep was boring.
> ⓔ I met the firefighter which saved your life.

① ⓐ, ⓒ, ⓔ ② ⓑ, ⓒ, ⓓ
③ ⓑ, ⓓ ④ ⓒ, ⓔ
⑤ ⓒ, ⓓ, ⓔ

04 U18_2
다음 빈칸에 들어갈 수 <u>없는</u> 것을 <u>모두</u> 고르시오. 2점

> • The girl _____ I met yesterday didn't give me her number.
> • This is the boy _____ I play with in the field.

① who ② whom
③ that ④ which
⑤ whose

05 U19_4+GP
밑줄 친 부분을 생략할 수 <u>없는</u> 것은? 2점

① This is the house <u>which</u> Mike lives in.
② The boy <u>that</u> you met is my cousin.
③ This is the girl with <u>whom</u> we are going to live.
④ I don't know the singer <u>who is</u> on TV now.
⑤ This is the suit <u>which</u> I bought for her.

06 U18_1
함정
다음 문장들에 대해 바르게 설명한 학생을 <u>모두</u> 고르시오. 3점

> ⓐ This is the flower which he gave it to me this morning.
> ⓑ Did you go to the restaurant that I recommended it?

① 지수: ⓐ it이 앞의 flower이므로 지워야 한다.
② 상진: ⓐ which는 to which로 바꾸어야 한다.
③ 진하: ⓐ which를 삭제해야 한다.
④ 영희: ⓑ it이 앞의 the restaurant이므로 지워야 한다.
⑤ 윤희: ⓑ that을 where로 바꾸어야 한다.

07 U19_3+GP
다음 중 밑줄 친 부분의 의미가 <u>다른</u> 하나는? 2점

① <u>What</u> I can do for you now is nothing.
② Thanks for <u>what</u> you did for me.
③ Do you know <u>what</u> happened to John?
④ What you want is <u>what</u> I want.
⑤ Don't take <u>what</u> I put on the table.

08 U19_3
다음을 영작할 때 필요한 것은? 2점

> 사무실의 식물이 죽은 의사에게는 절대 가지 마라.
> never, have p.p.

① whom ② of which
③ whose ④ which
⑤ what

09 다음 빈칸에 that이 들어갈 수 있는 것은? (정답 최대 3개) 3점

U19_2+3

① _____ you dream becomes a reality.

② This is the singer _____ I like the most.

③ Do all the things _____ you love to do.

④ This is the largest temple _____ I've ever seen

⑤ I saw a movie in _____ the villain goes to jail.

10 빈칸에 알맞은 것끼리 짝지어진 것은? 2점

U20_2+3

• I remember the day _____ he first called me.

• We will visit the farm _____ his father lived.

① why – where ② that – when

③ when – how ④ how – that

⑤ when – where

11 다음 두 문장을 조건에 맞게 한 문장으로 완성하시오. 4점

U19_4

She is holding a bag. + It was made in Italy.

· 조건 l   생략 가능한 어휘는 생략할 것
· 조건 2   모두 8단어로 쓸 것

→ _____

12 다음 중 어색한 부분을 골라 바로 쓰시오. 3점

U18_1

ⓐ The tree which she cut was 100 years old.

ⓑ The countries which she has visited since last year is all in Europe.

(_____) _____ → _____

13 우리말과 같은 뜻이 되도록 주어진 조건에 맞게 영작하시오. 6점

U18_1+3

이것은 누구나 할 수 있는 흔한 실수이다.

· 조건 l   어휘 – a common mistake, anyone, make, can
· 조건 2   관계사를 넣을 것

→ This is _____

_____ .

14 다음 문장에서 생략된 관계사를 넣어 문장을 다시 쓰시오. 4점

U19_4

Correct the errors you made on the test.

→ _____

15 Rewrite the sentence correctly. 4점

U18_1

I brought the boy whom you wanted to talk with him.

→ _____

16 주어진 단어를 바르게 배열하시오. (한 단어를 지울 것) 3점

U19_3

taught, what, me, love, meant, He, which

→ _____

17 다음 두 문장을 한 문장으로 만들 때 빈칸에 알맞은 관계대명사를 쓰시오. 3점

> I met an athlete. + His record is unbeatable.

→ I met an athlete _____ record is
   unbeatable.

18 다음 밑줄 친 부분을 두 단어로 바꿔 쓰시오. 3점

> She won the contest, which surprised
> everybody.

→ _____ _____

19 다음 문장에서 생략된 말을 넣어 문장을 다시 쓰시오. 4점

> I don't know the girl wearing the red skirt.

→ _____

20 Look at the picture and translate the
sentence according to the conditions. 6점

꽃으로 가득 찬 그 방을 봐.
·Condition 1   어휘 – full of, flowers
·Condition 2   7단어로 쓸 것

→ _____

[21~22] 다음 글을 읽고 물음에 답하시오.

  Good News was the name of a newspaper that
ⓐ**published** in California. It was very different
from other newspapers ⓑ**that** printed stories about
robberies, crimes, deaths, and disasters. *Good News*
printed only (A)사람들이 듣고 싶어했던 것 such as heroic
acts and good fortune. However, no one wanted
ⓒ**to buy** it, and the newspaper went out of business
soon after ⓓ**it** started. We can conclude from this
ⓔ**that** good news is bad news in the newspaper
today.

21 윗글의 밑줄 친 ⓐ~ⓔ의 설명이 **틀린** 것은? (정답 최대 3개)
★ 고난도   3점

① ⓐ 과거에 발행된 것으로 적절하다.
② ⓑ 주격 관계대명사로 생략할 수 있다.
③ ⓒ 명사적 용법으로 쓰인 to부정사이다.
④ ⓓ 가리키는 것은 *Good News*이다.
⑤ ⓔ which로 바꿔 쓸 수 있다

22 윗글의 밑줄 친 (A)와 같은 뜻이 되도록 주어진 조건에 맞게 영작하시오. 5점
★ 고난도

·어휘   want, hear
·조건 1   필요시 어형 변화할 것
·조건 2   5단어로 쓸 것

→ _____

CHAPTER 09
비교 구문

21 비교 변화, 원급 이용 비교 구문

■ 아래 표의 빈칸에 알맞은 내용을 써 넣으세요. ⟫⟫ 정답 26쪽

개념이해책
108쪽 함께 보기

1 비교 변화

A 규칙 변화

	원급	비교급	최상급
대부분의 형용사, 부사	small	1)	2)
-e로 끝나는 경우	large	3)	4)
'자음+y'로 끝나는 경우	easy	5)	6)
'단모음+단자음'으로 끝나는 경우	big	7)	8)
3음절 이상의 형용사, 부사	interesting	9)	10)
2음절이어도 -ful, -ous, -less, -ish로 끝나는 경우	careful	11)	12)
-ing, -ed로 끝나는 경우(분사 형태의 형용사)	boring	13)	14)

B 불규칙 변화

good/well(좋은/잘) – 15)＿＿ – 16)＿＿
many/much(많은) – 17)＿＿ – 18)＿＿
late(시간이 늦은) – 19)＿＿ – 20)＿＿ (최근의)
far(거리가 먼) – 21)＿＿ – 22)＿＿

bad/ill(나쁜/아픈/나쁘게) – 23)＿＿ – 24)＿＿
little(작은, 적은) – 25)＿＿ – 26)＿＿
late(순서가 늦은) – 27)＿＿ – 28)＿＿ (마지막)
far(정도가 깊은) – 29)＿＿ – 30)＿＿

2 원급을 이용한 비교 구문

A ~ 31)＿＿ +원급+ 32)＿＿ B	A는 B만큼 ~하다
A ~ 33)＿＿ 34)＿＿ [35)＿＿]+원급+36)＿＿ B (= B ~ 비교급 than A)	A는 B만큼 ~하지 않다 (= B가 A보다 더 ~하다)
37)＿＿ +원급+38)＿＿ 39)＿＿ (= as+원급+as+주어+can [could])	가능한 한 ~한/하게

Level 1 Test

⟫⟫ 정답 27쪽

A 표의 빈칸에 비교급과 최상급을 쓰시오.

	원급	비교급	최상급
1	strange		
2	heavy		
3	helpful		
4	well		
5	much		
6	late(시간)		
7	thin		

B 우리말과 같은 뜻이 되도록 주어진 단어를 이용해서 문장을 완성하시오.

1 나의 아들은 그의 아들보다 더 게으르다. (lazy)
→ My son is ＿＿＿ ＿＿＿ his son.

2 나는 형만큼 열심히 공부한다. (hard)
→ I study ＿＿＿ ＿＿＿ ＿＿＿ my brother.

3 가능한 한 많은 문제를 풀어라. (many)
→ Solve ＿＿＿ ＿＿＿ questions ＿＿＿ ＿＿＿.

VOCA hard 어려운, 딱딱한; 열심히 | solve 풀다

01 다음 중 원급-비교급-최상급의 관계가 바르지 <u>않은</u> 것은? 2점

① ill – worse – worst
② strange – stranger – strangest
③ hot – hotter – hottest
④ pretty – prettier – prettiest
⑤ bored – boreder – boredest

02 다음 밑줄 친 단어를 올바르게 고친 것은? 3점

> ⓐ Math is <u>difficult</u> for me than science.
> ⓑ Ms. Choi is <u>a kindest</u> of my teachers.
> ⓒ Unbox it as carefully as <u>can</u>.

① more difficult – kindest – you can
② more difficult – the kindest – possible
③ most difficult – a kindest – could
④ most difficult – the kindest – possible
⑤ most difficult – kindest – you can

03 두 문장이 같은 뜻이 되도록 할 때, 빈칸에 알맞은 말은? 2점

> I am not as lucky as David.
> = David is _____ I am.

① luckier than
② not luckier than
③ not as lucky as
④ more lucky than
⑤ not more lucky than

04 다음 중 어법상 어색한 문장으로 짝지어진 것은? 3점

> ⓐ His house is larger than me.
> ⓑ My dad came home earlier than me.
> ⓒ This meat is fresher than that.
> ⓓ She looked more pretty than before.

① ⓐ
② ⓑ, ⓒ
③ ⓐ, ⓓ
④ ⓑ, ⓓ
⑤ ⓒ, ⓓ

05 두 문장이 같은 뜻이 되도록 할 때 빈칸에 알맞은 말을 쓰시오. 4점

서술형

> She is my age. (old)

→ She is _____ _____ _____ I am.

06 다음 문장에서 <u>어색한</u> 부분을 찾아 바르게 고치시오. 5점

서술형

> Danny can draw pictures well than Luke.

→ _____

07 우리말과 같은 뜻이 되도록 주어진 조건에 맞게 문장을 완성하시오. 6점

서술형

> 아이들은 할 수 있는 한 높이 그네를 타는 것을 좋아한다.
> · 조건 I   어휘 – children, swinging, high, possible
> · 조건 2   단어 수 7단어

→ _____

08 그림을 보고 빈칸에 알맞은 말을 쓰시오. 5점

서술형

Number of Ice Cream Cones Sold	
Monday	🍦🍦
Tuesday	🍦🍦🍦🍦🍦
Wednesday	🍦🍦🍦
Thursday	🍦🍦
Friday	🍦🍦🍦🍦🍦
Saturday	🍦🍦🍦🍦🍦
Sunday	🍦🍦🍦🍦🍦🍦

🍦 = 4 Ice Cream Cones   🍦 = 2 Ice Cream Cones

(1) Ice cream cones sell the _____ on Sunday.

(2) They sell the _____ on Thursday.

VOCA   bored 지루한 | unbox 상자에서 꺼내다 | lucky 운 좋은 | meat 고기(육류) | age 나이 | swinging 그네 타는 것

01 Which words are proper for the blanks? 2점

- Mina spent as _____ money on food as Duna did.
- Your coat is as light as _____.
- She was voted the _____ dresser.

① much – me – bad
② much – mine – worst
③ many – me – worse
④ many – my coat – bad
⑤ more – mine – worse

02 Which of the following is incorrect? 2점

① Psy is more popular than Crayon.
② Dad is thinner than Mom.
③ Coke sells better in summer than in winter.
④ My bag is smaller than yours.
⑤ My daughter studies less harder than my son.

03 Which sentence has the same meaning as the example? 2점

> 보기　Jjangu is not as funny as Geronimo.

① Jjangu is funnier than Geronimo.
② Geronimo is funnier than Jjangu.
③ Geronimo is not as funny as Jjangu.
④ Geronimo is as funny as Jjangu.
⑤ Geronimo is not funnier than Jjangu.

04 Which word CANNOT be used when translating the sentence? 2점

> 학생들은 가능한 한 집에서 많이 공부할 필요가 있습니다.

① as
② possible
③ many
④ can
⑤ much

05 According to the picture, choose ALL of the incorrect sentences. 3점

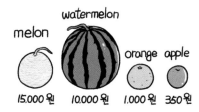

① Watermelons are more expensive than melons.
② Apples are the smallest fruit of the four.
③ Melons are not as expensive as watermelons.
④ Melons are bigger than oranges.
⑤ Oranges are more expensive than apples.

06 Which of the following best fits in the blank? 2점

> Please call us for _____ information.

① further
② farther
③ farthes
④ furthest
⑤ far

07 Which word is NOT suitable for the blank? 2점

> She will live _____ than me.

① closer
② farther
③ nearer
④ later
⑤ longer

08 Who corrects the incorrect sentence? 3점

> ⓐ Amy played the cello as good as a cellist.
> ⓑ Her book is thicker than mine.
> ⓒ Seattle is less crowded than New York.

① 도현: ⓐ good → well
② 승현: ⓑ mine → me
③ 연수: ⓒ crowded → more crowded
④ 미영: ⓐ good → better
⑤ 경원: ⓑ mine → my book

VOCA　coat 코트 | light 가벼운 | popular 인기 있는 | Coke 콜라 | watermelon 수박 | information 정보 | cello 첼로 | cellist 첼리스트

09 Which is grammatically **wrong**? (up to 3 answers) 2점

① The fast elevator in the world travels over 40km per hour.
② Music is much less boring than math.
③ Dynamite is most popular song of BTS's songs.
④ The new one is even worst than the old one.
⑤ Could you fax me the latest version?

Challenge! 주관식 서술형

10 Complete the sentence by using the given word. 3점

운동화가 슬리퍼보다 덜 편하다. (comfortable)

→ The sneakers are _____

_____ _____ the slippers.

11 Write the proper words for the blank so that the two sentences have the same meaning. 4점

The silk dress is smoother than the cotton dress.

→ The cotton dress is _____ _____ _____

as the silk dress.

12 Fill in the blanks to translate the sentence. 4점

가능한 한 많이 웃으려고 노력하십시오.

→ Try to laugh _____ _____

_____ _____.

13 After reading the following dialog, write a sentence according to the conditions. 6점

A: Which is higher, Mount Everest or K2?
B: Mount Everest is higher.

· Condition 1　Compare Mount Everest and K2.
· Condition 2　Use the word "as."
· Condition 3　Write a negative sentence with 8 words.

→ _____

14 Translate the sentence according to the conditions. 5점

내 전화기가 셋 중에서 가장 얇다.

· Condition 1　어휘 – thin, of the three
· Condition 2　빈칸에 6단어로 쓸 것

→ My phone _____.

15 Rewrite the **incorrect** sentence correctly. 4점

Milk and cheese are equally good for your health. Do you like milk? Then try cheese, too. It is just as well as milk.

→ _____

16 Fill in the blanks to complete the translation. 4점

가능한 빨리 그것을 해라. 아니면 가능한 빨리 그것을 그만둬라.

→ Do it _____ _____

_____ _____

_____.

= Drop it _____ _____

_____ _____

_____.

VOCA　sneaker 운동화 | comfortable 편안한 | silk 비단, 실크 | smooth 매끈한, 부드러운 | cotton 면직물, 목화 | Mount Everest 에베레스트 산 | equally 똑같이 | try 먹어보다, 시도해보다 | drop 그만두다, 떨어지다

여러 가지 비교 구문

■ 아래 표의 빈칸에 알맞은 내용을 써 넣으세요. ›› 정답 27쪽

개념이해책
111쪽 함께 보기

① 원급과 비교급을 이용한 최상급 표현

A ~ the+1)_____+단수 명사+2)_____[3)_____]…	A는 …(중)에서 가장 ~하다
A ~ 비교급+than any other+단수 명사+4)_____[5)_____]…	…(중)에서 A는 어떤 다른 것보다 더 ~하다
6)_____(other)+단수 명사 ~비교급+than A of[in]…	…(중)에서 A보다 더 ~한 것은 없다
7)_____(other)+단수 명사 ~8)_____[9)_____]+원급+10)_____ A 11)_____[12)_____]…	…(중)에서 A만큼 ~한 것은 없다

② 배수사를 이용한 비교 표현

A ~ 배수사+13)_____+14)_____+15)_____ B	…배만큼 ~한
A ~ 배수사+16)_____+17)_____ B	…배 더 ~한

③ 기타 비교 구문

18)_____+19)_____+주어+동사 ~, 20)_____+21)_____+주어+동사…	~하면 할수록, 점점 더 …하다
get/become/grow+22)_____+23)_____+24)_____	점점 더 ~한/하게 되다
25)_____[26)_____] ~ 비교급, A 27)_____ B?	A와 B 중 어느 것이[누가] 더 ~한가?
A ~ 28)_____ of the+29)_____+30)_____ 명사	A는 가장 ~한 것들 중의 하나이다
A ~ the+최상급+단수 명사+(that)+주어+have ever+p.p.	A는 주어가 …한 중에서 가장 ~하다

 Level **1** Test

›››› 정답 27쪽

A [ ]에서 알맞은 것을 고르시오.

1 The more we have, [the more / the most] we want.

2 The moon became [bigger and bigger / big and big].

3 Mary is the smartest person [of / in] my family.

4 The soap opera is one of the most popular [program / programs].

5 Kate is the most creative student [in / of] them.

B 두 문장이 같은 뜻이 되도록 빈칸에 알맞은 말을 쓰시오.

1 The dolphin is the smartest animal.

= No other animal is _____ than the dolphin.

= The dolphin is smarter _____ _____ _____ animal.

2 A human brain is three times larger than a gorilla's.

= A human brain is _____ _____ _____ _____ _____ a gorilla's.

VOCA **soap opera** 드라마 | **creative** 창의적인

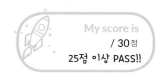
01 빈칸에 들어갈 말로 알맞은 것은? 2점

> Hitchcock's *Psycho* is the most frightening _____.

① of film
② in all film
③ in all films
④ of all film
⑤ of all films

02 다음 중 주어진 문장과 의미가 <u>다른</u> 것을 고르시오. 3점

> The cheetah is the fastest animal on land.

① The cheetah isn't as fast as any other animal on land.
② No other animal on land is faster than the cheetah.
③ The cheetah is faster than all of the other animals on land.
④ The cheetah is faster than any other animal on land.
⑤ No other animal on land is as fast as the cheetah.

03 다음 중 어법상 <u>어색한</u> 문장의 개수는? 3점

> ⓐ Micky is the smartest in us.
> ⓑ My backpack is the cheapest one of the store.
> ⓒ She has one of the oldest coin in history.
> ⓓ The warmer it is, the better I feel.

① 0개
② 1개
③ 2개
④ 3개
⑤ 4개

04 다음 중 밑줄 친 much 대신 쓸 수 <u>없는</u> 것은? 2점

> Deluxe taxis offer <u>much</u> better service than other taxis.

① even
② still
③ far
④ a lot
⑤ great

05 다음 중 <u>어색한</u> 부분을 바르게 고쳐 문장을 다시 쓰시오. 4점
서술형

> Hyde Park is one of the largest park.

→ _____

06 그림을 보고 주어진 단어를 이용해서 문장을 완성하시오. 5점
서술형

> The cactus is _____ me.
> (three times, tall)

07 우리말과 같은 뜻이 되도록 주어진 단어를 이용해서 문장을 완성하시오. 5점
서술형

> 점점 더 어두워지고 있다.
> get, dark

→ It is _____.

08 그림을 보고 빈칸에 알맞은 단어를 쓰시오. 6점
서술형

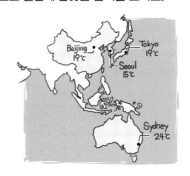

(1) Sydney is hotter _____ _____ _____ _____.

(2) _____ _____ _____ is colder than Seoul.

(3) Tokyo _____ _____ _____ as Beijing.

VOCA the Amazon 아마존 강 | backpack 배낭 | deluxe 고급의 | offer 제공하다 | Hyde Park 하이드 공원 | cactus 선인장

01 Which are the proper words for the blanks? 2점

> • He made the longest speech _____ them.
> • Nora is the most diligent student _____ my class.

① of – of   ② in – in
③ in – of   ④ of – in
⑤ by – in

02 Choose ALL of the grammatically incorrect sentences. 2점

> ⓐ Steve is one of the most creative student in my class.
> ⓑ The earlier you get up, more time you get.
> ⓒ Which is better, this or that?
> ⓓ I got more and more interested in food.

① ⓐ   ② ⓐ, ⓑ
③ ⓐ, ⓑ, ⓓ   ④ ⓑ, ⓒ
⑤ ⓒ, ⓓ

03 Which is NOT correct for any of the blanks? 2점

> ⓐ He is _____ stranger than his brother.
> ⓑ The shark is faster than _____ other animal.
> ⓒ Family is the most important thing _____ my life.
> ⓓ This screen is _____ as big as that screen.

① a lot   ② in
③ any   ④ all
⑤ three times

04 Which word is NOT necessary when translating the following sentence? 2점

> 차가 많아질수록 교통 체증은 더 심해진다.

① the   ② more
③ gets   ④ most
⑤ heavier

05 Which has a different meaning than the others? 2점

① KakaoTalk is the most popular smartphone application.
② KakaoTalk is more popular than any other smartphone application.
③ KakaoTalk isn't as popular as any other smartphone application.
④ No other smartphone application is more popular than KakaoTalk.
⑤ No other smartphone application is as popular as KakaoTalk.

06 According to the graph, which is NOT true? 3점

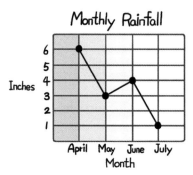

① No other month has more rainfall than July.
② It rains the most in April.
③ It rains the least in July.
④ The rainfall from June to July is getting less and less.
⑤ April has twice as much rainfall as May.

07 Who corrects the incorrect sentence? 3점

> ⓐ He is the funniest boy in my classmates.
> ⓑ The rose is more beautiful than any other flower.

① 미연: ⓐ classmates → classmate
② 광수: ⓑ flower → flowers
③ 경복: ⓑ more → the most
④ 세준: ⓐ the funniest → funniest
⑤ 수호: ⓐ in → of

VOCA   speech 연설 | diligent 부지런한 | creative 창의적인 | be interested in ~에 흥미가 있다 | strange 이상한 | application 응용 프로그램, 앱 | rainfall 강우량 | classmate 반 친구

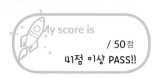
08 Which is grammatically <u>wrong</u>? (up to 3 answers) 2점

① Chicago is not bigger as New York.

② The blue whale is heavier than the elephant.

③ No other animal is as tall as the giraffe.

④ Blue whales are very heavier than elephants.

⑤ The longer snake ever found was over 10 meters long.

Challenge! 주관식 서술형

09 Write the proper words for the blanks to make the sentences have the same meaning. 4점

> The Smithsonian Institution is the world's largest museum complex.

→ _____ museum complex is _____ the Smithsonian Institution.

10 Complete the sentence according to the conditions. 6점

· Condition 1	*Romeo and Juliet* is the most romantic tragedy.와 같은 의미의 문장을 쓸 것
· Condition 2	비교급을 사용할 것
· Condition 3	6단어로 쓸 것

→ *Romeo and Juliet* is _____ _____ _____ .

11 According to the mathematical formula, write the proper words for the blank. 6점

> · Y = 5X
> · Y = 10
> · What is X? → X = 2
>
> Y is the number of yachts. X is the number of boats. There are _____ boats. If there are 10 yachts, how many boats are there? There are two boats.

12 Complete the sentence according to the picture. Use the given words. 5점

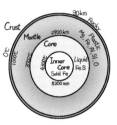

→ _____ _____ we go to the core of the Earth, _____ _____ the temperature becomes. (close, high)

[13~14] Read the following passage and answer the questions.

> ⓐDo you think that the largest pyramid in the world is in Egypt? ⓑActually, that is not right. ⓒ The great pyramids of Egypt are large. ⓓAnd the pyramid of Khufu in Egypt is the world's tallest. ⓔ But the pyramid of Quetzalcoatl in Mexico is larger than any other pyramids. ⓕIn fact, it's the largest monument in the world.

13 Find the sentence that has an error and correct it. 5점

(   ) _____

→ _____ _____

14 According to the passage above, write the proper words for the blanks. 6점

> · _____ _____ monument is larger than the pyramid of _____ _____ _____ .
> · The pyramid of _____ _____ _____ is the tallest of all the _____ in the world.

VOCA   Smithsonian Institution 스미소니언 협회 | complex 복합 건물; 복잡한 | tragedy 비극 | yacht 요트 | core 핵 | temperature 온도 | monument 건축물

U21_1A+U22_GP

01 빈칸에 들어갈 말이 바르게 짝지어진 것은? 2점

> • Mike studies _____ harder than John.
> • He is the _____ honest boy of us.

① much – more　　② much – most
③ very – more　　④ very – most
⑤ more – very

U21_1A

02 비교급을 만들 때 빈칸에 more가 들어갈 수 <u>없는</u> 문장을 2개 고르시오. 2점

① She has _____ money than I do.
② He came here _____ early than I did.
③ My books are _____ important than my bag.
④ I have a _____ difficult question than you do.
⑤ She got _____ healthy than before.

U22_3

03 다음 문장을 바르게 고친 학생은? 2점

> The elephant is one of the biggest animal.

① 서연: animal → animals
② 지호: biggest → bigest
③ 세미: the biggest → biggest
④ 명수: the biggest animal → the bigger animals
⑤ 철수: 틀린 부분이 없다.

U21_1A+2

04 주어진 문장과 같은 의미의 문장을 고르시오. 2점

> A dog isn't as dangerous as a wolf.

① A wolf is more dangerous than a dog.
② A wolf is dangerouser than a dog.
③ A dog is more dangerous than a wolf.
④ A dog is dangerouser than a wolf.
⑤ A wolf isn't as dangerous as a dog.

U21_1A+1B

05 Which sentences are grammatically <u>incorrect</u>? 2점

★고난도

> ⓐ My doll is even cuter than yours.
> ⓑ This book isn't as hard as that one.
> ⓒ Busan is hoter than Seoul.
> ⓓ This is the most difficult question.
> ⓔ She got a more better score than you.

① ⓐ, ⓑ　　② ⓑ, ⓔ
③ ⓒ, ⓓ　　④ ⓒ, ⓔ
⑤ ⓒ, ⓓ, ⓔ

U21_1A+U22_3

06 Which of the following is best for the blank? 2점

> The darker it became, _____ she was.

① more scared　　② the scareder
③ the more scared　　④ the scared
⑤ scareder

U22_2

07 우리말과 같은 뜻이 되도록 빈칸에 알맞은 것을 <u>모두</u> 고르시오. 3점

> 미국 쌀은 한국 쌀 값의 4배이다.
> = American rice costs _____.

① four times much as Korean rice
② as four times much as Korean rice
③ four times as much as Korean rice
④ four times more than Korean rice
⑤ more than four times Korean rice

U21_2

08 빈칸에 들어갈 말로 알맞은 것은? 2점

> He can't dance as _____ as you can.

① good　　② well
③ better　　④ best
⑤ more

132

09 U22_2

다음은 선민이네 반 학생들의 과일 선호도를 나타낸 차트이다. 이 차트를 잘못 분석한 것은? 3점

Favorite Fruit

① The students like apples the most.

② The students like cherries more than grapes.

③ The students like bananas five times as much as apples.

④ The students like grapes more than bananas.

⑤ The students don't like cherries as much as apples.

10 U21_2

Rewrite the sentence correctly. (2 answers) 4점

> Please sit down as low as can.

(1) _____

(2) _____

11 U22_3

우리말과 같은 뜻이 되도록 영작하시오. 4점

> 그녀는 가장 인기 있는 학생 중 하나이다.

→ _____

12 U22_3

Complete the sentence by using the given words. 3점

> _____ _____ we go to the North Pole, _____ _____ it becomes. (close, cold)

[13~15] 다음 표를 보고 물음에 답하시오.

	Star Phone	Apple Phone	Noke Phone
Screen Length	15cm	12cm	13cm
Design	★★★☆☆	★★★★★	★★☆☆☆
Cost	$1,200	$1,500	$900

13 U22_GP

위의 표에 알맞게 주어진 단어를 이용해서 문장을 완성하시오. 3점

> The Star phone has _____ _____ screen of all three _____ . (long, phone)

14 U21_GP

Compare the designs of the Star phone and the Apple phone. 3점

> The Star phone is _____ _____ _____ the Apple phone. (stylish)

15 U22_1

위 표를 보고 주어진 조건에 맞게 영작하시오. 6점

> · 조건 1 Apple phone의 가격에 대해 쓰시오.
> · 조건 2 비교급을 이용하여 최상급의 의미로 쓰시오.
> · 조건 3 어휘 – expensive

→ _____

_____

16 U21_2

주어진 문장과 같은 뜻이 되도록 문장을 완성하시오. 4점

> A whale doesn't live as long as a turtle.

→ A turtle _____ .

17
U21_1

After reading the following dialog, write a correct sentence according to the conditions. 6점

> A: Which is wider, the Amazon or the Nile?
> B: The Amazon is wider.
>
> · Condition 1 Compare the Amazon and the Nile.
> · Condition 2 Use the word "as."
> · Condition 3 Write a negative sentence with 8 words.

→ _____

18
U22_1

다음 문장과 같은 의미가 되도록 빈칸에 알맞은 말을 쓰시오. 4점

> Turkey is the most beautiful country that I have ever visited.

→ Turkey is more beautiful _____ _____

_____ _____ that I have ever visited.

[19~20] 다음 그래프를 보고 물음에 답하시오.

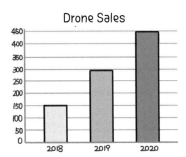

Drone Sales

19
U22_2

주어진 단어를 이용해서 빈칸에 알맞은 말을 쓰시오. 3점

> _____ _____ more drones were sold in 2020 than in 2018. (times)

20
U22_3

주어진 단어를 이용해서 그래프를 설명한 문장을 완성하시오. 4점

> Drone sales are _____ _____
> _____ _____. (grow, big)

[21~22] 다음 글을 읽고, 물음에 답하시오.

Recently in India, people ⓐ**have made** a healthy ice cream. They make this new ice cream from camel's milk, ⓑ**that** is very different from cow's milk. (A)(**three, has, milk, more, cow's, times, It, than, vitamin C**). It is also a rich source of iron and vitamin B. The fat in the ice cream is ⓒ**very** lower than that in average ice cream. Lots of people in India ⓓ**are** enjoying the ice cream. They believe that camel's milk is the ⓔ**most healthy** and that it can help to fight diseases.

21
U08_1+U18_4+U22_GP+U22_1

윗글의 밑줄 친 ⓐ~ⓔ 중 어법상 틀린 것을 찾아 바르게 고친 것은? (정답 최대 3개) 3점

① ⓐ have made → made
② ⓑ that → which
③ ⓒ very → much
④ ⓓ are → is
⑤ ⓔ most healthy → healthiest

22
U22_2

윗글의 (A)에 주어진 단어를 어법과 문맥에 맞게 배열하시오. 3점

→ _____

_____

CHAPTER 10
형용사, 부사, 분사

UNIT 23 형용사와 부사

개념이해책
118쪽 함께 보기

■ 아래 표의 빈칸에 알맞은 내용을 써 넣으세요. >>> 정답 29쪽

CONCEPT 1 형용사

소수 읽기	정수, 소수 → 기수+point+한 자리씩	3.14: 1)_____
분수 읽기	분자 → 기수 분모 → 서수(-s)	1/2: 2)_____ = (a) half 2/3: 3)_____
형용사의 후치 수식	−4)_____, −5)_____, −6)_____ +형용사	I'd like to meet someone tall.
the+형용사: ~한 사람들	the+7)_____ +복수 동사	The seat is for the old. (= old 8)_____)

CONCEPT 2 부사

A 접속부사와 연결사

9)_____	하지만	10)_____	그러므로	11)_____	다시 말해
12)_____	사실은	13)_____	그 결과	14)_____	반면에
15)_____ (= 16)_____)	마침내	17)_____ (= 18)_____)	게다가	19)_____ (= 20)_____)	예를 들면

B 타동사+부사

타동사+21)_____ +22)_____	Put the jacket on. (○)	타동사+23)_____ +24)_____	Put that on. (○)
타동사+25)_____ +26)_____	Put on the jacket. (○)	타동사+27)_____ +28)_____ (×)	Put on it. (×)

Level 1 Test

>>> 정답 29쪽

A 숫자를 바르게 읽으시오.

1 51.458 → _____

2 9,246 → _____

3 5/7 → _____

4 3 7/14 → _____

B [ ]에서 알맞은 것을 고르시오.

1 The rich [is / are] getting richer, and the poor [is / are] getting poorer.

2 I just saw [black something / something black] behind you.

3 I've never [given up it / given it up].

VOCA behind ~의 뒤에 | give up 포기하다 | attend 참석하다 | festival 축제 | protect 보호하다 | traffic 교통량 | make it (약속 등에) 가다

C [보기]에서 알맞은 말을 골라 쓰시오.

보기	Therefore	However
	Besides	For example

1 Mary was sick yesterday. _____, she couldn't attend the festival.

2 We can protect nature in our daily lives. _____, we can ride our bikes or walk to school.

3 Traffic was heavy this morning. _____, I got to work on time.

4 This weekend? I can't make it. I have to clean my room. _____, my parents are going to be away from home.

My score is
/ 30점
25점 이상 **PASS!!**

01 다음 중 주어진 숫자를 <u>잘못</u> 읽은 것은? 2점

① 3/4 – three-fourths

② 1/3 – a quarter

③ 2 1/2 – two and a half

④ 1,033 – one thousand and thirty–three

⑤ 0.542 – zero point five four two

02 다음 우리말을 영어로 바르게 옮긴 것은? 2점

> 가난한 사람들이 더 가난해지고 있나요?

① Do the poor getting poorer?

② Are the poors getting poorer?

③ Does the poor getting poorer?

④ Are the poor getting poorer?

⑤ Are poors getting poorer?

03 다음 두 문장 중 <u>어색한</u> 것을 찾아 바르게 고친 것은? 3점

> ⓐ He asked me to turn the light on.
> ⓑ Customers picked up it from the shelf.

① ⓐ to turn → turn

② ⓐ turn the light on → turn on the light

③ ⓑ picked up it → picked it up

④ ⓑ it from → from it

⑤ ⓑ from the shelf → the shelf from

04 빈칸에 들어갈 말로 알맞은 것은? 2점

> A: I hear that you're a doctor.
> B: Well, _____, I'm a dentist.

① beside   ② in fact

③ however   ④ as a result

⑤ finally

05 다음을 분수로 쓰시오. 4점

서술형

(1) a half ➡ _____

(2) five-elevenths ➡ _____

06 [보기]에서 알맞은 말을 골라 쓰시오. 5점

서술형

보기		
Besides		Therefore
For example		However

Nancy studied very hard.

(1) _____, she got a terrible grade.

(2) _____, she won first place.

07 우리말과 같은 뜻이 되도록 주어진 조건에 맞게 영작하시오. 6점

서술형

> 오늘 결석한 사람은 아무도 없었다.
>
> · 조건 1   There be 구문으로 시작할 것
> · 조건 2   어휘 – absent, nobody

➡ _____

08 밑줄 친 ⓐ~ⓓ 중 <u>어색한</u> 것 2개를 찾아 고치시오. 6점

서술형

 Excuse me. Will you ⓐ <u>pick up the pen</u>?

 Why do I ⓑ <u>have to</u>? Can't you ⓒ <u>pick up it</u> yourself?

 My hands are full, and I think the pen is yours.

 Oh, I'm sorry. I'll ⓓ <u>pick them up</u>.

( ) _____ → _____

( ) _____ → _____

VOCA customer 고객 | shelf 선반 | dentist 치과 의사 | absent 결석한 | pick up 줍다

01 Which of the following is correct? 2점

① My father's office is on the 3층. (→ three floor)
② Today is my 12번째 birthday. (→ twelve)
③ The cat drank about 3/5 of my milk. (→ three-fifths)
④ She was born in 1994. (→ nineteen ninetyfourth)
⑤ It is 5.46cm long. (→ five point forty-six)

02 Who reads the underlined fraction correctly? 2점

My father still loves the song "1 1/2" by TwoTwo.

① 현수: one and a half
② 수빈: one point a half
③ 빈이: one and one two
④ 이지: one point a second
⑤ 지후: one and first two

03 Which is NOT necessary when translating the sentence? 2점

뭔가 매우 부드러운 것이 내 왼쪽 다리에 닿았어.

① touched   ② very
③ something   ④ softly
⑤ left

04 Which translation is correct? 2점

She spent her life _____ . (약자들을 도우면서)

① to help weak people
② to help the weak
③ helping weak peoples
④ helping the weaks
⑤ helping the weak

05 When translating the sentence in the present perfect tense, which word comes fourth? 2점

이 근처에서 누구 유명한 사람 봤니?

① anybody   ② near
③ here   ④ seen
⑤ famous

06 Which is NOT suitable for the blank?
(2 answers) 2점

Some visitors _____ into the pond and just walked away.

① put empty cans
② tossed out those
③ threw away them
④ dumped candy wrappers
⑤ threw some plastic bottles

07 Which is suitable for the blank? 2점

Mika auditioned for a Korean girl group ten times in the last three years. _____ , she got selected.

① However   ② In fact
③ At last   ④ For instance
⑤ On the other hand

08 Who finds ALL of the errors? 3점

The deafs uses sign language to communicate with each others.

① 승은: uses
② 성은: to, with
③ 경선: deafs, uses
④ 민지: deafs, others
⑤ 세현: deafs, uses, others

VOCA floor 층 | soft 부드러운 | weak 약한 | toss out 툭 던지다 | throw away[out] 던져버리다 | dump 버리다 | candy wrapper 사탕 포장지 | audition 오디션; 오디션을 보다 | select 선택하다 | deaf 귀가 들리지 않는 | sign language 수화 | communicate 의사소통하다

09 How many sentences are correct? 3점

> ⓐ The coach called off it.
> ⓑ They experienced something unusual.
> ⓒ Seven-ninths are bigger than a half.
> ⓓ They told us something strange.
> ⓔ I have your phone. Are you looking for it?

① one   ② two
③ three   ④ four
⑤ five

10 How many sentences are grammatically correct? 3점

> ⓐ I feel like drinking hot something.
> ⓑ It was a really interesting movie.
> ⓒ 3 3/4 is read three and three fourths.
> ⓓ They had to put off their wedding.

① 0개   ② 1개
③ 2개   ④ 3개
⑤ 4개

Challenge! 주관식 서술형

11 Fill in the blanks with the proper words. 3점

> If you change 16/100 into a decimal, it is zero
> _____ _____
> _____.
>
> *decimal: 10진법

12 Find the error and correct it. 3점

> 집 없는 사람들은 도움과 지지가 필요하다.
> = The homeless needs help and support.

→ _____ → _____

13 Choose the necessary words and rearrange them to make a complete sentence. 4점

> useless, buying, should, you, buy, uselessly, not, anything, something

→ _____

14 Look at the picture and complete the sentence. 5점

→ Somebody ate o_____-
f_____ of my cake, so
t_____-q_____ are left.

[15~16] Translate the sentence according to the conditions. 각 6점

15

> 아픈 사람들은 간호사들에 의해 돌보아졌다.
>
> · Condition 1   관사로 시작할 것
> · Condition 2   수동태로 쓸 것
> · Condition 3   어휘 – sick, take care of, the nurses
> · Condition 4   주어진 어휘를 포함하여 9단어로 완성할 것

→ _____

16

> 노인들은 규칙적으로 운동을 해야 한다.
>
> · Condition 1   어휘 – elderly, regularly, has, exercise
> · Condition 2   The를 반드시 쓸 것
> · Condition 3   주어진 한 단어를 변형할 것
> · Condition 4   총 6단어로 완성할 것

→ _____

VOCA   call off 취소하다 | experience 경험하다 | unusual 드문 | homeless 집이 없는 | useless 쓸모 없는 | take care of ~을 돌보다 | elderly 나이 든 | regularly 규칙적으로

24 분사

■ 아래 표의 빈칸에 알맞은 내용을 써 넣으세요. ››› 정답 30쪽

개념이해책
121쪽 함께 보기

1 분사의 의미와 종류

현재분사	동사원형 +1)____	능동: 2)____	I saw a barking dog outside.
		진행: 3)____	We are having fun, aren't we?
과거분사	• 규칙: 동사원형 +4)____ • 불규칙: 동사의 과거분사형	완료: 5)____	The lady has just repaired the chair.
		수동: 6)____ , 7)____	They were raised in the countryside.

2 분사의 수식

| 단독 수식 | 8)____ +9)____ | The dancing cowboy is my father.
The broken smartphone is mine. |
| 어구 수식 | 10)____ +11)____ | The dog wagging its tail is friendly.
The song sung by EM Duo was fantastic. |

3 동명사와 현재분사의 비교

| 현재분사(12)____) | 13)____ 역할
(14)____ , 15)____) | The boy is playing baseball alone.
Did you see the swimming seal over there? |
| 동명사(16)____) | 17)____ 역할
(18)____ , 19)____) | I bought a new pair of running shoes.
His only hobby is collecting old coins. |

4 감정을 나타내는 분사

| -ing(~하는) | 주로 20)____ , 21)____ | -ed(~되는, 지는) | 주로 22)____ |

Level 1 Test

››› 정답 30쪽

A [ ]에서 알맞은 것을 고르시오.

1 Look at the [sleeping / slept] bears.

2 Who is the girl [stood / standing] at the gate?

3 The money [finding / found] on the floor is not yours.

4 The pictures hanging on the wall [are / is] from Santa Monica.

VOCA gate 문 | floor 바닥 | hang 걸려 있다 | jar 독, 단지 | armchair 안락의자

B 우리말과 같은 뜻이 되도록 문장을 완성하시오.

1 그녀는 물을 독에 채운 후에 피곤함을 느꼈다.
→ She felt ____ after ____ a jar with water.

2 그는 잡지를 읽으며 안락의자에 앉아 있었다.
→ He ____ ____ in an armchair ____ a magazine.

3 경찰에 의해 붙잡힌 그 남자는 내 돈을 훔치지 않았다.
→ The man ____ by the police ____ ____ my money.

Level 2 Test

>>> 정답 30쪽

My score is
/ 30점
25점 이상 PASS!!

---

01 빈칸에 들어갈 말로 알맞은 것은? 2점

> The girl _____ the hamburger is my sister.

① eat　　　　　② ate
③ eaten　　　　④ eating
⑤ eats

02 다음 중 어색한 것을 찾아 바르게 고친 학생은? 2점

> The German visitors bought hundreds of computers making in Korea.

① 수빈: German → Germany
② 하윤: bought → buying
③ 아연: hundreds → hundred
④ 아영: computers → computer
⑤ 상은: making → made

03 다음 중 밑줄 친 부분이 어색한 것을 모두 고르면? 3점

① I was surprising by the noise.
② The baseball game was so excited.
③ The road signs are pretty confusing.
④ Dogs often feel frightened by fireworks.
⑤ Sato was shocked to hear the news.

04 다음 중 어법상 옳은 문장의 개수는? 3점

> ⓐ He can't read books writing in Greek.
> ⓑ The lady standing there is smiling at us.
> ⓒ My father had a very depressing day.
> ⓓ He was looking for a sleep bag.
> ⓔ The monkeys swinging from the branches was funny.

① 1개　　　　　② 2개
③ 3개　　　　　④ 4개
⑤ 5개

05 우리말과 같은 뜻이 되도록 주어진 단어를 바르게 쓰시오. 5점 _{서술형}

> 나나(Nana)라는 이름의 여자가 어제 그를 방문했다.
> name, call

→ A woman _____ Nana
_____ on him yesterday.

06 주어진 문장과 의미가 통하도록 알맞은 말을 쓰시오. 5점 _{서술형}

> The results satisfied the director.

(1) The results were _____ .
(2) The director _____ _____
_____ the results.

07 다음 두 문장 중 어색한 것을 찾아 바르게 고치시오. 4점 _{서술형}

> ⓐ I have baking French toast for breakfast.
> ⓑ This is a poem written by a famous poet.

(　　) _____ → _____

08 그림을 보고 우리말과 같은 뜻이 되도록 주어진 단어를 이용해서 영작하시오. 6점 _{서술형}

> 짖는 개들은 좀처럼 물지 않는다.
> bark, seldom, bite

→ _____

VOCA　road sign 이정표 | firework 불꽃놀이 | depress 우울하게 하다 | swing 흔들다 | call on ~을 방문하다 | director 감독 | bark 짖다 | bite 물다

UNIT **24**　141

01 Which set has the correct words for the blanks? 2점

> A: I saw a very _____ old movie on TV last weekend. It was *Spartacus*. Did you see it?
>
> B: Yes, but it wasn't that good. It was a little _____.
>
> A: Do you think so? I'm _____ you didn't like it.

① touching – disappointed – surprised

② touched – disappointed – surprising

③ touched – disappointing – surprising

④ touching – disappointed – surprising

⑤ touching – disappointing – surprised

02 Which TWO words are NOT necessary when translating the sentence? 2점

> 아빠에 의해 구워진 쿠키들이 맛있는 냄새가 난다.

① the   ② baking

③ by   ④ smells

⑤ tasty

03 Which correction is right? 2점

> Here are some pictures painting by my father when he was a little boy.

① are → is   ② some → any

③ painting → painted   ④ by → with

⑤ little → few

04 Who understands the sentence correctly? 2점

> People lived in cities is very busy these days.

① 주원: lived는 people을 꾸며주는 말로 맞아.

② 하린: cities는 주어가 복수라서 -es가 붙은 거야.

③ 상근: 주어가 people이니까 is는 are로 써야 해.

④ 상은: very는 바로 앞의 is를 꾸며주는 형용사야.

⑤ 준선: these days에서 these를 this로 써야 해.

05 Which underlined part is used **differently**? 2점

① She was taking care of the <u>crying</u> baby.

② His only hobby is <u>going</u> fishing alone.

③ Do you know the girl <u>staring</u> into the air?

④ There was nobody <u>working</u> in the field.

⑤ Who are the people <u>waiting</u> outside?

06 Which is correct for each blank? 2점

> • The popera singer amazed us.
> → The popera singer was _____.
> • The last question confused the boys.
> → The boys were _____ by the last question.

① amazing – confusing

② amazed – confusing

③ amaze – confused

④ amazed – confused

⑤ amazing – confused

07 Whose correction is correct? 2점

> Minho is a very bored man because he always talks about himself.

① 민선: very → really

② 준형: bored → boring

③ 희수: because → so

④ 지희: always → never

⑤ 관우: himself → him

08 Which is grammatically **incorrect**? 2점

① The man sitting next to Jaeyoung is Sungjin.

② The children playing in the garden are cute.

③ The ideas presented in the book sound good.

④ Do you know the woman singing on TV now?

⑤ Mrs. Lee lives in a house making of wood.

VOCA a little 조금 | smell ~한 냄새가 나다 | popera 팝페라(pop+opera) | amaze 놀라게 하다 | confuse 혼동시키다 | present 제시하다

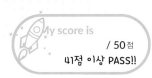

09 How many sentences are <u>incorrect</u>? 2점

> ⓐ Hockey is a very fascinating sport, isn't it?
> ⓑ Look at the little girl danced in the room.
> ⓒ The meals at the restaurant is satisfying.
> ⓓ I read comic books written in Japanese.

① none   ② one
③ two   ④ three
⑤ four

10 Who finds ALL of the errors? 3점

> ⓐ The answer chosen by the girls are number 4.
> ⓑ What is the language speaking in Guyana?
> ⓒ The girls wearing aprons roasted the *galbi*.

① 준아: ⓐ chosen, ⓑ speaking
② 승미: ⓐ chosen, ⓒ wearing
③ 철웅: ⓐ are, ⓑ speaking
④ 치환: ⓐ are, ⓑ roasted
⑤ 정민: ⓑ speaking, ⓒ roasted

Challenge! 주관식 서술형

11 Fill in each blank by using the given words. 4점

> The man _____ in the middle of the row _____ _____ on the phone. It was so _____.
> (sit, keep, talk, annoy)

12 Find the sentence that has an error and correct it. 3점

> ⓐ We were the only guests stayed at the hotel.
> ⓑ The girl walking toward me was Lucy.

(   ) _____ ➡ _____

13 Translate the sentence according to the conditions. 6점

> 헤밍웨이(Hemingway)가 쓴 여섯 단어짜리 이야기를 읽어본 적 있니?
> · Condition 1   현재완료로 쓸 것
> · Condition 2   단수 및 복수에 유의할 것
> · Condition 3   아라비아 숫자를 쓰지 말 것
> · Condition 4   어휘 – ever, story, write

➡ _____

14 Find ALL of the errors and correct them. 5점

> Harry went to the dinosaur museum. The exhibits looked so real that they were frightened. However, the guide dressing like a dinosaur explained everything kindly and clearly. Now, Harry wants to bring his friends there the next time.

➡ _____
_____

15 Translate the sentence by using the given words. 6점

> · Condition 1   Answer with 8 words.
> · Condition 2   Add words if necessary.
> · Condition 3   Do not change the given words.
> 나는 내게 온 이메일을 열어보지 않았다.
> the, me, to, sent, email

➡ I haven't opened _____.

16 Find the one who marks the sentence <u>incorrectly</u> and correct it. 5점

> 루나: ⓐ(○) The man talked with Cathy looks bored.
> 수아: ⓑ(×) Cathy felt tiring after talking with the man.

(1) 잘못 채점한 사람: _____

(2) 틀린 곳: _____

(3) 고친 것: _____

VOCA   fascinating 매혹적인 | meal 식사 | row 줄, 열 | dinosaur 공룡 | exhibit 전시품 | explain 설명하다 | clearly 명확히

My score is
/ 70점
60점 이상 PASS!!

U23_1A

01 다음 숫자를 잘못 읽은 것을 바르게 고친 것은? 2점

> 3,025.104 is read three thousand twenty-five point ten zero four.

① three → third
② thousand → thousands
③ twenty-five → two five
④ ten → one
⑤ four → fourth

U23_1B

02 다음 중 분수를 바르게 읽은 학생은? 2점

① 백김치: 1/2 → one two
② 박시개: 3/5 → three and five
③ 마진가: 1 2/3 → one and two-third
④ 방국봉: 2 7/9 → two and seven-ninths
⑤ 최고야: 3 9/13 → three and nine-thirteens

U23_2A

03 빈칸에 들어갈 말로 알맞은 것은? 2점

> I enjoy listening to heavy metal. _____, my parents don't like it. They only like trot music.

① Finally   ② However
③ In other words   ④ For example
⑤ In fact

U23_1D

04 Which pair is correct for the blanks?

(2 answers) 2점

> Is it true that _____ must now learn from _____?

① elderly – young
② elderly – young people
③ the elderly – the young
④ the elderly – the youngs
⑤ elderly people – young people

U23_1C

05 Which is grammatically incorrect? 2점

① Something exciting happened to you, right?
② He found something wrong with the plan.
③ I have nothing interesting to do today.
④ Can you think of new something?
⑤ I used to like to eat anything cold.

U24_3+GP

06 다음 중 밑줄 친 부분의 쓰임이 다른 하나는? 2점

한눈에 쏙

① We saw a <u>dancing</u> bear at the zoo.
② A <u>sleeping</u> baby is like an angel.
③ He enjoys <u>opening</u> bottles with a spoon.
④ The girl <u>doing</u> an interview is Mary Kelly.
⑤ The man <u>lying</u> on the bench is my father.

U24_GP+U13_GP

07 어색한 부분을 찾아 바르게 고친 것은? 2점

> The women having dinner next to us is Chris's English teacher and her daughter.

① women → woman   ② having → had
③ us → ours   ④ is → are
⑤ Chris's → Chris'

U24_4

08 빈칸에 들어갈 말이 바르게 짝지어진 것은? 2점

> We were _____ by the _____ news.

① frustrating – disappointed
② frustrating – disappointing
③ frustrated – disappointed
④ frustrated – disappointing
⑤ frustrate – disappoint

144

09 밑줄 친 부분의 쓰임이 같은 것끼리 분류한 것은? 3점

U24_3+GP

ⓐ The cat sitting on the sofa is a Persian.
ⓑ Your sister was dancing on the street.
ⓒ Are you good at playing baseball?
ⓓ The game was so exciting that I couldn't stop watching it.

① ⓐ, ⓒ – ⓑ, ⓓ
② ⓐ, ⓓ – ⓑ, ⓒ
③ ⓑ – ⓐ, ⓒ, ⓓ
④ ⓐ, ⓑ – ⓒ, ⓓ
⑤ ⓐ – ⓑ, ⓒ, ⓓ

10 How many sentences are incorrect? 2점

U24_4
고난도

ⓐ Mom looked pleased, didn't she?
ⓑ I was disappointed to hear the comment.
ⓒ He often does something shocked.
ⓓ Is it surprised that I passed the math test?
ⓔ Everyone was shocked by the landslide.

① zero
② one
③ two
④ three
⑤ four

11 Write the following as fractions. 3점

U23_1B

(1) three-quarters ➡ _____

(2) two over seven ➡ _____

(3) three and seven-ninetieths ➡ _____

12 다음 대화에서 어법상 어색한 것을 찾아 고치시오. 3점

U23_1C
함정

 Do you have special anything to do tonight?

 No, I have nothing special to do.

_____ ➡ _____

13 Find the error and correct it. 4점

U23_1D

The homeless is taken good care of by the volunteers at the shelter.

_____ ➡ _____

14 다음 주어진 단어를 배열하시오. 5점

U23_2B

them, you, like, to, out, would, try

➡ _____

15 주어진 우리말 표현을 각각 한 단어의 영어로 쓰시오. 4점

U23_2A+U24_1

Vincent van Gogh painted almost 900 paintings. He sold, (A) 그렇지만, only one painting during his lifetime. *The Red Vineyard* is the only piece (B) 팔린 by the artist while he was alive.

(A) _____

(B) _____

16 문장의 의미가 같도록 할 때 빈칸에 알맞은 말을 쓰시오. 4점

U24_4

The findings pleased scientists.

*finding: 연구 결과

(1) The findings _____ _____ to scientists.

(2) Scientists _____ _____ by the findings.

17 우리말과 같은 뜻이 되도록 주어진 단어를 이용해서 조건에 맞게 영작하시오. 6점

U24_4

> 아뇨, 저 당황 안 했는데요.
>
> embarrass
>
> · 조건 1   현재 시제로 쓸 것
> · 조건 2   -ed, -ing형에 유의할 것
> · 조건 3   5단어로 쓸 것

→ _____

U24_1

18 어법상 어색한 문장의 첫 글자를 배합하여 주어진 단어를 완성하시오. 5점

함정

> ⓐ All the girls inviting to my party came.
> ⓑ There was no food leaving for the hungry.
> ⓒ A dog showing its teeth is angry.
> ⓓ The Jeonju team called With Us won.
> ⓔ English is a language speaking in many countries.
> ⓕ I have a watch made in Switzerland.

→ B ☐ ☐ U ☐ Y

U24_1+GP

19 Fill in each blank with the proper words. 4점

> 이 사진 속에서 피아노를 치는 소년이 지금은 유명한 피아니스트란다.

→ The boy _____ the piano in this

picture _____ now a famous pianist.

U24_4

20 다음 문장들 중 어색한 것을 모두 찾아 고치시오. 4점

> ⓐ I am interesting in this interesting story.
> ⓑ The match was exciting, so we were excited.
> ⓒ My partner was boring, so I felt bored.
> ⓓ I was annoyed because her voice was annoyed.

(   ) _____ → _____

(   ) _____ → _____

[21~22] 다음 글을 읽고 물음에 답하시오.

   A smile is usually a sign of friendliness and interest. However, some people smile just to be polite. ⓐ**To get** another clue from people's faces, watch their eyes. Friendliness and interest ⓑ**are expressed** when a person's eyes meet yours ⓒ**direct**. If your listener looks away for a moment and then back again, the person is probably ⓓ**paid** attention to you. If this person continues to look away, he or she might not be ____(A)____ or shy. Remember that when someone keeps ⓔ**pointing** at you, it probably means the person feels superior to you or angry with you.

U24_1

21 윗글의 밑줄 친 ⓐ~ⓔ 중 어법상 어색한 것은?

고난도

(정답 최대 3개) 3점

① ⓐ

② ⓑ

③ ⓒ

④ ⓓ

⑤ ⓔ

U24_4

22 윗글의 빈칸 (A)에 들어갈 적절한 말을 다음 영영뜻풀이를 참조하여 쓰시오. 4점

> _____: adjective. wanting to give one's attention to something and to discover more about it

CHAPTER 11
접속사

25 명사절, 때의 부사절, 상관 접속사

■ 아래 표의 빈칸에 알맞은 내용을 써 넣으세요. >>> 정답 32쪽

개념이해책
128쪽 함께 보기

① 명사절을 이끄는 접속사

that	1)_____	I think (that) he is a great hero.
if	2)_____	I don't know if it is wrong.
whether	3)_____	I wonder whether he is married (or not).

② 때의 부사절을 이끄는 접속사

| 4)_____ | ~할 때 | 5)_____ | ~하기 전에 | 6)_____ | ~하는 동안 | 7)_____ | ~하자마자 |
| 8)_____ | ~할 때, ~하면서 | 9)_____ | ~한 후에 | 10)_____ | ~할 때까지 | 11)_____ | ~한 이래로 |

③ 명사절을 이끄는 접속사

12)____ A 13)____ B	A와 B 둘 다	Both my sister and I wear glasses.
14)____ A 15)____ B	A와 B 둘 중의 하나	Either she or I have to go there.
16)____ A 17)____ B	A도 B도 아닌	Jane likes neither math nor English.
18)____ 19)____ A 20)____ (21)____) B	A뿐만 아니라 B도	Not only you but also he was wrong.
22)____ A 23)____ B	A가 아니라 B	It is not red but yellow.

Level 1 Test

>>> 정답 32쪽

A 빈칸에 알맞은 말을 [보기]에서 골라 쓰시오.

> 보기 that   whether   before   since
>
> but   and   or   nor

1 Wash your hands _____ you eat.

2 We hope _____ you enjoy the ride.

3 I have known her _____ she was a child.

4 I'm not sure _____ she likes this picture.

5 Answer either yes _____ no.

6 Neither you _____ she is wrong.

7 Both Tom _____ Bill are soccer players.

8 She is not only honest _____ also diligent.

B 우리말과 같은 뜻이 되도록 문장을 완성하시오.

1 그녀에게 그것이 사실인지 아닌지 물어볼게.

→ I'll ask her _____ _____

_____ _____ _____ .

2 운전하는 동안 휴대 전화를 사용하지 마.

→ Don't use your cell phone _____

_____ _____ _____ .

3 그는 키가 크지도 작지도 않다.

→ He is _____ tall _____ small.

4 내가 들어왔을 때 그녀는 TV를 보고 있었다.

→ She was watching TV _____

_____ _____ _____ .

VOCA honest 정직한 | diligent 부지런한 | cell phone 휴대 전화

148

My score is
/ 30점
25점 이상 PASS!!

01 빈칸에 들어갈 말로 알맞은 것은? 2점

> My cat was sleeping on my lap _____ I
> was reading a book.

① until   ② since

③ that   ④ while

⑤ if

02 다음 빈칸 중 어느 것에도 들어갈 수 없는 것은? 2점

> • Neither she _____ he is happy.
> • I will buy either apples _____ oranges.
> • She began to cry as soon _____ she saw me.
> • He is not only an artist _____ also a scientist.

① or   ② as

③ and   ④ but

⑤ nor

03 밑줄 친 부분의 쓰임이 다른 하나는? 3점

① Bake the cake <u>until the top is brown</u>.
② They got up <u>before the sun came up</u>.
③ It has been a long time <u>since I met her</u>.
④ I'm not sure <u>if she can forgive him</u>.
⑤ Turn off the lights <u>when you leave the room</u>.

04 밑줄 친 부분이 어법상 어색한 것은? 3점

① Either you or he <u>has</u> to stay at home.
② Both Brian and Jane <u>are</u> from Australia.
③ Neither she nor I <u>am</u> going to the movies.
④ Not only his sister but also he <u>play</u> the piano.
⑤ When I <u>go</u> to London, I will visit the Tower Bridge.

05 우리말과 같은 뜻이 되도록 주어진 단어들을 이용해서 영작하시오. 5점
서술형

> 나는 그녀가 올지 안 올지 궁금하다.
> wonder, whether, or not

→ _____

06 우리말과 같은 뜻이 되도록 주어진 조건에 맞게 영작하시오. 6점
서술형

> 미나(Mina)와 나 둘 중 하나가 우승자가 될 것이다.
> ·조건1   either를 활용할 것
> ·조건2   be going to를 쓸 것
> ·조건3   10단어로 쓸 것

→ _____

07 우리말과 같은 뜻이 되도록 문장을 완성하시오. 4점
서술형

> 그녀는 테니스뿐만 아니라 야구도 한다.

→ She plays _____ _____
     tennis _____ _____
     baseball.

08 다음 두 문장이 같은 뜻이 되도록 빈칸을 채우시오. 5점
서술형

> Jessica is smart. Billy is smart, too.

→ _____ Jessica _____ Billy
     _____ smart.

[01~02] **Choose the proper word for the blank.** 각 2점

01

I was cleaning the house _____ he visited me.

① while
② that
③ if
④ when
⑤ whether

02

He is not only young _____ rich.

① and
② or
③ nor
④ either
⑤ but also

03 **Choose the proper words for the blanks.** 2점

• We need to go home _____ it gets dark.
• Can I have dessert _____ I finish my dinner?

① before – after
② before – until
③ until – after
④ after – since
⑤ since – before

04 **Choose the proper words from the brackets.** 3점

• I wonder [if / that] you can help me.
• I like [either / neither] cats nor dogs.
• You can have [either / neither] coffee or tea.

① if – either – neither
② if – neither – either
③ if – neither – neither
④ that – neither – either
⑤ that – either – neither

05 **Which translation is correct?** 2점

그곳에 도착하자마자 너에게 전화할게.

① I call you as soon as I got there.
② I call you as soon as I'll get there.
③ I'll call you as soon as I get there.
④ I'll call you as soon as I'll get there.
⑤ I called you as soon as I've gotten there.

06 **Which is grammatically incorrect?** 2점

① It ② has been ③ three years ④ as I ⑤ left my hometown.

07 **Choose the sentences in which "that" has the same usage.** 3점

ⓐ Look at that girl smiling at me.
ⓑ Don't you think that it's too expensive?
ⓒ I know some girls that are soccer players.
ⓓ She said that book was quite interesting.
ⓔ I'm sure that she's coming to the party.

① ⓐ, ⓑ
② ⓑ, ⓒ
③ ⓑ, ⓔ
④ ⓑ, ⓒ, ⓓ
⑤ ⓑ, ⓓ, ⓔ

08 **Which of the answer choices best fits in the blank?** 2점

We will go on a picnic _____.

① while it is raining
② as soon as it rains
③ until it stops raining
④ if it stops raining
⑤ before it stopped raining

VOCA visit 방문하다 | handsome 잘생긴 | get dark 어두워지다 | dessert 디저트, 후식 | get there 거기에 도착하다 | hometown 고향 | expensive 비싼 | quite 꽤, 매우 | interesting 흥미로운 | go on a picnic 소풍 가다

09 Choose ALL of the correct translations. 2점

> 그녀가 이 케이크를 좋아하는지 잘 모르겠어.

① I'm not sure as she likes this cake.
② I'm not sure if she likes this cake.
③ I'm not sure when she likes this cake.
④ I'm not sure since she likes this cake.
⑤ I'm not sure whether she likes this cake or not.

10 How many sentences are <u>incorrect</u>? 3점

> ⓐ Both you and he have to go there.
> ⓑ I think either he or she is hiding something.
> ⓒ Neither Jane nor her brother are tall.
> ⓓ Not only you but also I are exhausted.

① zero   ② one
③ two   ④ three
⑤ four

Challenge! 주관식 서술형

11 Fill in the blanks to make the two sentences have the same meaning. 4점

> She is not only beautiful but also kind.

→ She is kind _____ _____ _____ beautiful.

12 Complete the sentence by using the given words. 4점

(1) I'll wait until he _____ work. (finish)
(2) Neither Susan nor I _____ to attend the meeting. (plan)

13 Find the error and correct it. 4점

> I'll ask her that she will accept his proposal.

_____ → _____

14 Translate the sentence by using the given word. 5점

> Thomas와 James 둘 다 Alice를 사랑한다. (both)

→ _____

15 Rearrange the given words in the correct order. 4점

> not only, are, she, but also, you, intelligent

→ _____

16 Look at the picture and complete the sentence by using the given words. 6점

→ _____,
you should wear your helmet.
(when, ride a bike)

VOCA   tell a lie 거짓말하다 | exhausted 지친 | attend 참석하다 | accept 받아들이다, 수락하다 | proposal 청혼, 제안 | intelligent 똑똑한, 지적인 | helmet 헬멧

26 조건, 양보, 이유, 결과의 부사절

개념이해책
131쪽 함께 보기

■ 아래 표의 빈칸에 알맞은 내용을 써 넣으세요. ››› 정답 33쪽

CONCEPT 1 조건의 부사절을 이끄는 접속사

1)＿＿＿＿	만약 ～한다면	2)＿＿＿＿ you take the subway, you will get there on time.
3)＿＿＿＿ (= if ～ not)	만약 ～하지 않는다면	I will not go 4)＿＿＿＿ you go with me.

CONCEPT 2 양보의 부사절을 이끄는 접속사

5)＿＿＿ , 6)＿＿＿ ,	～하지만, ～일지라도	9)＿＿＿ [10)＿＿＿ , 11)＿＿＿ 12)＿＿＿]
7)＿＿＿ 8)＿＿＿		they are poor, they seem happy together.

CONCEPT 3 이유의 부사절을 이끄는 접속사

13)＿＿＿		I had no time to text you 14)＿＿＿ I was busy.
15)＿＿＿	～하기 때문에, ～해서	16)＿＿＿ it's raining, we'll have to stay inside.
17)＿＿＿		18)＿＿＿ she was tired, she didn't feel like going out.

CONCEPT 4 결과의 부사절을 이끄는 접속사

19)＿＿＿ ～ 20)＿＿＿ ...	너무 ～해서 …하다	The monkeys looked 21)＿＿＿ funny 22)＿＿＿ everybody laughed.

Level 1 Test

››› 정답 33쪽

A [ ]에서 알맞은 것을 고르시오.

1 [If / Unless] you study harder, you will fail.

2 [As / Though] I was busy, I couldn't help him.

3 The movie was [as / so] sad that she cried.

4 [Although / Because] it was raining, he went jogging.

B 두 문장이 같은 뜻이 되도록 빈칸에 알맞은 말을 쓰시오.

1 I put on my coat because it was cold.

= It was cold, ＿＿＿＿ I put on my coat.

2 As the air is dirty, many people become sick.

= Many people become sick ＿＿＿＿

＿＿＿＿ the dirty air.

C 우리말과 같은 뜻이 되도록 빈칸에 알맞은 말을 쓰시오.

1 TV 안 보면 꺼.

→ ＿＿＿＿ you are watching TV, turn it off.

2 네가 노력하지 않으면 어떤 것도 알 수 없다.

→ You won't know anything ＿＿＿＿ you try.

3 그의 말이 너무 빨라서 나는 그의 말을 이해할 수 없다.

→ He speaks ＿＿＿＿ fast ＿＿＿＿ I can't understand him.

VOCA jog 조깅하다 | put on ～을 입다 | try 노력하다

Level 2 Test

>>> 정답 33쪽

[01~02] 빈칸에 들어갈 말로 알맞은 것을 고르시오. 각 2점

01
_____ she felt tired, she kept on cleaning.

① If ② So
③ Unless ④ Though
⑤ Because

02
_____ you help me, I can't do the work.

① If ② When
③ Since ④ Unless
⑤ Because

[03~04] 빈칸에 공통으로 들어갈 말로 알맞은 것을 고르시오.
각 3점

03
· I studied hard, _____ I got a good score.
· Samson was _____ arrogant that he believed he was invincible.

*invincible: 무적의

① as ② so
③ that ④ though
⑤ because

04
· I'll do the dishes _____ you cook dinner.
· I don't know _____ it will be fine tomorrow.

① whether ② when
③ if ④ that
⑤ because

05 그림을 보고 두 문장이 같은 뜻이 되도록 빈칸에 알맞은 말을 쓰시오. 4점

서술형

Today is her birthday, so I sent her some flowers.

→ I sent her some flowers _____
today is her birthday.

06 우리말과 같은 뜻이 되도록 주어진 단어를 배열해서 문장을 완성하시오. 5점

서술형

날씨가 너무 추워서 나는 밖에서 놀 수 없었다.
play, I, that, cold, outside, couldn't, so

→ It was _____ .

07 우리말과 같은 뜻이 되도록 주어진 단어를 이용해서 문장을 완성하시오. 5점

서술형

비가 그치지 않으면 나는 외출하지 않을 거야.
stop

→ If it _____ _____ raining, I won't go out.

→ Unless it _____ raining, I won't go out.

08 다음 조건에 맞게 우리말을 영작하시오. 6점

서술형

내일 시험이 있어서 나는 공부를 해야 해.

· 조건 1 어휘 – have, test, so, must
· 조건 2 현재 시제로 쓸 것
· 조건 3 9단어로 완성할 것

→ _____

VOCA keep on+-ing 계속해서 ~하다 | score 점수 | arrogant 오만한 | believe 믿다 | do the dishes 설거지하다

Level 3 Test

»» 정답 33쪽

[01~02] Choose the proper word for the blank. 각 2점

01

_____ I had a cold, I had to stay home.

① If   ② So
③ Unless   ④ Because
⑤ Although

02

I love her _____ she doesn't love me.

① if   ② as
③ when   ④ because
⑤ even though

03 Choose the common word for the blanks. 2점

• _____ I was sleeping, the phone rang. • _____ the room was dark, he turned on the lamp.

① As   ② If
③ When   ④ Though
⑤ Because

04 Which is the correct word for the blank? 2점

If I _____ up early tomorrow morning, I'll wake you up.

① get   ② got
③ will get   ④ to get
⑤ getting

05 Which word for the blanks is <u>different</u> from the others? 3점

① She doesn't like him _____ he is selfish.
② I'm upset _____ I lost my cell phone.
③ Jim likes winter _____ he can go skiing.
④ I got up late, _____ I was late for school.
⑤ Dad is working late _____ he has a lot of work to do.

[06~07] Choose the sentence that has the same meaning as the one in the box. 각 2점

06

The lemon is so sour that I can't taste it.

① As the lemon is so sour, I can taste it.
② If the lemon is so sour, I can't taste it.
③ Although the lemon is sour, I can taste it.
④ The lemon is very sour, so I can't taste it.
⑤ The lemon is so sour because I can't taste it.

07

Unless it is too hot, we'll play baseball.

① If it is cold, we'll play baseball.
② If it is too hot, we'll play baseball.
③ If it isn't too hot, we'll play baseball.
④ If it will be too hot, we'll play baseball.
⑤ If it won't be cold, we'll play baseball.

08 Among the underlined "If[if]," which is <u>different</u> in usage? 3점

① I'll have pizza <u>if</u> I go out for lunch.
② I'm not sure <u>if</u> she can understand me.
③ <u>If</u> you hurry up, you can catch the bus.
④ Come to my office <u>if</u> you want to see me.
⑤ <u>If</u> I'm not busy, I'll go to the movies tonight.

VOCA ring (전화가) 울리다 | wake up 깨우다, 깨다 | selfish 이기적인 | upset 속상한 | sour 신, 시큼한 | taste 맛보다 | go to the movies 영화관에 가다

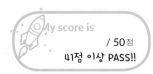

09 Which is appropriate for the blanks? 3점

> I couldn't go to school _____ I was sick.
> = I couldn't go to school _____ my sickness.

① because – because

② because – because of

③ because of – because

④ because of – because of

⑤ because of – because that

10 Choose ALL of the proper words for the blank. 3점

> _____ she was busy, she couldn't join us.

① As   ② If

③ Unless   ④ Though

⑤ Because

11 Choose the proper words from the brackets. 3점

> • [As / Because] I opened the door, I saw a cat.
> • [Though / If / Unless] the room is small, it has a nice view.

① As – If   ② Because – If

③ As –Though   ④ Because –Though

⑤ As – Unless

Challenge! 주관식 서술형

12 Fill in the blanks to make the two sentences have the same meaning. 4점

> The box is very heavy, so I can't carry it.

→ The box is _____ heavy

_____ I can't carry it.

13 Translate the sentence according to the conditions. 6점

> 그는 아침을 먹었지만, 여전히 배가 고팠다.
>
> • Condition 1   though를 활용할 것
> • Condition 2   과거 시제로 쓸 것
> • Condition 3   8단어로 완성할 것
> • Condition 4   though가 있는 절을 먼저 쓸 것

→ _____

14 Rewrite the sentence correctly. 4점

> If you will get home earlier than me, please turn on the heater.

→ _____

_____

15 Look at the picture and complete the sentence by using the given word. 5점

→ _____,

I couldn't play soccer with my friends. (broken)

16 Write the common word for the blanks. 4점

> • Cathy hasn't phoned _____ she went to Berlin.
> • _____ you lied to me, I don't trust you anymore.

→ _____

VOCA   sickness 질병 | view 전망, 경관 | heavy 무거운 | carry 나르다 | heater 난방기, 히터 | broken 부러진 | lie 거짓말을 하다

01 U25_1
빈칸에 들어갈 말로 알맞은 것은? 2점

> I think _____ the blouse is a little too large for you.

① if   ② when
③ because   ④ that
⑤ though

02 U25_2
Which is suitable for the blank? 2점

> You have to go home _____ it gets dark.

① when   ② before
③ until   ④ while
⑤ after

03 U25_3+GP
다음 중 어법상 옳은 것을 <u>모두</u> 고르시오. 2점

① Both my mother and I like to hike.
② Neither they nor she want to eat out.
③ Not only he but also we has to go there.
④ Not you but she are wrong.
⑤ Either she or I am to blame for the mistake.

04 U25_1+U26_1
Which is the common word for the blanks? 2점

> • I wonder _____ Jane is married.
> • _____ it snows a lot, my father won't drive.

① That[that]   ② Whether[whether]
③ So[so]   ④ Until[until]
⑤ If[if]

05 U26_1
다음 중 주어진 문장과 뜻이 같은 문장은? 2점

> If I am not busy, I'll stop by.

① When I am not busy, I'll stop by.
② Unless I am busy, I'll stop by.
③ Though I am busy, I'll stop by.
④ As soon as I am not busy, I'll stop by.
⑤ I am not busy, so I'll stop by.

06 U26_GP+U25_1
Which word for the blanks is <u>different</u> from the others? 2점

① It rained, _____ I didn't go to school.
② The traffic was _____ heavy that I went there on foot.
③ They helped me, _____ I said, "Thank you."
④ She is a very good swimmer, _____ I can't catch her.
⑤ I think _____ she speaks Spanish very well.

07 U25_2+GP
다음 문장에서 어법상 <u>어색한</u> 부분을 찾아 바르게 고친 학생은? 2점

> When Mr. Smith will retire, he will move to a small town.

① 세진: When → Though
② 민희: will retire → won't retire
③ 주영: will move → moves
④ 준이: will retire → retires
⑤ 소라: to → for

08 U25_2
우리말과 같은 뜻이 되도록 할 때 빈칸에 알맞은 말은? 2점

> 사자가 나타나자마자 모든 동물들이 도망갔다.
> = _____ the lion appeared, all of the animals went away.

① After   ② Until
③ As soon as   ④ Since
⑤ While

09 다음 중 어법상 <u>어색한</u> 것끼리 짝지어진 것은? 3점

U26_GP+U25_GP

고난도

ⓐ If it will rain, I will take my umbrella to school.
ⓑ I really like my older sister because of she's so nice.
ⓒ He as well as I go to London on business on Friday.
ⓓ You can pay with either cash or a credit card.

① ⓐ, ⓑ   ② ⓑ, ⓒ
③ ⓐ, ⓓ   ④ ⓐ, ⓑ, ⓒ
⑤ ⓐ, ⓑ, ⓓ

10 빈칸에 알맞은 표현을 3가지 쓰시오. 3점

U26_2

Piper missed the train _____ she took a taxi to the station.

→ _____

11 우리말과 같은 뜻이 되도록 빈칸에 알맞은 말을 쓰시오. 3점

U25_1

의사들은 숲 속을 걷는 것이 건강에 좋다고 말한다.

→ Doctors say _____ walking in the woods _____ good for your health.

12 주어진 단어를 빈칸에 알맞은 형태로 쓰시오. 3점

U25_2+GP

I will leave for Praha as soon as he _____. (arrive)

13 우리말과 같은 뜻이 되도록 주어진 단어를 배열하시오. 4점

U25_3

Robert는 커피숍 아니면 도서관에 있을 것이다.
in the coffee shop, either, will be, Robert, in the library, or

→ _____

_____

14 주어진 단어들 중 필요한 것만 골라 재배열해 문장을 만드시오. 4점

U26_3

보기 that   whether   because
      while   though

Everybody likes him he is polite.

→ _____

15 Rewrite the sentence starting with the given word. 4점

U26_1

If I don't wear my glasses, I can't see well.

→ Unless _____,

_____.

16 가장 알맞은 접속사를 [보기]에서 찾아 다음 두 문장을 연결하시오. 4점

U26_2

보기 Even   though   Until
      Whether   Since

I sneezed a lot. + I didn't catch a cold.

→ _____

_____

17 다음 문장에서 <u>어색한</u> 부분을 찾아 바르게 고치시오. 3점

> Neither my parents nor my sister are at home.

_____ → _____

18 Write the common word for the blanks. 3점

> • The river is polluted, _____ fish can't live there.
> • He is _____ young that he cannot ride a bike.

→ _____

19 다음 조건에 맞게 우리말을 영작하시오. 6점

> Ken뿐만 아니라 Jenny도 감기에 걸렸다.
>
> · 조건 1   not only를 사용할 것
> · 조건 2   어휘 – catch
> · 조건 3   9단어로 쓸 것

→ _____

20 그림을 보고 주어진 조건에 맞게 문장을 완성하시오. 6점

> · 조건 1   시간의 접속사를 사용할 것
> · 조건 2   과거 진행형으로 쓸 것
> · 조건 3   5단어로 쓸 것

→ She hurt her leg _____.

[21~22] 다음 글을 읽고 물음에 답하시오.

　(A)우리는 말을 통해서 뿐만 아니라 몸짓 언어를 통해서도 <u>의사소통을 할 수 있다.</u> Body language are all forms of gestures, postures, ⓐ_____ body movements. It can say a lot about you. If your posture is slumped, this could mean ⓑ_____ you are sad or that you have ⓒ_____ confidence. If your posture is straight, you are expressing confidence. A smile is a sign of friendliness. However, there are people ⓓ_____ smile just to be polite. Friendliness is expressed ⓔ_____ a person's eyes meet yours directly.

*slumped: 구부정한

21 Which is NOT proper for the blanks? 3점

고난도

① until
② and
③ little
④ who
⑤ that

22 윗글의 밑줄 친 (A)와 같은 뜻이 되도록 주어진 단어를 배열하시오. 5점

고난도

> only, through, not, but, also, through, body language, we, words, can communicate

→ _____

CHAPTER 12
의문문

선택의문문, 부가의문문

개념이해책
138쪽 함께 보기

■ 아래 표의 빈칸에 알맞은 내용을 써 넣으세요. >>> 정답 34쪽

CONCEPT 1 선택의문문

be동사	1)_____+주어 ~, A 2)_____ B?	Is she a dentist 3)_____ a surgeon?
조동사	4)_____+주어+동사원형 ~, A 5)_____ B?	Does she play the violin 6)_____ the cello?
의문사	7)_____+8)_____+주어+동사원형 ~, A 9)_____ B?	Which do you like better, *kimbap* 10)_____ ramen?
	의문사 ~ 11)_____, A 12)_____ B?	Which is more delicious, pizza 13)_____ hamburgers?

CONCEPT 2 부가의문문

긍정 → 14)_____ (항상 줄임말로) 부정 → 16)_____	Jack is energetic, 15)_____? You don't have English class today, 17)_____?
be동사/조동사 → 18)_____	It's cold, 19)_____? Jane can ski and snowboard, 20)_____?
일반동사 → 21)_____/22)_____/23)_____로	You have a bus card, 24)_____?
완료형(have/has +p.p.) → 25)_____/26)_____	Joe has seen a panda, 27)_____?
Let's ~ → shall we?	Let's be optimistic, 28)_____?
명령문 → will you?	Go to bed right now, 29)_____?

Level 1 Test

>>> 정답 34쪽

A 우리말과 같은 뜻이 되도록 빈칸을 채우시오.

1 너는 부산에 버스로 가니, 아니면 기차로 가니?
→ Do you go to Busan by bus _____ by train?

2 미술과 음악 중 어느 과목을 좋아하니?
→ _____ subject do you like better, art _____ music?

B 빈칸에 알맞은 부가의문문을 쓰시오.

1 Penguins can't fly, _____?

2 Vera isn't interested in insects, _____?

3 Don't make any noise, _____?

4 Let's go to the history museum, _____?

VOCA subject 과목 | be interested in ~에 관심이 있다 | insect 곤충 | make noise 소란을 피우다 | history 역사

C 밑줄 친 부분을 바르게 고쳐 쓰시오.

1 These are your socks, aren't these?
→ _____

2 Nancy's report was excellent, was she?
→ _____

3 You haven't been on television, was you?
→ _____

D 우리말과 같은 뜻이 되도록 주어진 단어들을 이용해서 문장을 완성하시오.

1 이 펜은 네 것이니, 아니면 그의 것이니? (yours, his)
→ Is this pen _____ _____ _____?

2 너는 이 쿠키들을 만들었니, 아니면 샀니? (make, buy)
→ Did you _____ _____ _____ _____ _____?

>>> 정답 35쪽

[01~02] 빈칸에 들어갈 말로 알맞은 것은? 각 2점

01

Which is bigger, this _____ that?

① or
② and
③ so
④ if
⑤ who

02

Rick and Robert were in the same class last year, _____?

① do they
② will you
③ shall we
④ wasn't they
⑤ weren't they

03 다음 문장에서 <u>어색한</u> 부분을 찾아 바르게 고친 학생은? 2점

David doesn't like to read books, did David?

① 은채: did를 does로 고쳐야 해요.
② 하늘: 마지막의 David를 he로 고쳐야 해요.
③ 하민: did David를 don't he로 고쳐야 해요.
④ 희망: did David를 does he로 고쳐야 해요.
⑤ 송이: did David를 doesn't he로 고쳐야 해요.

04 Which is the proper answer for the question? (Find ALL.) 2점

Do you want to go camping or go skating?

① Yes, I want to go camping.
② I want to go camping.
③ Skating.
④ No, I don't want to go skating.
⑤ Yes, I want to go skating.

05 우리말과 같은 뜻이 되도록 주어진 단어를 배열해서 영작하시오. 5점

서술형

당신은 캐나다 출신입니까, 아니면 미국 출신입니까?
are, from, Canada, America, or, you

→ _____

06 다음 두 문장 중 어색한 것을 찾아 고치시오. 5점

서술형

ⓐ Jim speaks Spanish, doesn't he?
ⓑ You aren't scared, don't you?

(　　) _____ → _____

07 다음 표를 보고 그림에 맞게 대화를 완성하시오. 6점

서술형

River	Mississippi	Thames
Length	3,782km	346km

A: (1) _____ is longer, the Thames
River (2) _____ the Mississippi?
B: (3) _____

08 우리말과 같은 뜻이 되도록 주어진 조건에 맞게 영작하시오. 6점

서술형

지각하지 마, 알겠니?

· 조건 1　부가의문문을 쓸 것
· 조건 2　Don't로 시작할 것
· 조건 3　5단어로 쓸 것

→ _____

VOCA　**go+-ing** ~하러 가다 | **scared** 겁먹은, 무서워하는

01 Which is suitable for the blank? 2점

Those shoes are nice, _____?

① are they
② aren't they
③ are those
④ aren't those
⑤ do they

02 Which underlined choice is grammatically incorrect? 2점

① You've adjusted well, <u>didn't you</u>?
② You can help him, <u>can't you</u>?
③ You aren't a singer, <u>are you</u>?
④ She doesn't like him, <u>does she</u>?
⑤ They saw you there, <u>didn't they</u>?

[03~04] Which pair is correct for the blanks? 각 2점

03

• Tony couldn't do the job, _____?
• You have made a decision, _____?

① could he – have you
② couldn't he – haven't you
③ didn't he – did you
④ could he – haven't you
⑤ did he – have you

04

• Let's play baseball on Sunday, _____?
• Pass me the salt, _____?

① shall we – don't you
② will you – isn't you
③ have you – will you
④ shall we – will you
⑤ don't we – will I

05 Which are the proper words for the blanks? 2점

너희 오빠 어젯밤 9시쯤에 집에 없었지, 그렇지?
= Your brother _____ at home last night around nine, _____?

① is – wasn't he
② was – wasn't he
③ was – wasn't your brother
④ wasn't – was he
⑤ wasn't – was your brother

06 Who does NOT understand the sentence correctly? 3점

Mrs. Smith has taken care of her grandson, hasn't she?

① 민지: 부가의문문이 올바르게 쓰였어.
② 동훈: 주절이 긍정이라 부정의 부가의문문이 쓰였어.
③ 윤후: 주절의 동사가 has taken이라서 has를 이용해서 부정의 부가의문문을 만들었어.
④ 준수: Mrs. Smith는 여자여서 she로 받았어.
⑤ 길동: taken이 본동사니까 hasn't she?를 does she?로 고쳐야 해.

07 Which is grammatically incorrect? (Find ALL.) 3점

① A: Will you take the train or the bus?
   B: I will take the train.
② A: Which do you want, coffee or tea?
   B: Coffee, please.
③ A: Do you speak French or English?
   B: Yes, I speak French.
④ A: Will you rent or buy a yacht?
   B: I will buy a yacht.
⑤ A: Would you like soup or salad with your meal?
   B: No, I would like to have salad.

VOCA adjust 적응하다, 조정하다 | make a decision 결정을 내리다 | pass 건네다 | salt 소금 | take care of ~을 돌보다 | French 프랑스어 | rent 세내어 빌리다 | yacht 요트

08 Which sentences are grammatically **incorrect**? 3점

> ⓐ You will tell me the truth, won't you?
> ⓑ You couldn't lend me any money, could you?
> ⓒ Let's go to the park tomorrow, will you?
> ⓓ Mary likes reading novels, doesn't she?
> ⓔ She hasn't met him yet, hasn't she?

① ⓐ, ⓒ   ② ⓑ, ⓒ
③ ⓒ, ⓔ   ④ ⓓ, ⓔ
⑤ ⓔ

09 Which blank needs a **different** word? 3점

① _____ did you omit, this word or that one?
② _____ is the proper expression, a cottage or a cabin?
③ _____ is that kid in the yellow rain boots?
④ _____ athlete has strong muscles?
⑤ _____ city is more developed, Seattle or L.A.?

Challenge! 주관식 서술형

10 Fill in the blanks with the proper words. 5점

> A: He lives in Taiwan. He has never seen snow
> (1) _____?
> B: (2) _____. He has never seen snow.

11 Find the error and correct it. 4점

> It's terrible that Gandhi was murdered, wasn't it?

➡ _____

12 Translate the sentence by using the given words. 4점

> 문방구는 1층과 2층 중 어디에 있니?
> first floor, the stationery shop, second floor

➡ _____
_____

13 Rearrange the given words to make a complete sentence. 4점

> which, do, music, you, like, better, the blues, jazz, or

➡ _____
_____

14 Rewrite the sentence by adding the proper tag question. 5점

> They have known each other for a long time.

➡ _____
_____

15 Translate the sentence according to the conditions. 6점

> 산책하러 가자, 그럴래?
>
> ·Condition 1   어휘 – take a walk
> ·Condition 2   6단어로 쓸 것
> ·Condition 3   부가의문문을 쓸 것

➡ _____

VOCA   **tell the truth** 사실대로 말하다 | **novel** 소설 | **omit** 생략하다 | **expression** 표현 | **cottage** 시골에 있는 작은 집 | **cabin** 오두막집 | **athlete** 운동선수 | **muscle** 근육 | **developed** 개발된 | **murder** 살해하다 | **stationery shop** 문방구 | **for a long time** 오랫동안 | **take a walk** 산책하다

28 간접의문문

■ 아래 표의 빈칸에 알맞은 내용을 써 넣으세요. ≫≫ 정답 35쪽

개념이해책
141쪽 함께 보기

CONCEPT 1 간접의문문이란?

I wonder if he will come.
1)_____ +2)_____ (의문사 없는 경우)
I don't know where he lives.
3)_____ +4)_____ (의문사 있는 경우)

CONCEPT 2 의문사가 없는 간접의문문

5)_____ [6)_____]+7)_____ +8)_____ (or not)
Is Sora at home? → Do you know 9)_____ Sora is at home? = Do you know 10)_____ Sora is at home
(11)_____ 12)_____)?
Do you know Nick? → I wonder 13)_____ you know Nick (14)_____ 15)_____).

CONCEPT 3 의문사가 있는 간접의문문

의문사+주어+동사
Where is he? → Do you know 16)_____ 17)_____ 18)_____ ?

Level 1 Test

≫≫ 정답 35쪽

A [ ]에서 알맞은 것을 고르시오.

1 I wonder [if / that] Leo got a perfect score.

2 I want to know whether [he can / can he] swim.

3 I'm not sure what [Semi will / will Semi] buy.

4 Tell me how [did you reserve / you reserved] the ticket.

B 우리말과 같은 뜻이 되도록 주어진 단어를 배열하여 문장을 완성하시오.

1 너는 왜 그가 경기를 기권했는지 아니?
(why, gave up, he)

→ Do you know _____ the match?

2 너는 누가 그것을 할 것이라고 믿니?
(do, you, believe, who)

→ _____ will do it?

C 두 문장을 한 문장으로 쓰시오.

1 Can you tell me? + Will he be back?

→ Can you tell me _____ ?

2 I don't know. + When did Jack come?

→ I don't know _____ .

3 I wonder. + Where is my USB?

→ I wonder _____ .

4 Do you think? + What is it?

→ _____

D 어색한 부분이 있으면 바르게 고쳐 문장을 다시 쓰시오.

1 When do you know she can finish the work?

→ _____

2 Tell me who sings the best in your class.

→ _____

VOCA perfect score 만점 | reserve 예약하다 | give up 기권하다, 포기하다 | match 시합

01 빈칸에 들어갈 문장 형태로 가장 알맞은 것은? 2점

> A: When was your grandfather born?
> B: Well, I don't know _____.

① when my grandfather born was
② when my grandfather was born
③ when my was grandfather born
④ when was my grandfather born
⑤ when was born my grandfather

02 다음 중 밑줄 친 if의 쓰임이 다른 하나는? 3점

① I wonder if you can go there for me.
② He wanted to know if she was born in Italy.
③ I will go if he comes to the conference.
④ Do you know if we will join the club?
⑤ Can you tell me if I will have good luck?

03 다음 우리말에 맞게 주어진 단어들을 배열할 때 6번째 올 단어는? 2점

> 나는 BTS에 몇 명의 멤버들이 있는지 알고 있다.
> are, I, know, there, in, BTS, members, how, many

① how   ② many
③ members   ④ there
⑤ are

04 다음 문장들 중에서 어색한 부분을 바르게 설명한 학생은? 3점

> ⓐ I don't know what he will make for dinner.
> ⓑ Can you tell me where does she live?
> ⓒ Nobody knows when did the fire break out.

① 정훈: ⓐ what절에서 will은 쓸 수 없다.
② 지수: ⓑ where 대신에 if를 써야 한다.
③ 세호: ⓒ when절에서 did를 없애야 한다.
④ 단아: ⓑ where는 문장 맨 앞으로 가야 한다.
⑤ 현철: ⓒ did를 없애고 break는 broke로 쓴다.

05 다음 대화문에서 이어질 말을 완성하시오. 6점

서술형

Mom : What is your homework ?

I don't know _____

→ I don't know _____

_____ _____.

06 다음 두 문장을 합쳐서 한 문장으로 만들 때 빈칸에 알맞은 3단어의 영어를 쓰시오. 4점

서술형

> Do you guess? + What did he select?

→ What _____ he selected?

07 다음 문장에서 어색한 부분을 바르게 고쳐 쓰시오. 4점

서술형

> I wonder that I will become a second-generation *chaebol* or not.

_____ → _____

08 다음은 한 여자가 fortuneteller에게 찾아가 물어보는 말이다. 주어진 조건에 맞게 영작하시오. 6점

서술형

> 제가 이상형의 남자를 만날 것인지 말해줄 수 있나요?
>
> · 조건 1   어휘 – can, tell, Mr. Right
> · 조건 2   10단어로 쓸 것 (Mr. Right는 2단어로 침)
> · 조건 3   간접의문문으로 쓸 것

→ _____

VOCA   be born 태어나다 | conference 회의 | join 함께 하다, 가입하다 | luck 운 | break out (사건, 화재가) 발생하다, 일어나다 | select 고르다 |
generation 세대 | *chaebol* 재벌 | Mr. Right 이상형의 남자

01 Which is the common word for the blanks? 2점

> • I wonder _____ you can handle this.
> • The question is _____ there is life on Mars.

① that ② who
③ whether ④ what
⑤ which

02 Which is the correct order for the given words? 2점

> Can you tell me (ⓐ what, ⓑ is, ⓒ your ID)?

① ⓐ – ⓑ – ⓒ ② ⓐ – ⓒ – ⓑ
③ ⓑ – ⓐ – ⓒ ④ ⓑ – ⓒ – ⓐ
⑤ ⓒ – ⓐ – ⓑ

03 Which are the proper words for the blanks? 2점

> A: When did Jasmine _____ ?
> B: I don't know when she _____ .

① leave – left ② leave – leaves
③ leave – leave ④ left – left
⑤ leaves – leave

04 Which sentence combines the two given sentences correctly? 2점

> Do you think? + Where did your son hide his report card?

① Do you think did your son hide his report card?
② Where do you think your son hid his report card?
③ Do you think where your son hid his report card?
④ Where do you think your son hided his report card?
⑤ Where do you think did your son hide his report card?

05 Choose ALL of the grammatically incorrect sentences. 3점

① Do you think who am I?
② Tell me how you solved the puzzle.
③ Do you know what does Jay wants?
④ I don't know when will he come back.
⑤ I want to know if I can use your pool.

06 Which is the proper word for the blank? 2점

> A: When do you _____ the package will arrive?
> B: Maybe tomorrow.

① know ② need
③ want ④ believe
⑤ like

07 Which sentences are grammatically incorrect? 3점

> ⓐ Do you know how many letters Hangeul has?
> ⓑ Do you guess where does he live?
> ⓒ Do you know who King Sejong was?
> ⓓ How old do you think she is?
> ⓔ I wonder if he needs help.

① ⓐ, ⓑ ② ⓑ, ⓒ
③ ⓓ, ⓔ ④ ⓑ
⑤ ⓓ

08 Which word appears second in the blank when translating the sentence? 2점

> 남은 좌석이 있을지 의심스럽다.
> = It's doubtful _____ .

① there ② whether
③ will ④ any seats
⑤ be

VOCA handle 다루다 | life 생명체 | Mars 화성 | report card 성적표 | package 소포 | letters 글자, 편지 | King Sejong 세종대왕 | doubtful 의심스러운 | seat 자리, 좌석

09 Who finds ALL of the errors and corrects them? 3점

> ⓐ Do you know who is that man?
> ⓑ Ask Jimmy where the monkey went.
> ⓒ Tell me whether Julia will be here this Saturday.
> ⓓ I can't remember how much did it cost.

① 예민: ⓐ who that man is
② 기량: ⓑ where did the monkey go
③ 다해: ⓒ whether Julia is here
④ 진아: ⓐ who that man is, ⓓ how much it cost
⑤ 정민: ⓒ whether Julia is here, ⓓ how much it cost

10 Which of the following CANNOT make a grammatically correct sentence? 4점

① Do / you / ? / know / Phillip / where / is
② I / wonder / if / you / . / know / Sue
③ I / not / sure / am / whether / he / love / . / me
④ He / doesn't / know / the / window / who / . / broke
⑤ Can / ? / tell / me / they / who / are / you

Challenge! 주관식 서술형

11 Look at the picture and rearrange the given words to complete Grandma's line. 5점

> Grandma: Seyoung, I'm (not, if, valid, still, is, this, sure, ticket). My eyes are poor.
> Seyoung: It's still valid, Grandma. We can watch the movie for free.

→ Seyoung, I'm _____ .

12 Combine the two sentences into one. 5점

> I can't remember. + Who complained about the customs procedure?

→ _____
_____

13 Fill in the blanks to complete the dialog. 5점

> A: What did Mr. Yoon write on the board?
> B: I can't read _____ _____
> _____ . He has really bad handwriting.

14 Translate the sentence according to the conditions. 6점

> 너는 그가 왜 훌륭하다고 생각하니?
>
> · Condition 1 어휘 – so great
> · Condition 2 7단어로 쓸 것
> · Condition 3 간접의문을 사용할 것

→ _____

15 Rearrange the given words to make a complete sentence. 4점

> why, believe, were, a, criminal, did, he, you

→ _____

VOCA cost (비용이) 들다 | valid 유효한 | for free 무료로 | complain 불평하다 | customs 관세 | procedure 진행 절차 | handwriting 필체 | criminal 범인

CHAPTER 12
Review Test

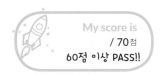
U27_2

01 빈칸에 들어갈 말이 바르게 짝지어진 것은? 2점

> • My brother made a mistake, _____?
> • You've gotten email, _____?

① did he – haven't you
② does he – have you
③ doesn't he – has you
④ did he – have you
⑤ didn't he – haven't you

U27_GP

02 다음 빈칸에 들어갈 말로 적절한 것은? (정답 최대 3개) 2점

> A: Is your brother older or younger than you?
> B: _____

① No, he isn't old.
② He is younger than me.
③ He is older than me.
④ Yes, he is older than me.
⑤ Sure. Do you have a brother?

U27_2

03 다음 중 어법상 옳은 문장을 모두 고르시오. 2점

함정

① You are hungry, aren't you?
② He could play chess, can't he?
③ Be calm, will you?
④ Mary bought a new car, don't she?
⑤ You haven't decided yet, do you?

U28_3

04 다음 시간을 묻는 표현에서 빈칸에 3번째로 올 단어는? 2점

> Could you tell me _____?

① what   ② is
③ time   ④ it
⑤ now

U27_1

05 다음 질문에 대한 대답으로 알맞은 것을 모두 고르시오. 2점

> A: Which do you like better, cash or checks?
> B: _____

① Yes, I do.   ② No, I don't.
③ I like cash better.   ④ Checks.
⑤ Yes, I like cash.

U28_3+GP

06 Which combines the two sentences correctly? 2점

한눈에
쏙

> Do you think? + Where did the birds go?

① Do you think where the birds went?
② Where do you think the birds went?
③ Do you think where did the birds go?
④ Where do you think the birds did go?
⑤ Where do you think did the birds go?

U28_2+U26_1

07 다음 중 밑줄 친 표현이 같은 의미인 것끼리 묶인 것은? 3점

> ⓐ We don't know if an earthquake will happen.
> ⓑ I wonder if the flight has arrived or not.
> ⓒ I can't open it if you lock the door.
> ⓓ I can't remember if I took the medicine.

① ⓐ, ⓑ   ② ⓑ, ⓒ
③ ⓐ, ⓑ, ⓒ   ④ ⓒ, ⓓ
⑤ ⓐ, ⓑ, ⓓ

U28_2

08 다음 중 어색한 문장을 고르시오. 2점

① I'm not sure whether is there a problem.
② I don't know what I should do.
③ Do you know what he wants?
④ Can you tell me where he is?
⑤ I asked her what John bought.

U28_3

09 다음 대화의 빈칸에 들어갈 말이 바르게 짝지어진 것은?

2점

> A: Hi, Sera. Did you study here in the library?
> Tell me what subject _____.
> B: Math. I have a math test. How about you?
> What subject _____?

① you studied – you studied

② you studied – did you study

③ did you study – you study

④ did you study – did you study

⑤ you studied – you did study

U27_1+2

10 Which sentences are grammatically correct?

★
고난도

3점

> ⓐ Don't fight with your friends, shall we?
> ⓑ You haven't met my mother, have you?
> ⓒ Which do you prefer, the cat and the dog?
> ⓓ Which girl has curly hair?
> ⓔ Let's eat out, will we?

① ⓑ, ⓓ   ② ⓐ, ⓑ, ⓓ

③ ⓒ, ⓔ   ④ ⓒ, ⓓ

⑤ ⓓ, ⓔ

U27_1

11 우리말과 같은 뜻이 되도록 주어진 단어를 배열하시오. 4점

> 창가 쪽 좌석을 더 좋아하시나요, 아니면 복도 쪽 좌석을 더
> 좋아하시나요?
> you, prefer, a window seat, an aisle seat, or,
> would

→ _____

_____

U27_1

12 Translate the sentence by using the given
words. (9 words) 4점

> 너는 스테이크와 버거 중에 어느 음식을 더 좋아하니?
> better, steaks, burgers

→ _____

_____

U27_GP

13 다음 문장에서 어법상 어색한 부분을 찾아 고쳐 쓰시오. 3점

> There was something strange in the yard,
> isn't it?

_____ → _____

U27_2

14 그림을 보고 주어진 조건에 맞게 다음 글을 완성하시오. 5점

LET'S

• Let's save energy.

• Let's not drive our cars as
much as possible.

• _____

_____

· 조건 1   부가의문문을 쓸 것

· 조건 2   어휘 – let's, our bikes

· 조건 3   6단어로 쓸 것

U27_2

15 Read the following situation and complete
the sentence by using the given expression.

4점

> You are trying on a dress. You look in the
> mirror, and you see the dress is too big. What
> do you say to your friend?

→ This dress _____

_____? (fit me well)

U28_3

16 우리말과 같은 뜻이 되도록 다음 의문문을 빈칸에 간접의
문문 형식으로 쓰시오. 3점

> What did he do?
> = I don't know _____.
> 나는 그가 무엇을 했는지 모른다.

17

U28_3

다음 그림은 공항에서 가방 무게를 측정하는 상황을 보여 주고 있다. 빈칸에 이어질 말을 쓰시오. 4점

Passenger: How much does my bag weigh?
Airline staff: What did you say?
Passenger: Could you tell me

_____?

18

U28_2

다음 두 문장을 한 문장으로 나타낼 때 빈칸에 알맞은 말을 쓰시오. 4점

Tell me. + Did you send a text message in class?

→ Tell me _____.

19

U28_3+GP

Rewrite the sentence correctly. 4점

함정

Did you think why was the film so amazing?

→ _____

20

U28_3

★
고난도

우리말과 같은 뜻이 되도록 주어진 조건에 맞게 문장을 완성하시오. 6점

엄마는 언제 전화기를 냉장고에 넣었는지 기억하지 못하신다.

· 조건 1　어휘 – remember, put, her phone, refrigerator
· 조건 2　간접의문문을 쓸 것

→ My mom _____

_____.

[21~22] 다음 글을 읽고 물음에 답하시오.

My seven-year-old son Brody ⓐwas warned never to leave our block. One day, however, he took a walk up by the railway tracks. I was very upset when I found out about that and said he ⓑhad to tell his dad about it. In the evening, ⓒhis dad arrived home, and I said, "Now tell Dad (1)네가 어디 있었는지." He didn't tell me ⓓwhere was he. Instead, he looked at me blankly, so I rephrased my words. "Where did you come from?" I asked again. "I'm not so sure, but I think ⓔthat I was born in Queens," Brody said.

*blankly: 멍하니　**rephrase: 바꿔 말하다

21

U15_3+U05_2+U11_GP+U28_3+U25_1

★
고난도

윗글의 밑줄 친 부분 ⓐ~ⓔ 중 어법상 어색한 것은? 3점

① ⓐ
② ⓑ
③ ⓒ
④ ⓓ
⑤ ⓔ

22

U28_3

윗글의 밑줄 친 (A)와 같은 뜻이 되도록 조건에 맞게 영작하시오. 4점

· 조건 1　3단어로 쓸 것
· 조건 2　어순에 유의할 것

→ _____

CHAPTER 13
가정법

UNIT 29 조건문과 가정법 과거

개념이해책
148쪽 함께 보기

■ 아래 표의 빈칸에 알맞은 내용을 써 넣으세요. **>>>** 정답 37쪽

① 가정법 과거

의미	1)_____과 반대되는 내용을 가정
형태	If+주어+ 2)_____ ~, 주어+조동사의 3)_____ + 4)_____ ···.
해석	5)_____

② 가정법 과거의 문장 전환

If+주어+ 6)_____ ~, 주어+조동사의 7)_____ + 8)_____ ···.
→ 9)_____ [10)_____]주어+ 11)_____ 동사 ~, 주어+ 12)_____ 동사 ···. [13)_____ ↔14)_____]
→ 주어+ 15)_____ 동사 ~, 16)_____ 주어+ 17)_____ 동사 ···. [18)_____ ↔19)_____]

③ 직설법 조건문과 가정법 과거

조건문 현재	If+주어+ 20)_____ 동사 ~, 주어+ 21)_____ +동사원형 ···.	22)_____ 현재와 미래를 가정
가정법 과거	If+주어+ 23)_____ 동사 ~, 주어+조동사의 24)_____ +동사원형 ···.	25)_____ 현재 사실의 반대를 가정

Level 1 Test

>>> 정답 37쪽

A [ ]에서 알맞은 것을 고르시오.

1 If you [got / get] there early, wait for me.

2 You [caught / could catch] the plane if you took a taxi to the airport.

3 [Did / Would] he do that if he were a wise man?

B 주어진 단어를 빈칸에 알맞은 형태로 쓰시오.

1 If Alex sold his old mobile phone, he _____ _____ a new one. (can, buy)

2 The boy would be on the national team if he _____ harder. (train)

3 If Carmen doesn't come, we _____ _____ _____ for dinner. (go out)

C 밑줄 친 부분이 어색하면 고치시오.

1 If I am you, I would follow his advice.

    → _____

2 Where do you visit if you were in Ulsan?

    → _____

D 우리말과 같은 뜻이 되도록 빈칸에 알맞은 말을 쓰시오.

1 내일 택배를 못 받으면 전화주세요.

    → If you _____ _____ the parcel tomorrow, please _____ me a call.

2 수업이 없으면 놀이공원에 갈 텐데.

    → If there _____ no class, I _____ _____ to an amusement park.

VOCA mobile 휴대 전화 | national team 국가대표 팀 | train 훈련하다 | follow 따르다 | advice 충고, 조언 | parcel 택배 | amusement park 놀이공원

My score is

/ 30점
25점 이상 PASS!!

01 빈칸에 들어갈 말로 알맞은 것은? 2점

> If she taught English, she _____ a good teacher.

① were ② will be

③ would be ④ had been

⑤ can be

02 두 문장의 뜻이 같도록 할 때 빈칸에 들어갈 말이 바르게 짝지어진 것은? 3점

> If I knew how to swim, I would go swimming with you.
> = As I _____ how to swim, I _____ swimming with you.

① knew – would go

② know – don't go

③ don't know – won't go

④ don't know – wouldn't go

⑤ didn't know – wouldn't go

03 다음 중 문장 전환이 어색한 것은? 3점

① If she listened to me, she wouldn't fail.

　→ She doesn't listen to me, so she will fail.

② If I knew her number, I could call her.

　→ As I know her number, I can call her.

③ If I had enough time, I could solve the problem.

　→ I don't have enough time, so I can't solve the problem.

④ If it were fine today, I would go jogging.

　→ It isn't fine today, so I won't go jogging.

⑤ If I cooked like her, I would be a chef.

　→ I'm not a chef because I don't cook like her.

04 우리말과 같은 뜻이 되도록 할 때 어법상 어색한 부분을 찾아 고치시오. 5점 서술형

> 그가 여기 있다면, 그들을 도울 수 있을 텐데.
> = If he is here, he could help them.

_____ ➡ _____

05 두 문장이 같은 뜻이 되도록 할 때 빈칸에 알맞은 말을 쓰시오. 6점 서술형

> If I had a lot of money, I could buy you the biggest house in the world.

→ As I _____ _____ a lot of

money, I _____ _____ you

the biggest house in the world.

06 다음 두 문장의 밑줄 친 부분 중 어색한 것을 찾아 고치시오. 5점 서술형

> ⓐ If you pay attention, I am so pleased.
> ⓑ If I were your mother, I would do the same thing.

( ) _____ ➡ _____

07 다음은 Eric Clapton이 어린 나이에 죽은 아들을 위해 부른 노래 'Tears in Heaven'의 일부분이다. 가사에서 어법상 어색한 것을 모두 찾아 고치시오. 6점 서술형

> Do you know my name
> If I saw you in Heaven?
> Is it the same
> If I saw you in Heaven?
> I must be strong and carry on
> 'Cause I know I don't belong here in Heaven.

→ _____

_____

VOCA fail 실패하다 | solve 풀다 | chef 요리사 | pay attention 주의를 기울이다 | heaven 천국 | carry on 계속 나아가다 | 'cause (= because) ~하기 때문에 | belong 속하다

01 Which is suitable for the blank? 2점

> I want to learn how to fix a car. If my car broke down now, _____.

① I would fix it
② I would know what to do
③ I will not know what to do
④ I would not know what to do
⑤ I would know anything about cars

02 Whose correction is right? 2점

> If there were no hungry people in this world, it will be a much better place.

① 미나: were → was ② 한지: no → not
③ 효령: will → would ④ 태섭: be → do
⑤ 병민: much → very

03 The following sentence is from the song "San Francisco" sung by Scott McKenzie. Who understands the sentence correctly? 3점

> If you're going to San Francisco, be sure to wear some flowers in your hair.

① 가경: if가 문장에 있으니까 가정법 문장이야.
② 병민: 조건문에서는 주절에 미래를 써야 하는데 틀렸어.
③ 민걸: 네가 샌프란시스코에 갈 가능성이 매우 적다는 소리야.
④ 사영: 조건문에서는 주절에 명령문도 사용할 수 있으므로 맞는 문장이야.
⑤ 지욱: if절에서 you're를 you'd be로 고쳐도 돼.

04 Which is correct for each blank? 2점

> I _____ Jandi the secret since I met her. She _____ angry if she _____.

① don't tell – is – knows
② didn't tell – would be – knew
③ didn't tell – would be – knows
④ haven't told – would be – knew
⑤ haven't told – would be – knows

05 Which change in the sentences is incorrect? 3점

① As he is too short, he can't be a good basketball player.
　→ If he were not too short, he could be a good basketball player.
② As it isn't sunny today, we won't go hiking.
　→ If it were sunny today, we would go hiking.
③ Because I like sweets, I don't have better teeth.
　→ If I didn't like sweets, I would have better teeth.
④ Colt isn't sociable, so he doesn't have many friends.
　→ Colt had many friends if he were sociable.
⑤ I'm not finished with my homework, so I can't go out with you.
　→ I could go out with you if I were finished with my homework.

06 When you change the sentence starting with "We would" which word comes ninth? 3점

> Because we are not working together, we don't do a better job.

① we ② were
③ not ④ working
⑤ together

07 How many sentences are grammatically incorrect? 3점

> ⓐ If my team won the championship, I'd bought you dinner.
> ⓑ If I had a chance to do it again, I would do it differently.
> ⓒ The kids would be happy if their mother allows them to climb up the tree.
> ⓓ If you give me some money, I'll pay you back tomorrow.
> ⓔ What did you do if you had more free time?

① one ② two
③ three ④ four
⑤ five

VOCA fix 고치다 | break down 고장 나다 | be sure to 꼭 ~하다 | sweet 단것 | sociable 사교적인 | championship 대회 |
allow A to B A가 B하게 허락하다 | climb 오르다 | pay back 갚다

08 Which word CANNOT be used when translating the sentence? 3점

> 아빠가 내게 강아지 한 마리만 사주시면 내가 잘 돌볼 텐데.

① if
② bought
③ took
④ would
⑤ puppy

09 Which is grammatically <u>incorrect</u>? 3점

① If she is honest, I will employ her.
② If I were you, I would sell this car.
③ I would fail the exam if I hadn't a tutor.
④ I would lend you some money if I had a lot of it.
⑤ What would you do if you knew his email address?

Challenge! 주관식 서술형

10 Fill in the blanks to make the sentences have the same meaning. 6점

> If it weren't raining, I could go out.

(1) _____ it _____
_____ , I _____ go out.
(2) It is raining, _____ I _____
_____ out.

11 Find the sentence that has an error and correct it. 4점

> ⓐ If everyone had clean water to drink, there would be a lot fewer diseases.
> ⓑ If we were in Paju today, we will go to the concert in Imjingak.

( ) _____ → _____

12 Fill in the blanks by using the given words. 5점

> 하지만 네가 여기 있다면 더 좋을 텐데.

→ However, _____ _____
_____ _____ , things
_____ _____
_____ . (be, good)

13 Translate the sentence according to the conditions. 6점

> 네가 아르바이트를 구하면 너에게 스마트워치를 사주겠다.
>
> · Condition 1   어휘 – a smartwatch, get, a part-time job, will
> · Condition 2   I로 시작할 것
> · Condition 3   주어진 어휘를 변형하지 말 것
> · Condition 4   주어진 어휘를 포함하여 총 12단어로 쓸 것

→ _____
_____

14 Complete the sentence so that it has the same meaning as the given one. 5점

> He is weak, so he cannot climb the mountain with us.

→ If he _____ weak, he _____
the mountain with us.

UNIT 30 I wish 가정법 과거, as if 가정법 과거

■ 아래 표의 빈칸에 알맞은 내용을 써 넣으세요. >>> 정답 38쪽

개념이해책
151쪽 함께 보기

❶ I wish 가정법 과거와 as if 가정법 과거

	I wish 가정법 과거	as if 가정법 과거
의미	현재나 미래의 실현될 수 1)_____ 소망을 표현	2)_____ 사실과 3)_____ 인 상황을 가정
형태	I wish+4)_____ +가정법 5)_____ 동사 ~	as if+6)_____ +가정법 7)_____ 동사
해석	8)_____	9)_____

❷ I wish 가정법 과거의 문장 전환

I wish+주어+가정법 과거 동사 ~. → 10)_____ +주어+11)_____ ~. [12)_____ ↔ 13)_____]
I wish I had a laptop computer. → I am sorry I 14)_____ a laptop computer.

❸ as if 가정법 과거의 문장 전환

as if+주어+가정법 과거 동사 → 15)_____ , 주어+현재 동사 ~. [16)_____ ↔17)_____]
I feel as if I were dreaming. → In fact, I 18)_____ dreaming.

Level 1 Test

>>> 정답 38쪽

A [ ]에서 알맞은 것을 고르시오.

1 I wish I [know / knew] everything.

2 I [want / wish] I could speak English well.

3 He treats her as if she [is / were] a baby.

4 It looks [even / as] if it were a precious jewel.

B 문장의 의미가 통하도록 빈칸을 채우시오.

1 He's sorry that he can't see the movie.

→ He wishes he _____ _____ the movie.

2 I'm sad because I don't have a smartphone.

→ I wish I _____ a smartphone.

3 He looks generous, but he isn't.

→ He looks as if he _____ generous.

4 Nari acts like a musician. However, she isn't a musician.

→ Nari acts as though she _____ a musician.

C 우리말과 같은 뜻이 되도록 빈칸을 채우시오.

1 오늘은 춥다. 더 따뜻했으면 좋겠는데.

→ It _____ cold today. I wish it _____ warmer.

2 내가 답을 알면 좋을 텐데, 난 몰라.

→ I wish I _____ the answer, but I _____.

3 네가 똑같은 실수를 하지 않으면 좋을 텐데. 할 것 같아.

→ I wish you _____ _____ the same mistake. I think you _____.

4 그는 나를 안 좋아하는 것처럼 말해. 사실은 좋아하면서.

→ He talks _____ he _____ _____ me. In fact, he _____ me.

VOCA email address 이메일 주소 | treat 취급하다 | precious 값비싼, 귀중한 | generous 관대한 | act like ~처럼 행동하다 | musician 음악가

>>> 정답 38쪽

01 빈칸에 들어갈 말로 알맞은 것은? 2점

> I wish I _____ thick glasses. They make me look stupid.

① wear ② worn
③ didn't wear ④ don't wear
⑤ can wear

02 다음 문장을 바르게 이해하고 있는 학생은? 3점

> Steve talks as if he didn't know Mia.

① 동준: talks가 현재니까 didn't을 doesn't로 써야 해.
② 석진: as if 대신에 if만 써도 같은 뜻이야.
③ 형우: Steve는 Mia를 알고 싶어 한다는 의미야.
④ 응국: Steve는 실제로 Mia를 알고 있어.
⑤ 규민: 이 문장은 In fact, Steve doesn't know Mia. 와 같은 뜻이야.

03 다음을 영작할 때 필요 없는 단어는? 2점

> 너의 엄마는 마치 슈퍼모델인 것처럼 걸으신다.

① walks ② as
③ if ④ is
⑤ were

04 다음 중 어법상 어색한 것은? 2점

① Do you wish you were a hero?
② I wish I could jump like a cat.
③ I wish she would text me every day.
④ Carol wishes it were a white Christmas.
⑤ He wishes he has a lot of good friends.

05 주어진 단어를 배열하여 영작하시오. 5점

서술형

> rich, spend, if, they, they, money, as, were

→ _____

06 우리말과 같은 뜻이 되도록 주어진 조건에 맞게 문장을 완성하시오. 6점

서술형

> 초등학교 때로 시간을 되돌릴 수 있으면 좋을 텐데.
>
> ·조건 1 I wish로 시작할 것
> ·조건 2 '능력'을 나타내는 조동사를 사용할 것
> ·조건 3 어휘 – turn back time to, my elementary school days

→ _____

07 그림을 보고 주어진 조건에 맞게 여우가 할 수 있는 말을 쓰시오. 4점

서술형

> A: I'm sorry you're not enjoying the meal.
> B: _____ a long beak like you.
>
> ·조건 wish와 have를 활용하여 4단어로 쓸 것

08 다음 문장을 주어진 조건에 맞게 다시 쓰시오. 6점

서술형

> I am sad because I can't see you more often.
>
> ·조건 1 실현 가능성이 희박한 소망을 나타내는 표현으로 쓸 것
> ·조건 2 위 문장에 있는 단어를 활용할 것
> ·조건 3 I로 시작할 것
> ·조건 4 8단어로 완성할 것

→ _____

VOCA glasses 안경 | spend 소비하다 | turn back time 시간을 되돌리다 | elementary school 초등학교 | beak 부리

01 Which is suitable for the blank? 2점

> The drawer is made of plastic. But it looks as if it _____ of wood.

① is made
② makes
③ is making
④ were made
⑤ made

02 Which of the following sounds unnatural? 2점

① Jerome can't see the future. He wishes he could see the future.
② Minki is not good at drawing. He wishes he were good at drawing.
③ Yuna has little free time. She wishes she didn't have more free time.
④ Mr. Baker can't cook pasta. He wishes he could cook pasta.
⑤ I don't have many friends like you. I wish I had many friends like you.

03 Which change in the sentences is incorrect? 3점

① Sakai talks too much. I cannot stand it.
   → I wish Sakai didn't talk too much.
② My family does not have a van. I want one.
   → I wish my family had a van.
③ I am sad because it is raining.
   → I wish it were not raining.
④ I am sorry it doesn't snow much in Busan.
   → I wish it snowed more often in Busan.
⑤ I have to work tonight. I don't like it.
   → I wish I had to work tonight.

04 Which TWO words are NOT necessary when translating the sentence? 2점

> 그녀는 그녀의 고양이가 자기 자식인 양 얘기한다.

① talked
② as
③ through
④ were
⑤ her

05 Which sentence has the same meaning as the one in the box? 2점

> Clint talks as if he could put together the puzzle in a minute.

① In truth, he has put together the puzzle in a minute.
② In a minute, he will put together the puzzle.
③ I'm sorry he can't put together the puzzle in a minute.
④ In fact, he can't put together the puzzle in a minute.
⑤ But he couldn't put together the puzzle in a minute.

06 Who finds ALL of the errors and correct them? 3점

> ⓐ If I had wings, I will fly away.
> ⓑ She behaves as if she owned the mall.
> ⓒ I wish our team has a different uniform.

① 가인: ⓐ will → would
② 나의: ⓑ if → though, ⓑ owned → owns
③ 다예: ⓐ will → would, ⓑ if → though
④ 라지: ⓐ will → would, ⓒ has → had
⑤ 마신: ⓐ will → would, ⓒ wish → wished

07 How many sentences are suitable for the blanks? 3점

> I know Jessie has no interest in ballet, but she talks _____ in front of boys.
>
> ⓐ as she is a ballerina
> ⓑ as if she liked it very much
> ⓒ as she doesn't enjoy teaching it
> ⓓ as if she were taking ballet lessons
> ⓔ as if she doesn't have a ballerino friend

① one
② two
③ three
④ four
⑤ five

VOCA   drawer 서랍장 | be good at ~을 잘 하다 | stand 견디다 | van 승합차 | put together 조립하다 | behave 행동하다 | own 소유하다

08 Which can come at the end? (2 answers) 3점

> It is raining, and I have to go out because I have an appointment. I don't like walking in the rain. _____

① I hope it was not raining.

② I wish it were not raining.

③ I wish I didn't have an appointment.

④ I wish I had an appointment.

⑤ I wish I don't have an appointment.

09 Which line in the dialog has a grammatical error? 2점

① A: Let's take a coffee break, shall we?

② B: I wish I can, but I couldn't.

③ A: What is making you so busy?

④ B: I have to finish this report today.

⑤ A: You'd feel better if you took a break.

10 Which is the correct word for the blank so that the two sentences have the same meaning? 2점

> I'm sorry I don't have a foreign friend.
> = I wish I _____ a foreign friend.

① have ② had

③ will have ④ have had

⑤ am having

Challenge! 주관식 서술형

11 Find ALL of the errors and correct them. 5점

> Sometimes I want I had a clone. If I have a clone, the other me will be with you forever.

→ _____

_____

12 Look at the picture and complete the boy's line with 6 words. 5점

→ I wish _____ _____ _____

_____ _____ you.

13 Translate the sentence according to the conditions. 6점

> 너는 네가 나이길 바라지 않니?

· Condition 1	부정 의문문임에 유의할 것
· Condition 2	실현 불가능한 현재 사실을 소망하는 표현으로 쓸 것
· Condition 3	6단어로 쓸 것

→ _____

14 Complete the sentence by using "as if". 5점

> Sam is angry with his boss, but he is talking to her _____.

15 Fill in the blanks to make the sentences have the same meaning. 5점

> He smiled at me as if he were sharing a secret.

→ In fact, _____. (5 words)

VOCA appointment 약속 | break 휴식 | clone 복제인간 | boss 상사

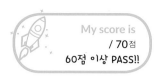

01 빈칸에 들어갈 말이 바르게 짝지어진 것은? 2점

If he _____ my son, I _____ happy.

① is – will be
② is – would be
③ was – will be
④ would be – were
⑤ were – would be

U29_2

02 주어진 문장과 의미가 가장 비슷한 것은? 2점

If I were you, I wouldn't go there with him.

① You'd better not go there with him.
② I want to go there with him.
③ You have to go there with him.
④ I want you to go there with him.
⑤ You don't need to go there with him.

U29_1

03 다음 중 어법상 어색한 것을 찾아 바르게 고친 것은? 2점

If she gotten more rest, she would feel better.

① If → As
② gotten → got
③ would → will
④ feel → felt
⑤ more → many

U29_2

04 빈칸에 들어갈 말이 바르게 짝지어진 것은? 2점

If I were rich, I could build a mansion.
= As I _____ rich, I _____ a mansion.

① was – could build
② were not – couldn't build
③ weren't – built
④ am not – can't build
⑤ am not – can build

U29_1+3+U30_1

05 다음 중 어법상 옳은 것끼리 짝지어진 것은? 3점

ⓐ He looks as if he lost everything.
ⓑ I wish I didn't have to study today.
ⓒ He can do it if she helped him.
ⓓ I hope she joins our diving team.
ⓔ If he is not afraid, he could do it now.

① ⓐ, ⓑ
② ⓓ, ⓔ
③ ⓒ, ⓔ
④ ⓐ, ⓒ, ⓔ
⑤ ⓐ, ⓑ, ⓓ

U29_1

06 Which correction is correct? 2점

네가 시간이 있으면, 그것에 대해 얘기할 수 있을 텐데.
= We can talk about it if you had time.

① can talk → talked
② can → could
③ if → unless
④ had → would have
⑤ time → a time

U30_2

07 주어진 문장과 가장 가까운 뜻을 갖고 있는 것은? 2점

I wish I could take away your sadness.

① I'm sorry I could take away your sadness.
② I'm sorry I'm able to take away your sadness.
③ I'm sorry I could not take away your sadness.
④ I'm sorry I can't take away your sadness.
⑤ I'm sorry I wasn't able to take away your sadness.

U30_1+U29_1

08 Find ALL of the grammatically <u>incorrect</u> sentences. 3점

① I wish there is no war in the world.
② Which would you buy if you are me?
③ He hopes everything is going well with you.
④ She treats me as if I were a serious patient.
⑤ If I had a driver's license, I will drive you home.

09 다음 문장을 실현 가능성이 희박한 현재의 소망을 나타내는 말로 바꿀 때 알맞지 <u>않은</u> 것은? 3점

U30_1

① I am too tall.
→ I wish I were a little shorter.

② I can't speak Italian.
→ I wish I could speak Italian.

③ I don't have enough money to buy medicine.
→ I wish I had enough money to buy medicine.

④ I drink too much soda.
→ I wish I didn't drink too much soda.

⑤ I have to finish my homework this evening.
→ I wish I don't have to finish my homework this evening.

U30_3

10 Choose the <u>necessary words</u> to complete the sentence. 4점

It seems to me (as, were, are, my coat, he, though, wearing, did).

→ _____

U29_2

11 두 문장의 뜻이 같도록 할 때 빈칸에 알맞은 말을 쓰시오. 4점

He is sick, so he cannot climb the mountain with us.

→ If he _____ sick, he _____
_____ the mountain with us.

U29_1

12 주어진 조건과 상황에 맞게 문장을 완성하시오. 5점

·조건 1   가정법 과거로 쓸 것
·조건 2   아래 상황에 쓰인 단어를 이용할 것
·상황   Kyle is not my friend. However, he is your friend. Any friend of yours is a friend of mine. So I will invite him.

→ I _____ _____ Kyle if he
_____ _____ your friend.

U29_1

13 다음 영작에서 어법상 <u>어색한</u> 것을 찾아 고치시오. 3점

만약 모든 멤버들이 같이 갈 수 있으면 더 좋을 텐데.
= It will be better if all the members could go together.

_____ → _____

U29_3

14 Look at the picture and complete the sentence by using the given words. 5점

(1) If I _____ hard, I _____
_____ the exam. (study, pass)

(2) If I _____ hard, I _____
_____ the exam. (study, pass)

U29_1

15 우리말과 같은 뜻이 되도록 주어진 단어를 배열해서 문장을 완성하시오. 5점

내가 너라면 이것을 절대 팔지 않을 거야.
I, I, never, you, would, were, this, sell

→ If _____, _____.

U30_4

16 대화의 빈칸에 알맞은 말을 쓰시오. 3점

A: Your ring looks as if it were made of gold.
B: Not at all. In fact, it _____
_____ plastic.

17 다음 상황 설명을 읽고 주어진 단어를 이용해서 문장을 완성하시오. 4점

> I have a friend named Seojoon. He and I have been good friends for a long time. However, he has one weak point. He uses my things without asking if it's okay or not. It sometimes makes me very angry. When he does this, what should I say to him?

→ I wish you _____ _____ _____ my things

without permission. (will, stop, use)

18 다음 문장을 아래와 같이 바꿀 때 빈칸에 공통으로 들어 갈 한 단어를 쓰시오. 3점

> • I don't have a good memory.
> → I wish I _____ a good memory.
> • Linda doesn't have a better answer.
> → Linda wishes she _____ a better answer.

→ _____

19 Find the error and correct it. 3점

> Mr. Sim is under a lot of pressure at the moment. He feels as if he has the weight of the world on his shoulders.

_____ → _____

20 Find the error in each sentence and correct them. 4점

한눈에 쏙

> ⓐ Sometimes I wish you are not my brother.
> ⓑ She says hi to me as if she knows me, but I don't know her.
> ⓒ If she's not careless, she wouldn't make errors.

( ) _____ → _____

( ) _____ → _____

( ) _____ → _____

[21~22] 다음 글을 읽고 물음에 답하시오.

Just think of the way ⓐ**an elephant uses its nose**. It uses its nose ⓑ**to carry things, to smell food, and to fight enemy**. When an elephant is thirsty, it can drink six liters with one noseful. It also uses its nose to take a bath. An elephant's nose has no bones. This ⓒ**makes it soft and easy to bend**. (A)그것이 구부리기가 쉽지 않다면, an elephant ⓓ**won't be able to hold** the little peanuts. Definitely, ⓔ**an elephant's nose is the most useful nose** in the world.

21 윗글의 밑줄 친 ⓐ~ⓔ 중 어법상 어색한 것은? 3점

★ 고난도

① ⓐ

② ⓑ

③ ⓒ

④ ⓓ

⑤ ⓔ

22 윗글의 밑줄 친 (A)를 주어진 조건에 맞게 영작하시오. 6점

> • 조건 1 어휘 – is, were, bend, bent
> • 조건 2 가정법 구문을 이용할 것
> • 조건 3 주어진 어휘 중 필요한 것만 쓸 것
> • 조건 4 총 7단어로 쓸 것

→ _____

불규칙 동사 변화표

불규칙 동사도
외우는 방법이 있다!

1 A – A – A 형태 동일

★표시는 필수 기본 동사들

원형	뜻	과거	과거분사
broadcast	방송하다	broadcast	broadcast
bet	돈을 걸다	bet	bet
burst	파열하다	burst	burst
cast	던지다	cast	cast
cost	비용이 들다	cost	cost
★cut	자르다	cut	cut
forecast	예고하다	forecast	forecast
★hit	치다	hit	hit
hurt	아프게 하다	hurt	hurt
let	~하게 하다	let	let
★put	놓다	put	put
quit	~을 그만두다	quit	quit
★read	읽다	read [red]	read [red]
rid	~을 제거하다	rid	rid
set	놓다	set	set
shed	흘리다	shed	shed
shut	닫다	shut	shut
spit	침을 뱉다	spit	spit
split	쪼개다	split	split
spread	펴다	spread	spread
thrust	찌르다	thrust	thrust
upset	뒤엎다	upset	upset

2 A – A – A' 과거분사만 살짝 바뀜

원형	뜻	과거	과거분사
beat	때리다, 이기다	beat	beaten

3 A – B – A 과거형에서 모음만 바뀜

원형	뜻	과거	과거분사
★come	오다	came	come
★become	되다	became	become
★run	달리다	ran	run

4 A – B – A' 과거형은 모음 변화, 과거분사형은 원형에 –n 붙임

원형	뜻	과거	과거분사
arise [əráiz]	(일이) 일어나다	arose [əróuz]	arisen [ərizn]
★be (am, is, are)	～이다	was, were	been
blow	불다	blew [bluː]	blown [bloun]
★do, does	하다	did	done
draw	당기다, 그리다	drew [druː]	drawn [drɔːn]
★drive	운전하다	drove [drouv]	driven [drivn]
★eat	먹다	ate	eaten
fall	떨어지다	fell	fallen
forbid	금지하다	forbade	forbidden
forgive	용서하다	forgave	forgiven
forsake	그만두다, 저버리다	forsook	forsaken
★give	주다	gave [geiv]	given [givn]
★go	가다	went [went]	gone [gɔːn]
★grow	자라다	grew [gruː]	grown [groun]
★know	알다	knew [njuː]	known [noun]
ride	(차, 말 등을) 타다	rode [roud]	ridden [ridn]
rise	일어서다	rose [rouz]	risen [rizn]
★see	보다	saw [sɔː]	seen [siːn]
shake	흔들다	shook [ʃuk]	shaken [ʃeikn]
show	보여주다, 보이다	showed	shown, showed
sow [sou]	(씨를) 뿌리다	sowed [soud]	sown [soun]
strive	노력하다	strove [strouv]	striven [strivn]
★take	잡다	took [tuk]	taken [teikn]
thrive	번영하다	throve [θrouv], thrived	thriven [θrivn], thrived
★throw	던지다	threw [θruː]	thrown [θroun]
withdraw	물러나다	withdrew [wiðdrúː]	withdrawn [wiðdrɔ́ːn]
★write	쓰다	wrote [rout]	written [ritn]

5 A – B – B 원형에 –t 붙임

원형	뜻	과거	과거분사
bend	구부리다	bent	bent
★build	세우다	built	built
burn	태우다	burnt, burned	burnt, burned
deal	다루다	dealt [delt]	dealt
dwell	거주하다, 살다	dwelt, dwelled	dwelt, dwelled
lend	빌려주다	lent	lent
mean	의미하다	meant [ment]	meant
★send	보내다	sent	sent
smell	냄새 맡다, 냄새가 나다	smelt, smelled	smelt, smelled

spend	소비하다	spent	spent
spoil	망쳐놓다	spoilt, spoiled	spoilt, spoiled

6 A – B – B 원형의 자음 + ought/aught

원형	뜻	과거	과거분사
*bring	가져오다	brought [brɔːt]	brought
*buy	사다	bought [bɔːt]	bought
*catch	잡다	caught [kɔːt]	caught
*fight	싸우다	fought [fɔːt]	fought
seek	찾다	sought [sɔːt]	sought
*teach	가르치다	taught [tɔːt]	taught
*think	생각하다	thought [θɔːt]	thought

7 A – B – B 원형의 자음 + ound

원형	뜻	과거	과거분사
bind	묶다	bound [baund]	bound
*find	발견하다	found [faund]	found

8 A – B – B 원형의 모음이 하나로 줄고 + t

원형	뜻	과거	과거분사
creep	기다, 포복하다	crept [krept]	crept
*feel	느끼다	felt	felt
*keep	유지하다	kept	kept
kneel [niːl]	무릎 꿇다, 굴복하다	knelt [nelt]	knelt
*leave	떠나다	left	left
*lose [luːz]	잃다	lost [lɔːst]	lost
*sleep	자다	slept	slept
sweep	쓸다	swept [swept]	swept

9 A – B – B 원형의 모음이 하나로 줄어듦

원형	뜻	과거	과거분사
feed	먹이다	fed [fed]	fed
*meet	만나다	met [met]	met
shoot [ʃuːt]	쏘다	shot [ʃɑt]	shot

10 A – B – B y를 i로 바꾸고 -d를 붙임

원형	뜻	과거	과거분사
lay	두다	laid [leid]	laid
*pay	지불하다	paid [peid]	paid
*say	말하다	said [sed]	said

11 A – B – B 원형에서 모음만 바뀜

원형	뜻	과거	과거분사
behold	~를 보다	beheld	beheld
bleed	피를 흘리다	bled	bled
breed	기르다	bred	bred
cling	달라붙다	clung	clung
dig	파다	dug [dʌg]	dug
fling	내던지다	flung	flung
hang	걸다	hung	hung
*hold	잡다, 손에 들다	held	held
lead	이끌다	led	led
shine	빛나다	shone [ʃoun]	shone
*sit	앉다	sat [sæt]	sat
spin	(실을) 잣다	spun [spʌn]	spun
*stand	서다	stood [stud]	stood
stick	찌르다	stuck	stuck
sting	쏘다	stung	stung
strike	때리다	struck [strʌk]	struck
*win	이기다	won [wʌn]	won
wind [waind]	감다	wound [waund]	wound
withhold	보류하다	withheld	withheld

12 A – B – B 모음 변화, 끝에 -d 붙임

원형	뜻	과거	과거분사
flee	도망치다	fled [fled]	fled
*have, has	가지다	had	had
*hear [hiər]	듣다	heard [həːrd]	heard
*make	만들다	made	made
*sell	팔다	sold	sold
slide	미끄러지다	slid	slid
*tell	말하다	told	told

13 A – B – B' 모음 변화, 과거형 + n

원형	뜻	과거	과거분사
awake [əwéik]	깨다	awoke [əwóuk]	awoken [əwoukn]
*bear [bɛər]	낳다	bore [bɔər]	born [bɔːrn]
bite	물다	bit [bit]	bitten [bitn]
*break	깨뜨리다	broke [brouk]	broken [broukn]
*choose	고르다	chose [tʃouz]	chosen [tʃouzn]
*forget	잊다	forgot [fərgát]	forgotten [fərgátn]
freeze	얼음이 얼다	froze [frouz]	frozen [frouzn]
*get	얻다	got [gɑt]	gotten [gɑtn]
*hide	감추다	hid [hid]	hidden [hidn]
*speak	말하다	spoke [spouk]	spoken [spoukn]
steal	훔치다	stole [stoul]	stolen [stouln]
swear	맹세하다	swore [swɔər]	sworn [swɔːrn]
tear [tɛər]	찢다	tore [tɔər]	torn [tɔːrn]
tread [tred]	걷다, 짓밟다	trod [trɑd]	trodden [trɑdn]
wake	깨다	woke	woken
*wear	입다	wore [wɔər]	worn [wɔːrn]

14 A – B – C

원형	뜻	과거	과거분사
*begin	시작하다	began [bigǽn]	begun [bigʌ́n]
*drink	마시다	drank [dræŋk]	drunk [drʌŋk]
*fly	날다	flew [fluː]	flown [floun]
lie	가로눕다	lay [lei]	lain [lein]
cf. lie (규칙 변화)	거짓말하다	lied	lied
*ring	울리다	rang [ræŋ]	rung [rʌŋ]
shrink	줄어들다	shrank [ʃræŋk]	shrunk [ʃrʌŋk]
*sing	노래하다	sang [sæŋ]	sung [sʌŋ]
sink	가라앉다	sank [sæŋk]	sunk [sʌŋk]
spring	튀다	sprang [spræŋ]	sprung [sprʌŋ]
*swim	수영하다	swam [swæm]	swum [swʌm]

15 조동사

원형	뜻	과거
*must	~해야 한다	(had to)
*can	~할 수 있다	could [cud]
*may	~해도 좋다	might [mait]
shall	~할 것이다	should [ʃud]
*will	~할 것이다	would [wud]

16 뜻에 따라 활용이 달라지는 불규칙 동사

원형	뜻	과거	과거분사
bear	참다	bore	borne
	낳다	bore	born
bid	명령하다	bade	bidden
	말하다	bid	bid
hang	걸다	hung	hung
	교수형에 처하다	hanged	hanged

17 혼동하기 쉬운 불규칙 동사와 규칙 동사

원형	뜻	과거	과거분사
bind	묶다	bound [baund]	bound
bound [baund]	되튀다	bounded	bounded
fall	떨어지다, 쓰러지다	fell	fallen
fell	쓰러뜨리다	felled	felled
find	발견하다	found [faund]	found
found [faund]	세우다, 창립하다	founded	founded
fly	날다	flew [flu:]	flown [floun]
flow	흐르다	flowed	flowed
lie	눕다	lay	lain
lay	눕히다, 낳다	laid	laid
see	보다	saw	seen
saw [sɔ:]	톱질하다	sawed [sɔ:d]	sawed, sawn [sɔ:n]
sew [sou]	바느질하다	sewed [soud]	sewed, sewn [soun]
sit	앉다	sat	sat
set	두다	set	set
wind	감다	wound [waund]	wound
wound [wu:nd]	상처를 입히다	wounded	wounded
welcome	환영하다	welcomed	welcomed
overcome	이겨내다, 극복하다	overcame	overcome

MEMO

MEMO

MEMO

신영주

2급 외국어 정교사 자격증, UCSD TESOL 취득(국제영어교사 교육자격증, University of California)
(전) EBSi 온라인 강사, 대치 시대인재, 이강학원 강사
(현) 프라우드 세븐 어학원 원장, 리딩타운 원장
저서: 체크체크, 올백(천재교육), 투탑 영어(디딤돌), Grammar 콕, VOCA콕(꿈을담는틀), 중학 영문법 클리어(동아) 등 다수의 교재 공저

이건희

쥬기스(http://jugis.co.kr) 대표
저서: 맨처음 수능 시리즈 – 맨처음 수능 영문법, 맨처음 수능 영어(기본, 실력, 독해, 완성)
　　　내공 시리즈 – 내공 중학영문법, 내공 중학 영어구문, 내공 중학영어듣기 모의고사 20회
　　　체크체크(천재교육), Grammar In(비상교육) 외 다수
instagram@gunee27

최신개정판
내신공략 중학영문법 **2** 문제풀이책

지은이 신영주, 이건희
펴낸이 정규도
펴낸곳 (주)다락원

개정판 1쇄 발행 2021년 3월 15일
개정판 7쇄 발행 2024년 12월 23일

책임편집 정지인, 김민주
디자인 구수정
조판 블랙엔화이트
영문 감수 Michael A. Putlack
삽화 김진용

다락원 경기도 파주시 문발로 211
내용문의: (02)736-2031 내선 532
구입문의: (02)736-2031 내선 250~252
Fax: (02)732-2037
출판등록 1977년 9월 16일 제406-2008-000007호

Copyright ©2021, 신영주, 이건희

저자 및 출판사의 허락 없이 이 책의 일부 또는 전부를 무단 복제·
전재·발췌할 수 없습니다. 구입 후 철회는 회사 내규에 부합하는
경우에 가능하므로 구입문의처에 문의하시기 바랍니다. 분실·파
손 등에 따른 소비자 피해에 대해서는 공정거래위원회에서 고시한
소비자 분쟁 해결 기준에 따라 보상 가능합니다. 잘못된 책은 바꿔
드립니다.

ISBN 978-89-277-0892-6 54740
　　　978-89-277-0888-9 54740(set)

http://www.darakwon.co.kr
다락원 홈페이지를 방문하시면 상세한 출판 정보와 함께 동영상 강좌,
MP3 자료 등 다양한 어학 정보를 얻으실 수 있습니다.

내공 중학영문법

신 공 략

신영주 ✦ 이건희 지음

최신개정판

신유형과 고난도 서술형 문제로
중학영어 내신 완벽 대비

문제풀이책

정답 및 해설

2

DARAKWON

내신공략
중학영문법

문제풀이책 2
정답 및 해설

CHAPTER 01
문장의 형식

UNIT 01 1형식, 2형식, 3형식

1) 주어	2) 동사	3) 동사
4) 주어	5) 형용사	6) 명사
7) 형용사	8) 형용사	9) 명사
10) 대명사	11) to부정사구	12) 동명사구

Level 1 Test
p. 12

A 1 There <u>was</u> <u>a portable computer</u> on the desk.
          V   S

2 <u>My little brother</u> <u>walks</u> to school.
          S   V

3 <u>He</u> <u>is becoming</u> <u>nervous</u>.
    S   V   C

4 <u>She</u> <u>didn't look</u> <u>intelligent</u>.
    S   V   C

5 <u>She</u> <u>was</u> <u>frightened</u> of him.
    S   V   C

B 1 bravely   2 safe
3 surprising   4 healthy
5 soft

C 1 2형식   2 1형식
3 2형식   4 1형식

D 1 playing   2 quickly
3 yellow   4 to do[doing]

Level 2 Test
p. 13

01 ②   02 ④ ⑤
03 ⑤   04 ③
05 The plan will work well.
06 (A) happily   (B) happy   (C) happy
07 He became a famous musician.
08 He has to look after his little brother.

≫ 해설

01 목적어로 to talk를 취할 수 없는 동사는 enjoy동사로 목적어로 동명사 talking이 와야 알맞다.
02 get은 상태동사로 다음에 형용사가 와서 보어 역할을 하는 2형식 동사이다.
03 감각동사 sound 다음에 형용사 perfect가 알맞다.
04 sound는 형용사를 보어로 취하므로 good이 옳다. well이 형용사이면 '건강한'이란 뜻이다.
05 work(실행되다, 작동하다)는 1형식 동사로 그 다음에는 부사 well이 알맞다.

06 1형식 문장에서 부사 happily, look 감각동사 다음에 형용사형 happy, 명사 life를 수식하는 형용사 happy가 알맞다.
07 상태 변화 동사 become(~해지다)은 2형식 동사로 보어로는 형용사 뿐만 아니라 명사도 올 수 있다. 여기서 주격 보어는 a famous musician이다. become의 과거형은 became이다.
08 look after(~을 돌보다)는 구동사로, 이 문장은 동사 다음에 목적어가 바로 오는 3형식 문장이다.

Level 3 Test
p. 14

01 ⑤   02 ⑤
03 ②   04 ④
05 ③   06 ⑤
07 ①   08 ③
09 ③   10 ① ② ③
11 ④
12 (A) heavily   (B) noisy
13 ⓒ to listen → listening
14 looks like a doll but looks sad
15 quiet → quietly
16 The new smartphone looked good and sold well.

≫ 해설

01 ⑤는 「주어+동사+주격 보어」의 2형식 문장이고, 나머지는 「주어+동사+수식어구」의 1형식 문장이다.
02 look은 3형식 동사로 angrily가 아닌 angry가 필요하다. → ⑤ The monster looks very angry.
① I need more time. ② She said hi to me. ③ Here comes Santa Claus. ④ They were at the starting line.
03 ⓐ 지각동사 sound 다음에 형용사가 와야 한다. (ridiculously → ridiculous) ⓒ 3형식 문장에서 '잘 대답하지 못했다.'이므로 부사가 와야 한다. (good → well)
04 lonely(외로운)는 형용사로 보어 역할을 하므로 2형식 동사가 와야 한다. live는 1형식 동사로 부사가 와야 한다. (alone은 형용사와 부사 둘 다 쓰일 수 있으므로 가능하다.)
05 의미상 '새로운 집으로 이사 가길 원해서 새로운 집을 찾는다.'는 의미이므로 look for(~을 찾다)가 알맞다.
06 be동사(~이다)는 2형식 동사로 보어 자리에 형용사나 명사가 온다.
07 2형식 문장의 보어로 명사, 분사, to부정사, 형용사, 동명사 등이 올 수 있다. 부사는 보어 역할을 할 수 없으므로 형용사로 바꾸어야 한다. ② peacefully → peaceful ③ badly → bad ⑤ patiently → patient ④는 1형식 문장으로 주어가 복수형 people이므로 동사는 were가 알맞다.
08 ⓓ ⓔ enjoy와 practice는 목적어로 동명사를 취한다. (to participate → participating, to play → playing)
09 solve는 목적어 the problem을 취할 수 있는 3형식 동사로 형용사 easy가 아니라 부사 easily가 와서 보충 설명할 수 있다.
10 ① few 다음에는 셀 수 있는 복수 명사가 오므로 fish는 복수형이고 동사는 were가 되어야 한다. ② 주어가 복수형(the teachers)이므로 동사는 come이 알맞다. ③ seem 다음에 형용사가 보어 역할을 하므로 happy가 되어야 한다.
11 promise동사는 목적어로 to부정사를, keep동사는 동명사를 취한다.
12 It rained ~.는 1형식 문장으로 부사 heavily가 알맞고, 감각동사 sound는 형용사가 보어 역할을 하므로 noise(소리)의 형용사형

noisy(시끄러운)가 알맞다.

13 enjoy는 목적어로 동명사를 취한다.

14 a doll은 명사이므로 '~처럼 보인다'는 의미의 look like를 쓴다. sad 는 형용사이므로 감각동사 look 뒤에 바로 온다.

15 read는 3형식 동사로, 목적어 the books 뒤에는 부사 quietly가 알 맞다.

16 look 다음에 형용사 good이 보어 역할을 하고, sell well은 '잘 팔린 다'는 의미이다. sell의 과거형은 sold이다.

UNIT 02 4형식, 5형식

1) to   2) for   3) of
4) 명사   5) 형용사

Level 1 Test
p. 16

A 1 I wrote her an email.
           IO   DO
  2 We made a birthday cake for Mom.
              O
  3 I named my hedgehog Ddochi.
             O   OC
  4 The results of the test made me disappointed.
                          O   OC

B 1 They lent their tent to us.
  2 I bought her a flower.
  3 Exercising every day makes you healthy.

C 1 My uncle sent a box of apples to me.
  2 He made colorful kites for them.
  3 She asked a personal question of me.
  4 The rabbit found a secret key for us.

Level 2 Test
p. 17

01 ①   02 ③
03 ③   04 ① ② ③
05 cooked ramen for   06 busily → busy
07 made / angry
08 The millionaire gave her a diamond bracelet.

》》 해설

01 bring은 간접 목적어 앞에 전치사 to를, buy는 전치사 for를 쓴다.

02 lent동사는 간접 목적어 앞에 전치사 to를, ask는 of를 쓴다.

03 ③은 5형식 문장이고 나머지는 4형식 문장이다.

04 ① ② write, teach 동사는 전치사 to를 쓴다. ③ 목적격 보어 자리에 는 형용사가 오므로 strong이 알맞다.

05 4형식 문장을 3형식으로 바꿀 때는 간접 목적어와 직접 목적어의 순 서를 바꾸고, 간접 목적어 앞에 전치사를 넣는다. cook은 전치사 for 를 쓴다.

06 kept의 목적어(me) 다음에 목적격 보어로 형용사가 알맞으므로 부사 busily가 형용사 busy로 바뀌어야 한다. (이 프로젝트는 지난 몇 주

동안 나를 계속 바쁘게 했다.)

07 5형식 동사 make(~을 …하게 만들다)의 목적격 보어로 형용사 angry를 쓴다.

08 주어진 단어에 전치사가 없으므로 「주어(the millionaire)+수여동사 (gave)+간접 목적어(her)+직접 목적어(a diamond bracelet)」의 순서가 알맞다.

Level 3 Test
p. 18

01 ②   02 ②
03 ⑤   04 ③
05 ③   06 ④
07 ②   08 ① ③
09 ①   10 ⑤
11 ⑤
12 buy a new CD for my sister
13 ⓑ to a scholar → a scholar
14 My science teacher asked it of us.
15 The trash makes the park messy.
16 This scent keeps me fresh all day.

》》 해설

01 ⓒ keep동사는 목적격 보어 자리에 형용사가 온다. (freshly → fresh) ⓓ inquire동사는 간접 목적어 앞에 전치사 of를 쓴다. (for → of)

02 give동사는 간접 목적어 앞에 전치사 to를, cook동사는 전치사 for 를 쓴다.

03 make동사는 간접 목적어 앞에 전치사 for를 쓴다.

04 주어진 문장과 ③은 「주어+동사+간접 목적어+직접 목적어」의 4형 식 문장이고, ①, ②는 「주어+동사+보어」의 2형식, ④는 「주어+동 사+목적어」의 3형식, ⑤는 「유도부사+동사+주어+수식어구」의 1 형식 문장이다.

05 3형식, 4형식(수여동사), 5형식(사역동사)에 모두 쓰이는 동사는 make이다.

06 buy동사는 간접 목적어 앞에 전치사 for를 쓴다.

07 give동사 다음에 전치사 없이 간접 목적어 me를 그대로 쓰는 것이 맞다.

08 ① 4형식의 경우 직접 목적어 자리에 대명사를 쓸 수 없다. (me it → it of me) ③ 목적격 보어 자리에 형용사가 와야 한다. (successfully → successful)

09 「동사(find)+목적어(your advice)+목적격 보어(useful)」의 순서를 취하는 5형식 문장이다.

10 대명사가 두 개 연속 나오면 3형식만 사용할 수 있다. ① him it → it to him ② her it → it to her ③ her them → them to her ④ us them → them to us

11 ⑤의 give는 4형식 동사로 명사가 직접 목적어 역할을 할 수 있고, 나 머지는 목적격 보어로 형용사를 쓸 수 있는 5형식 동사이다.

12 buy가 쓰인 3형식 문장으로 간접 목적어 앞에 for를 쓴다.

13 call동사는 목적어(him) 다음에 목적격 보어로 명사형(a scholar)을 쓴다. 전치사 to를 삭제해야 한다. (우리는 그를 학자라고 부른다.)

14 4형식의 경우 직접 목적어 자리에 대명사를 쓸 수 없으므로 3형식 문 장으로 바꾸어 써야 알맞다. ask는 전치사 of를 쓴다.

15 '쓰레기가 공원을 지저분하게 만든다.'라는 문장을 만들 수 있다. 주어 가 3인칭 단수(The trash)이므로 동사는 makes로 써야 하고, 이어

서 목적어(the park)를 쓰고 목적격 보어(messy)를 형용사 형태 그대로 쓴다.

16 '~를 …하게 유지하다'의 의미인 keep을 써서 5형식 구문으로 쓴다.

UNIT 03 5형식

1) to부정사　　2) to부정사　　3) 동사원형
4) 동사원형　　5) to　　　　 6) 동사원형
7) to　　　　 8) 동사원형　　9) 지각
10) 사역　　　11) 과거분사

Level 1 Test

p. 20

A　1　The audience found the performance <u>funny</u>.
　　2　The referee allowed him <u>to join the game</u>.
　　3　Mr. Lee saw his son <u>go into the Internet café</u>.
　　4　His mean words made her <u>angry</u>.

B　1　to clean　　　　　2　to keep
　　3　prepare　　　　　4　flying
　　5　get

C　1　Don't make me laugh.
　　2　We told her not to tell a lie.
　　3　I didn't see the kid steal the wallet.

Level 2 Test

p. 21

01　②　　　　　　　　02　① ④
03　④　　　　　　　　04　② ③ ④
05　I heard my neighbors argue
06　playing[play] basketball
07　repair → repaired
08　Dad made me read the newspaper every morning.

》》 해설

01　ⓒ 지각동사는 목적격 보어로 동사원형이나 현재분사를 쓴다. (to run → run[running])
02　지각동사 watch는 목적격 보어로 동사원형이나 현재분사를 취한다.
03　want동사는 3형식에서 목적어로 to부정사를 취하고, 5형식에서도 목적격 보어로 to부정사를 취한다.
04　① 사역동사 make는 목적격 보어로 동사원형을 취한다. (wiping → wipe) ⑤ help는 목적격 보어로 동사원형이나 to부정사가 온다. (going → go[to go])
05　「지각동사(heard)+목적어(my neighbors)+목적격 보어 (argue[arguing])」의 어순으로 쓴다.
06　「watch(지각동사)+목적어+목적격 보어」 구문이므로 목적어로 some children, 목적격 보어로는 진행의 의미를 강조하는 playing이 가장 적절하고, 동사원형 play도 가능하다.
07　내 시계가 수리되는 것이라서 목적어와 목적격 보어의 관계가 수동이므로 과거분사 repaired가 와야 알맞다.
08　「주어(Dad)+동사(made)+목적어(me)+목적격 보어(read)」의 순서로 영작한다.

Level 3 Test

p. 22

01　①　　　　　　　　02　③
03　① ②　　　　　　　04　①
05　① ② ③　　　　　　06　①
07　⑤　　　　　　　　08　②
09　③　　　　　　　　10　③
11　let me go outside
12　I heard him mumble[mumbling] to himself.
13　Her advice helped me make the right decision.
14　Green tea makes the body burn fat.
15　ⓑ carry → carried
16　My sister told me to feed the horse.

》》 해설

01　ⓐ 지각동사 watch의 목적격 보어로 동사원형이나 현재분사가 온다. (had → have[having]) ⓕ encourage동사는 목적격 보어로 to부정사가 온다. (work → to work)
02　지각동사 hear의 목적격 보어로 동사원형이나 현재분사가 오므로 make 또는 making이 알맞다.
03　지각동사(watch)는 목적격 보어로 동사원형이나 현재분사를 취한다.
04　준사역동사 help는 목적격 보어로 to부정사나 동사원형이 올 수 있고, 사역동사 make는 목적격 보어로 동사원형이 오므로 공통으로 올 수 있는 것은 동사원형이다.
05　④ 사역동사 had는 목적격 보어로 동사원형 bake를 써야 알맞다. ⑤ tell동사는 목적격 보어로 to clean이 와야 알맞다.
06　사역동사 let은 목적격 보어로 동사원형을 취한다.
07　⑤는 「수여동사+간접 목적어+직접 목적어」의 4형식이고, 나머지는 「동사+목적어+목적격 보어」의 5형식이다.
08　준사역동사 get과 tell동사는 둘 다 목적격 보어로 to부정사가 온다.
09　made는 목적격 보어 자리에 형용사, 명사, 동사원형이 올 수 있고, help는 to부정사나 동사원형이 올 수 있다. 현재분사 thinking이 쓰일 자리는 없다.
10　각각 「leave+목적어+목적격 보어(형용사)」, 「get+목적어+목적격 보어(to부정사)」 구문이다. open은 형용사로 '열려 있는'이라는 의미이고, 동사로 '열다'의 뜻이 있다.
11　「주어+let+목적어+동사원형」의 5형식 문장으로 부정어 don't가 들어가도 순서는 똑같다.
12　주어진 두 개의 문장을 합쳐서 지각동사가 쓰인 5형식 문장으로 만드는 문제이다. 「주어(I)+지각동사(heard)+목적어(him)+목적격 보어 (mumble 또는 mumbling)」의 형태로 만든다.
13　준사역동사 help는 목적격 보어로 to부정사나 동사원형을 취한다. 8단어로 쓰기 위해서는 to를 쓰지 않고 동사원형을 써야 한다.
14　사역동사 make는 목적격 보어로 동사원형을 취한다.
15　그녀의 가방이 옮겨져야 하는 수동의 관계이므로 과거분사형 carried를 쓰는 것이 알맞다.
16　tell동사는 목적격 보어로 to부정사가 온다.

Review Test

p. 24

01　①　　　　　　　　02　⑤
03　⑤　　　　　　　　04　③
05　②　　　　　　　　06　③ ⑤
07　① ③　　　　　　　08　②

4

09 ② 　　　　　　　　10 ③

11 There is

12 (1) brightly　 (2) bright

13 freshly → fresh

14 I saw my cellphone wash → I saw my cellphone washed

15 He told me to leave him alone.

16 ⓑ walk → to walk

17 he → him

18 I listened to her speak[speaking] in public.

19 He helped me (to) solve the math problem.

20 The soldiers didn't let them cross the border.

21 ③

22 won't make you a good player

》》 해설

01 감각동사 sound 다음에 형용사 sad가 와야 알맞다.

02 형용사 cool과 어울리는 2형식 동사들이 알맞다. change는 1형식 또는 3형식 동사이다.

03 smell은 감각동사로 뒤의 형용사와 함께 '~한 냄새가 나다'라는 의미가 된다. sweetly는 부사이므로 형용사인 sweet가 와야 한다.

04 동사 get이 사용된 4형식 문장을 3형식으로 전환할 경우 전치사 for를 간접 목적어 앞에 써야 한다.

05 ⓑ ⓕ give, send동사는 간접 목적어 앞에 전치사 to를 쓴다.

06 buy의 4형식 문장은 「주어＋동사＋간접 목적어＋직접 목적어」 순서이고, 3형식 문장은 간접 목적어가 문장 뒤로 가면서 전치사 for를 쓴다.

07 ② ④ 사역동사 make는 목적격 보어로 동사원형을 써야 한다. ⑤ tell 동사는 목적격 보어로 to buy가 와야 알맞다.

08 준사역동사 help, get과 advise, ask동사 모두 목적격 보어로 to부정사가 올 수 있다. ② 사역동사(make)는 목적격 보어로 동사원형이 온다.

09 ② 지각동사 watch는 목적격 보어 자리에 run이나 running이 알맞다.

10 첫 번째는 직원이 무대 조명을 나르는 능동의 관계이므로 carry, 두 번째는 무대 조명이 날라지는 수동의 관계이므로 carried가 알맞다.

11 셀 수 없는 명사는 단수 취급한다. 「there is＋단수 주어」: ~이 있다

12 (1) The sun shines ~.는 1형식 문장으로 부사 brightly가 알맞다.
(2) 5형식 동사 make는 목적어(the world) 다음에 목적격 보어 자리에 형용사 bright를 써야 알맞다.

13 감각동사 look은 형용사를 주격 보어로 취하므로 부사 freshly를 형용사 fresh로 고쳐야 한다.

14 '내 핸드폰이 세탁된 것을 보았다'에서 목적어와 목적격 보어의 관계는 수동이므로 과거분사 washed가 알맞다.

15 tell동사는 목적격 보어로 to부정사가 온다. (leave him alone 그를 혼자 내버려두다)

16 advise동사는 목적격 보어로 to부정사가 오므로 to walk가 되어야 알맞다.

17 「주어＋지각동사(saw)＋목적어(him)＋목적격 보어(change)」 구문이 되어야 하므로 목적어 자리에 있는 he를 목적격 him으로 써야 한다.

18 listen to는 「주어＋동사＋목적어＋목적격 보어(동사원형/현재분사)」 형태의 5형식 문장으로도 사용된다.

19 준사역동사 help는 목적어(me) 다음에 목적격 보어로 동사원형이나 to부정사를 쓸 수 있다.

20 영영풀이는 '누군가에게 무엇을 하라는 허락을 하다'로 let이다. 사역

동사이므로 목적격 보어로 동사원형을 쓰면 된다.

21 ⓑ want는 to부정사를 목적어로 취하므로 옳고, ⓒ 「지각동사＋목적어＋목적격 보어」에서 동사원형이 바르게 쓰였고, ⓔ and를 기준으로 pick up ~, bounce와 병렬구조이므로 적절하다. ⓐ 주어 자리이므로 Becoming 또는 To become으로 써야 한다. ⓓ 「give＋간접목적어＋직접목적어」 구문으로 to를 빼야 한다.

22 make가 4형식으로 쓰인 것으로 동사구 won't make를 쓰고 간접목적어(you) 직접목적어(a good player)순으로 쓰면 된다.

[21~22]

　하루 만에 무엇인가에 최고가 되는 것은 불가능하다. 예를 들어, 만약 네가 농구를 잘하고 싶으면, 너는 경험 있는 선수들이 경기를 하는 것을 보고 기초 기술을 배워야 한다. 하지만, 이것만으로는 너를 좋은 선수로 만들지 않을 것이다. 매일 연습해라. 그것은 너에게 더 좋은 선수가 될 기회를 줄 것이다. 너는 단지 농구공을 집어 들고, 그것을 몇 번 튕기고 한 두 달 만에 챔피언이 되길 바랄 수는 없다. 너는 뛰어난 선수가 되기 위해서 많은 시간과 에너지를 쏟아 부어야 한다. 따라서 속담에 있듯이, '연습을 하면 완벽해진다.'

• 어휘 • possible 가능한 | experienced 경험 있는 | basic 기초의 | skill 기술 | practice 연습하다 | chance 기회 | bounce 튕기다 | as the old saying goes 속담에 있듯이

CHAPTER 02
to부정사

UNIT 04 명사적, 형용사적, 부사적 용법

1) 주어	2) ~하는 것은
3) 보어	4) ~하는 것이다
5) 목적어	6) ~하는 것을
7) 명사	8) 대명사
9) ~하는, ~할	10) 목적
11) ~하기 위해	12) 감정의 원인
13) ~해서	14) 판단의 근거
15) ~하다니	16) 결과
17) ~해서 (결국) …하다	18) 형용사·부사 수식
19) ~하기에	

Level 1 Test
p. 28

A　1 ⓑ　　　　　　　　2 ⓔ
　　3 ⓖ　　　　　　　　4 ⓕ
　　5 ⓒ　　　　　　　　6 ⓓ

7 ⓐ

B 1 to buy   2 to eat[have]
   3 to write on   4 To speak

Level 2 Test

p. 29

01 ①   02 ③
03 ②   04 ③
05 It is dangerous to ride
06 what I should do
07 grew up to be[become]
08 ⓑ-ⓕ-ⓒ-ⓐ-ⓔ-ⓓ

》》 해설
01 '어떻게 해야 할지(~하는 방법)'에 관해 묻고 있으므로 「how+to부정사」가 적절하다.
02 ③은 부사적 용법(목적), 나머지는 명사적 용법이다.
03 [보기]와 ②는 형용사적 용법, ① ④ ⑤는 부사적 용법, ③은 명사적 용법이다.
04 ⓐ catching → catch ⓑ for → to ⓒ This → It
05 그림으로 보아 '얼음판에서 자전거를 타는 것은 위험하다.'이므로 「가주어-진주어」 구문을 사용하면 된다.
06 「의문사+to부정사」는 「의문사+주어+should+동사원형」으로 바꿔 쓸 수 있다.
07 부사적 용법 중 '~해서 (결국) …하다'의 '결과' 용법의 to부정사를 사용하면 된다.
08 so as to ~(~하기 위해)를 이용하여 완성하면 된다.

Level 3 Test
p. 30

01 ③   02 ⑤
03 ②   04 ② ⑤
05 ③   06 ③
07 ①   08 ① ⑤
09 ②   10 ③
11 ① ④
12 to become a governor
13 which way to go
14 in order[so as] to send the message
15 ⓐ it → 삭제
16 ⓑ make → making ⓓ where to do → what to do[what he should do]

》》 해설
01 ③ '그에게 그 상자를 어디에 둬야 하는지 물어봐.'로 해석해야 한다.
02 want to A and (to) B로 연결되므로 ⑤가 맞다.
03 ②는 형용사적 용법이고 나머지는 부사적 용법이다.
04 「의문사+to부정사」 또는 「의문사+주어+should+동사원형」으로 쓸 수 있다.
05 ③은 부사적 용법 중 '감정의 원인(~해서)'이고 나머지는 모두 '목적(~하기 위해)'이다.
06 ③은 지시대명사이고 나머지는 가주어이다.
07 ⓐ ⓒ 형용사적 용법 ⓑ ⓔ 부사적 용법 ⓓ ⓕ 명사적 용법
08 to부정사의 부사적 용법 중 결과 용법으로 I woke up to find

myself in the hospital.로 영작할 수 있다.
09 보기와 ⓐ ⓓ는 부사적 용법, ⓑ ⓒ 형용사적 용법 ⓔ는 가주어 진주어 구문으로 명사적 용법이다.
10 ⓑ It이 가주어 to 이하가 진주어이다. ① 형용사적 용법 ② of 그대로 ④ It은 가주어 ⑤ 명사적 용법
11 「의문사+to부정사」 구문을 이용하여 Kate and Edward are debating who(m) to invite to the next party.로 영작할 수 있다. 또는 who(m) to invite 대신에 who(m) they should invite도 가능하다.
12 to부정사의 부사적 용법 중 '결과'를 이용하여 표현할 수 있다. (그 여자아이는 커서 주지사가 되었다.)
13 '어느 길로 가야 할지 모른다'이므로 「의문사+to부정사」를 사용해 which way to go를 쓰면 된다.
14 '~하기 위해'는 in order[so as] to ~를 사용하여 나타낼 수 있다.
15 to부정사의 목적어가 문장 내에 있으면 생략해야 한다.
16 ⓑ singing, dancing, cooking, and even+-ing형으로 병렬구조로 연결되어야 한다. ⓓ '그는 무엇을 해야 할지 모른다'가 적절하므로 what to do로 써야 한다.

UNIT 05 의미상의 주어, 부정, 기타 용법

1) for   2) of   3) not
4) to   5) that   6) cannot
7) that   8) can

Level 1 Test
p. 32

A 1 for us   2 of Ryan
   3 for me   4 of him

B 1 not to fish   2 of you not to lock

C 1 generous enough   2 too scared
   3 so funny   4 어색한 곳 없음

D 1 so / that / couldn't stay
   2 so / that / could survive

Level 2 Test
p. 33

01 ①   02 ③
03 ④   04 ④
05 not to use
06 He was diligent enough to go swimming every morning.
07 The princess was brave enough to fight the dragon.
08 too expensive for me to buy

》》 해설
01 • hard가 일반 형용사로 for가 들어간다.
   • nice가 성품 형용사로 of가 들어간다.
02 Cathy promised not to delete my folder again.으로 영작할 수 있다. to부정사의 부정은 to 앞에 not을 쓴다.
03 too ~ to…는 「so ~ that+주어+can't」로 바꿔 쓸 수 있으므로 ④

의 can을 can't로 써야 한다.

04 시제가 과거이므로 can't를 couldn't로 써야 한다.

05 to부정사의 부정은 to 앞에 not을 붙여서 만든다.

06 「so ~ that+주어+can」은 ~ enough to...로 바꿔 쓸 수 있다.

07 '~할 만큼 …한'은 ~ enough to...로 표현할 수 있다.

08 too ~ to...(너무 ~해서 …할 수 없다) 구문을 사용해서 영작하면 된다.

Level 3 Test
p. 34

01 ③ ⑤	02 ⑤
03 ① ④ ⑤	04 ②
05 ④	06 ⑤
07 ③	08 ① ④
09 ③	10 ④
11 ① ③ ⑤	

12 The pizza was too cold for me to eat.

13 ⓑ enough simple → simple enough ⓔ solve it → solve

14 too → so 또는 that I can't → to

15 too tight to wear

》》 해설

01 성품 형용사는 of를 쓰고 일반 형용사는 for를 쓴다.

02 to부정사의 부정은 to 앞에 not을 쓴다.

03 tell A (not[never]) to B(동사원형)로 써야 한다.

04 ~ enough to...는 '…할 정도로 충분히 ~한'의 의미로 나머지와 다르다.

05 '…할 정도로 충분히 ~한'은 ~ enough to...를 쓴다.

06 to부정사의 목적어가 문장의 주어와 같으므로 생략해야 한다.

07 He speaks so fast that I can't understand him. 또는 He speaks too fast for me to understand.로 영작할 수 있다.

08 ① enough smart → smart enough ④ it 삭제

09 ⓐ young too → too young ⓓ enough warm → warm enough ⓕ very → so

10 careless라는 성품형용사가 있으므로 for 대신에 of가 필요하다. ① Everybody was too tired to cook. ② He didn't know what to do next. ③ Is the ice thick enough to walk on? ⑤ We ran so as not to miss his first performance.

11 ① to부정사의 목적어가 문장의 주어이므로 it을 생략해야 하고, ③ 시제가 과거이므로 can't를 couldn't로 ⑤ enough to는 so ~ that으로 전환하므로 too를 so로 고쳐야 한다.

12 일반 형용사인 경우 「for+목적격+to부정사」로 표현한다.

13 오류는 둘 다 ⓑ에 있다. enough는 형용사를 뒤에서 꾸며주며, to부정사의 목적어와 문장의 주어가 같으면 to부정사의 목적어는 생략한다.

14 too ~ to... 또는 「so ~ that+주어+can't」를 써야 한다.

15 '이 청바지는 너무 껴서 입을 수가 없어!'라는 의미를 그림에서 유추하여 too ~ to... 구문을 사용하여 완성하면 된다.

Review Test
p. 36

01 ③	02 ②
03 ① ⑤	04 ①
05 ③	06 ④
07 ②	08 ⑤

09 ③	10 ⑤

11 on

12 pleased to win a gold medal

13 too noisy for me to study

14 hope to be a nurse

15 ⓐ of → for

16 to train / not to play

17 It is possible for freshmen to join our club.

18 too small for the man to ride

19 I didn't know when to ask for her phone number.

20 He isn't strong enough to handle hatred.

21 ④

22 Vulcan didn't want people to bother him

》》 해설

01 식당에 갔으므로 내용상 ③이 적절하다.

02 ②는 형용사적 용법이고 나머지는 부사적 용법이다.

03 「의문사+to부정사」는 「의문사+주어+should+동사원형」으로 쓸 수 있다.

04 ①은 make의 목적어로 쓰인 지시대명사이고 나머지는 가주어이다.

05 성품형용사가 오면 의미상의 주어는 of를 쓴다.

06 to부정사의 목적어가 문장 내에 있으면 삭제해야 한다.

07 「so ~ that+주어+cannot」은 too ~ to...로 전환할 수 있다.

08 일반 형용사일 때 to부정사의 의미상의 주어는 for를 쓴다. (of → for)

09 enough는 형용사나 부사의 뒤에서 수식한다.

10 ⓑ talk to[with] someone이므로 talk → talk to[with] ⓓ It ~ to... 「가주어-진주어」로 써야 한다.

11 rely on a friend, write on some paper에서 on이 공통이다.

12 '금메달을 따다'는 win a gold medal로 표현하고, '감정의 원인'을 나타내는 to부정사를 이용하면 된다.

13 「so ~ that+주어+can't」는 too ~ to...로 쓸 수 있고, noisy가 일반 형용사이므로 의미상의 주어는 「for+목적격」으로 쓴다.

14 hope동사는 to부정사를 목적어로 취한다.

15 일반 형용사가 오면 의미상의 주어에는 for를 쓴다.

16 '~하기 위해'는 to부정사로 표현할 수 있고, to부정사의 부정은 「not to+동사원형」이다.

17 It ~ for... to 구문을 이용하여 바꾸면 된다. [보기]는 can't라 impossible이고, 문제에서 주어진 문장은 can이므로 possible로 쓰면 된다.

18 too ~ to...에 의미상의 주어를 넣어 「too ~ for+목적격+to...」로 쓰면 된다.

19 「의문사+to부정사」= 「의문사+주어+should+동사원형」인데 should를 쓰지 않아야 하므로 when to ask ~로 쓰면 된다.

20 주어와 동사는 She is이고 「형용사/부사+enough to+동사원형」의 구조로 쓰면 된다.

21 ⓓ saw는 지각동사이고 a mountain이 폭발하는 것이므로 능동의 현재분사 exploding으로 써야 한다.

22 「want+목적어+to+동사원형」의 구조로 쓰이고 부정문이다. 따라서 Vulcan didn't want people을 쓰고 to를 추가하여 to bother him으로 쓰면 된다. 주어가 people이면 People didn't want Vulcan to bother him이 되므로 어색함에 주의한다.

　　불카누스는 불과 대장간의 신이었다. 그는 금속을 다루는데 전문가였고, 그는 금속을 가열하기 위해 불을 사용했다. 불카누스는 사람들이 그를 귀찮게 하는 것을 싫어해서 산 속에서 혼자 일하는 것을 좋아했다. 그가 일할 때마다, 불꽃이 산에서 튀어 올랐다. 사람들이 산이 연기와 불꽃으로 폭발하는 것을 보았을 때, 그들은 불카누스가 일하고 있다고 생각했다. 그래서 그들은 폭발하는 산을 화산이라고 불렀다.

• 어휘 • expert 전문가 | deal with 다루다 | bother 귀찮게 하다 | spark 불꽃 | explode 폭발하다

CHAPTER 03
동명사

UNIT 06 동명사의 쓰임, 동명사와 to부정사

1) 주어
2) 보어
3) 동사의 목적어
4) 전치사의 목적어
5) 동명사
6) to부정사
7) to부정사 또는 동명사
8) ~한 것을 잊다
9) ~할 것을 잊다
10) ~한 것을 기억하다(과거)
11) ~할 것을 기억하다(미래)
12) 시험 삼아 ~해보다
13) ~하려고 노력하다
14) ~하는 것을 그만두다
15) ~하기 위해 멈추다

Level 1 Test
p. 40

A 1 Listening to others is important. → ⓐ
　 2 He didn't mind waiting for her. → ⓒ
　 3 I can't sing. I am poor at singing. → ⓓ

B 1 어색한 곳 없음 　　2 walking
　 3 to travel

C 1 to take 　　2 working
　 3 meeting 　　4 to tell

Level 2 Test
p. 41

01 ④ 　　　　　　　　02 ③
03 ② 　　　　　　　　04 ⑤
05 Her hobby is reading romance novels.
06 He was afraid of going into the cave.
07 ⓐ good → well ⓑ Play → Playing[To play]
08 (A) pulling　 (B) pushing

>>> 해설

01 plan은 to부정사를 목적어로 취한다.
02 동명사 주어는 단수 취급한다.
03 [보기]와 ②는 보어로 쓰인 동명사이다. ①과 ③은 동사구의 목적어로, ④는 전치사의 목적어로, ⑤는 주어로 사용된 동명사이다.
04 ⓐ to catch → catching ⓒ going → to go ⓔ to fly → flying
05 주어와 동사는 Her hobby is이고, 보어는 동명사를 사용해야 하므로 reading으로 쓴다.
06 be afraid of는 '~을 두려워하다'이고 전치사의 목적어로 동명사가 오므로 going ~을 이어서 쓰면 된다.
07 ⓐ good은 형용사이므로 '잘'의 뜻을 가진 부사 well이 적절하다. ⓑ 주어 역할을 할 수 있는 동명사나 to부정사로 바꾸어야 한다.
08 밀어야 하는 문을 계속 당기고 있으므로 그만 당기고 한번 밀어보라고 하는 내용이 와야 한다. 「stop+ing」는 '~하는 것을 멈추다'이고 「try+ing」는 '시험 삼아 한번 ~해보다'의 의미이다.

Level 3 Test
p. 42

01 ③ ④ 　　　　　　　02 ① ⑤
03 ④ 　　　　　　　　04 ①
05 ⑤ 　　　　　　　　06 ① ② ③ ⑤
07 ② 　　　　　　　　08 ⑤
09 ④ 　　　　　　　　10 ②
11 ⓐ to avoid → avoiding
12 Taking care of children is
13 finished doing her homework
14 Don't forget to attend the practice on Monday morning.
15 stop making noise
16 meet → meeting

>>> 해설

01 want와 expect는 to부정사를 목적어로 취한다.
02 ①은 주어, ⑤는 보어로 쓰였고, [보기]와 나머지는 동사의 목적어로 쓰인 동명사이다.
03 '~을 하기 위해 (하던 것을) 멈추다'는 「stop+to부정사」를 쓴다. (그녀는 거리에서 내가 걸어가는 것을 보고 나를 태워주기 위해 멈췄다.)
04 imagine은 동명사만 목적어로 취한다.
05 decide는 to부정사를, give up은 동명사를 목적어로 취하며, because 이하는 주어 역할을 해야 하므로 to부정사나 동명사 모두 가능하다.
06 like는 to부정사와 동명사 둘 다 목적어로 취할 수 있다. 그리고 당연히 명사도 목적어로 취할 수 있다.
07 '화를 내다'는 be angry이고, 주어 자리이므로 being 또는 to be로 써야 한다.
08 My cat likes to hide[hiding] in boxes.로 영작할 수 있다.
09 ① to hold → holding ② to do → doing ③ going → to go ⑤ studying → to study
10 ⓐ are → is ⓓ to buy → buying
11 keep동사는 동명사를 목적어로 취한다.
12 동명사를 사용해야 하므로 Taking care of children을 쓰고, 동명사 주어는 단수 취급하므로 동사를 is로 써야 한다.
13 finish는 동명사를 목적어로 취하고, 주어가 여자(Minhee)이므로 소유격은 her로 쓴다.

14 forget to ~는 '~할 것을 잊다'이고, '~하지 마'는 부정 명령문
(「Don't+동사원형」)을 사용하면 된다.

15 「stop+-ing」는 '~하는 것을 멈추다'이고 명령문이므로 동사원형으
로 시작해야 한다.

16 likes A(-ing) and B(-ing)로 이어져야 하므로 meeting으로 써야 한
다.

07 동명사와 현재분사, 관용적 표현

1) 동사원형
2) -ing
3) 명사
4) ~하는 것, ~하기
5) 형용사
6) 진행형
7) ~하고 있는, ~하는
8) 현재분사
9) 동명사
10) ~하러 가다
11) ~하느라 바쁘다
12) ~에 싫증이 나다
13) ~할 가치가 있다
14) ~하고 싶다
15) ~하는 게 어때?
16) ~하느라 시간[돈]을 쓰다[낭비하다]
17) ~하기를 고대하다
18) ~하는 데 어려움을 겪다

Level 1 Test   p. 44

A 1 swimming   2 Singing
  3 drinking

B 1 G   2 P
  3 P

C 1 waiting   2 camping
  3 to have

D 1 feel like sleeping
  2 isn't[is not] worth downloading
  3 spends his free time listening

Level 2 Test   p. 45

01 ④   02 ④
03 ③   04 ④
05 ⓑ 동명사
06 ramen time
07 is busy catching
08 I had a hard time persuading him.

>>> 해설

01 ⓒ와 ⓓ는 현재분사가 명사를 수식하는 형태이고 나머지는 모두 「동
   명사+명사」이다.

02 [보기]와 ④는 동명사이고 나머지는 현재분사이다.

03 앞의 smoking은 진행형으로 쓰인 현재분사이고, 뒤의 smoking은
   용도를 나타내는 동명사이다.

04 「be worth+-ing(~할 가치가 있다)」, 「feel like+-ing(~하고 싶다)」
   형태로 쓴다.

05 [보기]는 용도·목적을 나타내는 동명사, ⓑ는 보어로 쓰인 동명사이다.

06 ⓐ Her hobby is cooking ramen. ⓑ The cooking time is
   about five minutes.로 배열하면 된다.

07 「be busy+-ing」는 '~하느라 바쁘다'의 뜻이다.

08 '~하는 데 어려움을 겪다'는 「have a hard time[difficulty]+-ing」다.

Level 3 Test   p. 46

01 ④   02 ④
03 ① ② ⑤   04 ③ ⑤
05 ① ② ⑤   06 ③ ④
07 ④   08 ②
09 ①   10 ⑤
11 being
12 (1) G (2) P (3) G
13 (1) ⓐ ⓔ (2) ⓑ ⓒ ⓓ
14 to plan → planning / visit → visiting
15 Which movie is worth watching?
16 I spent ₩500[500 won] downloading the song.

>>> 해설

01 hope는 to부정사를 목적어로 취한다.

02 ⓐ와 ⓕ는 현재분사이고 나머지는 동명사이다.

03 [보기]와 ① ② ⑤는 현재분사이다. [보기]의 is becoming은 진행형
   으로 쓰였다.

04 「feel like+-ing」는 '~하고 싶다'의 의미이다.

05 ⓐ He is playing baseball. ⓑ His hobby is playing baseball.
   로 영작할 수 있다.

06 watching은 진행형으로 쓰인 현재분사이고, waiting은 용도·목적
   을 나타내는 동명사이다.

07 • 전치사의 목적어로 동명사가 사용된다.
   • 진행형으로 쓰인 현재분사의 형태가 들어가야 한다.

08 ②의 drinking은 보어로 쓰인 동명사(G)이다.

09 ② to have → having ③ to read → reading ④ to buy →
   buying ⑤ meet → meeting

10 ⓐ~ⓓ에서 -ing는 모두 동명사이다.

11 「be tired of+-ing」는 '~에 싫증이 나다'이며, 광고 속에 'BE'가 있
   으므로 이를 활용해서 동명사형(being)으로 쓰면 된다.

12 (1)과 (3)은 목적어로 쓰인 동명사이고 (2)는 명사를 수식하는 현재분
   사이다.

13 ⓐ 'go+-ing」로 관용적으로 쓰인 동명사이다. ⓔ 주어로 쓰인 동명사
   이다. 나머지는 진행형의 현재분사이다.

14 「be busy+-ing」 / 「look forward to+-ing」 형태로 쓴다.

15 「be worth+-ing」는 '~할 만한 가치가 있다'의 뜻이다.

16 「spend+목적어+-ing」 구문을 사용하여 영작하면 된다.

Review Test   p. 48

01 ①   02 ①
03 ③   04 ②
05 ④   06 ④
07 ③   08 ③
09 ②   10 ④
11 Drinking a lot of water makes you healthy.
12 ⓑ to have → having

13 I don't mind watching the movie again.

14 are → is

15 She was afraid of making mistakes.

16 Are / tired of drinking

17 to lock / to shut

18 ⓒ-ⓐ-ⓓ-ⓑ-ⓕ-ⓔ

19 Please stop talking and listen to me.

20 My first job was protecting the president.

21 ④

22 Riding a bike can be fun

≫ 해설

01 practice는 동명사만 목적어로 취한다. 나머지 동사들은 to부정사와 동명사 모두 취할 수 있다.

02 decide는 to부정사를 목적어로 취한다.

03 mind는 동명사를, want는 to부정사를 목적어로 취한다.

04 전치사(before) 다음에는 동명사를 쓴다.

05 ④는 현재분사이고 나머지는 동명사이다.

06 「stop+to부정사」는 '～하기 위해 (하던 일) 멈추다'이고, 「stop+-ing」는 '～하는 것을 멈추다'이다.

07 「remember+to부정사」는 '～할 것을 기억하다'이므로 to pay를 paying으로 써야 한다.

08 ⓐ Becoming ⓓ changing은 동명사이고, ⓑ dancing ⓒ baking은 현재분사이다.

09 ⓐ seeing → to see ⓔ to chase → chasing

10 go to hiking을 go hiking으로 써야 한다.

11 첫 문장의 동사를 동명사로 고쳐 주어가 되도록 하면 된다.

12 전치사 뒤에는 동명사를 써야 한다.

13 mind(꺼리다)는 동명사를 목적어로 취한다.

14 동명사 주어는 단수 취급한다.

15 주어는 she이고, '～을 두려워하다'는 be afraid of ～이며, 전치사 뒤에는 동명사를 써서 연결하면 된다.

16 '～에 싫증나다'는 be tired of ～이다. 현재형의 의문문으로 쓰고 of 다음에는 동명사형을 쓰면 된다.

17 「remember+to부정사」는 '～할 것을 기억하다'이고, 「forget+to부정사」는 '～할 것을 잊다'이다. 나올 때 문은 닫혔지만 창문을 닫지 않았다는 내용이다.

18 「spend+목적어+-ing」 구문을 이용하여 The poor guy spent all his money buying presents for his girlfriend.로 배열할 수 있다.

19 「stop+-ing」는 '～하는 것을 멈추다'이다. 병렬구조 stop A and B로 이어지므로 listen으로 써야 한다.

20 보어 역할을 할 수 있는 동명사 protecting을 이용한다.

21 ⓒ '～할 것을 기억하다'가 돼야 하므로 「remember to+동사원형」 구조로 써야 한다. ⓔ enjoy는 동명사를 목적어로 취하므로 riding으로 고쳐야 한다.

22 주어, 동사, 보어의 구조이므로 ride a bike, can be, fun으로 배열하고 6단어이므로 ride를 to부정사가 아닌 동명사로 변형해서 쓰면 된다.

[21~22]

　　자전거를 타는 것은 매우 재미있을 수 있지만, 안전 지침을 배우는 것은 중요하다. 여기에 안전한 자전거 타기를 위한 약간의 조언이 있다. 너의 머리를 보호하기 위해 항상 자전거 헬멧을 착용해라. 네가 도로에서 자전거를 탈 때, 교통규칙을 따라야 한다.

운전자와 보행자들이 너를 쉽게 볼 수 있도록 반드시 밝은 색의 옷을 입어라. 네가 속도를 줄이고 안전하게 멈출 수 있도록 브레이크와 타이어를 점검해라. 이러한 조언들을 기억하고 자전거 타기를 즐겨라.

• 어휘 • safety 안전 | guideline 지침 | tip 조언 | protect 보호하다 | traffic 교통 | keep ～ in mind 기억하다

CHAPTER 04
현재완료

08 현재완료의 의미와 용법

1) have
2) has
3) not
4) never
5) p.p.
6) Have
7) Has
8) p.p.
9) have
10) has
11) haven't
12) hasn't
13) 막 ～했다
14) ～한 적이 있다
15) ～해오고 있다
16) ～해버렸다(그래서 지금은 …하다)

Level 1 Test
p. 52

A 1 thought　　　2 hasn't
　3 done　　　　4 since

B 1 Has she volunteered　2 haven't tasted
　3 No / I haven't.

C 1 hasn't arrived → 완료　2 has lost → 결과
　3 has stayed → 계속　4 have ridden → 경험
　5 has forgotten → 결과　6 Has, replied → 완료

Level 2 Test
p. 53

01 ⑤　　　　　　　　　02 ④

03 ①　　　　　　　　　04 ③

05 has taught / since

06 (1) All the players haven't[have not] done their best.
　(2) Have all the players done their best?
　(3) Yes, they have.

07 she has just stepped out

08 has waited / for

≫ 해설

01 과거부터 현재까지 이어지는 시제로 현재완료를 써야 한다.

02 과거의 동작이 현재에 영향을 미치므로 현재완료를 쓴다. (drink - drank - drunk)

03 [보기]와 ①은 경험, ②와 ③은 완료, ④와 ⑤는 계속 용법이다.

04 ⓐ did → has ⓑ readed → read ⓔ since → for

05 과거의 동작이 현재까지 영향을 미치므로 현재완료를 쓰고, 「since+과거 시점」의 형태로 쓴다.

06 현재완료의 부정문은 「have/has+not+p.p.」이며, 의문문은 「Have/has+주어+p.p. ~?」이다.

07 just는 have와 과거분사(p.p.) 사이에 쓰며, step out은 '짧은 시간 동안 어떤 장소를 떠나다'라는 영어 풀이를 보면 알 수 있다.

08 말풍선에서 10분이 지났음을 알 수 있으므로 현재완료로 쓰며, 「for+기간」의 표현으로 쓴다.

Level 3 Test
p. 54

01 ⑤   02 ③
03 ⑤   04 ③
05 ②④   06 ⑤
07 ⑤   08 ④
09 ④
10 has bitten
11 has been interested in / since
12 somebody has taken it
13 Lucy hasn't downloaded the app, but I have downloaded the app.
14 Have you ever looked at the sun on a hot and clear day?

≫ 해설

01 ⓓ swim – swam – swum ⓗ rise – rose – risen로 써야 하고, ⓕ 는 found(설립하다) – founded – founded로 맞다.

02 과거의 일이 현재까지 이어지므로 현재완료를 쓰고, 「since+과거 시점」으로 쓴다.

03 긍정문에서는 already가, 부정문에서는 yet이 주로 쓰인다.

04 의문문이나 부정문에서 문장 끝에는 yet이 사용된다.

05 [보기]와 ②④는 계속의 용법이고, ①은 경험, ③은 완료, ⑤는 결과 또는 완료의 용법이다

06 ⓐ 계속 ⓑ ⓕ 경험 ⓒ ⓔ 완료 ⓓ 결과

07 ① 완료 – 완료 ② 결과 – 결과 ③ 계속 – 계속 ④ 경험 – 경험 ⑤ 완료 – 경험의 용법이다.

08 ⓐ doesn't → hasn't (또는 rained → rain) ⓑ eatten → eaten ⓒ since → for ⓔ Have → Has

09 ④ Ellie has played the guitar for 2018.에서 for 2018이 아니라 since 2018이 옳다. ① Have you seen her today? ② I have not spoken to him yet. ③ Has her cat ever caught a mouse? ⑤ Have they received their Children's Day presents?

10 그림을 보면 개가 남자아이의 팔을 문 것이므로 A dog이 주어이고, 주어의 수에 맞게 「has+p.p.」를 쓰면 된다. bite동사의 변화형은 bite – bit – bitten이다.

11 과거의 상태가 현재까지 이어지므로 현재완료를 쓰며, since 다음에는 「주어+동사」가 올 수 있다.

12 누군가 자전거를 가져가버려서 지금도 없으므로 결과 용법의 현재완료를 사용하면 된다.

13 Lucy는 앱을 다운로드하지 않았고 나는 했으므로 각각 hasn't downloaded와 have downloaded를 써서 문장을 완성한다.

14 '~해본 적 있니?'는 Have you ever ~로 묻고 요일 앞에는 on을 쓴다.

UNIT 09 주의해야 할 현재완료

1) 가본 적이 있다   2) 가버렸다   3) 없음
4) 있음

Level 1 Test
p. 56

A 1 arrived   2 since
   3 How long   4 did he meet
   5 twice

B 1 been   2 been
   3 gone   4 gone / been

C 1 went   2 in
   3 have / since   4 has / stayed

D 1 has gone   2 has lived / for
   3 have been / since

Level 2 Test
p. 57

01 ①⑤   02 ①⑤
03 ②③   04 ②③④
05 has gone to
06 I lost your backpack
07 No, we haven't met yet.
08 How long has she run the company?

≫ 해설

01 명백한 과거 시점을 나타내는 과거 부사는 현재완료와 함께 쓸 수 없다.

02 경험을 나타내고 서울에 못 가봤으므로 ①과 ⑤가 적절하다.

03 since가 있으므로 현재완료로 써야 한다. 또는 in 2011로 하고 단순 과거로 써도 된다.

04 ② since → for ③ has been → was ④ has he come → did he come

05 친구가 부산으로 가버렸으므로 have/has gone to를 쓴다.

06 과거 부사(two days ago)가 있으므로 과거형으로 써야 한다.

07 과거부터 현재까지 만나지 않았으므로 현재완료로 쓰며, 부정문에서 yet은 '아직'이란 뜻이다.

08 B의 대답이 기간을 말하고 있으므로 현재완료로 묻는 것이 적절하다.

Level 3 Test
p. 58

01 ②③④⑤   02 ④
03 ①   04 ③
05 ②   06 ⑤
07 ②⑤   08 ④
09 ②④   10 ③
11 (A) Have you seen her?   (B) she has just gone to Canada.
12 ⓐ has lived → lives[is living] ⓑ lived → has lived
13 has the delivery person visited → did the delivery person visit

14 has been

15 (A) I teach English.   (B) I have taught it for five years.

16 has not taken a shower for a month

≫ 해설

01 명백한 과거를 나타내는 부사는 현재완료와 함께 쓸 수 없다.

02 • 과거 부사(last weekend)가 있으므로 과거형
   • 경험을 나타내므로 have been to
   • Tom이 은행으로 가버렸는지 묻고 있으므로 have gone to가 맞다.

03 어제 늦게 잔 것은 과거이고, 아직 침대에서 나오지 않은 것은 현재완료로 써야 한다. get동사의 변화형은 get – got – gotten이다.

04 A가 과거로 물었으므로 B도 과거(I visited ~)로 답해야 한다.

05 과거 부사(last semester)가 있으므로 과거형을 써야 한다. / 지금까지 참석할 시간을 갖지 못했으므로 현재완료형이 와야 하며 내용상 부정이 와야 한다.

06 ⓐ 과거 시제이므로 과거형이 제대로 잘 쓰였다. ⓑ 특정한 시점을 묻는 when은 현재완료와 어울리지 않는다.

07 단순 과거형을 쓰거나, 「since + 과거 부사」를 써서 현재완료형으로 쓸 수 있다.

08 과거 부사(this morning)가 있으므로 과거형(went)으로 써야 한다.

09 ② Have로 물었으므로 I have로 답해야 하고, ④ 과거부사 (yesterday)가 있으므로 have seen을 saw로 써야 한다.

10 When have you become a U.S. citizen?으로 배열되는데 when은 현재완료형과 어울리지 않으므로 have를 did로 고쳐야 한다. ① Where has the kid gone to? ② Have you ever been to Quebec? ④ We got home very late last night. ⑤ She hasn't eaten anything since yesterday.

11 각각 경험과 완료를 나타내는 현재완료로 써야 한다.

12 ⓐ 현재 시제는 현재로 쓴다. ⓑ 과거부터 현재까지 이어지는 시제는 현재완료로 쓴다.

13 특정한 과거 시점을 나타내는 어구는 과거 시제와 함께 쓴다.

14 경험을 나타내므로 has been을 써야 한다.

15 각각 현재 시제와 현재완료로 묻고 있으므로 이에 맞게 대답하면 된다.

16 not과 함께 쓸 수 있는 것은 has이고, '샤워를 하다'는 take a shower, '1개월 동안'이라고 해야 하므로 for a month를 현재완료형에 맞게 쓰면 된다.

Review Test

p. 60

01 ②   02 ③
03 ⑤   04 ①
05 ②   06 ③
07 ③   08 ④
09 ④   10 ②③⑤

11 (1) You haven't[have not] had a hamster.
   (2) Have you had a hamster?
   (3) No, I haven't.

12 The printer has broken down.

13 have grown

14 Ally hasn't[has not, has never] worn *hanbok*.

15 I have already eaten[had] lunch with my friends.

16 ⓐ thinked → thought ⓑ has she knocked → did she knock

---

17 How long have you lived here?

18 (A) has come → came   (B) didn't see → haven't seen

19

	C			
B	R	A	I	N
	Y			

20 (A) Been   (B) go   (C) been   (D) gone

21 ③

22 Have you ever heard of tree-climbing goats?

≫ 해설

01 ⓑ swim – swam – swum ⓕ draw – drew – drawn ⓗ hide – hid – hidden

02 「go+-ing」는 '~하러 가다'이고, have가 있으므로 현재완료 시제로 쓴다. many times는 '여러 번'이라는 뜻의 부사이다.

03 얼마나 자주 배우는지는 주어진 문장을 통해 알 수 없다. 현재완료는 과거의 정보뿐만 아니라 현재의 정보도 알 수 있으므로 ①은 Yes, he is.로 답할 수 있다.

04 '~ 전에'라는 의미의 부사는 ago로 과거 시제와 함께 쓰고, 「for + 기간」은 현재완료와 함께 쓰여 '~ 동안 …해 왔다'는 의미를 나타낸다.

05 finish는 동명사를 목적어로 취하고, 현재완료 의문문은 「Have/Has + 주어 + p.p. ~?」 형태로 쓴다.

06 차 씨가 콜롬비아로 가고 없으므로 has gone을 써야 한다.

07 [보기]와 ⓒ ⓓ는 경험, ⓐ는 결과, ⓑ는 완료, ⓔ는 계속 용법이다.

08 ① finish → finished ② have → has ③ saw → seen ⑤ since → for

09 ⓑ는 1인칭이고 경험을 나타내므로 have been to를 써야 한다.

10 ① has invented → invented ④ has just broken → broke

11 현재완료의 부정문은 「have/has+not+p.p.」이고, 의문문은 「Have/Has + 주어 + p.p. ~?」이며, 이에 대한 부정의 대답은 「No, 주어 + haven't/hasn't.」로 한다.

12 주어가 3인칭 단수이므로 has를 쓰고, break – broke – broken에서 과거분사 broken을 쓰면 된다.

13 1년에 1센티미터가 자랐다는 내용으로 현재완료가 적절하다. grow 동사의 변화형은 grow – grew – grown이다.

14 한복은 입어보지 않았으므로 부정으로 쓰면 된다. (wear – wore – worn)

15 긍정문에서는 already가 have와 p.p. 사이에 들어가며, 식사명 앞에는 관사를 쓰지 않는다.

16 ⓐ think – thought – thought ⓑ what time은 현재완료 시제와 어울리지 않으므로 과거형으로 써야 한다.

17 B가 2년 동안 여기에 살았다는 것으로 보아 '얼마나 오랫동안 여기에 살았나요?'라는 의미의 문장을 현재완료 시제로 영작하면 된다.

18 과거 부사 last night이 있으므로 과거 시제로 써야 한다. / 어제부터 지금까지 보지 못했으므로 현재완료로 쓴다.

19 ⓓ는 경험, ⓕ는 계속이고 나머지는 모두 결과의 용법이다. 따라서 C, B, I, Y를 적절히 단어 퍼즐에 넣으면 된다.

20 be동사의 변화형은 am/is/are – was/were – been이며, go동사의 변화형은 go – went – gone이다. 주어가 어떤 장소에 갔다가 돌아왔으면 been, 어떤 장소에 가서 돌아오지 않았으면 gone을 쓴다.

21 ⓐ 주어가 The goats이므로 have로 고쳐야 한다. ⓓ after가 전치사이므로 전치사의 목적어가 될 수 있는 동명사 eating으로 고쳐야 한다.

22 현재완료를 사용하면서 의문문이므로 Have you ever heard of 그리고 of의 목적어로 tree-climbing goats를 쓰면 된다.

[21~22]

　　나무 타는 염소들에 대해 들어본 적이 있는가? 모코로의 아르간 숲에 있는 염소들은 특별한 기술을 가지고 있다. 그들은 베리를 먹기 위해 나무에 오른다. 그 베리는 올리브와 비슷하다. 그 베리는 안에 견과가 있고 사람들은 그것들을 만들기 위해 그것들을 사용한다. 농부들은 이러한 특별한 염소를 따라가는데, 왜냐하면 그 염소들은 베리를 먹은 후에 견과를 내뱉기 때문이다. 농부들은 나무에 오르지 않고 쉽게 그것들을 모을 수 있다. 그들은 수세기 동안 아르간 견과로 아르간 오일을 만들어 왔다.

• 어휘 • skill 기술 | berry 베리 | nut 견과 | cooking oil 식용유 | spit out 내뱉다 | collect 모으다

CHAPTER 05
조동사

〰〰

UNIT 10 can, may, will

1) 동사원형
2) cannot
3) can't
4) 동사원형
5) be able to
6) be not able to
7) may
8) may not
9) 동사원형
10) may not
11) 동사원형
12) can
13) cannot
14) 동사원형
15) will not
16) won't
17) 동사원형
18) be going to
19) be not going

Level 1 Test
p. 64

A 1 could
2 may not
3 may not
4 will be able to

B 1 have not → not have
2 can't → couldn't
3 late → be late
4 is able to → will be able to
5 speaks → speak

Level 2 Test
p. 65

01 ⑤
02 ③
03 ① ②
04 ④
05 We're going to be late for the concert.
06 (1) may not

(2) cannot
07 may → may be
08 I won't make that mistake again.

》》 해설

01 ⓓ와 ⓔ는 허락이고 나머지는 추측을 나타낸다.
02 ⓒ ⓓ ⓕ는 '허락'이고 나머지는 '능력'을 나타낸다.
03 큰 축제가 있을 것이라 많은 손님이 올 것이라는 긍정의 미래 표현을 만드는 will 또는 are going to가 들어가야 알맞다. 주어가 복수이므로 is going to는 옳지 않다.
04 상대방에게 요청하는 표현과 제안하는 표현에 공통으로 알맞은 것은 Would you ~?이다.
05 '늦을 것이다'라는 의미의 미래 조동사 be going to 다음에 be late for(~에 늦다)가 따라 와야 알맞다.
06 may not = cannot: ~하면 안 된다
07 may 다음에 동사원형이 와야 하는데, 형용사 tired가 있으므로 may be very tired가 되어야 한다.
08 '~하지 않겠다'는 미래의 부정형 will not을 사용해야 하는데, 단어 수를 맞추기 위해서는 줄임말 won't를 써야 한다.

Level 3 Test
p. 66

01 ③
02 ⑤
03 ②
04 ① ③
05 ②
06 ③
07 ③
08 ⑤
09 ③
10 ① ④
11 His opinion can't[cannot] be right.
12 wasn't going
13 The bag may not be found.
14 (B) Will → Can[May]
15 can't[cannot]
16 ⓑ may → may not

》》 해설

01 ③은 '~해도 좋다'는 허락을 나타내고, 나머지는 '~일지도 모른다'는 추측을 나타낸다.
02 ⓓ와 ⓕ는 허락을 나타내고, ⓒ의 can은 not과 함께 쓰여 부정의 추측을 나타내며, 나머지 ⓐ ⓑ ⓔ는 능력을 나타낸다.
03 ⓐ taking → take ⓔ may → may be
04 허락을 물을 때는 can 또는 may를 쓸 수 있다.
05 첫 번째는 능력을 나타내는 긍정의 can 또는 추측을 나타내는 may가 알맞다. 두 번째는 부정적인 의지를 나타내는 won't가 알맞다.
06 [보기]와 ③은 추측이고, ① ④ ⑤는 능력, ②는 허락을 나타낸다.
07 추측의 may가 문맥상 알맞다. (그가 옳을지도 모르지만 나는 그를 이해할 수 없다.)
08 May I ~?로 허락을 묻는 질문에 대한 대답으로 may와 can 둘 다 가능하다. ⑤ won't(~하지 않을 것이다)라고 대답하는 것은 어색하다.
09 마지막에 Tom의 말을 듣고 기뻤다고 했으므로 긍정의 표현이 들어가야 하며, said가 과거 시제이므로 빈칸에는 will의 과거형 would가 들어가는 것이 알맞다.
10 허가를 요청할 때는 may, can, could를 사용할 수 있다.
11 '~일 리가 없다'라는 강한 부정의 추측을 나타내는 can't[cannot]를 써서 영작한다.

12 will = be going to로 바꿔 쓸 수 있다. 여기서는 과거 부정형이므로 주어 He에 따른 be동사는 was이고 부정형은 wasn't가 알맞다.

13 「주어(the bag)+조동사(may)+not+동사원형 ~(be found)」의 순서로 배열한다. (그 가방은 발견되지 않을지도 모른다.)

14 스웨터를 입어봐도 되는지 허락을 묻는 표현으로는 Will I ~?가 아니라 Can[May] I ~?가 알맞다.

15 첫 번째는 불가능을 나타내는 can't이고, 두 번째는 강한 부정의 추측을 나타내는 can't이다.

16 '교통량이 많아서 제시간에 공항에 도착하지 못할지도 모른다.'는 의미가 되어야 하므로 may not을 써야 한다.

UNIT 11 must, have to, should, ought to

1) have/has to
2) don't/doesn't have to
3) don't/doesn't need to
4) need not
5) must not[mustn't]
6) may not
7) cannot
8) ought to
9) should not
10) shouldn't
11) 동사원형
12) ought not to

Level 1 Test
p. 68

A 1 do I have to
2 have to
3 go
4 had to

B 1 have[ought]
2 must be
3 must[should, may] not

C 1 He must be a plainclothes police officer.
2 He had to go to the dentist yesterday.
3 Children must not[should not, ought not to] talk to strangers.
4 We must[have to] book the tickets online.

Level 2 Test
p. 69

01 ③
02 ④
03 ②
04 ①
05 Harry must be excited.
06 We must not use violence.
07 You ought not to eat food too fast.
08 She didn't have to attend the meeting yesterday.

≫ 해설

01 문맥상 '다시 건강해지려면 그것을 먹어야 해.'라는 내용이 자연스러우므로, 긍정의 의무를 나타내는 「must[have to]+동사원형」이 들어가는 것이 알맞다.

02 should와 같은 의미인 ought to의 부정형은 ought not to로 나타낸다.

03 '~할 필요 없다'는 don't have to로 쓴다.

04 ⓐ must 다음에 동사원형이 와야 하므로 형용사(sad) 앞에 be를 붙여야 한다. ⓑ yesterday가 과거이므로 had to로 써야 한다.

05 I'm sure는 확신을 나타내는 조동사 must로 표현할 수 있다.

06 '폭력은 증오를 증가시킬 뿐이다.'라는 포스터의 내용상 금지를 나타내는 must not이 알맞다.

07 ought to의 부정형은 ought not to이다.

08 '~할 필요 없다'는 의미의 don't have to를 사용해야 하는데 yesterday가 있어서 과거 시제로 써야 하므로 didn't have to가 알맞다.

Level 3 Test
p. 70

01 ①
02 ③
03 ④
04 ③
05 ③
06 ④
07 ②
08 ③
09 ①
10 ②
11 ③ ⑤
12 You ought not to use paper cups here.
13 should cover your mouth when you are sneezing
14 You don't need to write it down.
15 No, you don't have to.
16 (1) should not
(2) don't have to

≫ 해설

01 '핫초코가 너무 뜨거우니 아직 먹지 말고 식을 때까지 기다리라.'는 의미이므로 「must not+동사원형(~해서는 안 된다)」을 쓴다.

02 '~할 필요가 없다'라는 불필요의 의미는 don't have[need] to 또는 need not으로 나타낸다.

03 문맥상 '도둑임에 틀림없다'가 되어야 하므로 강한 추측을 나타내는 must be a thief가 적절하다.

04 내용상 '~해야 한다'라는 의미의 조동사 should가 알맞다.

05 ⓒ ago가 과거 부사이므로 과거형 had to로 쓴다. ⓓ ought to의 부정은 ought not to이다. ⓔ 주어가 3인칭 단수 He이므로 doesn't have to로 바꾸어야 알맞다.

06 강한 추측을 나타내는 must는 have/has to로 나타낼 수 없다.

07 불필요를 나타내는 need not 다음에는 동사원형을 써야 한다.

08 ③은 '~임에 틀림없다'는 강한 추측을 나타내고, 나머지는 '~해야 한다'는 의무를 나타낸다.

09 • must는 '~임에 틀림없다'는 강한 추측을 나타낸다.
• must not은 '~해서는 안 된다'는 강한 금지를 나타낸다.

10 ②는 수업 시간에 떠들어야 한다는 뜻이고, 나머지는 수업 시간에 조용히 해야 한다는 뜻이다.

11 ③ yesterday가 과거를 나타내므로 didn't have to가 알맞다. ⑤ ought to의 부정은 ought not to이다.

12 to가 들어가고 '~하면 안 된다'는 의미의 표현은 ought not to이다.

13 「should+동사원형(cover 가리다)+목적어(your mouth)」의 순서로 적고, 시간 부사절 「when(~할 때)+주어(you)+동사(are sneezing)」를 쓴다. (재채기를 할 때는 입을 가려야 한다.)

14 '~할 필요 없다'는 「don't need to+동사원형」으로 쓴다.

15 대답에서 다른 것을 받아들일 수 있다고 했으므로 부정의 대답이 와야 알맞다. 의무 must의 부정은 불필요를 나타내는 don't have to(~할 필요 없다)이다.

16 (1) 의미상 '입에 (음식이) 가득 든 채 말하면 안 된다.'이므로 should

not(~하면 안 된다)이 알맞다.

(2) '그 고급 음식점에서는 네가 직접 음식을 가져다 먹을 필요가 없다.'이므로 don't have to(~할 필요 없다)를 쓴다.

UNIT 12 would like to, had better, used to

1) would like to
2) would not[wouldn't] like to
3) had better
4) had better not
5) used to
6) didn't use to
7) Did
8) use to
9) ~하곤 했다
10) used to
11) didn't use to
12) used not to
13) Did
14) use to
15) 예전에 ~이었다
16) used to
17) did not use to
18) used not to
19) Did
20) use to

Level 1 Test
p. 72

A 1 had better put on
2 There used to be flowers
3 would not like to go
4 You had better not sleep

B 1 I would[I'd] like to rest after school.
2 My grandparents used to drink coffee after breakfast.
3 You had better not eat too many beans.

Level 2 Test
p. 73

01 ③
02 ②
03 ①
04 ⑤
05 There used to be a statue here.
06 would like to be
07 She is used to mixing with foreigners.
08 had better

>>> 해설

01 '밖이 매우 추우니 목도리를 하는 게 낫다.'는 충고이므로 had better가 알맞다.

02 • 「used to+동사원형」: ~하곤 했다
• 「be used to+-ing」: ~하는 데 익숙하다

03 ① 「used to+동사원형」: ~하곤 했다 ⑤ 「be used to+-ing」: ~하는 데 익숙하다

04 「had better not+동사원형」은 '~하지 않는 것이 낫다'는 의미로 틀린 부분이 없다.

05 「used to+동사원형」은 '(전에) ~이었다'라는 의미로 과거에 있었는데 지금은 없는 경우를 나타낸다.

06 want to = would like to ~하고 싶다 (나는 너그러운 부모가 되고 싶다.)

07 「be used to+-ing」: ~하는 데 익숙하다 (아빠가 외교관이라 여러 나라에서 살아왔고 외국인과 어울리는 것에 익숙하다.)

08 손님이 귀여운 머리 스타일을 원해서 미용사가 앞머리를 자르라고 조

언하는 것이 알맞으므로 「had better+동사원형(~하는 것이 낫다)」을 쓴다.

Level 3 Test
p. 74

01 ①
02 ① ②
03 ①
04 ⑤
05 ①
06 ③
07 ⑤
08 ③
09 ③
10 ① ③ ⑤
11 ⓐ had not better → had better not
12 I would not like to see you become a pianist.
13 I would rather die than do it.
14 I would like to donate all my organs after death.
15 There used not to be a bookstore on the corner.
16 used to have

>>> 해설

01 「used to+동사원형」 또는 「would+동사원형」은 과거의 습관을 나타낸다.

02 would like는 to부정사가, had better에는 동사원형이 온다.

03 '많은 사람들이 나를 좋아했으면 좋겠다.'고 말한 것에 대해 '~하는 것이 좋다'는 had better를 이용한 충고의 표현이 알맞다.

04 Nuclear energy is used to produce electricity.로 영작할 수 있다. 「be used to+동사원형(~하기 위해 사용되다)」를 쓴다.

05 ⓐ 「used to+동사원형(~하곤 했다)」이므로 going → go ⓑ ought to의 부정은 ought not to이다.

06 몰이 너무 거대하고 붐비고 복잡해서 길을 잃기 쉬우므로 아이를 데리고 가는 것은 위험하다고 충고하고 있다. had better의 부정은 had better not이다.

07 used to의 의문문은 「Did+주어+use to+동사원형」이므로 틀린 곳이 없다.

08 ③ 「be used to+-ing(~하는 것에 익숙하다)」로 draw는 drawing이 되어야 한다.

09 ③ 「used to+동사원형」: ~하곤 했다 (→ He used to go to the library.) ① She used to be healthy. ② I would rather stay home than go out. ④ Would you like to leave a message? ⑤ You had better not go out.

10 ① had better(~하는 것이 좋다) She had better not use my computer. ③ 「used to+동사원형(~하곤 했다)」이므로 I used to be thin. ⑤ 「wouldn't like to+동사원형(~하고 싶지 않다)」 I wouldn't like to be in your shoes.
② 「be used to+-ing(~하는 것에 익숙하다)」 ④ would rather not(~하지 않는 것이 낫겠다)

11 had better의 부정은 had better not이다.

12 would like to의 부정문은 「would not like to+동사원형」으로 나타내며 '~하고 싶지 않다'는 의미이다. (나는 네가 피아니스트가 되는 것을 보고 싶지 않다.)

13 「would rather+동사원형(A)+than+동사원형(B)」: B 하느니 차라리 A 하겠다

14 I'd는 I would의 줄임말이고 would like to로 쓰이므로 to를 더하면 된다.

15 상태를 나타내는 there used to be의 부정문은 there used not to be이다.

16 과거에는 도마뱀을 길렀으나 지금은 기르지 않는다는 내용이므로 「used to＋동사원형(~하곤 했다)」을 쓰는 것이 알맞다.

Review Test

p. 76

01 ③	02 ④
03 ⑤	04 ①
05 ③	06 ④
07 ④	08 ①
09 ④	10 ③

11 can't[cannot]　　　　　12 may[might]
13 you ought to find something exciting
14 ⓑ ought to not → ought not to
15 You had better get some rest.
16 wouldn't
17 used to compare
18 Children would rather watch YouTube than read books.
19 (1) must not
　　(2) had better
20 can't[cannot] be a model / must be a beggar
21 ④
22 you may even disappear

≫ 해설

01 ③에서는 can이 not과 함께 쓰여 '~일 리가 없다'는 부정의 추측을 나타내고, 나머지는 '~할 수 있다'는 능력을 나타낸다.

02 첫 번째 문장은 but의 연결어로 보아 부정의 능력을 나타내는 can't가 알맞고, 두 번째 문장은 추측을 나타내는 조동사 may 또는 might가 알맞다.

03 조동사 will로 시작하는 의문문으로 뒤에 동사원형이 와야 하므로 able 앞에 be가 와야 한다.

04 능력을 나타내는 can't는 「be동사＋not able to」로 바꿔 쓸 수 있다.

05 차를 옮기겠다는 내용으로 보아 '~해서는 안 된다'는 금지를 나타내는 must not이 알맞다.

06 첫 번째 문장은 과거의 의무를 나타내는 had to(~해야 했다)를 쓰고, 두 번째 문장은 충고를 나타내는 had better(~하는 게 낫다)가 알맞다.

07 ⓑ 조동사는 나란히 쓸 수 없다. (will can → will be able to) ⓓ 「need not＋동사원형」(to read → read) ⓔ 「had better＋동사원형」(to bring → bring)

08 「be used to＋(동)명사」: ~하는 데 익숙하다

09 허락(may = can)을 묻는 질문에 불필요로 대답하는 것은 어색하다. don't have to: ~할 필요 없다 / must not = may not: ~하면 안 된다

10 used to 다음에는 동사원형이 온다. → ③ You'd better not look back.
① You had better think it over. ② Where would you like to go? ④ I didn't use to like Indian food. ⑤ There used to be a theater here.

11 첫 번째 빈칸에는 불가능을 나타내는 can't[cannot]가, 두 번째 빈칸에는 강한 부정의 추측을 나타내는 can't[cannot]가 알맞다.

12 약한 추측을 나타내는 조동사 may 또는 might(~일지도 모른다)가 알맞다.

13 「ought to＋동사원형」: ~해야 한다 / 형용사가 something을 수식

할 때 「something＋형용사」의 순서로 쓴다.

14 ought to의 부정은 ought not to이다. (ⓐ 너는 여기서 조심스럽게 주차하는 것이 낫다. ⓑ 사람들은 동물들에게 잔인하게 행동하면 안 된다.)

15 「had better＋동사원형」: ~하는 것이 좋겠다

16 be going to는 현재일 때 will로, 과거일 때 would로 바꾸어 쓸 수 있다. (그는 그녀를 떠나지 않을 것이라고 말했다.)

17 과거에 했지만 지금은 하지 않는 일을 나타낼 때는 「used to＋동사원형(~하곤 했다)」으로 나타낸다. (엄마는 나와 형을 비교하곤 했다.)

18 「would rather＋동사원형(A)＋than＋동사원형(B)」: B 하느니 차라리 A 하겠다

19 ① 의미상 '빨간 불에 길을 건너면 안 된다.'이므로 must not(~하면 안 된다)이 적절하다. ② '길을 건너기 전에 몇 초 기다리는 것이 좋다.'이므로 had better(~하는 것이 낫다)가 적절하다.

20 can't be: ~일 리가 없다 / must be: ~임에 틀림없다

21 ⓐ 가주어 it으로 바르게 쓰였고, ⓒ '~하기 위해 노력하다'의 「try to＋동사원형」으로 적절하고, ⓓ '~하는 것을 멈추다'의 「stop＋-ing」로 적절하다. ⓑ 문장의 동사가 없으므로 Keeping을 Keep으로 고쳐서 명령문으로 만들어야 한다. ⓔ 앞에 나온 일반동사 remain을 대신해야 하므로 do로 써야 한다.

22 영영풀이는 '이것은 일반적으로 가능성을 표현하는 데 사용되는 조동사이다. 이것은 또한 허락을 하거나 요청할 때도 사용될 수 있다.'는 뜻으로 주어와 조동사 may를 추가하면 된다.

[21~22]

다른 어떤 모래와는 달리, 유사(流砂)는 매우 위험하다. 만약 네가 그 안으로 걸어 들어간다면, 너는 점점 가라앉아서 마침내는 심지어 사라질 수도 있다. 하지만, 유사에서 인간이 물에서 뜨는 것처럼 뜨는 것이 가능하다. 만약 유사에 들어간다면 신체로부터 팔을 멀리 유지해라. 다리를 움직이려고 노력하지 마라. 그러면 너는 곧 가라앉는 것을 멈출 것이다. 그러고 나서, 팔을 천천히 움직여라, 그러면 단단한 땅을 향해 움직일 수 있다. 가장 중요하게, 침착함을 유지해라. 네가 만약 그렇게 한다면, 아마도 '배고픈 모래'는 계속 배고플 것이다.

● 어휘 ● sink 가라앉다 | disappear 사라지다 | float (둥둥) 뜨다 | remain (~인 채로) 남다 | calm 침착하는

CHAPTER 06

명사, 부정대명사

UNIT 13 명사의 종류, 수량 표현, 소유격

1) 있는   2) 보통   3) 집합
4) 고유   5) 없는   6) 물질
7) 추상   8) many   9) a few
10) few   11) much   12) a little
13) little   14) cup   15) glasses
16) pieces   17) bottle   18) slices[pieces]
19) pounds   20) sheet   21) spoonfuls
22) bowls   23) lumps   24) loaves
25) bars   26) 's   27) of

Level 1 Test
p. 80

A 1 A few   2 many
   3 little

B 1 bowls   2 bars[pieces]
   3 glasses   4 pieces[slices]

Level 2 Test
p. 81

01 ⑤   02 ③
03 ④   04 ④
05 ① pair ② dollars ③ them
06 little → few   07 ten-thousand-won
08 Nara's cat takes a five-minute nap every day.

》》 해설
01 egg와 strawberry는 셀 수 있는 명사이므로 복수형을 만들 수 있다.
02 homework는 셀 수 없는 명사이며 a lot of[lots of = plenty of = much]로 수식을 받는다.
03 My older[elder] sister gives me a little pocket money[spending money = allowance] every week.로 영작할 수 있다. 또는 me를 pocket money 뒤로 보내면서 전치사 to를 쓸 수 있다.
04 Alanis에서 -s는 복수형 어미가 아니므로 -'s를 붙여야 한다.
05 ① a가 왔으므로 a pair of가 맞다. ② won(원)은 셀 수 없지만 dollar는 셀 수 있다. ③ boots를 가리키므로 them으로 써야 한다.
06 friends가 셀 수 있는 명사이므로 few로 써야 한다.
07 만 원짜리 지폐는 a ten-thousand-won bill로 쓰고 thousand에 -s를 붙이지 않는다.
08 Nara의 소유격은 Nara's로 표현하고 하이픈을 이용한 '5분의 낮잠'은 a five-minute nap으로 쓴다.

Level 3 Test
p. 82

01 ④   02 ③
03 ④   04 ① ② ③
05 ① ⑤   06 ④
07 ②   08 ① ⑤
09 ② ⑤   10 ⑤
11 ③
12 few → little / furnitures → furniture
13 girls' school
14 The younger brother had a lot of rice, but the older brother didn't have much.
15 a slice of
16 The 180-centimeter-tall woman is Kobe's grandmother.

》》 해설
01 ① bottle → bottles 또는 these → this ② cakes → cake ③ pair → pairs ⑤ piece → pieces
02 hair(머리)는 머리카락 한 올씩 셀 때를 제외하고는 셀 수 없는 명사이므로 a를 삭제해야 한다.
03 ⓐ 주어가 exercises라 동사를 are로 써야 한다. ⓑ these vases로 쓰거나 this vase로 써야 한다. ⓒ policemen이 주어이므로 동사를 are로 써야 한다.
04 ④ centimeter는 셀 수 있으므로 centimeters로 고쳐야 한다. ⑤ 하이픈(-)으로 연결해서 명사를 꾸밀 때는 형용사 역할을 하므로 복수형을 쓰지 않는다.
05 You need a few eggs and a little flour to make pancakes.로 영작할 수 있다.
06 무생물은 'B of A'가 'A의 B'이고, -s로 끝나는 복수형의 경우에 -'만 붙인다. Chris는 복수형이 아니므로 -'s를 붙인다.
07 I have sold plenty[lots, a lot] of items online.으로 영작할 수 있으므로 네 번째 단어는 plenty이다.
08 ① Charles의 s가 복수형이 아니므로 Charles's로 ⑤ 빵(bread)은 셀 수 없으므로 bread로 고쳐야 한다.
09 advise는 동사이고 advice로 써야 하며 soup은 piece로 세지 않는다.
10 ⓐ bottle ⓑ lump ⓒ pairs ⓓ pounds가 들어간다. 따라서 필요 없는 단어는 bar, sheets이다.
11 ⓐ are → is ⓒ much → many ⓔ pair of 삭제 (coat는 pair of로 세지 않는다.)
12 furniture는 셀 수 없는 명사이므로 복수형을 쓸 수 없고 little로 수식한다.
13 복수형 어미 -s로 끝나면 -'(apostrophe)만 붙인다.
14 쌀(rice)은 셀 수 없으므로 a lot of나 much로 수식할 수 있는데, much를 앞에 쓰면 뒤의 문장이 a lot of로 끝나므로 앞에 써야 한다.
15 레몬을 얇게 썬 조각은 a slice of lemon으로 나타낸다.
16 180센티미터를 하이픈으로 연결하여 명사를 꾸밀 때 단수형 centimeter로 써야 하고, Kobe의 소유격은 Kobe's로 표현한다.

UNIT 14 부정대명사

1) ones   2) it   3) each
4) each   5) everything   6) everyone
7) everybody   8) all   9) all
10) all   11) both   12) both
13) some   14) any   15) one
16) the other   17) one   18) another
19) the other   20) one   21) another
22) the[a] third   23) the other   24) some
25) others   26) some   27) the others

Level 1 Test
p. 84

A
1 어색한 곳 없음
2 is
3 scientists
4 Something horrible

B
1 Each / has[needs]
2 another / it
3 Anyone[Anybody]

Level 2 Test
p. 85

01 ⑤   02 ③
03 ③   04 ③
05 One[one]
06 toothbrush / one / toothpaste / the other
07 ⓐ something → anything
08 each other

》》 해설
01 둘 중 하나는 one, 나머지 하나는 the other로 표현한다.
02 Each 다음에는 단수가 오든 복수가 오든 관계 없이 단수로 취급한다.
03 The company needs something more exciting.으로 영작할 수 있다. anything과 than은 필요하지 않다.
04 두 아기가 웃고 있고 한 아기가 울고 있다.
05 • '또 다른 하나'는 another one으로 나타낸다.
   • 셋 중에서 첫 번째는 one으로 쓴다.
06 용이 한 손에는 칫솔을, 다른 한 손에는 치약을 들고 있다. 손이 두 개니까 one ~, the other...를 이용해야 한다.
07 부정문에서는 anything을 쓴다. 형용사(useful)가 뒤에서 꾸며주는 것은 맞다.
08 '서로'를 나타내는 표현에는 each other와 one another가 있는데 빈칸의 첫 글자에 따라 each other를 쓰면 된다.

Level 3 Test
p. 86

01 ⑤   02 ①
03 ③   04 ②④
05 ②   06 ⑤
07 ④   08 ③
09 ④   10 ②⑤
11 ④

12 the other → another / one → it
13 the others
14 ⓒ the others ⓔ is
15 Why are some stars brighter than the others?
16 Some students speak German, others speak Dutch, and the others speak both.

》》 해설
01 ⓐ 「every+단수 명사+단수 동사」 ⓑ 「each of+복수 명사+단수 동사」 (ⓐ의 unique는 발음이 반자음으로 시작하기 때문에 a가 맞다.)
02 ② wish → wishes ③ tries → try ④ some → any ⑤ questions → question
03 막연한 것은 one으로, 특정한 것은 it으로 쓴다.
04 What does each of these signs mean?(이 표지판[기호] 각각의 의미는 뭐지?)으로 써야 한다. each of 다음에는 복수 명사가 온다.
05 봉투에 오렌지가 총 몇 개인지는 모르나, 처음에 꺼낸 두 개 중 한 개는 one, 다른 하나는 the other이고, 또 다른 하나를 꺼냈으므로 another, 그리고 그것을 나에게 줬으므로 it을 써야 한다.
06 3개 중 2개를 말하였고 나머지는 하나이므로 the others가 아닌 the other로 써야 한다.
07 It's not ₩3,000 for both of them, but each of them costs ₩3,000. 등으로 영작할 수 있으므로 every는 필요 없다.
08 ⓐ man → men, dollar → dollars ⓑ have → has
09 ⓐ children's → child's ⓒ semesters → semester ⓔ wears → wear
10 차례대로 one, the other, one, other가 들어간다.
11 ④ 2개 items → item, them → it ① 1개 are → is ② 1개 both → each 또는 corner → corners ③ 1개 Do → Does ⑤ 1개 others → other
12 '또 다른 하나'는 another로, 특정한 것은 it으로 받아 쓴다.
13 셋 중 하나는 one, 나머지는 the others로 표현한다.
14 ⓒ 9명 중 1명을 제외한 나머지이므로 the others가 알맞다. ⓔ Everybody는 단수 취급하므로 is로 써야 한다.
15 일부는 some, 나머지는 the others이고, bright의 비교급은 brighter이다.
16 일부는 some, 다른 일부는 others, 나머지 일부는 the others로 표현한다.

Review Test
p. 88

01 ②   02 ②
03 ⑤   04 ①⑤
05 ⑤   06 ④
07 ④   08 ①②④
09 ③   10 ④
11 (1) buying
   (2) little
12 The cook needs two cups of flour to bake cookies.
13 were few
14 ⓐ The computer of the speakers → The speakers of the computer
15 18-years-old → 18-year-old
16 They are looking for someone intelligent to work with.
17 Some / egg / others / some cheese

18 One / another / the others

19 One / another / the other

20 it, other, the other, both, some

21 ③ ④ ⑤

22 each / tries to show the other

>>> 해설

01 너무 바빠서 답문을 할 수 없다는 것은 답문할 시간이 거의 없다는 것과 마찬가지이므로 ②가 적절하며, little에 부정의 의미가 있으므로 doesn't를 쓰면 안 된다.

02 slice는 셀 수 있지만 ham은 셀 수 없으므로 hams를 ham으로 고쳐야 한다.

03 blouse는 pair로 세지 않는다.

04 furniture는 a piece of로 세고, a pair of 다음에는 짝을 이루는 복수 명사가 온다.

05 each와 every는 단수 취급한다.

06 '서로'는 each other 또는 one another로 쓴다.

07 여러 개 중 하나를 제외한 나머지이므로 the others가 맞다.

08 동사(were)가 복수형이므로 복수로 쓰이는 부정대명사를 찾으면 된다.

09 셋을 나타낼 때는 one, another, the other로 쓴다.

10 everybody는 단수 취급하므로 are를 is로 써야 한다. ①의 Everybody는 호격(부르는 말)이라 raise가 명령문으로 쓰인 것이다.

11 ① 「spend/waste+목적어+-ing」 구조로 쓰이고, 돈은 셀 수 없으므로 little이 와야 한다.

12 '그 요리사는 과자를 굽기 위해 밀가루 두 컵이 필요하다.'이므로 주어(the cook)와 동사(needs)를 쓰고 나머지를 이어서 쓰면 된다. 밀가루 두 컵은 two cups of flour로 쓴다.

13 사람이 거의 없었으므로 few를 쓰고, 주어가 복수(people)이므로 be 동사는 were를 써야 한다.

14 무생물의 소유는 B of A로 쓰고 'A의 B'로 해석한다.

15 하이픈으로 연결된 명사는 형용사 역할을 하므로 복수형이 없다.

16 -one, -body, -thing의 단어들은 형용사가 뒤에서 꾸며준다.

17 불특정 다수 중 일부는 some, 또 다른 일부는 others로 쓴다. 계란 하나는 an egg, 약간의 치즈는 some cheese로 쓴다.

18 넷 중 하나는 one, 다른 하나는 another, 나머지는 the others이다.

19 넷을 나타낼 때는 one, another, the third, the other 순으로 표현한다.

20 ⓐ 긍정문에서 any는 '~라두'라는 의미이다 ⓑ 단수 동사(has)가 왔으므로 each가 알맞다. ⓒ 「a+명사」는 one으로 받는다. ⓓ 다섯 개 중 두 번째는 another, 세 번째는 the third, 나머지 두 개는 the others를 쓴다.

21 ⓐ 셀 수 있는 명사이므로 many로 써야 한다.
ⓑ 복수동사인 wear가 쓰였으므로 each를 both로 고쳐야 한다.

22 '각'에 해당하는 each, 그리고 each는 단수 취급하므로 tries, '~하기 위해 노력하다'는 「try+to 동사원형」으로 쓰이므로 to show, 선수는 두 명이므로 상대를 의미하는 the other를 쓰면 된다.

[21~22]

　　복싱은 많은 나라에서 인기가 많다. 복싱 경기에서는 종이 울릴 때 두 선수는 손에 장갑을 끼고 서로 친다. 하지만 태국 복싱은 다르다. 이 복싱 경기는 음악과 함께 시작한다. 음악이 진행될 때, 두 선수들은 무릎을 꿇고 신에게 기도를 한다. 다음에 그들은 춤

을 추기 시작한다. 이 춤 동안에, 각 선수는 다른 선수에게 자기가 최고라는 것을 보여주려고 노력한다. 그 후에, 싸움이 시작된다. 태국 복싱에서, 선수들은 발로 찰 수고 팔꿈치나 무릎으로 서로 칠 수도 있다. 물론, 그들은 손으로도 친다.

• 어휘 • kneel 무릎을 꿇다 | pray 기도하다 | elbow 팔꿈치

CHAPTER 07
수동태

UNIT 15 수동태의 개념과 시제

1) 하는 주체　　2) ~을 하다　　3) 받는 대상
4) ~되다[~지다]　5) be　　6) p.p.
7) by　　8) 주어　　9) be
10) p.p.　　11) by　　12) am/is/are
13) was/were　　14) will be　　15) 일반인
16) 불분명한　　17) 불필요한

Level 1 Test
p. 92

A　1　were believed　　2　were not
　　3　be delivered　　4　witnessed

B　1　The gate is opened (by someone) every day.
　　2　The workers are paid in peso (by them).
　　3　All of the applicants will be hired (by the company).

Level 2 Test
p. 93

01　⑤　　　　　　　　02　④
03　③　　　　　　　　04　④
05　not → was not　　06　ⓐ sent → be sent
07　(1) painted
　　(2) Was / painted
　　(3) wasn't[was not] painted
　　(4) painted
08　The room wasn't cleaned by her.

>>> 해설

01 두 문장 모두 수동태이며, 두 번째 문장은 주어가 복수라 복수 동사(were)가 들어가야 한다.

02 수동태의 부정문은 「be+not+p.p.」이고, 수동태의 주어가 복수이므로 were를 써야 한다.

03 didn't bring은 수동형은 was/were not brought이다.

04 ⓑ not was → was not ⓒ took → taken ⓓ made → were

made

05 「be not+p.p.」에서 be동사가 없으므로 was를 써야 한다.

06 수동태의 미래형은 「will be+p.p.」이다.

07 ①과 ④는 능동이면서 과거이므로 painted이다. ②는 의문문, ③은 부정문으로 쓰면 된다.

08 수동태이므로 「be+p.p.+by+목적격」의 틀을 먼저 완성해야 한다. 수동태의 부정은 「be+not+p.p.」이다.

Level 3 Test

01 ② ④   02 ②
03 ④   04 ③
05 ④   06 ④
07 ②   08 ②
09 ②   10 ②
11 ① ③ ⑤
12 The food is going to be served soon.
13 ⓑ by → to
14 This well is not used anymore.
15 I'm sorry, but you're[you are] not invited.
16 (1) clean
(2) was cleaned

≫ 해설

01 die는 '죽다'의 자동사로 능동형으로 쓰고, kill은 '죽이다'의 타동사로 수동형으로 써야 한다.

02 Two mice were caught by my cat yesterday[yesterday by my cat].으로 전환할 수 있다. 동사의 목적어는 yesterday가 아님에 유의한다.

03 break의 과거분사는 broken이다.

04 첫 번째 문장은 일반동사의 의문문으로 동사원형이 필요하다. 두 번째 문장은 개가 찾아진 것으로 수동태로 써야 한다. 세 번째 문장에서 전치사 뒤에는 동명사를 쓴다.

05 8단어로 영작해야 하므로 Then, the wine is stored in the bottles.로 영작할 수 있으므로 by는 불필요하다.

06 by people은 불필요하므로 생략해도 무방하다.

07 미래 시제의 수동태는 「will be+p.p.」로 쓴다. (will eaten → will be eaten)

08 ⓐ are played → play ⓑ singing → sung ⓓ discovered → was discovered ⓕ held → were held

09 ⓑ 「by+them(일반인)」 ⓔ 「by+someone(불필요)」하므로 생략할 수 있다.

10 ② The image is going to be printed.가 되어야 하므로 be가 없다. ① The mouse isn't used anymore. ③ Pines are found everywhere in Korea. ④ This helmet was worn by many people. ⑤ The robbers were caught by the police.

11 수동태의 형태에 맞게 각각 ① hold → held ③ destroyed → were destroyed ⑤ was → were로 고쳐야 한다.

12 '음식이 곧 제공될 것입니다.'를 영작하면 되며, 「be going to be+p.p.」의 형태로 배열하면 된다.

13 「by+행위자」가 생략된 형태이므로 '빨간색으로'라는 뜻의 to red로 써야 한다.

14 일반인을 나타내는 「by+행위자」는 생략 가능하다.

15 '초대받지'로 해석되어 수동태로 써야 하며, 수동태의 부정형은 「be

---

not+p.p.」이다.

16 (1)은 일반동사의 의문문으로 동사원형이 필요하다.
(2)는 과거에 청소된 것이므로 수동태의 과거형이 와야 한다.

UNIT
16 여러 가지 수동태(1)

1) 조동사   2) be   3) p.p.
4) be동사   5) 주어   6) p.p.
7) 의문사   8) be동사   9) p.p.
10) by   11) By   12) be동사
13) p.p.   14) to   15) for
16) of

Level 1 Test

A 1 be   2 was
   3 Is   4 to

B 1 can't be fixed   2 am given
   3 was given to

C 1 has to be decided 2 Was / invited
   3 were sent to

Level 2 Test

01 ②   02 ③
03 ②   04 ③
05 Can the flowers be delivered
06 Then, what[which] language is spoken here?
07 ⓑ seen → be seen
08 (1) were shown the picture
(2) was shown to us

≫ 해설

01 조동사의 수동태는 「조동사+(not) be+p.p.」이다.

02 When was the electric guitar sold (by them)?으로 전환할 수 있다.

03 Will my apology be accepted by her?로 전환할 수 있다.

04 bring의 직접 목적어가 수동태의 주어가 되면 전치사 of가 아니라 to를 쓴다.

05 조동사의 의문문 수동태는 「조동사+주어+be+p.p.」 순으로 쓴다.

06 「의문사+be동사+주어+p.p.」 순으로 쓰면 된다.

07 조동사의 수동태는 「조동사+be+p.p.」이다.

08 (1)은 간접 목적어를, (2)는 직접 목적어를 수동태의 주어로 전환한 것이다. show는 전치사 to를 쓴다.

Level 3 Test

01 ④   02 ③ ④
03 ⑤   04 ⑤
05 ②   06 ④

07 ⑤ 08 ② ④
09 ② 10 ⑤
11 is had to use → has to be used
12 Is everything made in China?
13 (1) were given
(2) was given to
14 Where was this robot cleaner made?
15 Vietnamese noodles were cooked for me by my mom.
16 By what were you touched today?
또는 What were you touched by today?

》》 해설

01 주어가 동작을 받는 것이므로 수동태로 써야 한다.
02 「조동사+be+p.p.」로 쓰면 되며 '~해서는 안 된다'는 should not 또는 ought not to이다.
03 Where was this artifact found by you?로 재배열하면 된다.
04 I gave my girlfriend a pretty doll yesterday.에서 간접 목적어를 주어로 수동태로 전환한 문장으로 to가 아니라 by로 써야 한다. 직접 목적어를 주어로 전환하면 A pretty doll was given to my girlfriend by me yesterday.이다.
05 By whom was this picture drawn?으로 전환된다.
06 (Where) she bought the cap.을 수동태로 바꾸고 의문문으로 바꾼 것이 주어진 문장이다.
07 What did he buy at that store?를 수동태로 바꾼 것으로 볼 수 있으므로 「by+행위자」로 고치면 된다. What was bought (at that store) for him?으로 해도 가능하나 답에는 없다.
08 ② Did the question be understood → Was the question understood ④ finished → be finished
09 ⓐ paid → be paid ⓒ who → whom ⓓ for → at
10 make는 to가 아닌 for가 필요하다. ⑤ A paper plane was made for the boy. ① By whom were you told this? ② Are grapes grown in California? ③ The money wasn't given to me. ④ The video will be posted online.
11 have to를 하나의 조동사로 취급해서 수동태로 전환한다.
12 주어는 everything으로 단수 취급하며, 동작을 받는 수동태로 만들어 의문문으로 배열하면 된다.
13 (1)은 간접 목적어를 주어로 전환한 수동태이고, (2)는 직접 목적어를 주어로 한 것으로 전치사 to를 써야 한다. (1)에서 the police는 집합 명사로 복수 취급한다.
14 B의 대답이 '미네소타에서 만들어졌다'이므로 '장소'를 묻는 수동태의 질문이 와야 한다.
15 cook은 직접 목적어만 주어로 전환 가능하며, 이때 전치사는 for를 쓴다.
16 의문사가 주어인 의문문의 수동태로 「By+의문사+be동사+ 주어+p.p. ~?」로 쓰면 된다. (오늘 당신은 무엇에 의해 감동받았나요?) 이때 by는 뒤로 보낼 수 있다.

UNIT 17 여러 가지 수동태(2)

1) be interested in 2) be located in[at] 3) be caught in
4) be disappointed at[in, with]
5) be surprised at[by]
6) be shocked at[by]
7) be excited about[at, by]
8) be worried about
9) be amazed at[by]
10) be covered with
11) be satisfied with 12) be scared of
13) be filled with 14) be pleased with
15) be married to 16) be crowded with
17) be dressed in 18) be tired of 19) be made of
20) be made from 21) be known for 22) be known to
23) be known as 24) be known by
25) are taken care of

Level 1 Test
p. 100

A 1 was pleased with 2 is known for
3 is scared of

B 1 was run out of 2 be picked up by

C 1 is never satisfied with 2 is made from

Level 2 Test
p. 101

01 ④ 02 ④
03 ⑤ 04 ⑤
05 had to be put off by
06 (1) is made of
(2) are made from
07 The plan is not going to be carried out.
08 Is she pleased with my choice?

》》 해설

01 '~로 덮여 있다'는 be covered with로 쓴다.
02 She put on the mannequin's hat.의 수동태로, 동사구는 한 묶음으로 전환한다.
03 be crowded with, be surprised at[by]으로 쓴다.
04 ⓒ a bike → by a bike ⓓ as → for ⓔ in → with
05 have to는 하나의 조동사이고 동사구 put off도 한 묶음으로 인식해서 수동태를 만들어야 한다.
06 집은 과자로 만들어졌으므로 물리적 변화인 be made of로 쓰고, 과자는 밀가루로 만들어지는 화학적 변화로 be made from을 이용하여 쓴다.
07 동사구는 한 묶음으로 전환하며 be going to도 will처럼 조동사의 역할을 하므로 「be going to be+p.p.」형태로 쓰면 된다.
08 be pleased with(~이 마음에 들다)로 쓰며, 의문문이므로 be동사를 먼저 쓴다.

01 ⑤   02 ③
03 ⑤   04 ①
05 ③   06 ②
07 ④   08 ④
09 ②   10 ①
11 ① ④ ⑤
12 will be taken care of by
13 The twin bed will be taken out by the girls.
14 By whom are national parks looked after?
15 were taken care of
16 I am tired of the weather in London.

≫ 해설

01 be filled with, be covered with로 쓴다. ①은 in, ②는 of, ③은 to, ④는 of(질린) 또는 from(지친)이 알맞다.

02 I was made fun of by the girls in my class.로 전환할 수 있다.

03 The title wasn't paid attention to (by people).로 써야 한다.

04 be made of/from은 물리적 변화/화학적 변화로 제품이 앞에 오며 be made into는 재료가 앞에 오고 제품이 뒤에 온다.

05 He is known for his ability to train monkeys.로 영작할 수 있다. be known for가 '~로 유명하다'의 의미이다.

06 be crowded with를 써야 한다.

07 by everybody가 능동태의 주어가 되고 he가 look down on의 목적어인 의문문을 만들면 된다. (왜 모두가 그를 무시하는 거지?)

08 An Indian couple brought up the children.의 수동태로, 동사구는 한 묶음으로 전환한다.

09 ⓑ him → by him ⓔ looking → looked

10 be scared of로 쓰인다. ① Are you scared of the dark? ② Kathy is married to my brother. ③ They were caught in a dilemma. ④ We were shocked at his accent. ⑤ He was disappointed at the results.

11 ① from → at[by] ④ with → at ⑤ by → with

12 동사구의 수동태는 한 묶음으로 전환하고, 조동사의 수동태는 「조동사+be+p.p.」의 어순이다.

13 동사구는 한 묶음으로 취급해서 수동태로 쓰고 「by+행위자」를 써야 한다.

14 의문사(who)가 주어인 수동태는 「By whom+be동사+주어+p.p. ~?」로 바꾸며, 동사구는 한 묶음으로 수동태로 바꾼다.

15 '너의 이구아나들은 할머니에 의해서 돌봐졌다.'를 영작하면 된다. take care of(~을 돌보다)를 한 묶음으로 전환한다.

16 be tired of는 '~에 질리다(~이 지긋지긋하다)'라는 의미의 표현이다.

01 ③   02 ④
03 ②   04 ① ② ④
05 ⑤   06 ③
07 ⑤   08 ③
09 ⑤   10 ⑤
11 was delivered   12 to
13 The teacher always asks me difficult questions.
또는 The teacher always asks difficult questions of me.
14 It was[is] hidden inside the book.
15 from, in, about
16 check → be checked
17 I am not surprised at[by] a surprise party
18 ⓒ The dentist was taken to me by my uncle. → I was taken to the dentist by my uncle.
19 How long ago was the computer turned on?
20 (1) was given the wrong information
(2) was given to me by
21 ② ③
22 Our lives are filled with many things to do.

≫ 해설

01 주어가 동작을 받으므로 수동태로 써야 하며 will 다음에는 동사원형 be가 온다.

02 조동사의 의문문 수동태는 「조동사+주어+be+p.p. ~?」 순으로 쓴다.

03 의문사가 있는 수동태는 「의문사+be동사+주어+p.p. ~?」 순으로 쓴다.

04 ① is → are ② wrote → written ④ is → was (능동태에서 read에 -s가 없으므로 과거형임을 알 수 있다.)

05 be dressed in(~을 입다), be located in(~에 위치하다)으로 쓴다.

06 to를 삭제해야 한다. 간접 목적어가 주어가 되면 전치사를 쓰지 않는다.

07 ①~④는 with가 들어가고, ⑤에는 for가 들어간다.

08 「by+행위자」가 불분명, 불확실, 불필요할 때는 생략 가능하다.

09 Did you put off the plan?의 수동태로 Was the plan put off by you?로 써야 한다. (그 계획은 너에 의해 연기되었니?)

10 ① laughed → laughed at ② in → about ③ to → at ④ by → in ⑤ be known as ~로 알려져 있다

11 주어가 동작을 받는 것이고 과거 시제이므로 수동태로 was delivered라고 써야 한다.

12 be married to(~와 결혼하다), be known to(~에게 알려지다)로 쓴다.

13 4형식의 수동태에서 ask는 직접 목적어를 주어로 할 때 of를 쓴다.

14 I hid it inside the book.의 수동태에서 조건에 맞게 by me를 생략하면 된다. (숨긴 것은 과거지만 현재도 숨겨진 상태일 수 있으므로 be동사를 현재형 is로 쓸 수도 있다.)

15 be scared of, be shocked at, be covered with로 쓰인다.

16 ought to는 하나의 조동사처럼 사용되며, 「조동사+be+p.p.」 순으로 쓴다.

17 '~에 놀라다'는 be surprised at[by]을 쓴다.

18 took의 목적어가 me이므로 me[I]를 주어로 전환해야 한다.

19 의문사가 있는 수동태는 「의문사+be동사+주어+p.p.」로 쓴다. '얼마나 오래 전에'는 How long ago로 표현한다.

20 4형식 동사는 직접 목적어와 간접 목적어를 주어로 하는 두 개의 수동태로 전환할 수 있으며, give동사는 전치사 to를 쓴다.

21 ⓑ We가 부르는 것이 아니라 불리는 것이므로 수동형인 be called로 바르게 고쳤다. ⓒ 선택지 앞에 of not에서 of가 전치사이므로 전치사의 목적어로 쓰이는 동명사 having으로 바르게 고쳤다.

22 주어는 Our lives이고 '~로 가득 차 있다'는 are filled with로 쓴 후, with의 목적어인 many things가 오고 이것을 수식할 수 있는 to부정사인 to do로 쓰면 된다.

[21~22]

우리의 삶은 해야 할 많은 것들로 가득 차 있다. 우리가 가만히 앉아서 아무것도 하지 않는 것은 매우 어렵다. 심지어 몇 분 동안만이라도. 사람들은 더 이상 human being(존재하는 인간)이 아니다. 우리는 human doing(행동하는 인간)이라고 불려야 한다. 사실, 우리는 해야 할 어떤 것을 가지지 않는다는 생각에 종종 두려워한다. 하지만 우리의 신체처럼, 우리의 마음도 때때로 휴식이 필요하다. 휴식 후에, 우리의 마음은 강하고, 자유롭고, 창의적이게 된다.

• 어휘 • still 가만히 있는 | human being 인간 | as a matter of fact 사실 | break 휴식 | creative 창의적인

CHAPTER 08
관계사

UNIT 18 관계대명사 who, which

1) 사람
2) who
3) who(m)
4) whose
5) that
6) who[that]
7) who(m)[that]
8) whose
9) 사물
10) 동물
11) which
12) which
13) that
14) which[that]
15) which[that]
16) whose
17) of
18) which
19) whose
20) of which
21) 직접 수식
22) who
23) 보충 설명
24) comma(,)
25) 접속사
26) 대명사
27) who
28) and
29) he

Level 1 Test
p. 108

A 1 who 2 works
   3 that, which (둘 다 가능)

B 1 The customer liked the waitress who[that] was very friendly.
   2 The dictionary which[that] I'm using now has many new words.
   3 I know the man who(m)[that] you respect.

Level 2 Test
p. 109

01 ① ④   02 ②
03 ② ③ ④   04 ⑤
05 which   06 who / whom

---

07 We adopted a child whose parents were killed in an accident.
08 who[that] are sitting on the grass

》》 해설

01 선행사로 사람이 오면 주격 관계대명사로 who나 that 둘 다 가능하다.
02 선행사(an aunt)가 사람이므로 관계사는 who나 that이 적절하다.
03 ②는 명사절을 이끄는 접속사 that이고 ③ ④는 의문사이다.
04 ① that으로 써도 되지만 who도 맞다. ② 선행사가 a boy이므로 has가 맞다. ③ 주격이므로 생략할 수 없다. ④ who는 관계대명사이다.
05 선행사가 사물이고 목적격 관계대명사이다. 그런데 콤마(,)가 있으므로 계속적 용법이다. 따라서 which가 적절하다. which나 that이 알맞다. (우리가 지난 일요일에 본 영화 〈숨바꼭질〉은 매우 무서웠다.)
06 사람이 선행사인 목적격 관계대명사는 whom, who, that을 쓸 수 있다.
07 반복되는 명사 child가 소유격으로 쓰였으므로 소유격 관계대명사 whose를 the child's 대신 써서 한 문장으로 만든다.
08 선행사가 사람이므로 who나 that을 쓰고, children이 복수이므로 진행형의 be동사는 are이다. sit의 현재분사형은 sitting이다.

Level 3 Test
p. 110

01 ④   02 ③
03 ②   04 ② ③
05 ④   06 ② ③
07 ④   08 ②
09 ③   10 ④
11 that
12 The woman whom I take care of suffers from cancer.
13 will eat the pizza which[that] she left last night
14 Look at the calendar which is hanging on the wall.
15 and it
16 whose top was covered with snow

》》 해설

01 소유격 관계대명사가 사용된 관계절에서 주어(brothers)가 복수이므로 동사는 resemble이 되어야 한다.
02 주격 관계대명사가 쓰였으므로 종속절에 다른 주어는 필요 없다. which는 사물에 쓰는 관계대명사이므로 ⑤는 오답이다.
03 ②는 주격 관계대명사이고 나머지는 목적격이다.
04 [보기]와 ② ③은 관계대명사이고 ① ④ ⑤는 의문사이다.
05 「접속사+대명사」는 계속적 용법의 관계대명사로 고칠 수 있다. 선행사가 a gift이므로 which가 알맞다.
06 ② ③ 앞에 명사(선행사)가 있고 뒤에 동사가 있는 주격 관계대명사 ① 명사절을 이끄는 접속사 ④ 의문사(어떤 것) ⑤ 의문사(누구)
07 ⓒ 선행사가 a great book이므로 관계대명사 which나 that이 알맞다. ⓔ 소유격 관계대명사는 「명사+of which」나 「whose+명사」의 순서로 쓴다. which the leg → the leg of which 또는 whose leg
08 첫 번째는 사물이 선행사인 목적격 관계대명사로 which나 that이 알맞다. 두 번째는 사람이 선행사인 목적격 관계대명사 whom이나 that이 알맞다.
09 반복되는 명사인 선행사 a girl이 뒤 문장에서 소유격으로 쓰였으므로

알맞은 관계대명사는 whose이다.

10 「접속사＋명사」는 관계대명사로 바꿀 수 있다. 선행사가 앞 문장 전체이므로 which가 알맞다.

11 첫 번째와 두 번째는 각각 사물과 사람을 선행사로 할 수 있는 that, 세 번째는 목적절을 이끄는 접속사 that이 필요하다.

12 주어가 the woman이므로 동사 suffer는 suffers가 되어야 한다. (내가 돌보는 여자는 암을 앓고 있다.)

13 선행사 the pizza가 뒤 문장에서 목적어 역할을 하므로 관계대명사는 which나 that을 쓴다. 「주어＋동사＋선행사＋관계대명사＋주어＋동사 ～」

14 주격 관계대명사 which를 사용해서 두 문장을 합친 것이다. which 대신 that도 가능하다.

15 관계대명사의 계속적 용법은 「접속사＋명사」로 바꿀 수 있다. 여기서 내용상 접속사는 and가 알맞다.

16 the mountain과 its top을 연결하는 문장으로 소유격 관계대명사 whose를 쓴다.

UNIT 19 관계대명사 that, what

1) 소유　　　2) 계속　　　3) 전치사
4) 최상급　　5) 서수　　　6) very
7) only　　　8) same　　　9) all
10) every　　11) any　　　12) no
13) thing　　14) 주어　　　15) 보어
16) 목적어　　17) 목적　　　18) 목적
19) whom　　20) 목적　　　21) which
22) 주　　　23) be동사　　24) which is

Level 1 Test
p. 112

A　1　that, whom (둘 다 가능)　　2　what
　　3　which　　　　　　　　　　4　that
　　5　that　　　　　　　　　　　6　What
　　7　which, that (둘 다 가능)

B　1　I picked up the trash that[which] he threw out.
　　2　He gave me what he had.
　　3　the very car that[which] my father used to drive

Level 2 Test
p. 113

01　④ ⑤　　　　　　　　02　③
03　④　　　　　　　　　04　①
05　that
06　Look at the girls (who are) dancing on the stage.
07　ⓐ This is the thing which[that] you are looking for.
　　또는 This is what you are looking for.
08　I ate what he made for me.

》》 해설

01　① ② 주격 관계대명사 that ③ 접속사 that ④ 소유격 whose 필요
　　⑤ 전치사 앞에 that을 쓸 수 없다. (→ which)

02　③은 '무엇'이라고 해석되는 의문사이고, 나머지는 '～하는 것' 이라고

해석되는 관계대명사이다.

03　④ him은 the boy를 가리키는 것으로, 관계대명사가 쓰였으므로 없애야 한다.

04　① 주격 관계대명사는 생략할 수 없다. ② ③ ④ 목적격 관계 대명사는 생략할 수 있다. ⑤ 「주격 관계대명사＋be동사」는 같이 생략 가능하다.

05　첫 번째 문장은 선행사가 최상급이라 관계사 that이 주로 쓰인다. 두 번째는 목적절을 이끄는 접속사 that이다.

06　「관계대명사 주격＋be동사」는 같이 생략 가능하다. 둘 중 하나만 생략할 수는 없다.

07　the thing which[that]를 what으로 바꿔 쓸 수 있다.

08　선행사 the thing을 포함한 관계사 what을 넣어야 7단어로 문장을 완성할 수 있다.

Level 3 Test
p. 114

01　②　　　　　　　　　　02　①
03　⑤　　　　　　　　　　04　③ ④ ⑤
05　②, ⑤　　　　　　　　06　②
07　③　　　　　　　　　　08　⑤
09　①　　　　　　　　　　10　⑤
11　(A) that[which]　(B) what
12　Vanilla is a flavor I am fond of.
13　She is the very person that I want to work with.
14　He got the package which[that] was sent by me.
15　ⓐ He has a new car which[that] he drives every day.
　　ⓒ It is a crayon with which I drew this picture.
　　또는 It is a crayon which[that] I drew this picture with.
16　What made him angry was my mistake.

》》 해설

01　• 선행사를 포함한 관계사 what
　　• 선행사가 사물(bike)인 목적격 관계대명사 which나 that

02　that은 바로 앞에 전치사가 있으면 쓸 수 없다.

03　[보기]와 ⑤의 that은 주격 관계대명사이다. ① 지시대명사 ② ③ ④ 접속사

04　[보기]와 ③ ④ ⑤는 주격 관계대명사이고, ①은 It ～ that 강조 용법, ②는 목적절을 이끄는 접속사이다.

05　② 전치사 다음에 나오는 관계대명사는 생략할 수 없다. ⑤ 소유격 관계대명사는 생략할 수 없다.

06　ⓐ 앞에 명사가 있으므로 what은 that[which]으로 써야 한다. ⓑ 선행사 the temple이 주어로 쓰였으므로 동사는 gives이다.

07　③은 '～라는 것'이라고 해석되는, 목적절을 이끄는 접속사이고, 나머지는 명사 다음에 '～한'으로 해석되는 관계대명사이다.

08　⑤는 '무엇'이라고 해석되는 의문사이고, 나머지는 '～한 것'이라고 해석되는 관계대명사이다.

09　① 명사 the same thing 다음에 관계사 that이 알맞고, 나머지는 명사가 포함된 관계대명사 what이 들어간다.

10　선행사가 최상급일 때 관계사 that이 주로 쓰이며, it도 the biggest potato를 가리키므로 삭제해야 한다.

11　• 선행사가 -thing일 때 관계대명사 that이 주로 쓰인다.
　　• 선행사를 포함한 관계대명사 what이 알맞다.

12　관계대명사 목적격을 생략하기 위해서는 전치사가 문장 뒤로 가야 한다.

24

13 선행사에 the very가 쓰이면 관계대명사 that이 주로 쓰인다.

14 과거분사(sent)가 뒤에서 앞에 있는 명사를 꾸며줄 때는 「관계대명사 주격+be동사」가 생략된 것이다.

15 ⓐ 앞에 a new car가 있으므로 생략 가능한 목적격 관계대명사 which나 that이 알맞다. ⓒ 전치사 with가 있을 때는 목적격 관계대명사 which를 써야 하고, 전치사 with를 문장 뒤에 쓸 때는 생략 가능한 목적격 관계대명사 which나 that을 쓴다.

16 주어이면서 선행사를 포함한 관계대명사 what이 필요하다.

UNIT 20 관계부사

1) 전치사	2) 관계대명사	3) 전치사
4) 관계대명사	5) where	6) in
7) on	8) at	9) where
10) when	11) in	12) on
13) at	14) when	15) why
16) for	17) why	18) how
19) in	20) how	21) the way

Level 1 Test

p. 116

A
1 where
2 when
3 why
4 how
5 where
6 when

B
1 at which / at / where
2 in which / the way / how

Level 2 Test

p. 117

01 ② ⑤   02 ②
03 ⑤   04 ②
05 how
06 the place where I hang my keys
07 The reason (why) 또는 Why
08 the time when he had to call his mother

>>> 해설

01 [보기]와 ② ⑤는 '~한'으로 해석되는 관계부사이고, 나머지는 '어디에'로 해석되는 의문사이다.

02 ⓔ because는 앞에 why가 있으므로 that으로 쓰거나 생략해야 한다.

03 문장 끝에 전치사가 있는데 관계부사 where를 쓸 수 없다. 전치사를 없애든지 where를 which나 that으로 바꾸어야 한다.

04 첫 번째는 이유를 묻는 의문사 why이고, 두 번째는 이유를 설명하는 관계부사이다.

05 방법을 나타낼 때는 the way나 관계부사 how 둘 중 하나만 쓴다.

06 the place 다음에 관계부사 where를 놓고, 다음 문장이 the place를 꾸며줄 수 있도록 나열한다. (이것은 내가 열쇠를 거는 곳이다.)

07 뒤 문장에서 실패한 이유를 설명하고 있으므로 The reason이나 Why가 알맞다.

08 the time이 있으므로 관계부사 when을 써서 문장을 영작한다.

Level 3 Test

p. 118

01 ①   02 ①
03 ③   04 ④
05 ③   06 ①
07 ②   08 ②
09 (A) why   (B) that
10 I remember the way he looked at me
   또는 I remember how he looked at me.
11 Pyeongchang is the city in Korea where the Winter Olympics were held in 2018.
12 2005 was the year when we got married.
13 where he is standing is full of books
14 That's the reason which → That's the reason why[That's the reason 또는 That's why]

>>> 해설

01 ①은 앞에 시간을 의미하는 말이 없는 것으로 보아 '~할 때'라고 해석되는 접속사이고, 나머지는 시간을 나타내는 선행사와 함께 쓰인 관계부사이다.

02 [보기]와 ②~⑤는 관계부사이고, ①은 '어디에'로 해석되는 의문사이다.

03 ⓒ 선행사 many places가 뒤 문장에서 visit의 목적어 역할을 하므로 where는 which[that]가 되어야 알맞다. ⓔ 선행사 an office가 뒤 문장에서 부사 역할을 하므로 관계부사 where가 알맞다.

04 which를 where 또는 in which 고쳐야 한다. → ④ That's the restaurant where[in which] he has a part-time job.
① I knew why Claudia got upset. ② The city in which I live is beautiful. ③ The month when I was born is November.
⑤ I'm not satisfied with the way she cut my hair.

05 ③ the country가 뒤 문장에서 부사 역할을 하므로 which → where

06 ① situation은 때를 나타내는 것이 아니라 장소를 나타내므로 where가 알맞다.

07 ⓐ ⓒ 관계부사 where 다음에 전치사 in은 필요 없다.

08 ② 선행사 the place가 뒤 문장에서 목적어 역할을 하므로 관계대명사 which가 필요하고, 나머지는 관계부사 where가 필요하다.

09 첫 번째는 The reason이 뒤 문장에서 for the reason 부사 역할을 하므로 why이고, 두 번째는 동사 다음에 문장을 이끄는 접속사 that이 알맞다.

10 the way와 how는 같이 쓸 수 없고 둘 중 하나만 쓴다.

11 두 번째 문장의 부사 in the city를 관계부사 where로 바꾸어 연결한다.

12 주어(2005)와 동사(was)를 찾고 나머지 단어를 의미에 맞게 배열한다. 의미상 the year 다음에 관계부사 when을 넣어 8단어로 만든다.

13 the room이 다음 문장에서 장소 부사로 쓰였으므로 관계부사 where로 연결한다.

14 the reason이 뒤 문장에서 이유를 나타내는 부사로 쓰였으므로 관계부사 why를 써야 하고, 이때 둘 중 하나만 써도 된다.

Review Test

p. 120

01 ② ④   02 ① ⑤
03 ④   04 ④ ⑤
05 ③   06 ① ④

07 ③   08 ③
09 ② ③ ④   10 ⑤

11 She is holding a bag made in Italy.

12 ⓑ is → are

13 a common mistake which[that] anyone can make

14 Correct the errors which[that] you made on the test.

15 I brought the boy whom you wanted to talk with.

16 He taught me what love meant.

17 whose

18 and it

19 I don't know the girl who is wearing the red skirt.

20 Look at the room full of flowers.

21 ① ② ⑤

22 what people wanted to hear

≫ 해설

01 사람 선행사(a daughter)가 뒤 문장에서 주어 역할을 하므로 주격 관계대명사 who나 that이 알맞다.

02 ① 선행사(a bird)가 동물일 때는 which나 that을 쓴다. ⑤ 선행사가 복수형 questions이므로 동사는 were가 알맞다.

03 ⓒ 주어가 The dog이므로 동사는 looks가 되어야 한다. ⓔ 소방관은 사람이므로 관계사는 who가 알맞다.

04 선행사가 사람일 때 목적격 관계대명사는 who, whom, that 모두 가능하다.

05 ③ 전치사와 함께 있는 관계대명사는 생략할 수 없다.

06 ⓐ ⓑ 둘 다 반복되는 명사를 관계대명사 다음에 썼으므로 it을 없애야 올바른 문장이다.

07 ③은 의문사(무엇)이고, 나머지는 선행사가 포함된 관계대명사(~한 것)이다.

08 Never go to a doctor whose office plants have died.로 영작할 수 있다.

09 선행사로 all이나 최상급이 쓰이면 관계사 that을 주로 쓴다. ① → What ⑤ → which

10 첫 번째는 선행사 the day가 뒤 문장에서 on the day인 시간 부사 역할을 하므로 관계부사 when, 두 번째는 장소를 나타내는 where가 알맞다.

11 주격 관계대명사(which[that])와 be동사(was)는 생략할 수 있다.

12 ⓑ 선행사인 the countries가 복수이므로 동사는 is가 아니라 are가 알맞다.

13 a common mistake를 선행사로 하는 관계대명사 which[that]를 넣고 문장을 배열한다.

14 선행사 the errors 다음에 목적격 관계대명사 which[that]가 들어간다. (시험에서 네가 범한 오류들을 고치렴.)

15 the boy가 반복적으로 쓰여 관계대명사 whom을 쓴 것이므로 him을 없애줘야 한다. (나는 네가 이야기를 나누고 싶어 했던 남자애를 데려왔어.)

16 선행사가 없으므로 which를 지우고 what을 이용한다.

17 반복되는 명사가 His인 소유격으로 관계사 whose를 넣어 문장을 연결한다. (나는 깰 수 없는 기록을 갖고 있는 운동선수를 만났다.)

18 계속적 용법의 관계대명사는 「접속사+대명사」로 바꾸어 쓸 수 있다. 여기서는 의미상 접속사 and와 앞의 내용 전체(그녀가 대회에서 우승한 것)를 대신하는 대명사 it이 알맞다. (그녀는 그 대회에서 우승했는데, 그것이 모두를 놀라게 했다.)

19 현재분사가 뒤에서 앞에 있는 명사를 수식할 때는 「주격 관계대명

사+be동사」가 생략되어 있다. (나는 빨간 치마를 입은 소녀를 모른다.)

20 the room 뒤에 「주격 관계대명사+be동사」 which[that] is가 생략되어야 단어 수가 맞다.

21 ① 선행사가 a newspaper이고 발행된 것이므로 was published로 써야 한다. ② 주격관계대명사는 맞으나 생략할 수 없다. ⑤ 완전한 절을 유도하는 접속사 that이다.

22 '~하는 것'은 관계대명사 what으로, 시제에 맞게 wanted, 그리고 이것의 목적어로 to hear를 쓰면 된다.

[21~22]

> 'Good News'는 캘리포니아에서 발행되었던 신문의 이름이었다. 그것은 강도, 범죄, 죽음 그리고 재앙에 대한 이야기를 인쇄하는 다른 신문과는 매우 달랐다. 'Good News'는 영웅적 행동이나 행운 같은 사람들이 듣고 싶어했던 것만을 인쇄했다. 하지만, 아무도 그것을 사지 않았고, 그 신문사는 시작한지 얼마 안되어 곧 망했다. 우리는 이것으로부터 오늘날 신문에서 좋은 소식은 나쁜 소식이라는 결론을 내릴 수 있다.

• 어휘 • publish 발행하다 | robbery 강도 | crime 범죄 | death 죽음 | disaster 재앙 | heroic 영웅적 | act 행동 | good fortune 행운 | go out of business 망하다 | conclude 결론을 내리다

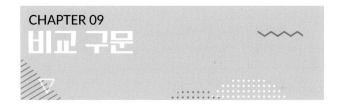

CHAPTER 09
비교 구문

UNIT 21 비교 변화, 원급 이용 비교 구문

1) smaller		2) smallest	
3) larger		4) largest	
5) easier		6) easiest	
7) bigger		8) biggest	
9) more interesting		10) most interesting	
11) more careful		12) most careful	
13) more boring		14) most boring	
15) better		16) best	
17) more		18) most	
19) later		20) latest	
21) farther		22) farthest	
23) worse		24) worst	
25) less		26) least	
27) latter		28) last	
29) further		30) furthest	
31) as		32) as	
33) not		34) as	

35) so   36) as
37) as   38) as
39) possible

Level 1 Test
p. 124

A 1 stranger / strangest   2 heavier / heaviest
   3 more helpful / most helpful
   4 better / best   5 more / most
   6 later / latest   7 thinner / thinnest

B 1 lazier than   2 as hard as
   3 as many / as possible

Level 2 Test
p. 125

01 ⑤   02 ②
03 ①   04 ③
05 as old as
06 Danny can draw pictures better than Luke.
07 Children like swinging as high as possible.
08 (1) best[most]
   (2) worst[least]

》》 해설
01 -ed로 끝난 분사 형태의 형용사는 more, most를 붙인다.
02 ⓐ than 앞에 비교급 more difficult가 와야 한다. ⓑ of 앞에 최상급
   the kindest가 알맞다. ⓒ '가능한 한'이라는 의미의 possible =
   you can이 알맞다.
03 「A ~ not as[so]+원급+as B」 = 「B ~ 비교급+than A」: A는 B
   만큼 ~하지 않다 = B가 A보다 더 ~하다
04 ⓐ me → mine (비교 대상이 His house이므로 같이 my house =
   mine으로 써야 한다.) ⓓ more pretty → prettier
05 같은 나이이므로 동등 비교 as old as를 쓴다.
06 부사 well의 비교급은 better이다.
07 「as+원급+as possible」: 가능한 한 ~한/하게
08 아이스크림이 일요일에 가장 잘 팔리고 목요일에 가장 안 팔린다. sell
   well(잘 팔리다)의 최상급 best, 가장 적게 팔릴 때는 worst를 쓴다.
   best 대신 most를, worst 대신 least를 써도 된다.

Level 3 Test
p. 126

01 ②   02 ⑤
03 ②   04 ③
05 ① ③   06 ①
07 ④   08 ①
09 ① ③ ④   10 less comfortable than
11 not as smooth   12 as much as possible
13 K2 is not as high as Mount Everest.
14 is the thinnest of the three
15 It is just as good as milk.
16 as soon as you can / as soon as you can

》》 해설
01 • 동등 비교 as ~ as 사이에 원급 much

• your coat와 비교 대상이 같아야 하므로 소유대명사 mine
• the 다음에 최상급 worst
02 less 열등 비교가 나왔으므로 비교급을 또 쓸 수 없다. less harder
   를 less hard 또는 harder로 고쳐야 한다.
03 「A ~ not as[so]+원급+as B」 = 「B 비교급+than A」: A는 B만
   큼 ~하지 않다 = B는 A보다 더 ~하다
04 Students need to study at home as much as possible[they
   can].로 many가 아니라 much를 쓴다.
05 ① 수박이 멜론보다 싸므로 more expensive → less expensive
   또는 cheaper ③ 멜론과 수박의 단어가 서로 바뀌어야 한다. '수박이
   멜론만큼 비싸지 않다.'가 알맞다.
06 의미상 far(정도)의 비교급 further가 알맞다. (더 많은 정보를 원하시
   면 저희에게 전화 주세요.)
07 '나보다 더 가까이/멀리/근처에/오래 살 것이다' (later는 '순서가 늦
   은'으로 '더 늦게 살 것이다'는 알맞지 않다.)
08 ⓐ '첼로를 잘 연주하다(play well)'로 형용사 good이 아니라 부사
   well이 알맞다. ⓑ ⓒ는 틀린 것이 없다.
09 ① fast는 the 다음에 최상급 fastest가 알맞다. ③ most popular
   최상급 앞에 the가 와야 알맞다. ④ worst(가장 나쁜)는 than과 함께
   비교급 형태인 worse가 알맞다.
10 comfortable(편리한)의 열등 비교 less comfortable(덜 편리한)이
   고 비교급 다음에 than을 쓴다.
11 「B ~ 비교급+than A」 = 「A ~ not as[so]+원급+as B」: B가 A
   보다 더 ~하다 = A는 B만큼 ~하지 않다
12 as much as possible: 가능한 한 많이
13 비교급을 동등 비교의 부정문으로 바꾸는 문제이다. (「B ~ 비교급+
   than A」 = 「A ~ not as[so]+원급+as B」: A는 B만큼 ~ 하지 않다)
14 「the+최상급+of+복수 명사」 thin의 최상급은 thinnest이다.
15 It is good.의 동등 비교이므로 well을 good으로 바꾸어야 한다.
16 빈칸 수에 맞게 「as+원급+as+주어+can」을 이용하며, 명령문이므로
   주어는 you로 쓴다.

UNIT 22 여러 가지 비교 구문

1) 최상급   2) of   3) in
4) of   5) in   6) No
7) No   8) as   9) so
10) as   11) of   12) in
13) as   14) 원급   15) as
16) 비교급   17) than   18) The
19) 비교급   20) the   21) 비교급
22) 비교급   23) and   24) 비교급
25) Which   26) Who   27) or
28) one   29) 최상급   30) 복수

Level 1 Test
p. 128

A 1 the more   2 bigger and bigger
   3 in   4 programs
   5 of

B 1 smarter / than any other 2 three times as large as

Level 2 Test
p. 129

01 ⑤ 02 ①
03 ④ 04 ⑤
05 Hyde Park is one of the largest parks.
06 three times taller than[three times as tall as]
07 getting darker and darker
08 (1) than any other city
(2) No other city
(3) is as cold

≫ 해설
01 「최상급＋of＋복수 명사」: ~중에 가장 …하다
02 ①은 '치타는 지상에서 다른 어떤 동물만큼 빠르지 않다.'는 뜻으로 최상급의 의미가 아니다.
03 ⓐ in us → of us ⓑ of the store → in the store ⓒ coin → coins
04 비교급 앞에 쓰인 much, even, still, far, a lot은 '훨씬'이라는 뜻으로 강조를 위해 쓰인다. great는 쓸 수 없다.
05 「one of the＋최상급＋복수 명사」: 가장 ~한 것 중 하나
06 「배수사＋비교급＋than」 = 「배수사＋as＋원급＋as」
07 「get＋비교급＋and＋비교급」: 점점 더 ~해지다
08 A ~ 최상급 = 「A ~ 비교급＋than any other＋단수 명사」 = 「부정 주어 ~ as[so]＋원급＋as」 / 「비교급＋A」로 표현할 수 있다. (① 시드니는 어떤 다른 도시보다 덥다. ② 어떤 도시도 서울보다 춥지 않다. ③ 도쿄는 베이징만큼 춥다.)

Level 3 Test
p. 130

01 ④ 02 ②
03 ④ 04 ④
05 ③ 06 ①
07 ⑤ 08 ① ④ ⑤
09 No other / as large as[larger than]
10 more romantic than any other tragedy
11 five times more yachts than[five times as many yachts as]
12 The closer / the higher
13 ⓔ larger than any other pyramids → larger than any other pyramid
14 • No other / Quetzalcoatl in Mexico
• Khufu in Egypt / pyramids

≫ 해설
01 최상급의 범위를 나타낼 때 「of＋복수 명사」 또는 「in＋집단이나 장소」 등의 단수 명사로 쓴다.
02 ⓐ 「one of the＋최상급＋복수 명사」로 student는 students가 되어야 한다. ⓑ 「the＋비교급 ~, the＋비교급…」으로 more 앞에 the가 필요하다.
03 ⓐ 비교급 앞에 much, even, still, far, a lot으로 강조 ⓑ 「비교급＋than any other＋단수 명사」 ⓒ in my life: 내 인생에서 ⓓ 「배수사＋원급/비교급」 (three times)
04 The more cars there are, the heavier traffic gets[becomes].

로 영작할 수 있다. 「The＋비교급＋주어＋동사 ~, the＋비교급＋주어＋동사…」는 '~하면 할수록 더욱 …하다'라는 의미이다.
05 ③ 동등 비교의 부정문은 열등 비교. (카카오톡이 다른 스마트폰 앱만큼 인기 있지 않다.) 나머지는 '카카오톡이 가장 인기 있는 스마트폰 앱이다.'라는 뜻이다.
06 ① '어떤 달도 4월보다 더 많은 강우량을 가지고 있지 않다.'가 알맞으므로 July는 April이 되어야 한다.
07 ⓓ '반 친구들 중에'라는 의미가 되도록 classmates가 복수형이어야 하고 앞에는 of를 쓴다.
08 ① bigger → as big ④ very → much (even, still, far, a lot) ⑤ longer → longest로 써야 한다.
09 「부정 주어＋원급/비교급 = 최상급 (스미소니언 협회는 세계에서 가장 넓은 박물관 건물이다.)
10 A ~ 최상급 = 「A ~ 비교급＋than any other＋단수 명사」
11 수학 공식상 5배수를 써야 한다. 배수사 다음에 비교급이나 원급을 써서 표현한다.
12 「The＋비교급＋주어＋동사 ~, the＋비교급＋주어＋동사…」: ~하면 할수록 더욱 …하다 (우리가 지구 핵 안쪽으로 가까워 질수록 온도는 더욱 높아진다.)
13 「비교급＋than any other＋단수 명사」이므로 pyramids는 pyramid가 되어야 알맞다.
14 「부정 주어＋원급/비교급」, 「최상급 of all the＋복수 명사」는 최상급을 나타내는 표현으로 세계에서 가장 덩치가 크고 웅장한(large) 피라미드는 멕시코에 있는 케잘코트 피라미드이고 가장 높은(high) 피라미드는 이집트의 쿠푸 피라미드이다.

Review Test
p. 132

01 ② 02 ② ⑤
03 ① 04 ①
05 ④ 06 ③
07 ③ ④ 08 ②
09 ③
10 (1) Please sit down as low as you can.
(2) Please sit down as low as possible.
11 She is one of the most popular students.
12 The closer / the colder
13 the longest / phones
14 less stylish than
15 The Apple phone is more expensive than any other phone.
또는 No other phone is more expensive than the Apple phone.
16 lives longer than a whale
17 The Nile isn't as wide as the Amazon.
18 than any other country
19 Three times
20 growing bigger and bigger
21 ② ③ ⑤
22 It has three times more vitamin C than cow's milk.

≫ 해설
01 비교급을 수식하는 부사로는 much, even, still, far, a lot이 있고, honest의 최상급은 the most honest이다.
02 early와 healthy는 비교급을 만들 때 earlier, healthier로 바뀐다.

03 「one of the＋최상급」 뒤에는 복수 명사가 와야 한다.

04 「A ~ not as[so]＋원급＋as B」＝「B ~ 비교급＋than A」: A는 B 만큼 ~하지 않다 ＝ B가 A보다 더 ~하다 / dangerous의 비교급은 more dangerous이다.

05 ⓒ hot의 비교급은 hotter이다. ⓔ better는 good의 비교급으로 more를 쓰지 않는다.

06 scared(무서워하는)의 비교급은 more scared이다. 「the＋비교급, the＋비교급」: ~하면 할수록 더욱 …하다

07 「배수사＋as＋원급＋as」 / 「배수사＋비교급＋than」: ~배만큼 …한

08 동작을 나타내므로 부사가 와야 하고, as ~ as이므로 원급을 써야 한다.

09 ③ 사과보다 바나나를 더 좋아하는 것이 아니라 바나나보다 사과를 더 좋아한다.

10 「as＋원급＋as＋possible」＝「as＋원급＋as＋주어＋can」: 가능한 한 ~한

11 「one of the＋최상급＋복수 명사」: 가장 ~한 … 중 하나

12 「The＋비교급＋주어＋동사 ~, the＋비교급＋주어＋동사…」: ~하면 할수록 더욱 …하다 (우리가 북극에 가까워질수록 추워진다.)

13 Star폰의 화면 길이가 가장 기니까 최상급 the longest이고 「of＋복수 명사(phones)」를 쓴다.

14 Star폰보다 Apple폰의 디자인 평점이 높으므로 열등 비교 less stylish than을 써야 한다.

15 「A ~ 비교급＋than any other＋단수 명사…」＝「No (other)＋단수 명사 ~ 비교급＋than A」 (모두 최상급을 나타내는 표현이다.)

16 「A ~ not as[so]＋원급＋as B」＝「B ~ 비교급＋than A」: A는 B 만큼 ~하지 않다 ＝ B가 A보다 더 ~하다

17 「B ~ 비교급＋than A」＝「A ~ not as[so] 원급＋as＋B」: A는 B 만큼 ~하지 않다 / 비교급을 동등 비교의 부정문으로 바꾸는 문제이다.

18 「최상급＋that＋주어＋have ever＋p.p.」＝「비교급＋than any other＋단수 명사＋that＋주어＋have ever＋p.p.」

19 「배수사＋원급/비교급」으로 표현한다.

20 「grow＋비교급＋and＋비교급」: 점점 더 ~하게 되다 (드론 판매량이 점점 더 커지고 있다.)

21 ⓑ that은 계속적 용법으로 쓸 수 없다. ⓒ very는 비교급을 수식하지 않는다. ⓔ healthy의 최상급은 healthiest이다. ⓐ Recently라는 표현으로 보아 현재완료는 적절하다. ⓓ 주어가 Lots of people이므로 are는 적절하다.

22 내용상 주어 It과 동사 has를 쓰고, 「배수사＋비교급＋than」 구문을 이용한다.

[21~22]

　　최근에 인도에서 사람들이 몸에 좋은 아이스크림을 만들었다. 그들은 낙타의 우유로 이 새로운 아이스크림을 만들었는데, 그것은 소의 우유와는 많이 다르다. 그것은 소의 우유보다 세 배 많은 비타민 C를 가지고 있다. 그것은 또한 철과 비타민 B의 풍부한 원천이다. 그 아이스크림의 지방은 보통 아이스크림의 것보다 훨씬 더 적다. 인도의 많은 사람들은 낙타 우유 아이스크림을 즐기고 있다. 그들은 낙타의 우유가 가장 몸에 좋은 아이스크림이고, 그것은 질병과 싸우는 것을 도울 수 있다고 믿는다.

• 어휘 • recently 최근에 | healthy 몸에 좋은, 건강한 | camel 낙타 | rich 풍부한 | source 원천 | iron 철 | fat 지방 | low 적은, 낮은 | average 보통의, 평균의 | disease 질병

CHAPTER 10
형용사, 부사, 분사

UNIT 23 형용사와 부사

1) three point one four　　　2) one[a] second
3) two-thirds　　　　　　　　4) one
5) body　　　　　　　　　　　6) thing
7) 형용사　　　　　　　　　　8) people
9) however　　　　　　　　　10) therefore
11) in other words　　　　　　12) in fact
13) as a result　　　　　　　　14) on the other hand
15) finally　　　　　　　　　　16) at last
17) in addition　　　　　　　　18) besides
19) for example　　　　　　　20) for instance
21) 명사　　　　　　　　　　　22) 부사
23) 대명사　　　　　　　　　　24) 부사
25) 부사　　　　　　　　　　　26) 명사
27) 부사　　　　　　　　　　　28) 대명사

Level 1 Test　　　　　　　　　　　p. 136

A　1　fifty-one point four five eight
　　2　nine thousand two hundred forty-six
　　3　five-sevenths 또는 five over seven
　　4　three and seven-fourteenths

B　1　are / are　　　　2　something black
　　3　given it up

C　1　Therefore　　　　2　For example
　　3　However　　　　4　Besides

Level 2 Test　　　　　　　　　　　p. 137

01 ②　　　　　　　　　　　02 ④
03 ③　　　　　　　　　　　04 ②
05 (1) 1/2
　　(2) 5/11
06 (1) However
　　(2) Therefore
07 There was nobody absent today.
08 ⓒ pick up it → pick it up ⓓ them → it

≫ 해설

01 1/3은 one[a] third로 읽는다. a quarter는 1/4이다.

02 the poor는 poor people의 의미로 복수 취급하므로 ④가 적절하다.

03 「동사＋부사」에서 대명사는 가운데 쓴다.

04 앞의 말에 자세한 내용을 덧붙일 때는 '사실은'이란 말을 사용한다.

05 (1) a half는 a[one] second(＝ 1/2)이다.

(2) 분자는 기수로, 분모는 서수로 읽는다. 분자가 복수이므로 분모에 -s를 붙인다.

06 (1) 열심히 공부했지만
   (2) 열심히 공부했으므로

07 -body는 형용사가 뒤에서 수식한다.

08 ⓒ 대명사는 동사와 부사 사이에 쓴다. ⓓ them은 the pen을 가리키므로 it으로 써야 한다.

Level 3 Test

p. 138

01 ③   02 ①
03 ④   04 ⑤
05 ①   06 ② ③
07 ③   08 ⑤
09 ③   10 ④
11 point one six
12 needs → need
13 You should not buy anything useless.
14 one-fourth / three-quarters
15 The sick were taken care of by the nurses.
16 The elderly have to exercise regularly.

≫ 해설

01 ① third floor ② twelfth ④ nineteen ninety-four ⑤ five point four six로 써야 한다.

02 대분수는 and로 읽고 1/2은 one[a] second = (a) half로 읽는다.

03 Something very soft touched my left leg.으로 영작할 수 있다. 「-thing＋부사＋형용사」의 어순으로 '부드러운'은 soft로 써야 한다.

04 「spend＋목적어＋-ing」로 쓰며, 약자들은 the weak 또는 weak people로 쓴다. peoples는 '민족들'이라는 뜻이다.

05 Have you seen anybody[anyone] famous near here?로 영작할 수 있다.

06 「동사＋대명사＋부사」 순으로 쓴다.

07 결국 오디션에 합격했다는 말로 At last(마침내)가 와야 한다.

08 deafs → deaf, uses → use, others → other

09 ⓐ called off it → called it off ⓒ are → is (Seven-ninths는 단일 개념으로 단수 취급해야 한다.)

10 ⓐ hot something → something hot

11 16/100을 십진법으로 나타내면 0.160이고 소수점 이하는 한 자리씩 읽는다.

12 「the＋형용사」는 '~한 사람들'로 복수 취급하므로 복수 동사가 필요하다.

13 '어떤 것이든 쓸데없는 것을 사서는 안 된다'가 적절하며, -thing은 형용사가 뒤에서 꾸며준다.

14 주어진 철자로 시작하여 1/4은 one-fourth, 3/4은 three-quarters로 쓴다.

15 「The＋형용사(sick)」로 시작하며, 복수 취급하고 take care of의 동사구를 한 묶음으로 해서 수동태로 쓰면 된다.

16 '노인들'은 The elderly로 쓰고 복수이므로 has를 have로 변형하여 쓴다.

분사

1) -ing   2) ~하는   3) ~하고 있는
4) -ed   5) ~한   6) ~되는
7) ~지는   8) 분사   9) 명사
10) 명사   11) 분사   12) ~하는
13) 형용사   14) 동작   15) 상태
16) ~하기   17) 명사   18) 용도
19) 목적   20) 사물   21) 사람
22) 사람

Level 1 Test

p. 140

A 1 sleeping   2 standing
   3 found   4 are

B 1 tired / filling   2 was sitting / reading
   3 caught / didn't steal

Level 2 Test

p. 141

01 ④   02 ⑤
03 ① ②   04 ②
05 named / called
06 (1) satisfying
   (2) was satisfied with
07 ⓐ baking → baked
08 Barking dogs seldom bite.

≫ 해설

01 소녀가 햄버거를 먹고 있으므로 능동의 현재분사를 쓴다. eats를 쓰면 본동사가 두 개라 어색하다.

02 본동사는 bought이고 컴퓨터가 만들어지는 것이므로 과거분사를 써야 한다.

03 ① 내가 놀란 것이므로 수동의 의미인 surprised로 써야 한다. ② 야구 경기가 감동을 주는 것이므로 능동의 의미인 exciting으로 써야 한다.

04 ⓐ writing → written ⓓ sleep → sleeping ⓔ was → were

05 첫 번째 빈칸은 나나가 '이름지어진' 것으로 수동의 관계라 과거분사를 쓰고, 두 번째 빈칸은 본동사 자리이므로 과거형으로 쓰면 된다.

06 (1) 결과가 만족을 주는 것으로 능동의 현재분사
   (2) 감독이 만족을 받는 것으로 수동의 현재분사가 와야 하며 be satisfied with로 쓴다.

07 프렌치 토스트가 구워지는 수동의 관계이므로 과거분사로 써야 한다.

08 개가 짖는 것이므로 능동의 현재분사(barking)가 오고, 빈도부사는 일반동사 앞에 쓰면 된다.

Level 3 Test

p. 142

01 ⑤   02 ② ④
03 ③   04 ③
05 ②   06 ⑤
07 ②   08 ⑤

09 ③　　　　　　　　　　　　10 ③
11 sitting / kept talking / annoying
12 ⓐ stayed → staying
13 Have you ever read a six-word story written by Hemingway?
14 frightened → frightening / dressing → dressed
15 the email sent to me
16 (1) 루나
　　(2) talked
　　(3) talking

》 해설
01 첫 번째 빈칸은 영화가 감동을 주는 것이므로 능동의 현재분사, 두 번째 빈칸도 영화가 실망을 시키므로 능동의 현재분사, 세 번째 빈칸은 내가 놀랐으므로 수동의 과거분사가 들어간다.
02 The cookies baked by my father[dad] smell tasty[delicious]. 로 영작할 수 있다.
03 pictures와 paint의 관계가 수동이므로 과거분사로 써야 한다.
04 lived는 living으로 써야 하고, is는 are로 써야 한다.
05 ②는 동명사이고 나머지는 현재분사이다.
06 • 팝페라 가수가 놀라게 하는 것이므로 현재분사가 와야 한다.
　　• 소년들이 혼란스러워진 것으로 과거분사가 와야 한다.
07 준형이 지루해진 사람이 아니라 지루하게 하는 사람이므로, 사람일지라도 -ing형을 써야 한다.
08 집이 나무로 만들어진 것으로 made로 써야 한다.
09 ⓑ danced → dancing ⓒ is → are
10 ⓐ are → is ⓑ speaking → spoken으로 고쳐야 한다.
11 '앉아 있는 남자'는 The man sitting으로 쓰고, 「keep+-ing」는 '계속 ~하다'라는 의미이다. 마지막 문장에서 시제가 과거임을 알 수 있고 앞의 상황이 짜증나게 한다는 능동의 의미이므로 annoy는 현재분사형으로 쓴다.
12 본동사(were)가 있고 손님들이 머무는 것이므로 능동의 현재 분사로 써야 한다.
13 현재완료로 Have you ever read로 시작하고 '여섯 단어짜리 이야기'는 a six-word story로 쓴다. 이야기가 쓰여진 것이므로 과거분사 written으로 수식하면 된다.
14 that절 안의 they는 전시품(exhibits)을 가리키고 능동이므로 현재분사가 필요하다. / 안내자가 옷을 입은 수동의 의미이므로 과거분사 drossed를 써야 한다.
15 분사가 어구와 함께 수식하면 명사 뒤에서 수식한다.
16 the man이 이야기를 하고 있으므로 능동의 현재분사 talking으로 고쳐야 한다. ⓑ는 tired가 되어야 하므로 맞게 채점했다.

Review Test
　　　　　　　　　　　　　　　　　　p. 144
01 ④　　　　　　　　　　02 ④
03 ②　　　　　　　　　　04 ③ ⑤
05 ④　　　　　　　　　　06 ③
07 ④　　　　　　　　　　08 ④
09 ④　　　　　　　　　　10 ③
11 (1) 3/4
　　(2) 2/7
　　(3) 3 7/90
12 special anything → anything special

13 is → are
14 Would you like to try them out?
15 (A) however　(B) sold
16 (1) were pleasing
　　(2) were pleased
17 No, I am not embarrassed.
18 B E A U T Y
19 playing / is
20 ⓐ I am interesting → I am interested
　　ⓓ her voice was annoyed → her voice was annoying
21 ③ ④
22 interested

》 해설
01 소수점 이하는 한 자리씩 읽는다.
02 ① one[a] second 또는 (a) half ② and five → fifths ③ third → thirds ⑤ thirteens → thirteenths
03 앞 문장과 반대되는 내용이 나오므로 ②가 적절하다.
04 '~한 사람들'은 「the+형용사」 또는 「형용사+people」로 나타낼 수 있다.
05 -thing은 형용사가 뒤에서 꾸며준다. (new something → something new)
06 ③은 enjoys의 목적어로 쓰인 동명사이고 나머지는 현재분사이다.
07 주어가 The women이므로 본동사는 are를 써야 한다. 복수형이 아닌 -s로 끝나는 단어의 소유격은 -s's로 나타내므로 Chris's는 맞다.
08 첫 번째 빈칸은 우리가 좌절된 것으로 수동의 과거분사가, 두 번째 빈칸은 소식이 실망을 시키는 것이므로 능동의 현재분사가 와야 한다.
09 ⓐ ⓑ는 현재분사이고 ⓒ ⓓ는 동명사이다.
10 ⓒ shocked → shocking ⓓ surprised → surprising
11 (1) a quarter는 1/4이고 three-quarters는 3/4이다.
　　(2) 분수는 「분자+over+분모」로 읽기도 한다.
　　(3)은 대분수를 읽는 법이다.
12 -thing으로 끝나는 단어는 형용사가 뒤에서 수식한다.
13 「the+형용사」는 '~한 사람들'로 복수 취급한다.
14 would like to(~하고 싶다)의 의문문이며, try ~ out(테스트해 보다)에서 대명사는 중간에 쓴다.
15 (A) '그렇지만'은 however이며 but은 중간에 쓸 수 없다.
　　(B) 그림이 팔린 것이므로 수동형의 과거분사를 쓰면 된다.
16 (1) 연구 결과가 기쁘게 해주는 것으로 능동의 현재분사가 와야 한다.
　　(2) 과학자들이 기뻐진 것으로 수동의 과거분사가 와야 하며, 각각 복수 주어이므로 과거형으로 were를 쓰면 된다.
17 주어가 당황하게 된 것으로 수동형의 과거분사로 써야 한다.
18 ⓐ inviting → invited ⓑ leaving → left ⓔ speaking → spoken 문장의 첫 글자는 각각 A, T, E이다. 이를 넣어서 단어를 완성하면 된다.
19 피아노를 치는 소년으로 능동의 현재분사(playing)가 필요하고, 주어가 the boy이므로 본동사는 is를 쓰면 된다.
20 ⓐ 내가 흥미 있어진 것이므로 수동의 과거분사가 알맞다. ⓓ 그녀의 목소리가 짜증을 나게 하는 것이므로 능동의 현재분사가 알맞다.
21 ③ 동사 meet을 꾸며주므로 부사인 directly로 고쳐야 한다. ④ the person이 주어이고 주의를 기울이고 있는 능동이므로 paying으로 고쳐야 한다.
22 영영풀이는 '형용사: 너의 관심을 무엇인가에 주고 그것에 대해서 더

발견하기를 원하는 것'이란 뜻으로 '관심 있는'이란 뜻이다. 따라서 i로 시작하는 단어인 interested를 쓰면 된다.

[21~22]

　　미소는 대개 친근함과 관심의 표시이다. 하지만, 어떤 사람들은 단지 공손하기 위해 미소 짓는다. 사람들의 얼굴에서 다른 단서를 얻기 위해서는 그들이 눈을 보아라. 친근함과 관심은 한 사람의 눈이 당신의 것(눈)을 직접 만날 때 표현된다. 만약 당신의 청자가 잠시 눈길을 돌렸다가 다시 돌아온다면, 그 사람은 당신에게 아마 주의를 기울이고 있을 것이다. 만약 이 사람이 계속 눈을 돌린다면, 그 또는 그녀는 관심이 없거나 부끄러움을 타고 있을지도 모른다. 누군가 당신에게 계속 손가락질을 할 때 그것은 아마도 그 사람이 당신보다 우월하다고 느끼거나 당신에게 화가 나 있다는 것을 의미할 수도 있다는 것을 기억해라.

• 어휘 | sign 표시 | polite 정중한, 예의 바른 | express 표현하다 | directly 직접 | pay attention to ~에게 주의를 기울이다 | point at ~에게 손가락질 하다 | superior to ~보다 우월한

CHAPTER 11
접속사

UNIT 25 명사절, 때의 부사절, 상관 접속사

1) ~하는 것, ~라고	2) ~인지(아닌지)
3) ~인지(아닌지)	4) when
5) before	6) while
7) as soon as	8) as
9) after	10) until
11) since	12) both
13) and	14) either
15) or	16) neither
17) nor	18) not
19) only	20) but
21) also	22) not
23) but	

Level 1 Test
p. 148

A
1 before		2 that	
3 since		4 whether	
5 or		6 nor	
7 and		8 but	

B
1　whether[if] it's true or not
2　while you are driving
3　neither / nor
4　when I came in

Level 2 Test
p. 149

01 ④　　　　　　　　02 ③
03 ④　　　　　　　　04 ④
05 I wonder whether she will come or not.
　또는 I wonder whether or not she will come.
06 Either Mina or I am going to be the winner.
07 not only / but also
08 Both / and / are

》》해설

01 '~하는 동안'이라는 의미의 접속사 while이 알맞다.
02 Neither A nor B: A와 B 둘 다 아닌 / either A or B: A와 B 둘 중 하나 / as soon as: ~하자마자 / not only A but also B: A뿐 아니라 B도
03 ④는 명사절, ① ② ③ ⑤는 부사절로 쓰였다.
04 ④ not only A but also B는 B에 동사를 일치시킨다. (play → plays)
05 「whether+주어+동사 ~ or not」 = 「whether or not+주어+동사」: ~인지 아닌지
06 either A or B(A와 B 둘 중 하나) 뒤에 동사가 나올 때 B에 동사를 일치시킨다.
07 not only A but also B: A뿐만 아니라 B도
08 both A and B: A와 B 둘 다 (복수 동사가 온다.)

Level 3 Test
p. 150

01 ④　　　　　　　　02 ⑤
03 ①　　　　　　　　04 ②
05 ③　　　　　　　　06 ④
07 ③　　　　　　　　08 ④
09 ② ⑤　　　　　　　10 ③
11 as well as
12 (1) finishes
　　(2) plan
13 that → if[whether]
14 Both Thomas and James love Alice.
15 Not only she but also you are intelligent.
16 When you ride a bike

》》해설

01 '그가 나를 방문했을 때'의 의미가 되어야 하므로 when이 알맞다.
02 not only A but also B가 되어야 하므로 but also가 알맞다.
03 • '어두워지기 전에'라는 뜻이 되어야 어울리므로 before가 알맞다.
　 • '저녁 식사를 끝낸 후에'라는 뜻이 되어야 어울리므로 after가 알맞다.
04 • '나를 도와줄 수 있는지'가 되어야 하므로 if가 알맞다.
　 • neither A nor B: A와 B 둘 다 아닌
　 • either A or B: A와 B 둘 중 하나
05 시간의 부사절은 미래를 표현할 때 현재 시제를 쓴다.
06 '고향을 떠난 이후로 3년이 지났다.'는 뜻이 되어야 하므로 as가 아니

라 since가 알맞다.

07 ⓐ ⓓ 지시형용사 ⓑ ⓔ 명사절을 이끄는 접속사 ⓒ 관계대명사

08 '비가 멈추면 소풍을 갈 것이다.'는 뜻이 되어야 가장 어울린다.

09 '~인지 (아닌지)'는 if[whether] ~ (or not)을 써서 표현할 수 있다.

10 ⓒ neither A nor B는 B에 동사를 일치시키므로 are는 is가 되어야 한다. ⓓ Not only A but also B는 B에 동사를 일치시키므로 are는 am이 되어야 한다.

11 not only A but also B = B as well as A: A뿐 아니라 B도

12 (1) 시간의 부사절에서는 미래를 표현할 때 동사의 현재형을 쓴다.
   (2) neither A nor B는 B에 동사를 일치시킨다.

13 '그녀가 그의 청혼을 받아들일지'의 뜻이 되어야 하므로 that이 아니라 if 또는 whether를 써야 알맞다.

14 both A and B(A와 B 둘 다)는 복수 취급한다.

15 not only A but also B(A뿐 아니라 B도)는 B에 동사를 일치시킨다. 동사가 are이므로 B 자리에는 you가 와야 한다. (그녀뿐 아니라 너도 똑똑하다.)

16 「when+주어+동사 ~」의 어순으로 쓴다. (자전거를 탈 때에는 헬멧을 써야 한다.)

UNIT 26 조건, 양보, 이유, 결과의 부사절

1) if
2) If
3) unless
4) unless
5) though
6) although
7) even
8) though
9) Though
10) Although
11) Even
12) though
13) because
14) because
15) as
16) As
17) since
18) Since
19) so
20) that
21) so
22) that

Level 1 Test
p. 152

A 1 Unless   2 As
   3 so   4 Although

B 1 so   2 because of

C 1 Unless   2 unless
   3 so / that

Level 2 Test
p. 153

01 ④   02 ④
03 ②   04 ③
05 because[since, as]
06 so cold that I couldn't play outside
07 doesn't stop / stops
08 I have a test tomorrow, so I must study.

해설
01 '피곤했지만 그녀는 계속해서 청소했다.'는 의미가 되어야 자연스러우므로 Though가 알맞다.

02 '네가 나를 돕지 않으면 그 일을 할 수 없다.'는 의미가 되어야 자연스러우므로 Unless가 알맞다.

03 • 결과의 부사절을 이끄는 so가 알맞다.
   • so ~ that...: 너무 ~해서 …하다

04 • 조건의 부사절을 이끄는 if(~하면)가 알맞다.
   • 명사절을 이끄는 if(~인지)가 알맞다.

05 「원인, so+결과」= 「결과+because[since, as]+원인」 (나는 오늘이 그녀의 생일이기 때문에 꽃을 좀 보냈다.)

06 so ~ that... couldn't: 너무 ~해서 …할 수 없었다

07 if ~ not = unless: ~하지 않는다면 / 조건의 부사절에서 미래를 표현할 때 현재 시제를 쓴다.

08 「이유, +so+결과」의 어순으로 쓴다.

Level 3 Test
p. 154

01 ④   02 ⑤
03 ①   04 ①
05 ④   06 ④
07 ③   08 ②
09 ②   10 ① ⑤
11 ③   12 so / that

13 Though he had[ate] breakfast, he was still hungry.
14 If you get home earlier than me, please turn on the heater.
15 Because[As, Since] my leg was broken
16 Since[since]

해설
01 '감기에 걸려서[걸렸기 때문에] 집에 있어야 했다.'는 의미가 되어야 자연스러우므로 Because가 알맞다.

02 '그녀가 나를 사랑하지 않는다 할지라도 나는 그녀를 사랑한다.'는 의미가 되어야 자연스러우므로 even though가 알맞다.

03 때를 나타내거나 이유를 설명할 때 as를 쓸 수 있다.

04 조건의 부사절에서는 미래를 표현할 때 현재 시제를 쓴다.

05 ④는 so, ① ② ③ ⑤는 because가 들어가야 자연스럽다.

06 so ~ that...: 너무 ~해서 …하다 / so: 그래서(결과의 부사절을 이끄는 접속사)

07 Unless = If ~ not: ~하지 않는다면

08 ②는 명사절을 이끄는 접속사, ① ③ ④ ⑤는 조건의 부사절을 이끄는 접속사루 쓰였다

09 「because+주어+동사 ~」= 「because of+명사」

10 '그녀는 바빠서 우리와 함께 할 수 없었다.'는 의미가 되어야 자연스러우므로 이유를 나타내는 접속사가 들어가야 알맞다.

11 • 내가 문을 열었을 때(As) 고양이 한 마리를 보았다.
   • 그 방은 비록 작지만(Though) 전망이 좋다.

12 '너무 ~해서 …하다'는 뜻이 되어야 하므로 so ~ that...을 쓴다.

13 「though+주어+동사 ~」의 어순으로 쓴다.

14 조건의 부사절에서는 미래를 표현할 때 현재 시제를 쓴다. (네가 나보다 일찍 집에 도착하면 히터 좀 틀어 줘.)

15 '다리를 다쳐 축구를 할 수 없었다.'는 뜻이 되어야 하므로 이유를 나타내는 because, as, since 등을 이용하여 문장을 완성한다.

16 '~이후로'와 '~ 때문에'의 두 가지 뜻을 가지고 있는 접속사 Since[since]가 알맞다.

01	④	02	②
03	① ⑤	04	⑤
05	②	06	⑤
07	④	08	③
09	④		

10 though, although, even though
11 that / is
12 arrives
13 Robert will be either in the coffee shop or in the library.
14 Everybody likes him because he is polite.
15 I wear my glasses / I can't see well
16 Even though I sneezed a lot, I didn't catch a cold.
17 are → is
18 so
19 Not only Ken but also Jenny caught a cold.
20 while she was playing basketball
21 ①
22 We can communicate not only through words but also through body language.

〉〉〉 해설

01 빈칸에는 think의 목적절을 이끄는 접속사가 필요하다. '~라고 생각한다'라는 뜻이 되어야 자연스러우므로 that이 알맞다.

02 문맥상 '너는 어두워지기 전에 집에 가야 한다.'라고 해석하는 것이 자연스러우므로 빈칸에 알맞은 것은 before이다.

03 Both A and B는 복수 취급하고, either A or B는 B에 수를 일치시키므로 옳은 문장은 ①, ⑤이다. neither A nor B, not only A but also B, not A but B는 B에 수를 일치시킨다. (② want → wants ③ has → have ④ are → is)

04 if의 두 가지 의미: ~인지 아닌지 / ~라면

05 Unless는 If ~ not의 의미이다.

06 ①~④는 so가 들어가고 ⑤에는 that이 들어간다.

07 시간의 부사절에서는 현재 시제가 미래를 대신하므로 will retire를 retires로 고친다.

08 as soon as: ~하자마자

09 ⓐ will rain → rains ⓑ because of → because ⓒ go → goes (as well as는 앞의 명사에 수 일치)

10 'Piper는 역까지 택시를 탔지만[탔음에도 불구하고] 기차를 놓쳤다.'라는 의미가 되어야 자연스러우므로 양보의 접속사를 써야 한다.

11 that은 명사절을 이끄는 접속사이다. that절의 주어는 동명사 walking이므로 동사는 is를 쓴다.

12 시간의 부사절에서는 현재 시제가 미래를 대신하므로 빈칸에는 arrives가 알맞다.

13 either A or B: A이거나 B

14 문맥상 '그가 예의 바르기 때문에 모든 사람들이 그를 좋아한다.'라고 해석하는 것이 자연스러우므로 because를 이용해서 문장을 다시 쓴다.

15 unless = if ~ not

16 '나는 재채기를 많이 했을지라도, 나는 감기에 걸리지 않았다.'라고 해석하는 것이 자연스러우므로 양보의 접속사로 연결한다.

17 neither A nor B는 B에 수를 일치시키므로 are를 is로 고쳐야 한다.

18 • so: 그래서

• so ~ that…: 너무 ~해서 …하다

19 not only A but also B: A뿐만 아니라 B도

20 농구를 하고 있는 동안에 다리를 다쳤으므로 '~하는 동안'이라는 의미의 시간의 접속사 while을 쓴다.

21 내용상 ⓔ에는 '~할 때'가 적절하므로 until이 아니라 when이 필요하다. ⓐ and ⓑ that ⓒ little ⓓ who

22 not only A but also B 구문을 이용한다.

[21~22]

> 우리는 말을 통해서 뿐만 아니라 몸짓 언어를 통해서도 의사소통을 할 수 있다. 몸짓 언어는 모든 형태의 몸짓, 자세, 그리고 신체의 움직임이다. 그것은 여러분에 관하여 많은 것을 말해줄 수 있다. 당신의 자세가 구부정하다면, 이것은 당신이 슬프거나 자신감이 거의 없음을 의미할 수도 있다. 당신의 자세가 곧다면, 당신은 자신감을 표현하고 있는 것이다. 미소는 친근함의 표시이다. 하지만, 단지 예의 바르기 위해서 미소 짓는 사람들이 있다. 친근함은 한 사람의 눈이 당신의 눈을 직접 마주할 때 표현된다.

• 어휘 • communicate 의사소통하다 | form 형태 | posture 자세 | movement 움직임 | confidence 자신감 | express 표현하다 | sign 표시, 징조 | polite 예의 바른 | directly 직접

CHAPTER 12
의문문

UNIT 27 선택의문문, 부가의문문

1) be동사	2) or	3) or
4) 조동사	5) or	6) or
7) 의문사	8) 조동사	9) or
10) or	11) 비교급	12) or
13) or	14) 부정	15) isn't he
16) 긍정	17) do you	18) 그대로
19) isn't it	20) can't she	21) do
22) does	23) did	24) don't you
25) have	26) has	27) hasn't he
28) shall we	29) will you	

Level 1 Test p. 160

A 1 or 2 Which / or

B 1 can they 2 is she
  3 will you 4 shall we

C 1 aren't they   2 wasn't it
  3 have you

D 1 yours or his
  2 make these cookies or buy them

Level 2 Test
p. 161

01 ①   02 ⑤
03 ④   04 ② ③
05 Are you from Canada or America?
06 ⓑ don't you → are you
07 (1) Which
   (2) or
   (3) The Mississippi (is longer).
08 Don't be late, will you?

≫ 해설
01 선택의문문이므로 빈칸에는 or가 알맞다.
02 주절이 긍정문이므로 부정의 부가의문문을 만든다. 주절의 주어가 Rick and Robert이고 동사가 were이므로 알맞은 부가 의문문은 weren't they이다.
03 주절이 부정문이므로 긍정의 부가의문문을 써야 한다. 주어가 David 이고, 동사가 doesn't like이므로 부가의문문은 does he로 써야 한다.
04 선택의문문은 Yes나 No로 대답하지 않는다.
05 be동사가 사용된 선택의문문은 「be동사+주어 ~, A or B?」로 쓴다.
06 주절이 부정문이므로 긍정의 부가의문문이 필요하다. 주절에 be동사 are가 쓰였으므로 부가의문문에서도 are를 쓴다.
07 '둘 중 어느 것이 ~하니?'라고 할 때는 「Which ~, A or B?」라고 한다.
08 명령문에 부가의문문을 쓸 때는 will you?라고 한다.

Level 3 Test
p. 162

01 ②   02 ①
03 ④   04 ④
05 ④   06 ⑤
07 ③ ⑤   08 ③
09 ③
10 (1) has he
   (2) No, he hasn't.
11 wasn't it → isn't it
12 Where is the stationery shop, (on the) first floor or (on the) second floor?
13 Which music do you like better, jazz or the blues[the blues or jazz]?
14 They have known each other for a long time, haven't they?
15 Let's take a walk, shall we?

≫ 해설
01 주절이 긍정문이므로 부정의 부가의문문으로 만들어야 한다. 주어가 Those shoes이고 동사가 are이므로 부가의문문은 aren't they가 된다.
02 주절이 현재완료(「have+과거분사」) 긍정이므로 부가의문문은

---

haven't you가 되어야 한다.
03 • 주어가 Tony이고, 조동사 couldn't가 있으므로 부가의문문은 could he가 알맞다.
   • 주어가 You이고, 동사가 have made이므로 부가의문문은 haven't you가 되어야 한다.
04 • Let's ~로 시작하는 문장에 대한 부가의문문은 shall we?이다.
   • 명령문에 대한 부가의문문은 will you?를 쓴다.
05 주절의 문장은 과거 부정형이고, 부가의문문은 긍정의 부가의문문이 되어야 한다.
06 주절에 완료 시제가 쓰이면 부가의문문은 완료 시제에 쓰인 조동사 have/has를 이용해서 부가의문문을 만든다.
07 선택의문문은 Yes나 No로 대답하지 않는다.
08 ⓒ Let's ~권유문은 shall we?를 붙여 부가의문문을 만든다. ⓔ 앞 문장이 현재완료 부정이므로 부가의문문으로는 긍정형 has she?가 와야 한다.
09 ③ '노란 장화를 신은 저 아이는 누구니?'에서 Who이고, 나머지는 선택의문사 Which이다.
10 현재완료 부정형의 부가의문문은 긍정형 「have/has+대명사 주어?」이다. 주어가 3인칭 단수 he이므로 has를 쓴다. 대답은 내용상 부정의 대답이다.
11 앞 문장의 주어는 It이고 동사는 is이다. that 이하는 목적절로 주절 현재 시제의 부가의문문에 영향을 미치지 않는다. (간디가 살해당했다는 것은 매우 유감스러운 일이야, 그렇지 않니?)
12 「의문사(Where)+be동사+명사, A or B?」의 순서이다.
13 「선택의문사(Which)+명사+조동사(do)+주어+동사원형+better ~, A or B?」의 순서이다. (넌 어느 음악을 더 좋아하니, 재즈니 블루스니[블루스니 재즈니]?)
14 주절이 긍정문이므로 부정의 부가의문문을 만들어야 한다. 주절의 주어는 they이고 조동사는 have가 쓰였으므로 부가의문문은 haven't they?가 되어야 한다.
15 Let's ~ 청유문의 부가의문문은 shall we?를 붙인다.

28 UNIT 간접의문문

1) 주절   2) 간접의문문   3) 주절
4) 간접의문문   5) if   6) whether
7) 주어   8) 동사   9) if
10) whether   11) or   12) not
13) whether   14) or   15) not
16) where   17) he   18) is

Level 1 Test
p. 164

A 1 if   2 he can
  3 Semi will   4 you reserved

B 1 why he gave up   2 Who do you believe

C 1 if[whether] he will be back
  2 when Jack came
  3 where my USB is
  4 What do you think it is?

D 1 Do you know when she can finish the work?
    2 어색한 곳 없음

Level 2 Test
p. 165

01 ②   02 ③
03 ④   04 ⑤
05 what my homework is
06 do you guess
07 that → whether[if]
08 Can you tell me whether[if] I will meet Mr. Right?

≫ 해설

01 간접의문문은 의문문이 문장의 한 요소가 되는 것으로 의문사가 있을 경우 「의문사＋주어＋동사」의 어순으로 쓴다.

02 ③은 조건절을 이끄는 접속사 if(만약 ~한다면)이고, 나머지는 간접 의문문을 이끄는 접속사 if(~인지)이다.

03 I know how many members there are in BTS. 의문사가 있는 간접의문문으로 의문사(how many members) 다음에 there are 가 알맞다.

04 ⓑ 「의문사＋주어＋동사」로 where she lives가 되어야 한다. ⓒ when the fire broke out이 알맞다.

05 간접의문문은 「의문사＋주어＋동사」의 어순으로 써야 한다. 여기서 A의 your는 B의 대답에서 my로 써야 함에 유의한다.

06 상상·추측 동사인 guess가 있으므로 간접의문문의 어순에서 의문사 는 문장 앞에 써야 한다.

07 wonder(궁금 동사) 다음에 의문사가 없는 간접의문문을 이끄는 접속 사 whether나 if를 쓴다.

08 의문사가 없는 간접의문문으로 「접속사 whether[if]＋주어 (I)＋동사 (will meet)＋목적어(Mr. Right)」의 순서로 쓴다.

Level 3 Test
p. 166

01 ③   02 ②
03 ①   04 ②
05 ①③④   06 ④
07 ④   08 ①
09 ④   10 ③
11 not sure if this ticket is still valid
12 I can't remember who complained about the customs procedure.
13 what he wrote
14 Why do you think he's so great?
15 Why did he believe you were a criminal?

≫ 해설

01 • 목적어 역할을 하는, 의문사 없는 간접의문문을 이끄는 접속사 whether
   • 보어 역할을 하는 간접의문문을 이끄는 접속사 whether

02 간접의문문으로 「접속사＋주어＋동사」의 어순으로 써야 한다. (너의 ID가 뭔지 말해 주겠니?)

03 첫 번째 직접의문문에서는 조동사 did가 있으므로 원형동사 leave를 쓴다. 두 번째 문장에서 when 이하는 간접의문문으로, A가 과거형으 로 묻고 있으므로 과거형 left가 알맞다.

04 동사가 think일 때의 간접의문문은 「의문사＋do you think＋주어＋

동사 ~?」의 순서로 써야 한다. hide의 과거형은 hid이다. (너는 너의 아들이 어디에 성적표를 숨겼다고 생각해?)

05 ①은 Who do you think I am?이 맞고, ③은 does를 없애야 한다. ④는 when will he come back을 when he will come back으 로 고친다.

06 간접의문문의 의문사가 문장 맨 앞에 있으므로 주절의 동사는 think, believe, guess 등이 되어야 한다.

07 ⓑ 동사가 guess일 때의 간접의문문은 「의문사＋do you guess＋ 주어＋동사 ~?」의 순서로 써야 한다.

08 whether there will be any seats left의 순서로 써야 하므로 두 번째 올 단어는 there이다.

09 ⓐ ⓓ 간접의문문이므로 「의문사＋주어＋동사」의 순서가 알맞다.

10 ③ I am not sure whether he loves me.가 알맞으므로 love가 loves가 되어야 한다.

11 의문사가 없는 간접의문문의 어순으로 「접속사(if)＋주어＋동사」의 순서로 쓴다.

12 의문사가 있는 직접의문문에서 의문사가 주어이므로 간접의문문이 되어도 어순은 똑같다. (나는 누가 세관 절차에 대해 불평했는지 기억 할 수 없다.)

13 의문사가 있는 간접의문문의 어순은 「의문사＋주어＋동사」의 순서로 쓴다. 시제가 과거이므로 wrote를 쓰는 것에 유의한다.

14 Do you think?와 Why is he so great?를 간접의문문으로 바꾸면, 주절의 동사가 think이므로 의문사 Why를 맨 앞에 쓰고, 「do you think＋주어＋동사」의 순서로 쓴다. 단어 수를 맞추기 위해 he is 를 he's로 줄여 쓴다.

15 동사가 believe일 때의 간접의문문은 「의문사＋do/did＋주어 ＋believe＋주어＋동사 ~?」의 순서로 써야 한다. were동사는 주어 로 you가 와야 한다.

Review Test
p. 168

01 ⑤   02 ②③
03 ①③   04 ④
05 ③④   06 ②
07 ⑤   08 ①
09 ②   10 ①
11 Would you prefer a window seat or an aisle seat?
12 Which food do you like better, steaks or burgers?
13 isn't it → wasn't there
14 Let's ride our bikes, shall we?
15 doesn't fit me well / does it
16 what he did
17 how much my bag weighs
18 if[whether] you sent a text message in class
19 Why did you think the film was so amazing?
20 doesn't remember when she put her phone in the refrigerator
21 ④
22 where you were

≫ 해설

01 앞 문장의 동사가 각각 과거형과 현재완료형인 긍정문이므로, 부가의 문문의 동사는 조동사의 부정형인 didn't와 haven't가 알맞다.

02 선택의문문으로 물으면 Yes/No로 답하지 않는다.

03 ② 앞에 조동사 과거형 could가 있으므로 couldn't he로 쓴다. ④ 과거형이므로 didn't she로 쓴다. ⑤ 현재완료 부정이므로 have you가 알맞다.

04 Could you tell me what time it is now?로 영작할 수 있다. What time is it now?가 간접의문문으로 문장 끝에 들어가므로 「What time+주어+동사 ~?」의 어순이어야 함에 유의한다.

05 선택의문문 Which ~, A or B?에는 Yes나 No로 답할 수 없다.

06 동사가 think일 때 간접의문문은 「의문사+do you think+주어+동사 ~?」의 순서로 써야 한다.

07 ⓐ ⓑ ⓓ의 if는 간접의문문을 이끄는 '~인지 (아닌지)'이고, ⓒ의 if는 조건절을 이끄는 '만약 ~한다면'의 의미이다.

08 whether 다음에 평서문의 순서로 there is a problem이 와야 한다.

09 첫 번째는 간접의문문으로 「주어+동사」의 순서이고, 두 번째는 직접의문문으로 「조동사+주어+동사」의 순서이다.

10 ⓐ 명령문이면 will you?를 쓴다. ⓒ 선택의문문에서는 and가 아니라 or를 쓴다. ⓔ Let's ~의 부가의문문은 shall we?이다.

11 「조동사(Would)+주어+동사원형+A or B?」

12 「선택의문사(Which)+명사+조동사(do)+주어+동사 ~, A or B?」

13 There was로 시작하는 문장의 부가의문문은 wasn't there?이다.

14 Let's 청유문의 부가의문문은 shall we?이다. (에너지를 절약합시다. 가능한 한 자동차를 운전하지 맙시다. 자전거를 탑시다, 그럴 거죠?)

15 입어본 드레스가 크므로 '이 드레스가 나에게 잘 맞지 않네, 그렇지?'라고 해야 한다. 부정의 평서문과 긍정의 부가의문문이 되어야 한다.

16 간접의문문의 어순은 「의문사+주어+동사」이다.

17 의문사가 있는 간접의문문의 어순으로 「의문사(how much)+주어+동사(weighs)」로 weigh의 3인칭 단수 변화형 weighs에 유의한다.

18 의문사가 없는 간접의문문이므로 접속사 if[whether]를 쓰고 평서문의 어순으로 조동사 did를 없애고 sent를 쓰는 것에 유의한다.

19 Did you think?와 Why was the film so amazing?을 간접의문문으로 바꾸면, 주절의 동사가 think이므로 의문사 Why를 맨 앞에 쓰고, 「did you think+주어+동사」의 어순으로 쓴다.

20 의문사가 있는 간접의문문으로, 「의문사(when)+주어+동사(put)」로 과거형 동사 put에 유의한다.

21 간접의문문이므로 어순에 맞게 where he was로 고쳐야 한다.

22 Where were you?의 간접의문문으로 어순에 맞게 본문의 어휘를 골라 where you were로 쓰면 된다.

[21~22]

　　　나의 일곱 살짜리 아들 Brody는 결코 우리 블록(동네)을 떠나지 말라고 경고를 받았다. 그런데, 어느 날 그는 기찻길까지 산책을 갔다. 그것에 대해 알았을 때 나는 매우 화가 났고, 그가 자신의 아빠에게 이것에 대해 말해야 한다고 말했다. 저녁에 그의 아빠가 집에 도착했고, 나는 "이제 아빠한테 네가 어디 있었는지 말해."라고 말했다. 그는 자신이 어디 있었는지 말하지 않았다. 오히려 그가 나를 멍하니 바라봐서, 나는 바꿔 말했다. "너 어디 있다가 왔어?(너 어디 출신이야?)"라고 나는 다시 물었다. "잘 모르겠어요. 하지만 내 생각에 난 Queens에서 태어났어요."라고 Brody가 말했다.

• 어휘 • warn 경고하다 | block 블록, 동네 | railway track 기찻길 | upset 화가 난

CHAPTER 13
가정법

UNIT 29 조건문과 가정법 과거

1) 현재 사실　　2) 과거 동사　　3) 과거형
4) 동사원형　　5) 만일 ~라면, …할 텐데.
6) 과거 동사　　7) 과거형　　8) 동사원형
9) As　　10) Because　　11) 현재
12) 현재　　13) 긍정　　14) 부정
15) 현재　　16) so　　17) 현재
18) 긍정　　19) 부정　　20) 현재
21) will　　22) 불확실한　　23) 과거
24) 과거형　　25) 확실한

Level 1 Test
p. 172

A　1　get　　　　　2　could catch
　　3　Would

B　1　could buy　　2　trained
　　3　will go out

C　1　were[was]　　2　would

D　1　don't receive[get] / give
　　2　were[was] / would go

Level 2 Test
p. 173

01　③　　　　　　　02　③
03　②　　　　　　　04　is → were[was]
05　don't have / can't buy
06　ⓐ I am so pleased → I will be so pleased
07　1행: Do → Would, 3행: Is it → Would it be

》》 해설

01 가정법 과거에서는 주절에 「would+동사원형」을 쓴다.

02 가정법 과거는 '긍정↔부정'으로 직설법 현재로 전환할 수 있다.

03 ②의 know와 can을 don't know와 can't로 바꿔야 한다.

04 가정법 과거에는 if절에 과거형 동사를 쓴다.

05 긍정의 가정법 과거는 부정의 직설법 현재로 전환할 수 있다.

06 직설법 조건문에서 if절에 현재, 주절에는 미래가 온다.

07 '천국에서 너(아들)를 본다'는 가정을 하고 있으므로 가정법 과거로 써야 한다.

Level 3 Test
p. 174

01　④　　　　　　　02　③
03　④　　　　　　　04　④
05　④　　　　　　　06　②

07 ③　　　　　　　　　　　08 ③

09 ③

10 (1) As[Because] / is raining / cannot[can't]
　　(2) so / cannot[can't] / go

11 ⓑ will → would

12 if you were here / would be better

13 I will buy you a smartwatch if you get a part-time job.

14 weren't[wasn't] / could climb

≫≫ 해설

01 차를 수리하는 법을 모르므로 가정법 과거 문장이다.

02 가정법 과거의 주절에는 will이 아닌 would를 쓴다.

03 조건문에서는 주절에 미래뿐만 아니라 명령문도 사용 가능하다.

04 첫 번째는 since가 있으므로 현재완료가, 두 번째와 세 번째에는 가정법 과거형이 들어가므로 ④가 적절하다.

05 ④에서 had는 가정법의 if절 동사이므로 would have로 써야 한다.

06 We would do a better job if we were working together.로 전환할 수 있다.

07 ⓐ bought → buy ⓒ would → will 또는 allows → allowed ⓔ did → would

08 If Dad bought me a puppy[a puppy for me], I would take good care of it.으로 영작할 수 있다. took는 쓸 수 없다.

09 가정법 과거의 if절에는 본동사의 부정을 해야 하므로 hadn't가 아닌 didn't have로 써야 한다.

10 가정법 과거는 As[Because] ~, ... 또는 ~, so...의 직설법으로 전환할 수 있다.

11 현재의 사실에 반대되는 가정이므로 가정법 과거로 써야 한다.

12 가정법 과거 문장으로 if절에는 were를, 주절에는 would be를 쓰고, '더 좋을 텐데'는 good의 비교급 better로 쓰면 된다.

13 주어진 단어(will)를 변형하지 말고 그대로 조건문 현재를 사용하면 된다.

14 직설법 현재는 반대의 가정법 과거로 전환할 수 있다.

UNIT 30 I wish 가정법 과거, as if 가정법 과거

1) 없는　　　　　　　　　　2) 현재

3) 반대　　　　　　　　　　4) 주어

5) 과거　　　　　　　　　　6) 주어

7) 과거　　　　　　　　　　8) ~하면 좋을 텐데

9) 마치 ~인 것처럼　　　　10) I am sorry

11) 현재 동사　　　　　　　12) 긍정

13) 부정　　　　　　　　　14) don't have

15) In fact　　　　　　　　16) 긍정

17) 부정　　　　　　　　　18) am not

Level 1 Test
p. 176

A　1　knew　　　　　　　2　wish
　　3　were　　　　　　　4　as

B　1　could see　　　　　2　had
　　3　were[was]　　　　4　were[was]

C　1　is / were[was]　　2　knew / don't
　　3　wouldn't make / will
　　4　as if[though] / didn't like / likes

Level 2 Test
p. 177

01 ③　　　　　　　　　　02 ④

03 ④　　　　　　　　　　04 ⑤

05 They spend money as if they were rich.

06 I wish (that) I could turn back time to my elementary school days.

07 I wish I had

08 I wish I could see you more often.

≫≫ 해설

01 I wish 가정법 과거 문장으로 동사의 과거형을 쓴다.

02 In fact, Steve knows Mia.의 의미로 응국이의 설명이 맞다.

03 Your mother walks as if she were[was] a supermodel.로 영작할 수 있다.

04 현재의 실현 가능성이 희박한 소망은 wish 가정법 과거로 표현하므로 has를 had로 써야 한다.

05 주어(They), 동사(spend), 목적어(money) 다음에 as if 가정법 과거를 쓰면 된다.

06 I wish 가정법 과거 구문을 사용하면 되며, '능력'은 could로 표현하면 된다.

07 여우가 할 수 있는 말은 '나도 너처럼 긴 부리를 가졌으면 좋을 텐데.'이다. I wish 가정법 과거로 쓰면 된다.

08 '너를 더 자주 볼 수 있으면 좋을 텐데.'의 의미로 전환하면 된다. 직설법 현재(부정)는 I wish 가정법 과거(긍정)로 바꿀 수 있다.

Level 3 Test
p. 178

01 ④　　　　　　　　　　02 ③

03 ⑤　　　　　　　　　　04 ① ③

05 ④　　　　　　　　　　06 ④

07 ②　　　　　　　　　　08 ② ③

09 ②　　　　　　　　　　10 ②

11 want → wish / have → had / will → would

12 I were as tall as

13 Don't you wish you were me?

14 as if[though] he were[was] not (angry with her)

15 he isn't sharing a secret

≫≫ 해설

01 실제로는 아닌데 서랍장이 나무로 만든 것처럼 보이므로 as if 가정법 과거 수동태로 써야 한다.

02 자유 시간이 거의 없어서 더 갖기를 원하는 것이 자연스러우므로 didn't have를 had로 써야 한다.

03 직설법 현재(긍정)는 I wish 가정법 과거(부정)로 바꿀 수 있으므로 had to → didn't have to로 바꿔야 한다.

04 She talks as if[though] her cat were[was] her child.로 영작할 수 있다. through는 '~을 통하여'이다.

05 as if 가정법 과거(긍정)는 In fact[In truth, But] 등과 함께 직설법 현재(부정)로 바꿀 수 있다.

06 ⓐ 가정법 과거이므로 would로 고쳐야 한다. ⓑ as if 가정법 과거이므로 owned가 맞다. ⓒ I wish 가정법 과거이므로 had로 고쳐야 한다.

07 as if 가정법 과거가 오며 현재 사실의 반대되는 내용이 와야 하며, 내용상 ⓑ ⓓ 두 개가 적절하다.

08 비가 오고 있고, 글쓴이는 약속이 있어서 나가야 하는데 빗속을 걷는 것을 좋아하지 않으므로 '비가 오지 않았으면 좋겠다' 또는 '약속이 없었으면 좋겠다'가 적절하다.

09 I wish I could take a break, but I can't take a break.의 의미로 I wish I could, but I can't.로 써야 한다.

10 I'm sorry 직설법 현재(부정)는 I wish 가정법 과거(긍정)로 바꿀 수 있다.

11 첫 번째는 실현 불가능한 소망이라 wish로 쓰고, 두 번째는 가정법 과거의 if절이므로 had로, 세 번째는 주절이므로 would로 써야 한다.

12 아버지의 말로 보아 아들의 말에는 '아빠만큼 키가 컸으면'이란 표현을 넣으면 된다.

13 일반동사(wish)의 의문문으로 Don't you wish로 시작하고 현재 사실의 가정이므로 가정법 과거형 동사(were)로 써서 완성하면 된다.

14 Sam이 상사에게 화가 나 있으나 화가 나지 않은 것처럼 말한다는 의미로 as if 가정법 과거를 쓰면 된다.

15 as if 가정법 과거(긍정)는 in fact 직설법 현재(부정)로 전환할 수 있다.

Review Test
p. 180

01 ⑤   02 ①
03 ②   04 ④
05 ⑤   06 ②
07 ④   08 ① ② ⑤
09 ⑤
10 It seems to me as though he were wearing my coat.
11 weren't[wasn't] / could climb
12 wouldn't invite / were[was] not
13 will → would
14 (1) study / will pass
    (2) studied / would pass
15 I were you / I would never sell this
16 is made of
17 would stop using
18 had
19 has → had
20 ⓐ are → were ⓑ knows → knew ⓒ she's → she were[was]
21 ④
22 If it were not easy to bend

>>> 해설
01 가정법 과거는 주절에 과거 동사를 쓰며, if절에는 were[was]를 쓴다.
02 '내가 너라면 그와 함께 그곳에 가지 않을 텐데.'는 혼자 가지 말라는 충고의 뜻이다.
03 가정법 과거의 if절에는 과거 동사가 온다.

04 가정법 과거는 반대로 직설법 현재로 바꿔 쓸 수 있다.

05 ⓒ can → could (또는 helped → helps) ⓔ is → were[was]

06 시간이 없어서 얘기할 수 없다는 뜻이므로 가정법 과거로 표현해야 한다.

07 I wish 가정법 과거(긍정)는 I'm sorry 직설법 현재(부정)로 바꿀 수 있다.

08 ① is → were[was] ② are → were ⑤ will → would

09 I wish 가정법 과거를 써야 하므로 don't을 didn't으로 써야 한다.

10 as though 다음에 가정법 과거형(were wearing)으로 쓰면 된다.

11 직설법 현재는 반대의 가정법 과거로 전환할 수 있다.

12 '네 친구가 아니면 Kyle을 초대하지 않을 거야.'에 맞게 가정법 과거로 본문의 단어를 이용하여 쓰면 된다.

13 가정법 과거의 주절에는 조동사의 과거형을 쓴다.

14 (1) 조건문 현재: 「If + 주어 + 현재 동사 ~, 주어 + will + 동사원형」
    (2) 가정법 과거: 「If + 주어 + 과거 동사 ~, 주어 + would + 동사 원형」

15 가정법 과거 문장으로 「If + 주어 + 과거 동사 ~, 주어 + would + 동사원형」 순으로 쓴다.

16 as if 가정법 과거(긍정)는 직설법 현재(부정)로 바꿔 쓸 수 있으나, B가 플라스틱으로 만들어졌다고 말하므로 내용상 긍정이 와야 한다.

17 I wish 가정법 과거로 '나의 물건을 허락 없이 빌리는 것을 그만했으면 좋겠다.'이므로 would stop using으로 써야 한다. 「stop + -ing」는 '~하는 것을 멈추다'이다.

18 직설법 현재(부정)는 I wish 가정법 과거(긍정)로 쓸 수 있다.

19 as if 가정법 과거가 오므로 had로 써야 한다.

20 ⓐ I wish 가정법 과거이므로 be동사의 과거형을 쓴다. ⓑ 실제로는 모르는 사이인데 아는 것처럼 인사하므로 as if 가정법 과거를 쓴다. ⓒ 가정법 과거이므로 if절에 과거 동사를 써야 한다.

21 현재 사실에 대한 반대를 가정하는 것이므로 가정법 과거완료 구문이 와야 한다. 따라서 won't를 wouldn't로 고쳐야 한다.

22 가정법 과거 구문으로 be동사는 주어가 3인칭 단수일지라도 were가 원칙이므로 If it were not easy를 쓰고 easy를 수식할 수 있도록 to bend를 쓰면 된다.

[21~22]

코끼리가 그것의 코를 이용하는 방법을 생각해 보라. 그것은 물건을 나르고, 식량의 냄새를 맡고, 적과 싸우는데 코를 이용한다. 코끼리가 갈증이 날 때, 그것은 코 한 가득 6리터를 마실 수 있다. 그것은 또한 목욕을 하기 위해 코를 사용한다. 코끼리의 코는 뼈가 없다. 이것은 그것을 부드럽고 구부리기 쉽게 해준다. 만약 그것이 구부리기에 쉽지 않다면, 코끼리는 작은 땅콩을 잡을 수 없을 것이다. 확실히 코끼리의 코는 세상에서 가장 유용한 코이다.

• 어휘 • enemy 적 | thirsty 갈증 나는 | noseful 코 한 가득 | bone 뼈 | bend 구부리다 | definitely 확실히

MEMO

내신공략
중학영문법 2
문제풀이책